YOUNG HENRY

Also by Robert Hutchinson

Last Days of Henry VIII
Elizabeth's Spy Master
Thomas Cromwell
House of Treason

YOUNG HENRY

The rise to power of Henry VIII

———•◦•———

ROBERT HUTCHINSON

Weidenfeld & Nicolson

LONDON

First published in Great Britain in 2011
by Weidenfeld & Nicolson

1 3 5 7 9 10 8 6 4 2

Text © Robert Hutchinson 2011

A CIP catalogue record for this book
is available from the British Library.

HB ISBN-13 978 0 297 85952 9

Typeset by Input Data Services Ltd,
Bridgwater, Somerset

Printed in Great Britain by
CPI Mackays, Chatham, Kent

Weidenfeld & Nicolson

The Orion Publishing Group Ltd
Orion House
5 Upper Saint Martin's Lane
London, WC2H 9EA
An Hachette UK Company

The Orion Publishing Group's policy is to use papers that
are natural, renewable and recyclable products and
made from wood grown in sustainable forests. The logging
and manufacturing processes are expected to conform to
the environmental regulations of the country of origin.

For Ciss and Eva

CONTENTS

LIST OF ILLUSTRATIONS

AUTHOR'S NOTE

Henry VIII is England's most famous monarch. The king's turbulent life, the traumas of his six marriages and his ruthless, despotic actions combine to provide the most compelling drama that any fiction author could hope, in their wildest dreams, to write.

His victims, Wolsey, Fisher, More and the Boleyns, weave their way through the narrative, entering and exiting like actors on the stage of Henry's court before the denouement of their disgrace or violent end in this most vivid of tragedies. In this king's story, historical fact is stranger than fiction.

Henry VIII has always aroused the strongest emotions. In the eighteenth century, for example, Jonathan Swift, the Irish satirist – and author of *Gulliver's Travels* – noted in the margin of one of his books his own vitriolic verdict on 'Bluff King Hal':

> I wish he had been flayed, his skin stuffed and hanged upon a gibbet. His bulky guts and flesh left to be devoured by birds and beasts for a warning to his successors for ever. Amen.

This book analyses the motives and needs that drove Henry both in his private life and in his policies directed towards his own people and his brother kings abroad.

Much of his personality traits and likes and dislikes were inherited from his father Henry VII – the love of magnificence, ostentation, the rituals of ceremony, the excitement of hunting and gambling, and the design and construction of a range of grand new palaces. A brazen rapaciousness in seizing the cash and property of some of their subjects is immediately recognisable in both.

It is truly a case of like father, like son, down to their unusual height – both were tall, the son over six feet and this, together with their striking red gold hair, marked them out among lesser men.

But where the father was cautious, the son was impulsive. Where the father was often magnanimous in victory, the son was merciless. These dubious qualities were passed on, via the Tudor gene pool, to Henry VIII's siblings, Edward VI, Mary I and Elizabeth I.

Two important drivers combined to dictate their course of action in almost everything the two king Henrys did. The first was an overweening dynastic pride and the second a chronic lack of assurance in their ability to achieve their ambitions of a long line of Tudor kings.

The nagging fear of losing the crown of England that gripped both father and son was born out of the uncomfortable knowledge that the Tudors' claim on the throne was fragile in its legality, secured only by right of conquest on the field of battle in 1485. Hence Henry VIII's immediate, angry reaction to any show of opposition, however insignificant, to his will.

His father's defeat and destruction of Richard III at Bosworth terminated the Plantagenet dynasty's hold on England, which had spanned fifteen monarchs and dated back to 1154. The Tudors planned to substitute their own line of succession, doubtless aiming to rule for just as long as their predecessors.

They needed a plentiful supply of male heirs to achieve this with any degree of certainty. Henry VII came close to losing everything when three of the four sons provided by Elizabeth of York died – most decisively Arthur, his sickly heir. When the Prince expired on Saturday 2 April 1502, she sought to comfort a stunned king by pointing out that 'God has lent them yet a fair and goodly ... young prince'.

Henry, as the 'spare heir', was never intended for the trials of kingship and the subsequent stifling protection of the teenager provoked his adolescent kicking of the traces after he succeeded to the throne in April 1509.

After those early glory days of feasting, jousting and fun, the continuing lack of a legitimate male heir runs like a thin line of poison through almost three decades of his reign and goes some way to explain his callous treatment of his first wife Katherine of Aragon (spelt with a 'K' incidentally throughout, as this is how she signed herself).

Henry VIII was the first English king to have insisted on the title of 'majesty' as a form of address. He may later have seen himself as God's deputy on earth with direct communication to the Almighty at local rates rather than via Rome. But behind all that bluff and bluster, tantrum and tyranny, he felt just as vulnerable as the most miserable of his disease-ridden subjects.

Betrayed by his allies and unable to fulfil his military ambitions, much of what Henry attempted left him with the bitter aftertaste of failure.

This book strives to provide insights into what turned this happy, playful Renaissance prince into the tyrant of his later years when the golden age heralded so optimistically by his accession was slowly transformed into a bleak human tragedy.

ACKNOWLEDGEMENTS

This book could not have been written without the very willing help of my dear wife Sally who, like me, has come to lead almost a double existence, immersed in the conspiracies and intrigues of Tudor life.

Like my other books on the period, much of the material for this work has been drawn from contemporary documents and other sources, where possible employing the written or spoken words used by those living in those tumultuous, dangerous times.

A great number of friends and colleagues have kindly given invaluable support and help in tracking down manuscripts and rare books. In particular, I would like to thank Robin Harcourt Williams, Librarian and Archivist to the Marquis of Salisbury at Hatfield House for his help with the Cecil Papers. Dr Andrea Clarke, curator of Early Modern Historical Manuscripts in the British Library, and Jessamy Sykes of the National Archives were very helpful in locating a manuscript once in the library of Wrest Park, Bedfordshire.

My thanks also go to Heather Rowland, head of library and collections, and Adrian James, assistant librarian, at the Society of Antiquaries of London; Kay Walters and her team at the incomparable library at the Athenæum in Pall Mall; the ever-willing staff at the University of Sussex library at Falmer and the always helpful teams at the National Archives and in the Rare Books, Humanities and Manuscripts reading rooms of the British Library at Euston. I am also very grateful for help given by my good friends the Revd Jerome Bertram, on Latin translation, and Dr Richard Robinson on forensic medicine issues. At Weidenfeld & Nicolson, Alan Samson has been encouraging and helpful, as has Lucinda McNeile, and I would like to thank Lisa Rogers my editor and Christopher Phipps for the index.

I must point out, however, that any errors are entirely my responsibility.

ROBERT HUTCHINSON
West Sussex, 2010

Prologue

THE UNCERTAIN CROWN

—•◦•—

'What ... should be if his grace departed ... who should have the rule in England then? Some spoke of my lord of Buckingham [and] said that he would be a royal ruler ... others spoke of the traitor Edmund de la Pole but none of them spoke of my lord prince.'

Sir Hugh Conway, Treasurer of Calais, [later than] 1503.[1]

After audaciously seizing the crown of England, Henry VII told his first Parliament on 9 November 1485 that his inalienable right to the throne was based not only on his lawful inheritance but on the dreadful judgement of God – delivered decisively in battle less than three months before.[2] But behind the bold, confident words of the victor of Bosworth Field that rang around the Painted Chamber at Westminster that winter's day lurked deep, dark fears in Henry's heart about the future, both of his own fledgling sovereignty and of the glorious dynasty of Tudor monarchs he intended to establish.

The new king muttered a profound and fervent 'amen' to the dutiful, diligent appeal made to the peers, bishops and commoners by the Lord Chancellor, John Alcock, Bishop of Worcester, to humbly pray on their knees for a long, happy and fertile reign.[3]

Shakespeare's brisk line 'Uneasy lies the head that wears a crown'[4] is grimly appropriate to the dysfunctional House of Tudor that went on to rule England for more than a century.

Insecurity always beleaguered Henry VII and his imperious descendants, who all faced rebellions during their lifetimes – some of which

1

came close to toppling them from an often precarious throne. Ruthless and brutal suppression of such opposition was part of the inherited Tudor genes.[5] Moreover, there were always hard questions about who would succeed them when omnipotent death finally knocked on the doors of the royal apartments within their opulent palaces. Frequently, only the copious shedding of noble English blood decided the issue.

Insecurity especially haunted Henry's second son who, as Henry VIII, slaughtered those who held latent claims to the throne as well as the many unfortunates trapped by his new catch-all treason laws. Above all, he agonised for decades over his inability to sire a legitimate male heir.

Henry VII had spent fourteen embittered years exiled in Brittany after the Yorkist defeat of the Lancastrian cause in the Wars of the Roses at the Battles of Barnet and Tewkesbury in 1471. His questionable, certainly tenuous, claim to the English throne was founded on the descent of his formidable mother Lady Margaret Beaufort from John of Gaunt, son of Edward III, and Katherine Swynford, his mistress of twenty-five years and later his third wife.[6] Their children were legitimised by Act of Parliament in 1397 but were barred from inheriting the throne in an order of dubious legality made by Henry IV a decade later.

The king's claim to the crown on his father's side was even more fragile. Edmund Tudor, First Earl of Richmond, was half-brother to Henry VI, born of an illicit union between Katherine of Valois, widow of the great English hero-king Henry V, and Owen Tudor,[7] her Welsh-born Keeper of the Wardrobe. Owen was beheaded in 1461 after Lancastrian forces were defeated at Mortimer's Cross, near Wigmore, Herefordshire.

Edmund died of the plague in November 1456 after being imprisoned by the Yorkists in Carmarthen Castle in South Wales. Henry, his only child, was born at Pembroke Castle in 1457, three months after his death, following a difficult confinement for his fourteen-year-old mother.

Claims by descent can always be challenged. But winning the throne by right of conquest was an undeniable fact of realpolitik. Henry triumphantly wore Richard III's regal circlet of gold after just two hours of intense fighting at Bosworth on 22 August 1485. The defeated king's bloody and mired body, stripped stark naked, was contemptuously thrown over a horse and carried off the battlefield 'trussed like a hog or calf'[8] to an ignominious burial in an unmarked grave two days later in the Church of the Greyfriars, Leicester.[9] In thanks for his victory, Henry offered up his red Welsh dragon standard at the high altar of St Paul's Cathedral in London and on Sunday 30 October was crowned at Westminster by the same archbishop who two years earlier had performed precisely the same role in Richard III's coronation.

Now Henry wanted to quash Richard's earlier scornful charge that he was 'descended of bastard blood, both [on his] father's side and mother's side . . . [so] no title can, nor may, [be] in him'.[10]

He therefore immediately introduced two Bills into Parliament. The first set out the king's style and title as 'King of England and France and Lord of Ireland'.[11] Expediently, it offered no explanation as to how Henry acquired it and contained the convenient legal canard that his reign began twenty-four hours *before* the Battle of Bosworth. Thus, all who fought against him that day were automatically deemed traitors and their lives and goods liable to be forfeit under attainder for treason.

The second repealed the notorious *Titulus Regius* statute of 1483 that ratified a petition bastardising Edward IV's children on the grounds that his marriage to Elizabeth Woodville was legally invalid.[12] The couple's children included the so-called 'Princes in the Tower', Edward V and his brother Richard, Duke of York, and this instrument effectively declared Richard III the true and lawful king.[13] The two boys disappeared mysteriously after passing through the gates of the Tower of London in June 1483, never to be seen again.

In this instance, foul murder did not shriek out. It was presumed they were either killed in the Tower or died from disease or privation behind its grim battlements. Whether Richard III himself was responsible for their deaths has been thoroughly clouded by clever Tudor propaganda and is still debated heatedly to this day. The puzzling ramification of Henry VII's repealing of the *Titulus Regius* was that he must have been certain sure that the two princes were already dead. Henry would have known that by re-legitimising Edward IV's children, he was also restoring the lost princes' birthrights to the succession. The risks to the new king's chances of survival would have been vastly increased if they were still living.

The real reason behind the Act was that Henry needed to buttress his battered kingdom after the destruction and division of the thirty-two years of the Wars of the Roses. To achieve that, he planned to marry Elizabeth of York, the eldest daughter of Edward IV, now deftly re-legitimised by his legislation, to finally unite the houses of York and Lancaster.[14] On 10 December 1485, immediately before it was prorogued, Parliament humbly petitioned him to fulfil his oath to marry her, sworn in the great cathedral of Rennes, in eastern Brittany, on Christmas Day 1483. The new Speaker Sir Thomas Lovell[15] hoped that God would bless the marriage 'with progeny of the race of kings to the great satisfaction of the whole world'.[16]

Henry intended to rule England in his own right as king-conqueror, rather than merely relying on his queen consort's own lineage to secure the throne. A papal dispensation for the marriage was granted on 16 January 1486 to end 'the long and grievous variance, contentions and debates' between England's warring factions. The Bull underlined Henry's legal claim to the crown – should Elizabeth die childless, the issue of any future marriage would inherit the throne – and furthermore threatened excommunication to any who should rebel against him or his lawful heirs.[17] It was printed and read out from church pulpits up and down the realm, in one of the earliest uses of the printing press to distribute government propaganda to the masses.[18]

Two days afterwards Henry and Elizabeth were married by Thomas Bourchier, the eighty-two-year-old Archbishop of Canterbury[19] at West-minster Abbey. Henry was ten days away from his twenty-ninth birth-day; Elizabeth was aged almost twenty. Bernard André, the blind French poet of Henry's court, reported that the king's subjects 'constructed bonfires far and wide to show their gladness and the City of London was filled with dancing, singing and entertainment' in celebration of the wedding.[20] More soberly, the chronicler Edward Hall wrote that:

> By reason of which marriage, peace was thought to descend out of heaven into England, considering that the lines of Lancaster and York ... were

now brought into one knot and connected together, of whose two bodies one heir might succeed, which after their time should peaceably rule and enjoy the whole monarchy and realm of England.[21]

The theme of divine intervention on behalf of Henry VII was deliberately promoted and widely believed. In Rome an English envoy delivered an elegant oration in breathless Latin to the Pope and cardinals, acknowledging Henry's great debt to God for His divine assistance in recovering the throne of his ancestors. He declared that the new king had agreed to marry the daughter of Edward IV 'to end all civil strife in England'.[22]

Subsequent events were to prove this expectation rather premature.

Throughout history, the first imperative for any monarch has always been to establish a male line of succession as early as possible in their reign. Henry VII was quick off the mark, as Elizabeth soon found herself pregnant, and preparations were made for her confinement and the delivery of the hoped-for prince at Winchester, the ancient capital of England, where the king was enjoying the local deer hunting after a gruelling royal progress in the west of England.

The king's mother, Lady Margaret Beaufort, jotted down the time of the birth in her devotional *Book of Hours*[23] as 'in the morning afore one o'clock after midnight' on 19/20 September 1486 – St Eustace's Day.[24] The child was a healthy boy, despite being born at least a month prematurely, and was promptly named Arthur.[25] In thanks for her safe delivery, Elizabeth founded a chapel dedicated to the Blessed Virgin Mary in Winchester Cathedral bearing her arms, surmounted by the jubilantly pious words *In Gloriam Dei*.[26]

There has been much learned debate about Henry's intentions behind this choice of name for his first-born son and heir.[27] The seventeenth-century historian Francis Bacon believed the king's objective was to bind his dynasty to 'that ancient worthy king of the Britons, in whose acts there is truth enough to make him famous, beside that which is fabulous [legendary]'.[28] Edward Hall considered that the name carried mythical potency before which 'Englishmen ... rejoiced ... and foreign princes trembled and quaked, so much was that name to all nations terrible and formidable'.[29] However, 'Arthur' was not a name regarded as especially significant by earlier English kings – Edward IV gave it to one of his bastard sons, Arthur Plantagenet, later Viscount Lisle – and in Henry VII's reign, there was no attempt to create a popular cult of King Arthur[30] other than the poetic conceits written at court, intended only to massage the greedy ego of Henry himself.[31]

The king might now have his heir, but threats to his crown from the defeated Yorkists had not vanished. As early as February 1486, his uncle Jasper Tudor[32] was sent into Wales 'to see to that country'[33] and the following month there were brief but violent riots in Westminster and north London apparently aimed at deposing Henry. Later that spring abortive rebellions sprang up in Yorkshire, Warwickshire and the West Midlands – the city of Worcester was briefly held against the king – but these minor insurrections fizzled out harmlessly, although sporadic sedition continued to simmer in the Thames Valley area.[34]

A more serious threat emerged in bizarre circumstances in 1487. After Bosworth, Henry VII had swiftly locked up the closest Yorkist claimant to the throne, ten-year-old Edward Plantagenet, Seventeenth Earl of Warwick,[35] in the Tower, but now a counterfeit Warwick appeared in Dublin. Lambert Simnel was the ten-year-old son of an Oxford joiner who had a passing resemblance to the imprisoned earl and had been schooled in the ways of the nobility by Richard Simons, a wily scholar-priest of Oxford. With rumours abounding that Warwick had escaped custody, Henry was forced to bring him out of the Tower and parade him in St Paul's for all to see, in a vain attempt to scotch the dangerous treasonous talk.

Another Yorkist nobleman, John de la Pole, First Earl of Lincoln, had taken part in the ceremonial of the christening of Prince Arthur on 24 September 1486 at Winchester. He now fled the court and crossed the English Channel to Burgundy, seeking support and tangible assistance from Margaret of York, dowager Duchess of Burgundy and sister to both Edward IV and Richard III. Lincoln raised a force of 2,000 German mercenaries – a highly disciplined brigade of *Landsknechte* armed with tall pikes, ably commanded by the swaggering Martin Schwarz[36] – and shipped them over to Ireland, arriving on 5 May. His defection was particularly dangerous to Henry Tudor, as his maternal uncle Richard III had named him as his legal heir to the throne of England.

Simnel was crowned as 'Edward VI, King of England', in Christ Church Cathedral, Dublin, on Ascension Day, 24 May 1487.[37] Coinage bearing his image was quickly minted and the always fractious Gerald Fitzgerald, Eighth Earl of Kildare, mustered a raggle-taggle army of Irish soldiers in support of the imposter's cause.

Lincoln was joined by another Yorkist exile, Francis Lovell, Viscount Lovell, and on 4 June they led the small German–Irish invasion force that landed at Piel Castle, on a small island around 1,000 yards (1 km) off the Furness Peninsula in Cumbria. They then marched eastwards over the Pennines towards York, seeking reinforcements from amongst the disaffected, and after a brief victorious skirmish at Tadcaster against royalist troops under Lord Henry Clifford, turned their horses' heads south towards London.

Henry VII had gathered a 12,000-strong royal army to defend his crown on the field of battle. As a precaution, he dispatched his queen, escorted by Peter Courtenay, the newly appointed Bishop of Winchester, to Farnham in Surrey to collect the infant heir-apparent Arthur. Prudently, contingency plans were also made for them to move on to a house of Benedictine nuns at Romsey, not far from the Hampshire coast, in case the king was defeated and the queen and the prince had to flee the shores of England.[38]

Henry confronted the rebels on ground abutting a wide bend of the River Trent at East Stoke, 3.7 miles (6 km) south of Newark, Nottinghamshire, on the morning of 16 June. The king entrusted tactical command of the battle to John de Vere, Thirteenth Earl of Oxford, the experienced commander of the 6,000 veterans in his vanguard, while he and his uncle, Jasper Tudor, led the 4,000 men of the main battle as a second echelon, with a reserve under George Stanley, Ninth Lord Strange, following up behind.[39]

The rebel army, swelled by Yorkist malcontents to perhaps 8,000 strong, extended across a front just over 1,000 yards (1 km) wide, with the battle-hardened German mercenaries stationed at Lincoln's centre, his English troops on the right and the lightly armed Irish *kerns* –

contemptuously described as 'beggarly, naked and almost unarmed' – on the left. They were destroyed by Oxford's troops in just three hours of vicious fighting, with his archers taking an especially heavy toll on the barefoot Irish. Lincoln and the mercenary captain Schwarz were killed at Stoke Field and Lovell was last seen swimming his horse across the wide river to escape Henry's waiting retribution.[40] Around 4,000 of the rebels were slaughtered – a nearby gully became known as the Red Gutter because of the blood that ran freely down it – and Lambert Simnel was captured. In a rare moment of Tudor compassion, he was spared because of his tender years. But with a finely judged level of disdain and disparagement, he was made a scullion in the royal kitchens (where Henry VII could keep an eye on him) and later was promoted to a humble falconer.[41] The victory was noted approvingly by the king's mother, Lady Margaret Beaufort, in her *Book of Hours*:

> The xvith day of June, the year of our lord 1487, King Henry the VIIth had victory upon the rebels in [the] battle of Stoke ... whereby was slain John Earl of Lincoln and others.[42]

Lincoln's younger brother, fifteen-year-old Edmund de la Pole, was also spared by Henry who now regarded the Yorkist threat as safely neutralised, a rash assumption he was later to regret. Henry VII felt secure enough to turn his attention to planning the coronation of his queen consort. In September 1487 writs were issued ordering peers to attend the ceremony in Westminster Abbey on 25 November.[43]

The previous Friday, Lady Margaret and Elizabeth sailed from Greenwich to watch an extravaganza on the Thames organised by the City of London. One of the pageants 'well and curiously devised to give [the queen] sport and pleasure' was a barge bearing a mechanical dragon spouting fire out of its mouth into the river.[44]

This excitement was but nothing compared to that of her coronation. Wearing a dress and mantle of purple velvet furred with ermine, Elizabeth of York stood at the great west door while the abbey's floor was overlaid with gold cloth (later slashed to pieces by the crowd for souvenirs). Then, escorted by a bareheaded Jasper Tudor, Duke of Bedford, who carried her crown, and supported by the Bishops of

Winchester and Ely on either side, Elizabeth entered and was duly crowned, watched by her husband and mother-in-law from a stage with latticed windows between the pulpit and high altar.[45]

Henry celebrated by having a new crown of gold 'set with many rich precious stones' made for himself, and wore it for the first time to mark the Feast of the Epiphany on 6 January 1488.[46] During that year, it is possible that Elizabeth gave birth to another son, reputedly named Edward, but the baby may only have lived a few short hours. By March 1489, the queen was pregnant again and on 29 November she delivered a daughter, Margaret. The next morning their first-born Arthur, now three years old, was created Prince of Wales and Earl of Chester in a ceremony in the Parliament Chamber and their baby daughter was afterwards christened in the adjacent church of St Margaret, Westminster.

Eighteen months later her third child, Henry, was born at Greenwich Palace, alongside the River Thames, five miles (8 km) east of London, on 28 June 1491.

Henry VII now had his 'spare heir' to the crown of England. Having ruthlessly crushed Yorkist aspirations to overthrow him, the prospects of a bright future for his Tudor dynasty looked even more secure.

Unhappily, his confidence proved to be wholly unfounded.

1

IN MY BROTHER'S SHADOW

———•◦•———

*'At about three of the clock . . . was conveyed through the city [of London]
with many lords and gentlemen, the Duke of York, second son of the
king, a child of about four years or thereabouts . . . sitting alone on a
courser, [he] was had unto Westminster to the king.'*

Henry's official entrance into London before being knighted by his father,
29 October 1494.[1]

Henry VIII was born into a very structured and disciplined world.
Comprehensive directives had been laid down for his mother's confinement, the fixtures and fittings of his nursery, and the pomp and
circumstance of a royal christening. Such minutely drawn strictures
were imposed upon almost every aspect of his life until his father died
eighteen years later.

In her arcane and pedantic style, his manipulative grandmother Lady
Margaret Beaufort had set out detailed ordinances[2] in 1486 governing
precisely how the arrival of a Tudor prince into this uncertain and
perilous world should be managed. These directions were repeated and
amended in a veritable lexicon of regal etiquette called *The Royal Book*.[3]

First, of course, was the ritual of the queen's confinement. Elizabeth
of York would have had her own private chapel accessible from adjacent
great and small chambers. (With only primitive medical care on hand,
childbirth in the Tudor period was always a hazardous experience. She
was sensible to seek the divine protection of the Almighty and His saints
to see her through the ordeal.) Her bedchamber would be 'hanged with
rich cloth of Arras, sides, roof, windows and all, except one window

11

which must be hanged so she may have light when it pleases her'.

Lady Margaret even listed all the necessary bedclothes and furnishings including 'two pairs of sheets ... every one of them four yards (3.66 m) broad and five yards (4.57 m) long; and square pillows of fustian[4] stuffed with fine [goose] down; a scarlet counterpane, furred with ermine and embroidered with crimson velvet or rich cloth of gold; a mattress stuffed with wool'. A pallet with a bolster of down was positioned alongside the great bed for the queen's midwife to sleep on.

When all was ready and her time drew nigh, two of the senior nobles of the realm would escort the queen into her darkened room and then depart respectfully, retreating slowly backwards with many an obeisance.

> Then all the ladies and gentlewomen to go in with her and none to come into the great chamber but *women* ... All manner of officers shall bring them all needful things unto the great chamber door and the women officers shall receive it there of them.[5]

After her flurry of organisation in this very female world, Lady Margaret seems to have been little moved by the birth of her second grandson on St Peter's day during the damp, dank summer of 1491. Her handwritten notes in her personal *Book of Hours* merely record the date, 28 June – and even then, she forgot to include the year and inserted it some time later.[6] Doubtless Arthur, the four-year-old heir to the throne, always remained uppermost in her thoughts and pious prayers, as he did for most of England's population. It is therefore not unexpected that for the first decade of the new prince's life, we only catch the occasional glimpse of him as he fleetingly emerges from the shadow cast by his elder brother's brilliant dynastic star.

A few days after his birth, Henry was baptised in the newly built church of the Order of the Franciscan Observants that adjoined Greenwich Palace immediately to the west.[7] Richard Fox, Bishop of Exeter and the Lord Privy Seal – one of Henry VII's old comrades from his days of tedious exile in Brittany[8] – performed the short ceremony, standing upon a circular tiered platform of wood beneath a glittering canopy of cloth of gold. As he named the child, Fox enthusiastically plunged the naked red-haired infant three times into the holy water, contained in a silver font specially brought from the great abbey at Canterbury. History does not relate whether the new prince cried out in protest at his triple immersion in the carefully warmed water. The baby was afterwards wrapped up in a mantle of crimson cloth 'with a long train [trimmed] with ermine' fur and carried triumphantly through the echoing church, a lighted candle clutched in his tiny right hand to symbolise his coming journey through this dark world. Payments totalling £6 3s 4d later made to Benjamin Digby, Yeoman of the Queen's Wardrobe of the Beds, suggest that the ceremonies followed Lady Margaret's instructions for the christening of a prince, including provision of the linen used to drape the font.[9]

Immediately after the christening, Mistress Anne Oxenbridge took charge of the baby as his wet nurse on a salary of £10 a year, or nearly £5,000 a year at current values.[10] This first important lady in Henry's life was a Launcelyn, an old gentry family entitled to bear arms,[11] who held the manor of Wood End in Cople, Bedfordshire, four miles (6.44 km) east of Bedford. Anne's husband Geoffrey Oxenbridge was Bailiff of the East Sussex Cinque Port of Winchelsea, but he died a few years after her royal appointment, some time between 1494–6. She married her second husband Walter Luke, a Sussex gentleman (and probably a lawyer) by 1504.

Anne cared for Henry for at least two years and his ever-careful grandmother ordered that her 'meat and drink be assayed [tasted] during the time that she gives suck to the child and that a physician do oversee her at every meal, [who] shall see that she gives the child season-able meat and drink'[12] after he had progressed to solid foods.

The wet nurse was assisted in her motherly duties by two official 'rockers' of the royal cradle – Frideswide Puttenham[13] and Margaret Draughton, each paid salaries of £3 6s 8d a year. Later, Anne was generously rewarded by a grateful Henry VII for her well-performed services.[14]

The baby had two cradles in his two-room nursery at Greenwich, together with other practical items for the best available infant care, including two 'great' pewter basins for washing the bed linen and the child's clothes and 'swaddling bands'. These were strips of linen or other material that were wound tightly around the infant from head to foot – restricting movement and popularly thought to promote sleep. It was also widely believed in Tudor times that these bands helped development of a correct posture in later life.[15] A silver basin was also supplied to bathe the child and a 'chafer' used to heat small quantities of water and later food. Anne Oxenbridge was equipped with a large leather cushion on which she sat while suckling her royal charge at her breast, surrounded by eight large carpets on the floor.[16]

The first cradle was the showy 'cradle of estate', five feet (1.52 m) long and three feet (0.9 m) wide, which gently rocked, suspended from a U-shaped wooden frame. It was covered with crimson cloth of gold, with four silver-gilt pommels or knobs decorated with the king and queen's heraldic arms. The cradle had a mattress, two pillows and a scarlet counterpane edged with ermine fur. Safely laid down in this, the infant Henry would receive his admiring and sycophantic visitors, each one bowing low on entering or leaving the royal baby's presence as he lay almost completely hidden in his swaddling bands of blue velvet or cloth of gold. The second, smaller cradle was for Henry to sleep in and was made of painted and gilded wood, forty-four inches (1.12 m) long and twelve inches (0.31 m) wide. Again, it was decorated with silver-gilt pommels and was supplied with two mattresses (in case of accidents . . .).[17]

Henry probably shared the royal nursery with his two-year-old sister Margaret, although they lived in separate accommodation and had their own female attendants. While the queen frequently stayed in the same building as her children, everyday care and love always devolved upon paid staff, as was normal in royal or noble houses. However, Elizabeth of York was probably well educated, and it may be that she taught Henry to read and write when he was about four years of age.

In their very early years, the royal children had a peripatetic existence, shifting from one palace to another as their mother travelled with the seasons, following the set regal diary of events, which was sometimes linked to religious festivals. As befitted the heir to the throne, their elder brother Arthur meanwhile had an entirely separate life, spending his first two years at Farnham Castle, the imposing seat of the Bishop of Winchester in Surrey, before his nursery was moved to Ashford in Kent around 1488. Five years later the seven-year-old prince was at Ludlow, learning the duties of a king, complete with his own household and council, administering his principality of Wales.

On 2 July 1492 Henry and Margaret were joined by another sister, Elizabeth, born at the Palace of Sheen, near Richmond, on the banks of the River Thames in Surrey.[18] She, of course, had her own wet nurse, Cecily Burbage, but warrants for payment also refer to the 'servants attending upon our right dearly well-beloved children, the Lord Henry and the ladies Margaret and Elizabeth'.[19]

While Henry VII was away briefly campaigning in northern France in October–November 1492, the infant Henry and his two sisters were with their mother at Eltham Palace, Kent (now swallowed up by the conurbation of south-east London), and their nursery remained a fixture there for some time. Four years later, it was placed under the control of a 'lady mistress' and one of the queen's ladies, Elizabeth Denton, was appointed to this post, although she continued as a royal attendant with an annuity of £20 per annum.[20]

Henry's early formative years were thus spent in a very cloistered and cosy feminine world at Eltham, with its impressive great hall built by Edward IV in the 1470s and set inside enclosed hunting parks extending to 1,265 acres (5.1 sq. km). Every day he played with his sisters, but was acknowledged as a first amongst equals by his adoring attendants. As the only boy in this royal nursery, he was thoroughly spoilt and tenderly protected from the hard knocks and bruises of childhood misfortune. The toddler prince was cosseted, his grumpiness and tears sweetly cooed away, and his every whim swiftly fulfilled by the doting matronly ladies who cared for him. Moreover Henry's grandmother, the redoubtable and pious Lady Margaret Beaufort, took a close interest in the children's conduct and education. Years later, when he ascended the throne, Henry did not forget those who cared for him in his early years and ensured they received generous incomes in their dotage.

Did this period in Henry's early life forge a deep psychological flaw within him that later created some of the personal difficulties that arose in his relationships with his wives? Some psychiatrists have detected in him an unconscious craving for a forbidden incestuous union – even signs of an Oedipus complex.[21] Certainly, that soft, compliant female world may have planted and nurtured the seeds of his terrible temper in adulthood; the breathtaking tantrums that assailed courtier or commoner when he was denied what he desired, or confronted by any kind of opposition, however feeble or insignificant the source.

But the young Henry was no effeminate sissy. He probably learnt to ride a pony before he could walk; on 1 January 1494 Henry VII paid fourteen shillings for horses purchased 'for my lord Harry'.[22] A sketch (Plate 5) of a young boy of two to three years of age wearing an ostrich-plumed cap,[23] which is traditionally believed to be Henry, shows a round-faced, chubby infant with fat forearms and a rather headstrong, if not wilful, look as he glances to the observer's left – as if distracted and diverted by a toy being suddenly waved at him just out of the picture.[24]

But all was not childhood rhymes, playthings and matronly routines in Henry's young life. Fresh fears over the insecurity of his father's crown invaded the peace and ordered existence of the royal nursery when Henry was only six months old. The harsh trumpet-call of insurrection against the Tudors again rang out, piercing even the cloistered, ordered calm of Eltham.

Another claimant to the English throne had surfaced – but this one was more dangerous than poor Lambert Simnel, still sweating away naked[25] as a turnspit in the stifling heat and noise of the royal kitchens. In November 1491, a French-speaking Flemish silk-trader arrived in Cork, on the south-west coast of Ireland. In looks, he bore more than a passing resemblance to Richard, First Duke of York, the younger of the two lost princes in the Tower – or was he yet another of Edward IV's many bastards?[26] He was named Perkin Warbeck, born around 1474 in Tournai (in today's Belgium), the son of a French official, Jehan de Werbecque.[27] He was the right age, the right height, and both literate and very personable.

After falling under the enthralling influence of Yorkist conspirators, he crossed the English Channel, seeking support from the French king

Charles VIII. However, the Treaty of Étaples, which had followed Henry VII's brief war with France in 1492, included a clause preventing Charles from providing shelter to any English rebels, so Warbeck and his followers fled to Malines (or Mechelen) also in present-day Belgium.

This town was within the domain of Margaret of York, the childless widow of the tyrannical Charles the Bold, Duke of Burgundy, who had died in battle in 1477. The canny and politically astute Margaret was sister to the two last Yorkist kings and therefore was understandably eager for a Yorkist to again wear the crown of England.[28]

Whether or not she suspected Warbeck to be a fraud is not known and probably does not matter. He posed a viable and costly threat to Henry VII across the sea in England, and as such was well worth her support. The duchess therefore immediately officially recognised him as her long-lost nephew Richard, miraculously returned from the dead. She set him up accordingly, with all the sad trappings of exiled, penniless royalty: paid-for halberdiers dressed in the Yorkist livery of blue and murrey,[29] an official residence in Malines and a comptroller of his meagre accounts. There was also his brand-new seal, bearing beneath the royal arms this proud inscription: 'Secret seal of Richard IV, King of England and France and Lord of Ireland'.[30] As presentation is half the battle, Margaret also carefully tutored him in the traditions and comportment of the Yorkist court. Did she really believe him to be an unfortunate victim of amnesia?

In August 1493 Warbeck had a chance to display his new-found courtly skills. He attended the funeral of the Holy Roman Emperor Frederick III[31] in the Stefankirche in Vienna, where he was acknowledged as King Richard IV by Maximilian I, the new Archduke of Austria and Imperial King of the Romans, who had married Margaret's stepdaughter.[32]

Back in England a rattled Henry VII railed against Duchess Margaret: 'That stupid brazen woman ... hates my own family with such bitterness ... she remains bent on destroying myself and my children.'[33] In a vain attempt to break her spirit, he imposed a trade embargo on Burgundy in retaliation for her support of Warbeck. Their income damaged, two angry English merchants hurled a bucket of night-soil at the pretender's house in Antwerp in protest at his activities. The king must have been positive in his own mind that Warbeck was an imposter, given his firm belief that the 'Princes in the Tower' were dead; certainly he was aware of Warbeck's antecedents by July 1495.[34] Henry probably reasoned that, imposter or not, the unwelcome reality was Warbeck's warm reception and recognition by the European courts – and news of this was stirring black, treacherous forces in his realm.

His trade sanctions were too little, too late.

Support for 'the king over the sea' was growing at home and ominously, it seemed that the lethal contagion of treason was spreading even within the royal household. In January 1493, Sir John Radcliffe, First Baron Fitzwalter and the First Steward of Henry's household, went over to the pretender. Two months later Henry VII's step-uncle Sir William Stanley, his Lord Chamberlain, also tentatively declared for Warbeck, unwisely pledging that he 'would not bear arms against King Edward's son'.[35] This was a humiliating setback for the king. Almost eight years earlier, Stanley's last-minute decision with his brother Thomas (later First Earl of Derby) to support Henry Tudor was a decisive factor in the defeat of Richard III at Bosworth. It was all too clear that Henry VII had to snatch the initiative in what was becoming an increasingly serious threat to his crown.

His immediate actions to counter the menace of Perkin Warbeck seem slight, if not insignificant. But if the king was habitually cautious, he was also shrewd. Arthur was already Prince of Wales, Duke of Cornwall and Earl of Chester, and in 1492 the six year old was allotted the figurehead role of King's Lieutenant – the 'Keeper of England' – when Henry was away in 'remote parts'. In February the following year, the heir was granted powers to administer justice in Shropshire, Herefordshire, Gloucestershire and Worcestershire and the Welsh borders.[36] The prince could also raise troops to assist the king and to enforce Henry's laws.[37] His commissioners' enthusiasm for enforcing Arthur's feudal rights led to a small but troubling insurrection in Meirionnydd, North Wales, in 1498.[38]

Henry reasoned it was now time to exploit the appeal and status of the second son. On 5 April 1493 the king made the infant Henry Lord Warden of the fourteen Cinque Ports on the south-east coast of England

and Constable of Dover Castle, that mighty fortress atop the white cliffs that guards the gates of England, facing the continent of Europe.[39]

It was a highly symbolic act. Not only was a royal prince now nominally in charge of the realm's defensive front line – a deputy, Sir Edward Poynings (another of Henry VII's loyal cronies from his exile), was the day-to-day operational commander – but the appointment was also deliberately linked with a name of famous memory. This possessed almost magical power in the history of the English monarchy: 'Henry of Monmouth, Prince of Wales', later King Henry V, was Lord Warden in 1409–12.[40]

Further prestigious offices followed: Earl Marshal of England and then, on 12 September 1494, his appointment as Lord Deputy of Ireland, the king's personal representative in that unstable and disorderly island with control of the Irish government executive – although, of course, the faithful Poynings[41] did all the hard work.[42] Prince Arthur was the Tudor figurehead in Wales and its marches; his younger brother fulfilled that role in Ireland. Henry was firmly stamping the Tudor dynasty upon the administration of his kingdom and dominions.

A more signal honour came just over six weeks later. Henry VII created his three-year-old son Duke of York and a knight of the Most Honourable Order of the Bath. His intention was quite transparent. Here was no mere Johnny-come-lately imposter. What price the pretender's claims when there was now a true Duke of York who was also a member of one of the most prestigious orders of chivalry of England? The king was determined to cut the ground from beneath Perkin Warbeck's feet, so gaudily shod by Burgundian money. Ceremony, the glittering and awesome spectacle of a grand state occasion, was his chosen weapon.

The toddler was confronted with a seemingly impossible test of infant nerve and stamina. He was to be at the centre of an unintelligible and interminable series of elaborate rituals, full of strange sounds and vibrant colours, and amid a host of strangers, all in the unfamiliar and intimidating surroundings of Westminster. We can only guess at the problems of coaching the little boy at Eltham in preparation for his ordeal during the twenty-seven days between 2 October 1494, when the writs for attending the initial ceremony of creating Henry a Knight of the Bath were issued by the royal household at Woodstock, Oxfordshire,[43] and the date Henry was scheduled to make his triumphant entry into the City of London as a curtain-raiser. What tears and tantrums there must have been as hour after hour he was patiently taught his oath of fealty and indeed, the most risky part – how to stand still and silent for long periods without betraying boredom or his pressing need for a pisspot.[44] The fun of trying on his coronet and robes and playing with his tiny sword surely alleviated the tedium of this training, but the ladies of his nursery probably frequently despaired of his performance on the day and must have shown considerable perseverance.

On 27 October, Henry VII travelled downriver from his Palace of Sheen to Westminster, together with the queen and his mother. Two days later he sent messengers to Eltham to summon little Henry to the ceremonies. At three that afternoon, the toddler rode a mighty warhorse through London, surrounded by representatives of the nobility. His horsemanship impressed the mayor, aldermen and members of the livery companies as the cavalcade clattered through the cobbled streets and on to Westminster.

The following day – Thursday 30 October – the child had his first taste of the ceremonial of being invested as a Knight of the Bath. At a small dinner[45] in the king's chamber at Westminster, he took part in the formalities of serving the king the main meal of the day. Happily, his was an easy task. Others tasted the food, brought in the dishes, poured the wine – Henry was involved in the simpler ritual of washing his royal father's hands before and after the meal. Henry, Tenth Baron Clifford, held the heavy silver basin as John Bourchier, Third Lord Fitzwarren, poured in the warmed perfumed water. The king rinsed his fingers and his son bashfully offered him a white damask towel with which to dry his hands. The task done, the smiling father returned the towel to his little son, who respectfully bobbed his head and gingerly backed away, no doubt seeking instant reassurance on his performance and advice about what to do next.[46]

His tribulations were far from over. Henry now had to undergo the rituals of his knighthood, which involved bathing in a wooden tub in the draughty king's chamber before a long vigil during the dark, silent hours. This barrel was 'royally dressed' with linen and covered with thick mantles and carpets against the cold of the late October evening. Twenty-two other knights were being created that night, all with their own barrels lined up in rows in the Parliament Chamber, with the exception of the Lords Harrington[47] and Fitzwarren who had theirs in the queen's closet. Unlike their young fellow postulant knight, the others would have their 'beards shaved and the heads rounded' – their hair trimmed. All now had to be spiritually cleansed.

After the naked Henry clambered awkwardly into the warm bath, John de Vere, Earl of Oxford and Great Chamberlain of England, stepped forward. Kneeling down, he read out the so-called 'advertisement' to the child – the formal creed or way of life that must be pursued by a new knight:

> Be ye strong in the faith of Holy Church, (steadfast and abiding in word, [a] manly protector unto Holy Church) and widows, and maidens oppressed relieve, as right commands.
>
> Give ye to each one his own, with all thy mind, above all things love and dread God and above all other earthly things love the King the sovereign lord, him, and his right defend unto thy power, and before all worldly things put him in worship ... [48]

This was pure gobbledygook to a child aged just three: only years later would he grasp the full import of these stentorian words concerning a subject's allegiance, loyalty and faithfulness to the wearer of the crown of England.

Then, out of the gloom appeared his father, his lean, fine-featured face lit by the bright golden candlelight. The king dipped his hand into the bathwater and with his finger made the sign of the cross on his son's right shoulder. He then bent down and kissed the mark. After a few reassuring words to the toddler, Henry VII departed to fulfil the same ritual for all the other knights, accompanied by Oxford.

The child was taken out of the bath by his 'governors', put into an adjacent bed and gently dried. But there was no respite or slumber for the little boy. He was dressed in the coarse robes of a pious anchorite and conducted in procession, the footfalls echoing through the silence of the labyrinthine Palace of Westminster, to St Stephen's Chapel[49] to pray. Like the others, Henry must have been given a gold coin – a noble, worth 6s 8d (33 pence) – to hand over to the Sergeant of the Royal Confectionary in return for a spiced cake to nibble and wine to sip, as tradition dictated. There in the flickering light of the chapel with its colourful wall paintings in gold, vermillion and blue and the central images of the Adoration of the Magi below the east window, the knights kept vigil on their knees. Each one then confessed to one of the thirteen chaplains or canons attached to the chapel, received absolution and finally all heard a short Mass. They were then allowed to return to their cold beds for the few hours left before dawn.

It would have seemed like a dream (or a nightmare) to such a small child. It is beyond belief that Henry stayed awake through those hours of cold, cheerless vigil unless there was an attendant alongside him to ensure that he did so, by means of a gentle, respectful prod at the appropriate moment. In the event, he enjoyed only a short nap before being woken by de Vere, the sixteen-year-old Algernon Percy, Fifth Earl of Northumberland,[50] and Henry Bourchier, Second Earl of Essex, a member of the king's Privy Council. They hurriedly dressed him in his shirt and robes.[51]

Two by two, the new knights rode into Westminster Hall, led by Henry. A contemporary account describes the scene in that ancient raftered building:[52]

> The Lord William Courtenay bore the Lord Henry's sword and spurs, the pommel [of the sword] upward and when he ... alighted from his horse, Sir William Sandys [carried] him to the king's presence.
>
> There, the Earl of Oxford took the sword and spurs and presented the right spur to the king [who] commanded the Duke of Buckingham to put it at the right heel of Lord Henry and likewise the left spur to the Marquis of Dorset.
>
> And then the king girded his sword about him and after dubbed him knight in manner accustomed, then set him upon the table.[53]

His spontaneous action, born out of natural paternal pride, was Henry's only public acknowledgement of the tender years of his second son. Perhaps it was also tempered by his relief that the ceremony had passed off so successfully.

The next day, Saturday 1 November, was the Feast of All Hallows, one of the great red-letter days in the calendar of the royal court.

It was the day selected for the creation of Henry as Duke of York and the king was up early, attending the religious office of matins in St Stephen's at cockcrow before returning to his chamber to don his robes of royal estate. He then processed to the Parliament Chamber and stood waiting on a dais beneath a great canopy of cloth of gold, surrounded by a throng of prelates, wearing their mitres and pontifical vestments, and the premier nobility of the realm. Ranged down the sides of the chamber were the judges in their coifs and red robes; Richard Chawry, Lord Mayor of London, and his aldermen, and 'a great press of knights and esquires'. Above, from a windowed chamber or closet, the queen and her mother-in-law looked down on the vibrant proceedings, probably in some anxiety lest the child now disgrace himself before all the spiritual and temporal peers and a host of commoners of England.

Amid the shuffling of feet and suppressed coughing, a small procession approached the king. Sir John Writhe, Garter King of Arms and principal herald, stepped forward and, bowing low, presented the letters patent – the document creating the new Duke of York. Three other nobles accompanied him, one carrying a 'rich sword', the hilt uppermost, another the ducal rod or staff of gold and the third an ermine cap of estate with a duke's coronet. Behind came Sir George Talbot, Fourth Earl of Shrewsbury, a veteran of the Battle of Stoke Field, carrying the toddler duke in his arms. He gently set him down, and the Marquis of Dorset and the Earl of Arundel helped the child walk through the chamber, halting him immediately in front of the king.

Oliver King, now Bishop of Exeter and the king's secretary, read out the letters patent, which included a handsome annuity of £1,000 a year (£538,000 in current values) to the holder of the dukedom. The king then solemnly invested his son with all the noble accoutrements of a duke – the sword, the cap and coronet and the rod of gold – and, the ceremony over, moved back into St Stephen's Chapel for a solemn High Mass. Much, much later, when he ruled England, Henry VIII carefully amended the herald's report of the ceremony, inserting a phrase demonstrating that he had, as a child, carried 'his verge [rod] of gold in his hand' and clarifying the difference in roles of John Lord Dynham, the Lord Treasurer of England, and Sir Thomas Lovell, now Treasurer of the Household.[54] This could not be just mere pedantry. It was a conscious decision to call for the manuscript and check its contents. Perhaps Henry was anxious to demonstrate his royal bearing, even at an early age. Certainly that occasion spawned his later delight in gaudy pageantry and lavish ceremonial.

Back in 1494, his father stood in the dean's pew in the choir stalls and organised the procession into St Stephen's Chapel, but four of his noblemen, cursed with a frightful sense of timing, bickered loudly over their order of precedence, an unseemly argument swiftly resolved by a few short, sharp words from the king. Mass was then celebrated by Cardinal John Morton, Archbishop of Canterbury and Henry's Lord Chancellor, assisted by eight bishops and a whole chant of mitred abbots.

All then processed through Westminster Hall, the Earl of Shrewsbury carrying a desperately tired, if not overexcited, new Duke of York in his arms.[55]

Substantial gratuities must have been provided to the heralds, for after the second course of a bewildering array of choice meat and fish dishes, Garter led his brother officers to thank the king. They also cried 'largess' for the generosity of the newly created duke – which naturally had been supplied by his father. In ringing tones, they then proclaimed young Henry's new style and title for the first time in French – 'the most high, mighty and excellent prince, second son of the king our sovereign lord, Duke of York, Lieutenant-General of Ireland, Earl Marshal, Marshal of England, Lord Warden of the Cinque Ports'.[56]

After the strain and exhaustion of all the official ceremonies, now came the reward of spectacular entertainment for the three year old. Celebratory jousts in his honour were held over three days at Westminster from 9 November – the first witnessed by the little boy.

These had been delayed for two days by Henry VII's decision to take advantage of the presence of most senior members of the English nobility to hold two impromptu council meetings, both attended by Sir William Stanley, even though the king was well aware of his suspect loyalty.

When the jousts were finally staged, little Henry must have wriggled and squirmed with excitement as he sat alongside his mother and father in a grandstand richly hung with blue Arras cloth decorated with gold fleur-de-lis, watching the armoured contestants ride out of Westminster Hall, their horses trapped with the Tudor colours of green and white, tiny bells tied to the coursers' manes. It must have been an especial thrill to see the challengers wearing the Duke of York's new personal livery of blue and tawny brown.

Henry's five-year-old sister Margaret presented the prizes to the winning knights after three days of jousting, which included a diamond-studded gold ring to the leading challenger, Edmund de la Pole, Sixth Earl of Suffolk, younger brother of the rebel Earl of Lincoln who had been killed seven years before at Stoke Field.

The thunder of the steeds' hooves; the jingling of their harness; the splintering crashes as the competitors' lances 'shivered' (broke) against shield, body or helmet; and the screeching clash of sword on armour: all must have thrilled the toddler – and imbued Henry with his future passion for the chivalry and spectacle of the tournament.

The following month he was appointed the figurehead Warden of the Scottish Marches, covering the vulnerable border region with England's sometimes truculent neighbour.

That Christmas was spent at Greenwich, but less than a week after Twelfth Night – 6 January 1495 – Henry VII moved back upriver to the Tower of London. Messengers had brought the startling news that one of Warbeck's supporters, Sir Robert Clifford, had seemingly turned coat and held important information about the extent of the domestic conspiracy against the Tudor crown. In reality, Clifford – who had fought for Henry at Stoke and had been knighted afterwards – was almost certainly one of the king's spies. The historian Polydore Vergil claimed the move to the Tower was to enable Henry VII to 'imprison in that safe place any members of the plot whom [Clifford] might name'.[57]

Stanley was 'suddenly arrested and put under sure keeping', as were a number of others, including William Worsley, Dean of St Paul's, and William Richford, the Provincial of the Dominican Order of the Black Friars, 'one of the most famous preachers at that time about London'. The last two were pardoned but died shortly afterwards.[58] Stanley was arraigned on treason charges at the Court of King's Bench in Westminster Hall on 6/7 February and was beheaded nine days later.[59] The life of the former Lord Steward, Sir John Radcliffe, Baron Fitzwalter, was spared and he was sentenced to life imprisonment, but was executed in November 1495 in Calais after a failed escape. Clifford received an opportune royal pardon for his evident offences and £500 in cash for information received.[60] He was later rewarded with the appointments of Knight of the Body and Master of Henry VII's Ordnance.[61] This fresh plot against the Tudor crown seemed to have been nipped in the bud, but Warbeck remained in Burgundy, a dormant threat beyond the reach of the king.

He was quick to take advantage of Henry VII's absence on royal progress in Lancashire and the North. After becoming becalmed, the pretender had arrived off Deal in Kent on 3 July 1495, with troops and ships paid for by Burgundian cash. Warbeck mistakenly expected to rally popular support for his cause. The partisan historian Edward Hall was contemptuous of this forlorn hope of an invasion force:

> So gathering a great army of valiant captains of all nations … some English sanctuary men, some thieves, robbers and vagabonds which [desired] only to live of[f] robbery and rapine, came to be his servants and soldiers.
>
> The Kentish men, hearing that this feigned duke was come and … that he was but a painted image … thought it neither expedient or profitable … to aid and assist him.[62]

Warbeck – wisely, perhaps – decided not to disembark from his ship, as the four hundred troops who came ashore were quickly cut off by the local militia and one hundred and fifty hacked to pieces before the handful of survivors were driven back in panic to their ships. A further one hundred and sixty were taken prisoner and dragged off to London 'railed in ropes like a team [of] horses drawing ... a cart'.[63] These riff-raff soldiers of fortune were executed, some in London and others in towns along the coasts of Kent, Sussex and Norfolk, and their corpses were left hanging to rot near the high-water mark as a terrible warning to those who contemplated insurrection.

Warbeck may have been down, but he was not out. He sailed on to Ireland and there, with support from Maurice Fitzgerald, Ninth Earl of Desmond, besieged Waterford that August. His ships, however, were driven off after eleven days' determined resistance by the city and he fled to Scotland and the protection of King James IV, who was always delighted to be a thorn in England's side.[64] He promptly fed and clothed 'Prince Richard of England' and provided him with spending money. Furthermore, Warbeck married the king's cousin, Catherine Gordon, daughter of George Gordon, Second Earl of Huntly – 'a young virgin of excellent beauty and virtue' – on 13 January 1496 and was granted the munificent pension of £112 a month. It was the closest he came to any pretence of royalty.

Warbeck was certainly dogged in his attempts to claim the English crown; some might have considered him almost suicidally so. If he hoped for more than half-hearted Scottish military support, James was too crafty to supply it, even though Warbeck had promised him the handsome prize of the border fortress town of Berwick-upon-Tweed.[65] In September 1496 the pretender led just 1,400 men into England, hoping to rally the population of Northumberland to his standard.[66] It quickly became merely another tiresome border raid. After just three days of pillaging and burning, it was obvious that his cause was as unpopular in the north as it had been in Kent and he quickly retreated to Scotland, his tail between his legs.[67]

Far away from the alarums of the north, family life for the real Duke of York still centred on his nursery at Eltham Palace. He was to see little of his elder brother and lived away from his father for much of his young life.

There are only fleeting glimpses of father and son together during this period. On 17 May 1495, young Henry received the Garter, the highest order of chivalry in England. He wore a long crimson velvet gown and bonnet of the same material, specially made for the occasion.[68] Later that year the king paid out £7 10s for 'diverse yards of silk bought for my lord of York and [his sister] my lady Margaret'. The royal accounts for 1496–7 also record purchases of a furred gown in black camlet,[69] a black satin coat and a scarlet petticoat for Henry. Thriftily, an old lambskin garment of his was repaired so it could be used as a gown, as good as new. There was an order on 4 December for a crimson velvet gown trimmed with black lamb's wool, possibly intended for little Henry to wear that coming Christmas, as a present from his father.[70]

The child would have noticed the increasing absences from play of his younger sister Elizabeth. Unknown to the royal physicians, she was suffering from atrophy, a wasting disease caused by the breakdown of her body's tissues, and on Saturday 14 September 1495 Henry's sibling and playmate died at Eltham Palace, aged three years and two months.

Her funeral, attended by one hundred poor men in black gowns and hoods, was arranged by Cardinal Morton; the newly appointed Lord Chamberlain, Giles, Lord Daubeney; and the Lord High Treasurer, John, Lord Dynham, at an unusually high cost for a child of £318.[71] She was buried in Westminster Abbey, as close as possible to the sacred shrine of St Edward the Confessor, beneath a Purbeck marble tomb-chest with her effigy in gilded copper placed on the black marble cover-stone. Her Latin epitaph read:

> The royal child lies after death in this sarcophagus,
> A young noble Elizabeth, an illustrious princess,
> The daughter of King Henry VII
> Who holds the flourishing sceptres of two kingdoms.
> Atropos, the severe messenger of death, took her away
> But may there be eternal life for her above in heaven.[72]

The loss of Elizabeth was eased by the birth of another sister, Mary, on 18 March 1496, who joined Margaret and Henry in the nursery at Eltham.

Henry's first public duty came at Windsor on 21 September 1496, when he was aged five. This was his formal witnessing of a royal grant of a charter to the abbot and convent of Glastonbury to hold two annual fairs in the Somerset town.[73] Paradoxically, forty-three years later as king, he destroyed the abbey during the Dissolution of the Monasteries and had its last abbot brutally hanged for high treason.[74]

Meanwhile in Cornwall, discontent was mounting over the additional taxation levied on the population to pay for a planned retaliatory war against Scotland. Disgruntlement morphed into insurrection in mid-May 1497 and a Cornish host, totalling around 15,000, marched towards London via Salisbury, Winchester and Guildford. This may have been a fearsome sight, but a tactician would have wryly noted their lack of any cavalry or artillery.

Even so, something akin to panic swept the streets of the capital at the approach of the rebel army. Edward Hall recorded that there was 'great fear through the city and cries were made, "every man to harness, to harness" [armour]. Some ran to the gates, others mounted the [city] walls so that no part was undefended.'[75]

Henry had journeyed with his mother from Sheen on 6 June to stay at his grandmother's London home, 'The Coldharbour' in Thames Street, as a discreet precaution. Six days later he and the queen were hustled off to the nearby Tower of London for safety as the rebels passed south of the Thames and concentrated their forces at Blackheath, only a few miles to the south-east and near both Greenwich and Eltham Palaces. It was Henry's first experience of the acrid stench of rebellion and one, as a six year old, that he was never to forget.

Continual watch was kept by the city's magistrates 'lest the rebels, being poor and needy, would descend from their camp and invade the city and spoil, and rob the riches and substance of the merchants'. It was ever thus – the city was seemingly worried more about its wealth than providing patriotic support for the government of the day.

As they nervously awaited battle with the royalist forces, many Cornishmen deserted, fearful of Henry VII's vengeance if they were defeated. When the 25,000-strong royalist army under the king attacked on Saturday 17 June 1497, the Cornish were quickly surrounded by Henry's three 'battles' (or battalions) of archers and armoured men-at-arms on the battlefield alongside the River Ravensbourne. It was no contest and all over within hours. Hall recounts how

> there were slain of the rebels which fought and resisted, 2,000 men and more and taken prisoners an infinite number and amongst them Michael Joseph, surnamed 'the blacksmith' one of the captains of this dung hill and draught-sacked ruffians.[76]

The royalists lost about three hundred men in the fighting.

The king rode through the streets of the City of London in triumph at two o'clock that afternoon. The leaders of the Cornishmen were executed, but most of the rebels were allowed to return home un-molested.

A few months later, Warbeck decided on his final throw of the dice. He landed on the broad, flat sweep of Whitesand Bay, near Land's End in Cornwall, on 7 September, with the three-hundred-strong remnant of his force, pledging to the restless and still truculent Cornish that he would halt Henry VII's tide of taxation. This time he received an enthusiastic welcome and was proclaimed 'Richard IV' by his new supporters on Bodmin Moor before he tried unsuccessfully to capture the city of Exeter at the head of an army of 8,000. After several costly assaults on the city's walls and gates, Warbeck and his Cornish sup-porters headed for Taunton in Somerset.

Henry VII now had the measure of the pretender and knew that he could finally quash the threat he posed to the Tudor crown. The king claimed to be 'cured of those privy stitches which ... had long [been] about his heart and had sometimes broken his sleep'[77] and he lost £9 coolly playing cards while he awaited his forces to muster at Taunton.[78] Despite his bravado, Queen Elizabeth, again accompanied by Prince Henry, was quietly packed off on a pilgrimage to the Shrine of Our Lady at Walsingham, five miles (8.1 km) from the north coast of Norfolk, well away from any likely fighting.[79]

But when Warbeck heard that advanced elements of the royal army were sending out scouting parties, he panicked and fled with three companions to the Cistercian monastery of Beaulieu – possibly hoping to escape from England by a small boat from one of the many little creeks splintering that part of the Hampshire coastline. He had a bounty of 1,000 marks (£666 – or £357,000 at today's values) on his head. There he was found and seized by royalist forces on or about 5 October, either by violating the sanctuary offered by the monks, or by luring Warbeck out of it with tempting yet specious offers of a free pardon.[80]

Warbeck was now safely in Henry's grateful hands – as was his wife, Catherine, captured as she hid in the Church of St Bryan, near Marazion, Cornwall. The king, after admiring 'her beauty and amiable countenance', dispatched her to London to his queen 'as a true and undoubted token of his victory'.[81] The most serious threat to Henry VII and his dynasty had at last been neutralised.

Like his Tudor descendants, the king was not altogether magnanimous in victory. He brought Warbeck back to London and subjected him to the derision and taunts of the mob. He also appointed

> certain keepers to attend on him which should not (the breadth of a nail) go from his person, to the extent that he might not neither convey himself out of the land, nor fly any[where], nor yet ... be able to sow again no new sedition nor seditious tumult within his realm[82]

although he did manage to escape custody. He was eventually thrown into the Tower and kept 'with the greatest care' in a cell 'where he sees neither sun nor moon'.[83] A fellow prisoner was that other claimant to the throne, Edward Plantagenet, Seventeenth Earl of Warwick, who had languished as Henry's prisoner since the king's accession after Bosworth, when the earl was aged just ten. Warwick had grown into a handsome youth, though sadly somewhat mentally impaired.[84] He was held in a room above Warbeck and Warwick knocked a hole through the floor to communicate with his fellow pretender, who was chained securely by the leg to the wall. 'How goes it with you? Be of good cheer!' the earl called merrily through the opening.[85]

In February 1499, another claimant appeared to tax Henry VII's depleted store of patience. Ralph Wilford, the nineteen-year-old son of a shoemaker who traded under the sign of the bull in London's Bishopsgate Street, also declared himself to be the imprisoned Warwick. He was swiftly arrested, tried and hanged, as was the priest who promoted his cause from the pulpit.

Furthermore, Edmund de la Pole, the Sixth Earl of Suffolk and a surviving nephew of the Yorkist kings through his mother, fled England for France that July after being indicted for murdering Thomas Crue, in the parish of All Hallows next to the Tower, a man involved in litigation against him in the King's Council.[86] Another potential claimant was therefore on the loose in Europe and Henry ordered that he should be persuaded to return, or at worst, be brought back forcibly.

Henry VII was told by a priest that 'his life would be in great danger' throughout that year and the tension created by this prophecy and the strain of putting down seemingly constant rebellions was beginning to tell on him. The Spanish ambassador in London reported: 'Henry has aged so much during the last two weeks that he seems to be twenty years older. The king is growing very devout. He has heard a sermon every day during Lent and has continued his devotions during the rest of the day.'[87]

Wilford may have been the last straw for Henry Tudor, who by now had had more than his fill of impersonators. If the king sought divine guidance, he received it. In August, Warwick and Warbeck were accused of trying to escape from the Tower. It may have been that Henry had shrewdly manufactured the ideal excuse to rid himself finally of these politically sensitive prisoners. On 12 November, a sixty-strong meeting of his council advised the king to impose harsh justice on this unlikely pair of prisoners.

Warbeck was hanged at Tyburn[88] beyond the western walls of London on Saturday 23 November, after reading out a carefully worded confession on the scaffold that duly confirmed that he had impersonated Richard, First Duke of York.

Five days later, Warwick was beheaded on Tower Hill. It was only the second time he had been outside the gates of the Tower – the first being when Henry paraded him to scotch talk of his impersonation by Lambert Simnel in 1487. With that blow of the headsman's axe, the last Plantagenet in the legitimate male line was judicially murdered. Perhaps even the weather gods were affronted by this palpably unjust act on

Henry VII's part. That day there were 'great floods, winds, thunder, lightning which did much harm and hurt in diverse places and countries in England'.[89]

Henry VII could now afford the time to look overseas to seek spouses for his children and alliances to secure England's rightful place in the cockpit of European diplomacy.

Already his heir Arthur had been betrothed to Princess Katherine, the fourteen-year-old daughter of King Ferdinand II of Aragon and Queen Isabella I of Castile, and they were married by proxy on 19 May 1499 at Bewdley in Worcestershire. The Spanish ambassador in London, Don Pedro de Ayala, told the Spanish monarchs: 'There does not remain a drop of doubtful royal blood; the only royal blood being the true blood of the king, the queen and, above all, of the Prince of Wales.'[90]

The Milanese ambassador Raimondo de Soncino presented his letters of credence to Henry and Arthur at Woodstock in September 1497:

> The king was standing and remained so until our departure.
>
> There was also ... [the] Prince of Wales, almost eleven years of age, but taller than his years would warrant, of remarkable beauty and grace and very ready in speaking Latin.
>
> His majesty, in addition to his wonderful presence, was adorned with a most rich collar, full of great pearls and many other jewels, in four rows, and in his bonnet he had a pear-shaped pearl which seemed to be something most rich.[91]

No wonder the king looked relaxed and 'in a most quiet spirit'. For the first time in fourteen years on the English throne, he could sleep easier at night. There remained only the still latent threat posed by the Earl of Suffolk.

Furthermore, Elizabeth of York had given birth to another son, named Edmund after the king's father, on Friday 20 February.[92]

There were now three sons in direct line of succession to the Tudor crown.

2

THE SPARE HEIR

'In the midst stood Prince Henry then nine years old and having already something of royalty in his demeanour, in which there was a certain dignity combined with singular courtesy.'

The Dutch humanist scholar Desiderius Erasmus meets the royal children during his stay in England, 1499.[1]

A painted and gilded terracotta bust of a laughing child, just over one foot (31.8 cm) in height of *c*.1498 probably portrays a boisterous young Henry at the age of seven.[2] It seems to have been part of the Royal Collection since it was carved, and may have been the result of a special commission by Henry VII himself.

The bust (Plate 6) has been attributed to the Modenese sculptor Guido Mazzoni (1450–1518) who submitted designs and estimates for Henry VII's grandiose tomb at Westminster Abbey. These were rejected[3] and this commission may have been awarded as something of a consolation prize. It takes the form of the head and shoulders of a young boy dressed in a high-collared green tunic and a gold lace skullcap – originally it had a green glaze over a tinfoil layer to imitate a rich cloth of gold for the garment. But it is the face that instantly captures our attention. Here is a rumbustious, mischievous child, with dimpled, chubby red cheeks, his blue-grey eyes cast downwards to the left, seemingly pondering on what impish prank to indulge in next. He has a broad, knowing grin – as if he is well aware that he will always evade punishment for any transgressions, as Henry, sequestered within his adoring, tolerant female world at Eltham, would know and slyly exploit all too easily. It is a charming sculpture, redolent of boyish high spirits and rude, youthful health.

As noted earlier, his mother, Elizabeth of York, probably taught Henry to read and write – as she did his sisters. When the boy was almost five years old, his father paid £1 on 2 November 1495 'for a book bought for my lord of York',[4] doubtless a simple reading primer, full of colourful pictures. Henry, Margaret and Mary's handwriting all closely resemble one another's, although later examples of the young duke's letters are bolder, more deeply inscribed and angular, resembling the fashionable Italianate style.[5]

In the seventeenth century it was claimed, without any evidence, that the king intended Henry to be a future Archbishop of Canterbury – a prince of the church, rather than of the realm.[6] If this is true, it would be characteristic of the king's scheming and cunning persona. Perhaps Henry VII believed his dynasty should rule England both regally and ecclesiastically, with Tudor hands safely gripping the two main levers of power controlling his subjects' faith, lives and finances, through tithes and taxation. Not for him a repetition of the catastrophic tensions between church and state suffered by Henry II with Thomas Becket in the twelfth century. One cannot help wondering what would have happened to the Reformation in England if Prince Henry had been in charge of Mother Church, given his devotion to the old liturgies in his later years.

Around 1496, the king appointed his mother's protégé John Skelton as tutor to Henry. He had been created Poet Laureate nine years before, entitled to wear the green and white Tudor livery, and he was now to teach his young charge English grammar and Latin – the international language of diplomacy, religion and scholarship – and instruct him in the standard classical works. He was a satirist, his views making him something of a loose cannon, and very fond of extolling his own skills and virtues.

One of the histories that Skelton is known to have used in teaching Henry was a fifteenth-century manuscript chronicle of France, the *Chronique de Rains*, now in the library of Corpus Christi College, Cambridge.[7] This was copiously annotated by the tutor – a bad habit acquired by his pupil who later demonstrated a proclivity for writing marginalia in his own books and paperwork.

Henry had a hard act to follow in his elder brother. His tutor, the blind poet Bernard André, boasted that before he had reached the age of sixteen, Arthur 'had either committed to memory or read with his own eyes and leafed with his own fingers' twenty-four books by the ancient Greek and Roman authors, including the favourites of the fashionable Italian humanist scholars: Guarino of Verona, Lorenzo Valla and Cicero.[8] Lady Margaret Beaufort gave her elder grandson a copy of Cicero's *De Officiis*, printed on vellum at Mainz in Germany in 1465, for his private edification. This pinnacle of moral philosophy was personalised by the insertion of colourful Tudor heraldic badges, and on one folio there is a tiny illuminated initial containing a picture of Arthur, standing rather sheepishly in his red and ermine robes in front of his tutor who is seated behind his desk, surrounded by books.[9] The prince does not look too happy – possibly he has stumbled over the words of his set recitation.

Perhaps in reaction to André's bragging, Skelton was far from reticent about his own success in schooling Henry: one of his later poems boasted of his teaching skills with the little duke – notably with his spelling:

> The honour of England I learned to spell
> In dignity role that doth excel ...
> I gave him drink of the sugared well
> Of Helicon's[10] waters crystalline
> Acquainting him with the Muses nine.
> It comes ... well [for] me to remorde [recall]
> That creausner [tutor] was [I] to thy sovereign lord.
> It pleases that [a] noble prince royal
> Me as his master for to call
> In his learning primordial.[11]

In August 1501 Skelton wrote a handy guide to proper princely behaviour for his pupil, entitled *Speculum Principis* ('A First Mirror')[12] which, to modern eyes, reads like a code of morality written for the estimable Boy Scout movement.

It bulges with earnest, if not trite, maxims: 'Do not deflower virgins; do not violate widows' (reflecting the oath Henry took as a Knight of the Bath); 'Avoid drunkenness'; 'Above all, loathe gluttony' (was Henry already prone to greediness?). Not much camera-fodder here for far future Hollywood scriptwriters!

Then there are the principles of conduct more pertinent to royal life: 'If you want to excel all others in majesty and find glory you should lead in learning and virtue.' Henry was also urged not to rely wholeheartedly on his councillors in adulthood – they will be 'either learned or ignorant, either indecisive or weak'. True wisdom came only from books and the careful study of the past: 'Peruse the chroniclers – seek out histories and commit them to memory.'

Finally, there was also an injunction that was to echo hollowly down the sad and sterile years of Henry VIII's reign: 'Choose a wife for yourself; prize her always and uniquely.'

All these – and more – the young prince probably learnt by rote, repeating them ad nauseam until Skelton believed they had been committed fully to his heart and mind. How much influence they had in Henry's later years is more doubtful, judging by his many lapses from kingly probity.

Then there was the French language, taught by the Fleming Giles D'Ewes (later royal librarian), who also taught Henry how to play the lute.[13] Another musical teacher was 'Guillam', an expert in the playing of wind instruments such as the trombone-like 'sackbut' and the shawm flute, with its six finger keys and one for the thumb.

A contemporary description of the royal children as they gathered in Edward IV's great hall at Eltham Palace has come down to us. The compelling word picture was written by the Dutch humanist scholar Desiderius Erasmus, who accompanied his former pupil William Blount, Fourth Baron Mountjoy, to England in the summer of 1499. Mountjoy had already been appointed a companion to Henry and had shared in his studies of Latin and history. He and Erasmus were staying at Sayes Court, near Greenwich, and one day the Dutchman's new-found friend, twenty-one-year-old Thomas More (whom he called *mellitissime Thoma*, 'sweetest Thomas'), visited them. The trainee lawyer[14] took the scholar 'for a walk as far as the next village [Eltham], where all the king's children (except Prince Arthur) were being educated'. Years later, Erasmus recalled:

When we came into the hall, the attendants not only of the palace but also of Mountjoy's household were assembled.

In the midst stood Prince Henry, then nine years old [*sic*] and having something of royalty in his demeanour, in which there was a certain dignity combined with singular courtesy.

On his right was Margaret, about eleven years of age ... and on his left played Mary, a child of four.

Edmund was an infant in arms.

More walked across to the group, bowed low to Henry and presented him with some of his writings. This was the small beginning of a long and tumultuous friendship between prince and pious lawyer – More was already wearing a hair shirt next to his skin to mortify his flesh – that was to end tragically on the Tower Hill scaffold thirty-six years later.

Erasmus had brought nothing with him to offer the prince and was angry with More for not warning him that he would meet the royal children, 'especially as the boy sent me a little note while we were at dinner, to challenge something from my pen'.[15]

Afflicted by a stultifying attack of writer's block, Erasmus took three days to cobble together a suitable poem in Latin to send in recompense. The ten-page, rather tedious *Prosopopeia Britanniæ* (in which Britannia heaps praises upon her princes as well as immodestly on herself) bears the telling stigmata of its writer's frustration and haste.[16] His covering letter, headed 'Erasmus to the most illustrious prince, Duke Henry', emphasises the lasting importance of poetry and learning and hints at Henry's inspiring future:

We have for the present dedicated these verses, like a gift of playthings, to your childhood and shall be ready with more abundant offerings, when your virtues, growing with your age, shall supply more abundant material for poetry.

I would add my exhortation to that end, were it not that you are of your own accord, as they say, underway with all sails set and have with you Skelton, that incomparable light and ornament of British Letters, who can not only kindle your studies, but bring them to a happy conclusion.

Erasmus ends: 'Farewell and may Good Letters be illustrated by your splendour, protected by your authority and fostered by your liberality.'[17]

Henry VII may have been a distant, rarely seen father, but in his second son's early years, he kept him well clothed in the manner of a prince. John Flight was paid 4s 4d for a tippet of sarsenet (thin, light-weight silk) for Henry in April 1498.[18] It was followed by a green velvet riding gown lined with black satin and a crimson doublet. The new outfit came with knee-high tawny buskin boots.[19] A set of formal robes was made for Henry that November consisting of a long crimson velvet gown splendidly decorated with 2,800 ermine tails, together with another gown of black velvet, lined with sable fur. This grand ensemble was completed by crimson velvet bonnets and scarlet petticoats. The same month he received four pairs of knitted hose and two pairs of long hose to keep his chubby legs warm during the long winter nights.[20]

So who was Henry VII – many of whose character traits were inherited by his second son? The king's sombre portraits depict a dignified, haughty and driven man with a sallow complexion and aquiline features (Plate 1). Behind the sparkling brilliance of his blue eyes are hints of a certain craftiness, if not slyness, in his personality.[21]

The Italian-born contemporary chronicler Polydore Vergil described Henry VII as slender in body

but well built and strong, his height above the average.

His face was cheerful especially when speaking. His mind was brave and resolute and never, even at moments of the greatest danger, deserted him. He had a most pertinacious memory.

In government he was shrewd and prudent so that no one dared to get the better of him through deceit or guile.

Those of his subjects who were indebted to him and did not pay him due honour or were generous only with promises, he treated with harsh severity.[22]

Given his turbulent life and the repeated threats to his crown, it is not surprising that he was a self-centred king who kept his distance from those around him – indeed, a Milanese ambassador described Henry VII as someone who 'has no need of no one, while everyone needs him ... his majesty can stand like one at the top of a tower looking on at what is passing in the plain'.[23]

The security of his precarious crown must have consumed his thoughts almost daily throughout his reign. After the joy of the birth of his third son, Edmund, Duke of Somerset, in February 1499, the child's death on 19 June the following year must have been a crushing blow.[24] But he still had two sons living and had good cause to hope that at least one would live to succeed him.

The Spanish ambassador Don Pedro de Ayala reported that Henry was disliked by his subjects 'but the queen is beloved because she is powerless. The king looks old for his years but is young for the sorrowful life he has led ...' Henry was also 'much influenced by his mother [Lady Margaret Beaufort] and his followers in affairs of personal interest and in others. The queen ... does not like it.'

Then there is the issue of his legendary and notorious meanness and love of money. The envoy added:

> The King of England is less rich than generally said. He likes to be thought very rich because such a belief is advantageous to him in many respects. His revenues are considerable ... [with] great impoverishment of the people by the great taxes laid on them. The king himself said to me that it is his intention to keep his subjects low, because riches would only make them haughty ...
>
> He spends all the time he is not in public, or in his council, in writing the accounts of his expenses with his own hand.[25]

He also handled the cash himself. In his own handwriting, he itemised the moneys delivered in one day to John Heron, the treasurer of his chamber: 'sov[er]eigns of gold ... diverse coins of gold ... old weighty crowns ... good crowns ... [Venetian] ducats' and 'Spanish gold', all amounting to several thousands of pounds.[26]

A year later, de Ayala sneered that if 'gold coin once enters his strong boxes, it never comes out again. He always pays in depreciated coin . . . All his servants are like him; they possess quite a wonderful dexterity in getting other people's money.'[27] On just one day – 5 February 1509 – the king paid eleven individuals a total of £5,000 *all in pennies*, amounting to 1.2 million coins weighing more than 1,800 lbs (837 kg), which posed an immense and laborious task in counting it out.[28] Did he miserly begrudge the payment of every coin?

Aside from regular taxation, Henry VII collected money through a pernicious system of written legal obligations and recognisances imposed on many subjects, both high- and low-born, to guarantee their absolute allegiance to the crown. These were administered by two notorious royal servants, the lawyers Sir Richard Empson and Edmund Dudley. If any suspicion surrounded the victims, no matter how flimsy the evidence, they were forced to pay substantial cash penalties to the crown or face imprisonment. Many suffered both.

This insidious process of wealth generation accelerated after 1502 to the extent that of the sixty-two families in the English peerage that survived the butchery of the Wars of the Roses, forty-seven were at the king's mercy, either by living under attainder[29] or forfeiting substantial sums to the crown to guarantee their good behaviour. Only fifteen noble families were entirely free of this regal financial coercion.[30]

Some bonds or recognisances were imposed on what seem to us today to be absurdly slim pretexts. A one-time royal favourite, George Neville, Third Baron Abergavenny,[31] was liable for the remainder of his life under a bond for £5,000 should he ever enter the counties of Kent, Sussex, Hampshire or Surrey without the king's permission. This was on top of existing recognisances for £100,000 that he faced for unlawfully maintaining retainers and to assure his loyalty to the Tudor crown. Richard Grey of Ruthven, Earl of Kent from 1505,[32] had a £10,000 bond imposed on him to make no sale, lease or grant of any land, offices or annuities without the king's explicit consent. He also had to be seen in the king's house at least once a day and could not leave court without a royal licence, except for an agreed eight days away every three months.

This was all easy money: Dudley alone brought in nearly £219,500 to the royal coffers from sureties guaranteeing these bonds in the period

1504–8 – worth more than £113 million at today's prices. Henry VII knew full well how to not only keep his nobility submissive, but also how to squeeze the last silver groat[33] out of their depleted purses and those of his other hapless, complaining subjects.

Vergil alleged that:

[Henry] began to treat his people with more harshness and severity than had been his custom, in order ... to ensure they remained more thoroughly and entirely in obedience to him.

The people themselves had another explanation ... for they considered they were suffering not on account of their own sins but on account of the greed of their monarch ...

[Henry] gradually laid aside all moderation and sank into a state of avarice.

Empson and Dudley realised 'they had been given the job by the king not so much to administer justice as to strip the population of its wealth without respite, and by every means fair or foul, vied with each other in extorting money'. Moreover, Vergil added, 'they devised many fresh ways of satisfying their king's avarice while they were eagerly serving as the ministers of their own private fortunes.'[34]

Historians have debated long and hard over whether Henry VII was truly guilty of charges of rapacity and avarice,[35] but documentary evidence suggests strongly that the king was responsible personally for many of the decisions to extort money and Dudley, years later, acknowledged that the king's chief aim was 'to have many persons in his danger at his pleasure'.[36] This was state blackmail, pure and simple.

At Henry's death, most of his abundant treasure was held 'in secret places under his own key and keeping' at his new riverside palace at Richmond, Surrey.[37] Potential revenue from recognisances during the king's reign has been estimated at £954,790 – or £495 million at 2011 prices – which was over and above the £142,000 the royal coffers received annually in later years from more traditional sources of income under the wise guidance of the Lord Treasurer of England, Thomas Howard, Earl of Surrey.[38] This grossly swollen exchequer was an extraordinarily rich legacy to Henry's son and heir, who all too diligently learnt at his father's knee the delights of sequestering cash and property from those who fell victim to kingly power.

Much of the king's revenues was consumed by an ambitious building programme begun in the 1490s, which was designed to emphasise shamelessly the prestige of the new Tudor dynasty. A disastrous fire on 21 December 1497 at the old palace at Sheen destroyed a 'great substance of richness, as well as jewels and other things'[39] along with most of the wooden buildings. The blaze

> about nine of the clock began suddenly ... within the king's lodging and so continued till midnight. By violence whereof ... [a] great part of the old building was burnt and much more harm done upon costrings [curtains] and hanging beds of cloth of gold and silk and much other rich apparel with plate and manifold jewels belonging to such a noble court.
>
> How well loving thereof be to God [that] no living creature was there perished.[40]

Divine intervention had indeed truly shielded and protected the Tudor family. They had gathered at Sheen for the Christmas festivities but fortunately the king, his wife and mother, together with 'my lord of York [and] my lady Margaret' all escaped from the fire unhurt. What excitement for the young Henry: hustled away from his warm bed into the cold darkness of the night, amid the crackling flames and flying sparks piercing the night sky and the panicked shouts and confusion of the royal household. His father may have feared the fire was the prologue to another attempted *coup d'état*; his son probably saw it as an adventure after the well-ordered serenity of his nursery at Eltham Palace.

Henry VII immediately began construction of a huge new palace on the site, renamed Richmond (after the family earldom), alongside the Thames – finishing the major phase by 1501. The royal apartments, rebuilt and refurbished, were still within the largely undamaged fifteenth-century donjon or keep, moated and battlemented. Evidently Henry continued to prize his security. Its opulence – it had a bowling alley and tennis courts – and the splendour of its furnishings led it to be popularly nicknamed 'Rich Mount' by his more truculent citizens downstream in London.[41]

In the same period, Henry rebuilt Baynard's Castle at the confluence of the Rivers Fleet and Thames on the western edge of the City of London,[42] constructed a fine new brick courtyard house at Greenwich Palace[43] and undertook building projects at Windsor Castle and the Tower of London. The delight of designing and raising palaces was clearly part of the Tudor inheritance, as Henry VIII also became a prolific builder, first completing his father's works at Hanworth, Middlesex; Woking, Surrey; Wanstead, Essex; Ditton, Buckinghamshire; and Leeds Castle in Kent, before embarking on his own grandiose schemes, beginning at Bridewell, off Fleet Street in London, Eltham Palace and Beaulieu in Essex. Many more were to follow.

Some of those around Henry VII, such as Bishop Richard Fox, had been his comrades in exile and these, together with gentry from the king's native Wales, found favour at his court. Fox, having been at Bosworth, was appointed Lord Privy Seal in February 1487. He was notoriously loyal to his master. Thomas More was told later that to serve the king, Fox 'would not stick [fail] to agree to his own father's head [being struck off]'.

Yet Henry remained a secretive, chronically suspicious king, frequently making notes during his conversations with courtiers, counsellors and diplomats and writing private aides-memoires to himself. One day his favourite pet, a spider monkey that lived in his library, 'tore his principal notebook all to pieces. Whereat the court (which liked not these pensive accounts) was almost tickled with sport.'[44]

Aside from his shrewd, if not wily, administration of the realm, the king was not the dour, glum or dreary monarch that many have been taught to believe him to be. Far from it: he loved hunting, gambling and, from 1494, playing real tennis within a closed court. In June of that year, a payment of £4 was made to a 'Spaniard, the tennis player' who may have been the king's private coach.[45] (Tennis was to become another favourite sport of his second son, although like his father, his first passion was hunting.) In May 1499, the Milanese ambassador complained ruefully that Henry VII 'attends to nothing but pleasure and the enjoyment of the infinite treasure he has accumulated and continues to pile up'.[46] In September 1507, the king was reported to be out 'every day to hunt deer and other game in forests and in parks. Besides, he often went out hawking.'[47]

Three months earlier, perhaps because of his deteriorating eyesight, he shot a farmyard cock in error with his crossbow at Chesterford, Essex, and had to pay four shillings to an aggrieved farmer named Whiting.[48] The compensation culture, unfortunately all too familiar today, is nothing new. For example, in October 1496, Henry's Privy Purse had to pay a man called Rede four shillings to replace his colt 'that was slain by the greyhounds', and in August 1505, 3s 4d was paid to a 'poor man that had his corn eaten by the king's deer' near the hunting lodge at Woking, Surrey.[49]

But Henry VII's hard fiscal heart did have some capacity for generosity. When one of his Esquires of the Body remained unpaid because he was absent due to his 'great diseases', the king ordered the annuities to be reimbursed immediately because of the courtier's 'long continued s[er]vice done unto us to our singular good pleas[u]r[e]'.[50] Loyalty in that most turbulent of reigns was a virtue always worth rewarding as it sometimes seemed in such short supply.

In September 1495 he must have suffered an attack of conscience – or, more cynically, made an attempt to appease or assuage continuing Yorkist resentment. Henry VII commissioned a tomb costing £10 from the Nottingham mason James Keyley[51] to hold the mortal remains of Richard III. The alabaster effigy and tomb-chest were duly set up in Greyfriars, Leicester, where the deposed king was so contemptuously buried in the aftermath of Bosworth.[52]

During the evenings and idle moments, Henry VII gambled at chess, cards and dice – a favourite amusement also inherited by Henry VIII – and bet on the potential winner of archery contests and tennis matches. Whatever the pastime, he seems to have enjoyed poor luck and rarely won.[53] Card games of the period have especially intimidatory names: Plunder, Pillage, Triumph, Condemnation, Cuckolding and Torment. There was also a game called *Totem Nihil* ('All or Nothing') in which a four-sided object was spun to determine the winner.[54]

The royal accounts from 1500 onwards record the king's losses at gambling: for example, the 8s 4d paid in August of that year to [Richard] 'Weston', a Groom of the Chamber; the 24s 4d given to James Braybroke 'for the king's play'; and an additional forty shillings for the lucky Weston in September 1502 after losing at 'gleek', a three-handed card game played with a forty-four-card pack.[55] Henry VII even lost 6s 8d at cards to seven-year-old Prince Henry on 23 May 1498.[56] No wonder the child was depicted with a broad grin! Was this the king's customary bad luck – or was this a doting father allowing his young son to win? One can almost hear young Henry's boyish squeals of delight as the cards were dealt and turned over by a chuckling king. A total of 66s 8d was also paid 'to my lord of York to play at dice' in January 1502, but perhaps this was funding games over a length of time, as the considerable sum – equivalent to around £1,500 in today's monetary values – might have annoyed the financially careful king if this represented his son's gambling losses at a single session.[57]

We have already met Henry's grandmother, Lady Margaret Beaufort, (Plate 3) fussing and fretting over the arcane arrangements for court ceremonial. She had been married three times: firstly to Edmund Tudor, First Earl of Richmond, whom she wed at the age of twelve; after his death in November 1456 she gave birth to her single child on 28 January 1457 – but only after a lonely and perilous confinement in which mother and baby son came close to death. Her second husband was her cousin, Sir Henry Stafford, son of Humphrey, First Duke of Buckingham. She married him in 1462 and enjoyed a happy and close union with him before he died from wounds sustained fighting for Edward IV at the Battle of Barnet on 14 April 1471. Lastly, at the age of thirty in June 1473, Margaret married Thomas Stanley, later First Earl of Derby, whose eleventh-hour intervention at Bosworth, together with his younger brother William (executed for treason in 1495), had won the day for Henry VII.

Margaret was famously pious. In 1499, with her husband's permission, she swore a vow of chastity in the presence of Richard Fitzjames, Bishop of London, and retired to a separate establishment at Collyweston, Northamptonshire, three miles (4.83 km) south-west of Stamford,

Lincolnshire. It was an idyllic spot, on the south side of the valley of the River Welland, and she extended the existing early-fifteenth-century manor house originally built by Sir William Porter.[58] Given her sacred vow, her husband was thoughtfully provided with separate rooms on the rare occasions when he visited, travelling down from his seat at Lathom Hall, near Ormskirk, West Lancashire.

Gradually the house at Collyweston was turned into a palace fit for a lady whose official title was 'the King's Mother'.[59] By special permission of her son, she was allowed to sign herself 'Margaret R' – the 'R' for *Regina,* the feminine form of '*Rex*' – and was also licensed to keep her own retainers, all wearing the silver and blue Beaufort livery and her portcullis badge on their chests. At one stage she had four hundred servants and dependants. Like the king, she employed spies and informers, and the string of castles and manor houses across England granted her by her son became operating bases for her agents, ever vigilant for treachery and treason.[60]

Lady Margaret also maintained a large London townhouse, granted by the king. Coldharbour, in Thames Street, was an ancient mansion with its own river frontage and a pleasant 'summer house' overlooking the water.[61]

Their letters testify to the close, loving relationship between the politically shrewd only son and equally guileful mother. One from Henry VII begins:

> Madam, my most entirely well beloved Lady and mother, I recommend me unto you in the most humble and lowly ways that I can, beseeching you of your daily and continual blessings . . .
>
> I shall be glad to please you as your heart can desire it and I know well that I am as much bounden so to do to any creature living for the great and singular motherly love and affection that it has pleased you at all times to bear towards me.[62]

Such filial love was gushingly reciprocated. A letter from mother to son, probably written in January 1501, begins:

> My own sweet and most dear king and all my worldly joy, in as humble

manner as I can think I recommend me to your grace and most heartily beseech our Lord to bless you.[63]

Another starts with a fervent 'My dearest and only desired joy in this world' and refers to Henry VII in the text as 'my dear heart' and 'my good king'. The same letter archly requests the king's permission to reserve some of her tenants in north-west England to be 'kept for my lord of York, your fair sweet son' as his retainers.[64]

Portraits of Lady Margaret depict her in the drab, dark clothes of a vowess, her lean, high-cheekboned face staring out with hooded eyes from beneath a linen headdress with a white or grey coif and a wimple covering her head and throat like a nun. A pleated barbe stretches down from her chin onto her chest. She is invariably seen either on her knees devoutly praying, or holding an open missal in her hands. She was the principal patron behind the rebuilding of Great St Mary's Church in Cambridge, and in 1505 she refounded the impoverished Godshouse there as Christ's College;[65] later she founded another Cambridge college, St John's. She also established readerships (later professorships) in Divinity at Oxford and Cambridge Universities.

In about 1501, she appointed Dr John Fisher, Master of Michaelhouse, Cambridge, as her chaplain. Shortly afterwards he became her confessor.

Henry VII was impressed by Fisher and decided to make him Bishop of Rochester. He sought his mother's permission to offer the appointment:

> Madam: And [if] I thought I should not offend you, which I would never do, I am well minded to promote Master Fisher, your confessor, to a bishopric ... for none other cause but for the great and singular virtue that I know and see in him.
>
> Howbeit, without your pleasure known, I will not move him nor tempt him ... [66]

She clearly agreed as Fisher was appointed by papal Bull on 14 October 1504.

He later described her daily ritual of piety:

> In prayer every day at her uprising which commonly was not long after

five of the clock, she began certain devotions and so after them, with one of her gentlewomen, the matins of Our Lady. Then ... she came into her closet, where with her chaplain she said also matins of the day.

After that [she] daily heard four or five Masses upon her knees, so continuing in her prayers and devotions unto the hour of dinner which was ... of ten of the clock and upon a fasting day, eleven.

After dinner full truly she would go her stations to three altars daily [and] daily her dirges and commendations[67] she would say and her evensongs before supper, both of the day and of Our Lady, besides many other prayers and psalters ... [68]

Twelve poor or injured people lived under her roof whose wounds she regularly tenderly dressed with her own hands. She wore 'lacerating garments of hair cloth' next to her skin to mortify her flesh.[69]

But behind all that strait-laced sobriety and holiness, Lady Margaret had a lighter side. She kept a troupe of minstrels – Henry VII paid 10s to them on 18 February 1494 for performing before him – and her own fool, or jester, called 'Skip', who wore a pair of 'start-ups' or high-heeled shoes. There was also 'Reginald the idiot' to provide her with hours of innocent entertainment, if necessary. The vowess liked a little wager at times also, betting – like her son – on the outcome of games of chess. On one occasion, she dispatched a man from Buckden, Cambridgeshire, to deputise for her on a pilgrimage while she gambled at cards.[70]

Lady Margaret must have presented a grim, formidable figure to her grandchildren, but she was extremely fond of all of them, although her favourite was her godchild and namesake Margaret.[71] Her imperious nature and very rigid views must have overawed all of them, particularly young Henry, who lived under her controlling influence, especially in regard to his behaviour and education. She certainly was a dominant mother-in-law: a Spanish envoy, the sub-prior of Santa Cruz, wrote in 1498 that Elizabeth of York – 'a very noble woman' – was 'kept very much in subjection by the mother of the king'. He respectfully suggested to the Spanish monarchs, Ferdinand and Isabella, that 'it would be a good thing to write often to her and to show her a little love'.[72]

Henry, Duke of York, was now going to play a major role in a spectacular and expensive show of pageantry, carefully stage-managed by his father as a showcase for the glamour and glory of the House of Tudor: the glittering wedding of the heir-apparent, Arthur, to Princess Katherine of Aragon (Plate 9).

Negotiations for the wedding match had been continuing for years, complicated by the frequent bitter bickering between the Spanish ambassadors in London[73] and the complexities of the marriage settlement. There were endless niggling details to sort out. One Spanish envoy, Dr Roderigo de Puebla, reported in July 1498 that the queen, Elizabeth of York, and the king's mother desired that Katherine

> should always speak French with Princess Margaret who is now in Spain in order to learn the language and to be able to converse in it when she comes to England.
>
> This is necessary because these ladies do not understand Latin, much less Spanish.
>
> They also wish that the Princess of Wales [Katherine] should accustom herself to drink wine. The water of England is not drinkable and even if it were, the climate would not allow of it.[74]

Meanwhile Arthur and his intended bride could only write forlorn and studiously polite love letters to each other, delivered via the squabbling diplomats in London.[75]

At last in 1501, Katherine left Granada at the start of her long journey to England for the wedding, with a fifty-two-strong entourage, including a cook, a baker and even her own floor sweeper.[76] She was delayed first by the unusually fierce heat of Spain and then by terrible weather off Ushant, including storms and hurricanes, forcing her ships to return to port. Henry VII was so worried that he sent one of his best captains, Stephen Butt, out into the Bay of Biscay to escort her to England. Katherine, he added, was 'impatiently expected by me, the queen, by the Prince of Wales and by the whole nation'.[77]

At three in the afternoon of Saturday 2 October, the fleet carrying the bride finally entered Plymouth harbour to 'great rejoicings, as if she had been the Saviour of the world', one of her many Spanish gentlemen reported.

As soon as she left the boat, she went in procession to the church, where, it is to be hoped, God gave her the possession of all these realms for such a period as would last long enough to enable her to enjoy life and to leave heirs to the throne.[78]

As it would turn out, these words were more of a curse than a blessing. Lady Margaret Beaufort used far plainer words. As was her habit, in her *Book of Hours* she noted against the date: 'This day my lady princess landed.'

Although very elaborate arrangements had been made for Katherine's stately progress to London, after all those turgid and tedious years of negotiation, Henry VII could not wait for her to arrive in his capital city. Impulsively, he rode out from Richmond with Arthur to meet her and at about two or three o'clock on the afternoon of 4 November intercepted her cavalcade, which had arrived three hours before at a palace of the Bishop of Bath and Wells at Dogmersfield in Hampshire. Katherine was under firm instruction from her parents 'not to converse with him or the Prince of Wales until the day of the solemnisation of her marriage'.[79]

Arthur was miserably left outside in the November rain as his father sought to meet his son's bride. But the door of her lodgings remained firmly closed, with her attendants declaring that 'the lady infanta has retired to her chamber'. Henry VII was not a king lightly brushed aside by maidenly inconvenience or incomprehensible Spanish conventions. He insisted that 'if she were even in her bed, he meant to see and speak with her, for that was his mind and the whole intent of his coming'. Katherine therefore hurriedly dressed and prepared herself to meet her future father-in-law.

Neither could comprehend what the other was saying; Henry could not speak Spanish and Katherine not a word of English. Her carefully learnt Latin was fluent but her pronunciation was so bad that the king could not understand more than a few words that she uttered. The encounter was descending into pantomime. But interpreters assured them 'there were the most goodly words uttered to each other ... as to great joy and gladness as any persons conveniently might have'.[80] After half an hour, a dripping Arthur was admitted for his first glimpse of his bride.

She had probably remained veiled but now modestly lifted it with the assistance of her attendants. She curtsied low, a shy girlish smile flickering across her oval face. Katherine was six weeks off her sixteenth birthday. She was pink-cheeked with blue eyes and reddish-gold hair. Unkindly, it was noted that Katherine was slightly on the plump side and quite short, even tiny. Henry VII 'much admired her beauty as well as her agreeable and dignified manners'. Arthur afterwards told her parents, Ferdinand and Isabella, that he 'never felt such joy in his life as when he beheld the sweet face of his bride. No woman in the world could be more agreeable.' Dutifully, he promised to be a good husband.[81]

What Katherine made of her fifteen-year-old groom is not recorded. He was half a head shorter than her, with a pallor to his face and lips. In appearance, he took after his father and grandmother, with hooded eyes, finely drawn features and a long nose. He did not look very healthy (Plate 4).

On 14 November 1501 their marriage took place in St Paul's Cathedral. Ten-year-old Henry was granted the honour of giving the bride away. A wardrobe of new clothes had been ordered for him for the celebrations: six gowns, including one for riding; eight pairs of hose; five bonnets or hats; and new boots and spurs. Livery was also provided for his four footmen and two minstrels, and his lute-player and teacher D'Ewes was given sixteen yards (14.3 m) of black camlet[82] for a new gown 'for the solemnisation of the marriage of our dearest son'.[83]

Henry had escorted Katherine in her dazzling entrance into the city of London two days before the wedding. It was his first sight of the girl who was to preoccupy his life, for better, for worse, for more than three decades.

She wore a broad-brimmed round hat, tied with gold lace, and in the fashion of unmarried women allowed her long auburn hair to stream down over her shoulders.[84] In a carefully orchestrated spectacle, they led the Anglo–Spanish procession of nobles and clergy through Southwark, across London Bridge and on to the bishop's palace alongside St Paul's Cathedral. The roads had been sanded for the horses' hooves, and the timing was thought critical: Lord Abergavenny had been deputed to ensure there was not 'too much haste, nor too much tarrying'.[85]

Edward Hall was beside himself with excitement, stunned by the splendour of 'the rich apparel of the princess, the strange fashion of the Spanish nation, the beauty of the English ladies, the goodly demeanour of the young damsels, the amorous countenance of the lusty bachelors'.[86] Thomas More was less impressed. He believed Katherine's escort of swarthy Spanish grandees resembled 'pigmy Ethiopians'.[87]

Inside the cathedral, a circular tiered wooden platform was built for the wedding ceremony, connected to the quire door by a twelve-foot- (3.66 m) wide carpeted walkway, five feet (1.52 m) above the floor. There were to be no embarrassing accidents: 'Sir Charles Somerset and the comptroller of the king's house have taken upon them that the said work should be made sure and substantial.' The cathedral walls were resplendent with costly cloth of Arras, hanging down from seven or eight feet (2.14 to 2.44 m) above the ground. Over the west door, the king's trumpeters were told to 'blow continually' when the princess left her lodgings in the palace next door 'till she be in the church upon the high place'.[88]

Henry, dressed all in white satin like the groom, escorted the bride in by the great west door and they mounted the walkway. She wore a dress of white silk with a border of gold, pearls and precious stones and her train was carried by Lady Cecily, Elizabeth of York's eldest sister. Above, in the consistory, Henry VII, his queen, and his mother watched the marriage ceremony from a closet[89] while the nave was packed with English nobility. The flamboyant Edward Stafford, Third Duke of Buckingham, wore a gown said to be worth £1,500.

Many days of feasting and celebratory jousts followed. An entertainment was staged at Westminster Hall which included dancing by the guests. Henry, enlivened by all that had gone on before, danced with his older sister Margaret. Then boyish high spirits took over. He shrugged off his expensive gown and 'danced in his jacket' as his excitement swept aside any thought of courtly etiquette.[90] But this exuberance drew no chiding looks from his parents; brother and sister 'in so goodly and pleasant a manner' provided 'great and singular pleasure' to Henry VII and Elizabeth of York.[91]

Shortly before Christmas the newly-weds left the Palace of Richmond to begin their new life together on the Welsh borders at Ludlow Castle.

On 2 April 1502 – less than twenty weeks after that sumptuous wedding – Arthur was dead and cold in his bed.

3

PRINCE OF WALES

———•◦•———

'There is no finer youth in the world than the Prince of Wales. He is already taller than his father and his limbs are of a gigantic size. He is as prudent as is to be expected from a son of Henry VII.'

Spanish ambassador Roderigo de Puebla to King Ferdinand of Spain, 5 October 1507.[1]

Henry, Duke of York, spent the Christmas of 1501 with his parents at their new palace at Richmond. His elder brother and his new bride had departed for Ludlow[2] but the court was still buzzing with excitement and expectation over the forthcoming proxy marriage between the boy's elder sister Margaret, now aged twelve, and James IV, the King of Scotland, three weeks into the New Year.

England's new-found ally Spain had mediated in Henry VII's protracted disputes with his irascible neighbour to the north, resulting in a fragile peace treaty being signed in July 1498. It had been a difficult and elusive diplomatic assignment, as the Spanish ambassador Pedro de Ayala acknowledged afterwards: 'The old enmity is so great it is a wonder the peace is not already broken.'[3] Almost immediately, the notion of a marriage between Margaret and the Scottish king was mooted as a means to cement the alliance and build future amity between the traditional enemies. However, negotiations over the projected marriage had dragged on for three years, with Henry VII initially being opposed to the match. In 1498, he told the Spanish envoy de Puebla:

I have already told you more than once that a marriage between him

57

[James IV] and my daughter has many inconveniences.

She has not yet completed the ninth year of her age and is so delicate and weak that she must be married much later than other young ladies. Thus it would be necessary to wait at least another nine years.

Besides my own doubts, the queen and my mother are very much against this marriage. They say if the marriage were concluded we should be obliged to send the princess directly to Scotland, in which case they fear the King of Scots would not wait, but injure her, and endanger her health.

De Puebla confirmed to Ferdinand and Isabella that 'the daughter of Henry is, in fact, very young and very small for her years'.[4]

Three years later, diplomatic necessity had overcome Henry VII's nicer paternal scruples and a marriage treaty was finally signed on 24 January 1502 with a proxy wedding arranged in the queen's newly refurbished great chamber at Richmond the next day. Henry, Elizabeth of York and the king's mother still retained serious concerns about Margaret's delicate health: the treaty contained a clause stipulating a maximum delay of eighteen months before she could join her husband in Edinburgh.

The delightfully named Robert Blackadder, Archbishop of Glasgow, officiated at the ceremony, asking Margaret whether she was 'content without compulsion [to marry] and of her free will?'

[She answered:] 'If it please my lord and father the king and my lady, my mother the queen.' Then the king showed her that it was his will and pleasure and that she had the king's and queen's blessings.

Such was the dumb duty and predestined fate of a Tudor princess. Patrick Hepburn, First Earl of Bothwell and Lord High Admiral of Scotland, stood proxy for the Scottish king, promising

in his name and behalf and by his special commandment, [I] contract marriage with thee Margaret and take thee into and for the wife and spouse of my said sovereign lord James, King of Scotland ... during his and your lives natural ...[5]

Ten-year-old Henry watched his sister's proxy marriage, heading the list of many dignitaries who attended, which graciously included Catherine Gordon, widow of the pretender Warbeck and a cousin to James IV.[6]

The Duke of York was now of an age when he enjoyed the beginnings of his own small household and some clues to its membership occur in his mother's Privy Purse accounts and elsewhere. In March 1502, Elizabeth of York gave a shilling to 'John Goose, my lord of York's fool' for bringing a carp for her dinner table – this was probably the young master's nickname for the jester who was called John Goor.[7] Like his sister Margaret, Henry had his own company of minstrels[8] and there were other attendants. Three shillings and four pence were repaid to a 'footman to my lord prince' who donated alms to the poor on Henry's behalf at Abingdon in Berkshire in October that year. In the same month, 'one of his servants' was given 6s 8d after bringing a message from the prince to his mother.[9] Livery in Henry's personal colours of blue and tawny brown were supplied to his footmen, 'John Williams and Richard Wiggins', in October 1501 and the following May.[10] There were nobler companions as well, somewhat older than Henry and therefore not playmates: we have already met William Blount, Fourth Baron Mountjoy, who mentored the prince's studies in history and Latin. There was also Algernon Percy, Fifth Earl of Northumberland, who had woken Henry after his vigil in St Stephen's Chapel, Westminster, and afterwards regularly attended on the prince.[11]

Two numbing, sledgehammer blows now fell painfully upon Henry VII.

First, his fifteen-year-old heir apparent Arthur died in Ludlow Castle on Saturday 2 April 1502, having fallen sick in late March after attending the traditional ceremony of alms-giving to the poor on Maundy Thursday. There was no doubt about the seriousness of his affliction. A herald recorded him suffering

> a most pitiful disease and sickness that with so sore and great violence had battled and driven in the singular parts of him inwards; that cruel and fervent enemy of nature, the deadly corruption, did utterly vanquish

and overcome the pure ... blood without manner of physical help and remedy.[12]

His death seems to have come like a bolt from the blue. Lady Margaret had recently bought gold damask garters as gifts for both Arthur and Henry for a total of 12s 6d from 'Mistress Windsor', but Arthur's was never delivered.[13] He had not even received all his wedding presents; a magnificent window in Flemish glass depicting the Crucifixion had been given by the good magistrates and burghers of Dort in Gouda (in today's Netherlands), to be erected in Henry VII's new chapel at Westminster, but it arrived too late for Arthur to see it.[14]

Based on the scant and unreliable medical evidence surviving, three causes of death appear tenable. For two of the possible diseases, Henry VII himself may have been the unwitting agent of this crushing disaster to his dynasty.

The most probable is tuberculosis – an infectious disease that became the curse of the Tudor dynasty and one which had afflicted the king himself.[15] It may be that Henry VII passed it on to Arthur through the prince's inhalation of bacillus-infected droplets of saliva or mucus after a royal sneeze. Tuberculosis can lie dormant for years before eventually endangering the victim; symptoms include a persistent cough, breathlessness, fever, weight loss and fatigue. We know that the prince developed a recurrent fever shortly before his wedding – probably caused by a chronic and lingering chest infection.[16]

Secondly, it is possible that he succumbed to the *sudor Anglicus*, the so-called English sweating sickness. Again, it is cruel irony that this disease may have been introduced into England by the French mercenary soldiers of Henry Tudor, as the scourge made its first appearance shortly after he landed with his small army at Milford Haven, Pembrokeshire, on 7 August 1485 to snatch the crown from Richard III.[17] Dr John Caius, who fifty years later published a study of the disease, described its effects:

> It ... immediately killed some in opening their windows, some in playing with children in their street doors; some in one hour, many in two it destroyed.
>
> As it found them, so it took them, some in sleep, some in wake, some

in mirth [and] some in care. Some fasting and some full, some busy and some idle and in one house, sometimes three, sometimes five, sometimes more [died] sometimes all.

Of the which, if the half in every town escaped it was thought a great favour.[18]

Symptoms began with a fever and a sweat, accompanied by sharp pains in the back, shoulders and head. The disease then attacked the liver and the victim became leaden-limbed and drowsy. Delirium and vomiting followed together with palpitations of the heart. Death occurred within twelve to twenty-four hours of the onset of symptoms. Most at risk from this disease – now thought to be a pulmonary infection, such as an acute viral pneumonia – were young, rich males living in towns and cities. It was thus the original 'yuppie' sickness.[19] There were five major epidemics of the sweating sickness in this period – 1485, 1508, 1517, 1528 and 1551, so superficially it seems unlikely that Arthur was a victim of this disease, although there may have been localised outbreaks.

Thirdly, an undefined plague – almost certainly bubonic – was raging in Worcester, thirty-six miles (58.1 km) from Ludlow, and in Chester, seventy miles (112.3 km) away, around the time of his death.[20] Symptoms of this included fever, headache, nausea and vomiting, diarrhoea and the telltale tender 'buboes', up to four inches (10 cm) in diameter, found under the arms, in the groin and on the neck of sufferers, for which the disease is named.[21]

On the balance of the limited evidence, it seems most likely that tuberculosis finished off Prince Arthur. Symptoms of the 'sweating sickness' and plague were so familiar to the contemporary chroniclers that they probably would have identified either one of these as the cause of his death.

But there is one joker in this pack of the Grim Reaper's cards of mortality. There is hazy evidence that Arthur's already fragile constitution may have been undermined by his over-enthusiastic performance in the marital bed – an issue that was to cast such a black shadow over the middle portion of his younger brother's reign. More than three decades later, when the question of whether or not Arthur had consummated his marriage with Katherine of Aragon was on the prurient lips of most of England, testimony was taken from his attendants about the early love life of the newly-weds.

By favour of his father, who was steward of the king's household, Sir Anthony Willoughby was present when Arthur went to bed on his marriage night in the palace of the Bishop of London. He swore that

> in the morning, the prince ... said to him: 'Willoughby, bring me a cup of ale for I have been this night in the midst of Spain,' and afterwards said openly, 'Masters, it is a good pastime to have a wife.'[22]

These were merry, laddish words coming from a youth hitherto regarded as something of a swot – said to be 'studious and learned beyond his years'.[23] Edward Hall reports a similar brash boast, this time overheard by one of Arthur's household chamberlains: 'I have this night been in the midst of Spain which is a hot region and that journey makes me so dry. If you had been under that hot climate, you would have been drier than I.' Perhaps Arthur, with all his Tudor bragging and swagger, repeated this daring bon mot to all who would listen. It must eventually have become rather tiresome coming from a fifteen year old, even if he was heir to the throne.[24]

Another unidentified witness waited on Arthur during his breakfast after the wedding night. 'Sir,' he told his master, with the leer, nudges and winks of the trusted male servant, 'you look well upon the matter.' But he was later warned by one of the prince's officials, Maurice St John, a favoured great-nephew of Lady Margaret Beaufort, that

> after [Arthur] had lain with the Lady Katherine at Shrovetide[25] after his marriage, [he] began to decay and was never so lusty in body and courage until his death.
>
> St John said [this] was because he lay with the Lady Katherine.[26]

For her part, Katherine steadfastly maintained, years later, that they had shared their marital bed for only seven nights and that 'she [had] remained as intact and incorrupt as when she emerged from her mother's womb'.[27] So much for Arthur's gamecock bravura.

Whatever the cause, the heir was dead and his staff had the painful duty of informing the king. Sir Richard Pole, chamberlain of Arthur's household, sent letters off by messenger to Greenwich where the king and queen were staying.

Even riding post-haste, the courier took more than two days to reach London. With commendable sensitivity, Pole had insisted that the letters should first be seen by members of the king's council. Ducking an unpleasant task, they immediately sent for Henry's confessor, one of the Greenwich Friar Observants, to break the dreadful news to him.

On the Tuesday morning, 'somewhat before the time accustomed', the friar knocked at the king's bedchamber door. The attendants were instructed to leave, and in the awkward silence – Henry must have instinctively sensed imminent bad news – the Friar declared: '*Si bona de manu dei suscipimus mala autem quare non sustineamus*.' God, he said, in His wisdom, had decided to take the king's good son to be with Him and His divine judgement must be accepted.

Henry VII must have been left stunned and speechless by the friar's hesitant and stumbling Latin. The contemporary account by a herald of that tragic day's events says simply that 'when his Grace understood these sorrowful and heavy tidings, [he] sent for the queen, saying that he and his queen would take the painful sorrows together'.[28]

Amid her own deep grief, Elizabeth of York (Plate 2) sought bravely to comfort her distraught husband with 'full, great and constant comfortable words'. She told him that he should remember after God

the wealth of his own noble person, the comfort of his realm and of her and how [her mother-in-law, Lady Margaret] had never no more children but him only.

God had lent them yet a fair, goodly and towardly[29] young prince [Henry] and two fair princesses and over that, God is where He was.

Elizabeth pointed out: 'We both [are] young enough' to have more children. She then retired to her own chamber and 'natural and motherly remembrance of that great loss smote her so sorrowful to the heart that those that were about her [sent] for the king to comfort her'.[30]

Henry, Duke of York, was now the unexpected and untrained heir-apparent to the throne of England. In just over 1,000 days, Death had cruelly snatched two of the three Tudor princes.

A day of mourning was declared on the Friday following, with a general procession through the streets of London and a solemn dirge and requiem for Arthur's soul was sung in every city church. In St Paul's Cathedral, the mayor and aldermen attended a special Mass, dressed in black.

Meanwhile in Ludlow, Katherine was lying ill – the cause of her ailment is not known, but her confinement to her bed does lend some weight to the theory of some kind of prevalent epidemic.[31] Arthur's body had been embalmed and placed in a coffin covered with a black cloth. It remained in his presence chamber until the afternoon of 23 April – St George's Day – watched over day and night by the poor people who had received the royal alms on Maundy Thursday.[32] Then the corpse was carried in slow stages to Worcester for burial in the Benedictine abbey there (now the cathedral).[33] It was not an easy or comfortable journey:

> On St Mark's Day [25 April] the procession went from Ludlow church to Bewdley Chapel [Worcestershire]. It was the foulest cold, windy and rainy day and the worst way [road] that I have seen . . .
>
> In some places the car [carriage, with the prince's coffin] stuck so fast in the mud that yokes [teams] of oxen were taken to draw it out, so ill was the way . . .

reported the escorting herald.[34]

The funeral cost the large sum of £892 2s ½d, of which nearly forty per cent was for the cost of supplying black cloth for the mourners – probably enough for about five hundred and fifty individuals.[35] The chief mourner was Thomas Howard, Earl of Surrey, the Lord Treasurer of England, wearing a mourning hood over his head. Amongst the seven other official mourners was George Talbot, Fourth Earl of Shrewsbury. Maurice St John, who had worried that the joys of sex had sapped Arthur's energy, was one of the bearers of the canopy held over the coffin. A Purbeck marble tomb-chest was subsequently erected within a chantry chapel to the south of the high altar of the church.[36]

In London everyone at court was fitted with mourning outfits even though they were not attending the prince's obsequies at Worcester. 'Mr Geoffrey', Prince Henry's chaplain, was given 4.5 yards (4.1 m) of black cloth to make his mourning suit, as was John Skelton, also described as his chaplain. Ten of his yeomen and grooms were allowed three yards (2.7 m) of cloth each.[37]

In Spain, Ferdinand and Isabella's response to the news was prosaic. They immediately authorised their ambassador in London to reclaim the first instalment of Katherine's dowry, to insist that Henry VII hand over the lands and property that came with their daughter's marriage and to 'beg the King of England to send Princess Katherine to Spain in the best manner and in the shortest time possible'. Hours later, with an eye perhaps on the main chance, further instructions were sent to London 'to conclude with Henry, in their names . . . a marriage between our daughter and his son, Henry Prince of Wales'.[38]

It was only two days later that they sent a letter containing any semblance of regret to de Puebla:

> We have read with profound sorrow the news of the death of Prince Arthur. The will of God must be obeyed. We have heard that the Princess of Wales is suffering. She must be removed, without loss of time from the unhealthy place where she is now.[39]

Happily, after recovering from her sickness, she was removed safely to the Archbishop of Canterbury's palace at Croydon, Surrey – Elizabeth of York kindly providing a horse-drawn litter covered with black velvet and cloth for her bereaved daughter-in-law's slow-paced transportation.[40]

Katherine arrived there in late May and on the 25th of that month, Elizabeth of York sent Edmond Calverd, one of the pages of her chamber, to see her.[41] Almost certainly his was a delicate mission. He probably carried letters from the queen discreetly enquiring whether her daughter-in-law now found herself pregnant by her dead son. Her answer would have been: 'No.' That information was vital to the formalities of succession to the English crown: Henry could not be declared Prince of Wales until it was positively established that there was no heir in the offing from the union of Arthur and Katherine of Aragon.

Therefore on 22 June, 'Henry Prince of Wales' was granted the sine-cure post of Keeper and Chief Justice of the Forest of Galtres, north of the city of York.[42] The following October he succeeded Arthur as Duke of Cornwall.

After New Year 1503, the second grievous blow befell Henry VII.

As her words of comfort to the stricken king had prophesied, Elizabeth became pregnant again a few months after Arthur's death. With two daughters living, the king and queen had hoped desperately for a second boy to firmly secure the line of Tudor succession. Elizabeth had dreaded a difficult birth with Edmund in February 1499, but in the end his was easy. There were concerns now about her latest confinement as she had been ill throughout much of her pregnancy. The queen was rowed downriver in her barge from Westminster to take possession of her apartments on the upper floor of the White Tower, within the Tower of London, on 26 January 1503 – in good time before her expected confinement.[43] A monk from the Augustinian abbey at Bruton in Somerset had already been paid 6s 8d for bringing her a holy relic to bolster her during the birth.[44] This was 'Our Lady's Girdle' in red silk, piously supposed to be the very belt that encircled the Virgin Mary's stomach before the birth of Christ. It was believed to provide spiritual comfort during labour and divine assistance against miscarriage.[45] In addition, she had paid 3s 4d to a retainer who went on a pilgrimage to the shrine of Our Lady of Willesden in north-west Middlesex to seek the Mother of God's especial blessing on her behalf.

Henry was both optimistic and confident about the prospects of a new heir, emotions born out of his long-standing addiction to prog-nostications by those he superstitiously believed could see into the future. On New Year's Day, his Milanese astrologer William Parron, who had been employed by the king since 1498,[46] had presented him with a book that boldly predicted that Henry VII would go on to father many lusty sons and that the queen would live on until she was eighty or ninety.[47] Parron presented a second copy to Prince Henry, dedicated to the new heir, which contained prophecies that had been drawn up based on the date and time of his nativity.[48]

During the night of 2 February, the queen 'travailed suddenly of a child' but with the assistance of her midwife, Alice Massy, safely gave birth to a daughter, christened Katherine (perhaps named after her daughter-in-law), in St Peter ad Vincula, the parish church within the Tower, the following Saturday.[49]

A few days later Elizabeth fell ill, possibly of a puerperal fever arising from an infection picked up during the birth. Her condition rapidly worsened until her life hung in the balance. One of her attendants, James Nattres, was dispatched to Kent to collect urgently the physician Dr Halesworth to treat her. He travelled night and day. The queen's accounts record payments for his hire of a boat at the Tower to sail the twenty-five miles (39.3 km) down the River Thames to Gravesend in Kent (which cost 3s 4d) and the procurement of horses and guides to take him to and from Halesworth's home.[50]

The tides would have been a major factor affecting the timing of this frantic journey, but whether the good doctor arrived quickly or not became a matter of little consequence. The ministrations of her midwife (afterwards paid £10 for her services)[51] were to no avail. Early on the morning of Saturday 11 February 1503, Elizabeth died. It was her thirty-seventh birthday. The next day, twelve yards (10.97 m) of flannel were purchased for the baby's use.[52] A few days later the baby was also dead.

Henry VII had lost his gentle, blonde and fair-skinned wife of eighteen years, and of the eight children she had borne him, only three now survived – Margaret, Mary and Prince Henry.[53] She had lived true to the doctrine laid down by her personal motto: 'Humble and reverent'. The royal couple had enjoyed a happy and affectionate marriage, free of quarrels over politics or even over the frequent meddling by the king's dominant mother.[54] When Henry VII was told of her death he 'privily departed to a solitary place and would no man should resort to him'. Her passing was 'as heavy and dolorous to the king's highness as had been seen or heard of', commented one observer.[55]

Solemn Masses and requiems for her soul were ordered to be said in all the churches of the realm – six hundred and thirty-six Masses were said in London alone – and after lying in state at the Tower, her body was taken in procession, via Charing Cross, to Westminster Abbey where it was buried. Above the coffin was an effigy of the dead queen, wearing her rich robes of estate and a crown upon its head, with hair 'about her shoulders, her sceptre in her right hand and her fingers well garnished with rings of gold and precious stones'.[56] Richard Fitzjames, Bishop of London, preached on a text from the Old Testament Book of Job: 'Have pity upon me, my friends, for the hand of God hath touched me.'[57] The queen was dearly loved by her husband's hard-pressed subjects, and a watching herald declared: 'He spoke these words in the name of England and the lovers and friends . . . of that virtuous queen.'[58]

Thomas More wrote a resonant poem shortly after her death, *A Rueful Lamentation of the Death of Queen Elizabeth*, which has her addressing the living from her grave. In his sonorous words, she regrets not seeing the completion of Henry VII's magnificent new chapel under construction at Westminster:

> Where are our castles now, where are our towers?
> Goodly Richmond's son, art thou gone from me?
> At Westminster, that costly work of yours
> My own dear lord now shall I never see.
> Almighty God vouchsafe to grant that Ye
> For you and your children well me edify
> My palace builded is and now here I lie.

More has the queen ruefully bemoaning the false prophecies of the court astrologer, William Parron:

> Yet was I late promised otherwise
> This year to live in wealth and delice [joy].
> Lo! Whereto comes your blandishing promise
> O false astrology and devinatrice [divination]
> Of God's secrets making yourself so wise?
> How true is for this year your prophecy
> The year yet lasts and lo! Here I lie.

No surprise then that Parron fled the court and England immediately after the queen's death.[59] The poem also has Elizabeth urging her husband to provide love for their surviving children, and makes this farewell to Prince Henry, now almost twelve years old:

> Adieu lord Henry my loving son so dear
> Our Lord increase your honour and estate.[60]

Having lived very separate existences for so much of their young lives, Arthur's death may not have impinged too much upon young Henry's emotions, other than surprise or shock at the sudden dramatic change in his status within the royal household.

His mother's death was another matter. She had taught him to read and write, and most of his formative years had been spent very close to her at Eltham. Much later, in an elegant letter written in Latin to Erasmus in 1507, Henry wrote of his thoughts at the death of the King of Castile, but recalled his great grief at the loss of Elizabeth of York:

> For never, since the death of my dearest mother has there come to me more hateful intelligence.
>
> Your letter . . . seemed to tear open again the wound to which time had brought insensibility.[61]

Although Henry did not attend her funeral, he was kitted out with a mourning suit of black cloth, furred with lambskin, with a riding gown in the same material and a cloak bordered by black velvet. Twelve pairs of hose and twelve pairs of shoes and gloves were also provided.[62]

Aside from fulfilling the established formalities of mourning a lost queen and mother, the all-important Tudor dynasty had to be safeguarded. One week after his mother's death, on 18 February, Henry was created Prince of Wales, and Earl of Chester and Flintshire. And he was approaching the age when it would be imperative to choose a wife for a future King of England. Two years earlier, in 1501, Henry VII had made cautious enquiries about the prospects of marrying off his second son to Eleanor, the daughter of Philip, Duke of Burgundy, who was also the niece of Katherine of Aragon, whom Arthur was then about to wed.[63]

This idea was abandoned on Arthur's death as the Spanish suggestion of a re-match between Henry and Katherine looked diplomatically more inviting. But the present wearer of the crown also had ideas to remarry in the hope of siring more sons. He may have been deranged by the death of his beloved wife, but two months afterwards, he briefly considered marrying his eighteen-year-old widowed daughter-in-law.

Some scholars have questioned whether Henry VII was truly serious in this choice of potential bride[64] but Queen Isabella of Spain was incandescent at the scandalous suggestion:

> This would be a very evil thing – one never before seen and the mere mention of which offends our ears.
>
> We would not for anything in the world that it should take place.

She instructed her ambassador in London: 'If anything be said to you about it, speak of it as a thing not to be endured. You must likewise say very decidedly that on no account would we allow it, or even hear it mentioned.' She repeated her demand for the return of Katherine to Spain:

> Now the Queen of England is dead, in whose society ... the Princess might honourably have remained as with a mother and the king being the man he is ... it would not be right that the Princess should stay in England.[65]

In the face of such parental opposition, Henry VII speedily dropped any lustful claim on Katherine, and the marriage treaty of Henry, Prince of Wales, and the Spanish princess was signed on 23 June 1503,[66] with a formal betrothal two days later at the London mansion of Edmund Audley, Bishop of Salisbury, off Fleet Street, on the western edge of the city.[67] Katherine discarded her mourning black to appear at the ceremony dressed in a virginal white dress.

The new Prince of Wales' reaction to the prospect of marrying his brother's widow can only be guessed at. He hardly knew her – having seen her only during the brief few weeks between personally escorting the princess during her official welcome to London on 12 November 1501 and the couple's departure to freezing Ludlow Castle the following January. Having lived in Arthur's shadow for so long, Henry may have been more than a little piqued at now having to wed his hand-me-down wife after already being given much of his brother's wardrobe.

Doubtless, in the taciturn way of royal fathers, Henry VII pointed out that his son had little or no choice in the matter. It was only much later that his patriotic duty for England burgeoned into true love.

As far as Katherine was concerned, the betrothal probably came as a respite in her uncertain life: it had her parents' blessing and was a happy harbinger of the future in an alien existence in a foreign land, amid a host of strangers with unfamiliar customs and language.

There were still some obstacles to jump before Katherine's marriage to Henry could go ahead, which was planned to take place before the prince's fourteenth birthday in June 1505. Whether or not Arthur had consummated his marriage with Katherine, she was still Henry's sister-in-law – and this unnatural relationship, or affinity, had to be legally swept aside by a special dispensation from Pope Alexander VI. Ferdinand of Spain wrote to his ambassador in Rome:

> In the clause of the treaty which mentions the dispensation of the Pope, it is stated that the Princess Katherine *consummated her marriage with Prince Arthur.*[68] The fact, however, is that although they were wedded, Prince Arthur and the Princess ... never consummated the marriage.
>
> It is well known in England that the Princess is still a virgin.
>
> But as the English are much disposed to cavill [quibble], it has seemed to be more prudent to provide for the case as though the marriage had been consummated and the dispensation of the Pope must be in perfect keeping with the said clause of the treaty.
>
> The right of succession depends on the undoubted legitimacy of the marriage.[69]

It was a complicated process, even more thorny than the English and Spanish sovereigns feared, mainly because the Pope unexpectedly and inconveniently died in the Vatican. Alexander VI, one of the most corrupt of those who ever wore the papal triple tiara, expired on 18 August, aged seventy-two, after days of suffering convulsive fevers and intestinal bleeding, probably as a result of poisoning. Not for nothing was he a member of the notorious Borgia family. His last words were a plaintive, 'Wait a minute,' as if he was frantically fending off the hand of Death, and his passing triggered an unseemly scramble to secure the papal treasure. The frail and gout-ridden Cardinal Francesco Piccolomini of Siena was then consecrated as Pius III on 8 October 1503. He only lasted twenty-six days on the throne of St Peter before dying – supposedly from the effects of a leg ulcer, but in reality probably from poison. Finally, Cardinal Giuliano della Rovere was elected by a near-unanimous vote of the conclave of cardinals on 31 October to become Julius II.

Eventually the new Pope got around to the question of Henry and Katherine's marriage and dictated a one-page aide-memoire immediately after Christmas 1503 summarising his initial reactions:

> We have been informed that the Princess Katherine of Spain had contracted a marriage with Arthur, late Prince of Wales, and that this marriage has, perhaps, been consummated.
>
> Notwithstanding this, in his quality as the Head of the Church, [the Pope] authorises Henry Prince of Wales and the Princess Katherine to contract a lawful marriage.[70]

In the sixteenth century, the Vatican's civil service was notorious for its snail-like progress in processing paperwork, or indeed arriving at any kind of decision. To the clerks, bureaucracy was a creed almost as fervently followed as their devotion to the Catholic faith. The all-important process of unhurried 'mature consideration' was always the order of the day. The long-desired formal dispensation, with its weighty lead papal seal, or *bulla,* was frustratingly slow to arrive in both England and Spain. The following year, on 6 July, Julius wrote to Henry VII, regretting the delay.

> We never intended to withhold the dispensation and all that has been said to the contrary is an invention of ill-intentioned persons.
>
> It is true [there have been delays] to dispense with the obstacles to the marriage ... but this was done only from the wish to consider the case more maturely.

The document was to be handed over to Robert Sherborne, Dean of St Paul's and the English ambassador to the papal court:

There could not be a safer person to whom to entrust it and at the same time the life of that excellent man would be preserved by a journey to England, for a longer stay in Rome would prove fatal to him.[71]

Julius pointed out, a little primly, that there was absolutely no need to thank him 'as the Pope cannot be otherwise than gracious and benevolent'.[72]

Despite these august promises, nothing arrived.

Ferdinand, Duke de Estrada, the Spanish ambassador in London, was in abject despair: 'I had expected the brief of the Pope containing the dispensation would have come a long while ago,' he told Isabella. 'As it has not come, doubts have arisen whether the dispensation will be given and a [papal] brief even seems to confirm these doubts.' He told the English king that if it did not arrive by the end of August 1504, 'it would be clear that the Pope did not like to give it'.[73]

On 28 November, Henry VII wrote to Julius, expressing some barely restrained exasperation:

We had written to Pope Alexander VI and Pope Pius III, asking them to grant the dispensation necessary for the marriage ...

Both these Popes, your immediate predecessors, had received our demands so favourably that the dispensation would have been given long ago if they had not so suddenly died.

We have repeated our demands afterwards, very often, in our letters and by our ambassadors.

Julius, Henry reminded the Pope, had promised 'in different letters and by word of mouth' to send the dispensation to England with Robert Sherborne, but the envoy had returned empty-handed. 'It seems,' added the king with some asperity, 'as if nothing at all has been done in Rome in this matter.' He repeated his earnest prayers that permission for the marriage be granted 'as soon as possible' and the papal Bull be delivered 'at once to the English ambassadors who are remaining at Rome'.[74]

Back in London, Katherine meanwhile had fallen ill, suffering from a malarial fever and frequent stomach cramps. Whether her constitution had been weakened by worries over the Vatican's procrastination and her own future must remain a matter for conjecture. On 4 August 1504, Henry VII wrote to her in oily tones:

> As you were not well when we left Greenwich, the time which will have passed before we receive good news from you will in any case seem too long.
>
> We love you as our own daughter.
>
> We send one of our most trusty servants not only to visit you but also to do anything for you that may be desirable with respect to your health or that may give you some pleasure.[75]

After a brief improvement, Katherine suffered a relapse. The Spanish ambassador reported to Queen Isabella that the illness

> seems sometimes serious, for the Princess has no appetite and her complexion has changed completely ... [She] has had at intervals a bad cold and cough. The physicians have twice purged her and twice attempted to bleed her [in the arm and in the ankle] but no blood came. She desires very much that the operation be repeated, being persuaded that if she were bled, she would be well directly.[76]

It is likely that Katherine was not only suffering from anaemia but was also born with fragile veins, which went into spasm as the surgeon wielded his scalpel – hence the lack of blood.[77]

To compound all her troubles, there were quarrels within her largely Spanish household at her lonely home in the Bishop of Ely's residence, Durham House off The Strand, between the City of London and Westminster.[78]

Henry VII was now her paymaster, having refused to refund the first portion of her dowry for her marriage with Arthur. She had become a pawn in his diplomatic games, granting her money for her living expenses only when he needed Spanish political support. He brusquely rejected her pleas to settle the strife amongst her servants, pointing out that they were beyond his jurisdiction.[79]

In Spain, her mother Isabella was dying. A copy of the dispensation was delivered to her on her deathbed, as some kind of papal send-off on her journey to heaven. It arrived just in time: on 24 November 1504 she was dead. Her eldest surviving daughter Juana, as heir-apparent, became Queen of Castile. She was the wife of Archduke Philip, Duke of Burgundy, the son of Maximilian I, the Holy Roman Emperor. Unfortunately, she was also mad – she suffered from schizophrenia – and Ferdinand moved swiftly to retain control.

At last, in March 1505, Henry VII heard that the original dispensation was on its way to England. Silvestro de' Gigli, Bishop of Worcester, reported from Rome that it had

> pleased his Holiness to command him to go to England with the original Bull of the dispensation for the marriage.
>
> It had grieved his Holiness to learn that copies had been sent from Spain to England of the Bull, which under seal of secrecy, had been sent to Queen Isabella only for her consolation when on her deathbed.

The bishop was to set out on his journey 'within a few days'.[80]

But Henry VII had grown tired of waiting. He needed to put pressure on the Spanish to speed payment of the second instalment of Katherine's marriage dowry. Perhaps William Warham, the new Archbishop of Canterbury and the king's Lord Chancellor, who harboured serious doubts about the wisdom of the marriage, suggested a dramatic new tactic. The king, after his customary cautious consideration, issued a new command to his son and heir.

On 27 June 1505, the eve of his fourteenth birthday, his son made his 'protestation' – his firm renouncement – of his marriage with Katherine. It was very much a covert, hole-in-the-corner affair. The prince swore a statement before Richard Fox, Bishop of Winchester and Lord Privy Seal; Giles, Lord Daubeny, Lord Chamberlain;[81] Thomas Ruthal, the king's secretary; and James Read, a public notary, in a bizarre formal ceremony hidden away in a cellar below the eastern end of Richmond Palace. After he appended his signature in Latin – 'Henricum Walliæ Principeu' – he read out the document, declaring that

> ... whereas I being under age was married to the Princess Katherine, yet now coming to be of age, I do not confirm that marriage but retract and

75

annul it and will not proceed in it, but intend in full form of law to void it and break it off which I do freely and without compulsion.[82]

Katherine, penniless, lonely and frequently ill, knew nothing of this repudiation by her husband-to-be. In November, Henry VII stopped paying her the parsimonious monthly allowance of £100 for her frugal existence at Durham House.

Her fate seemed entirely hopeless.

4

KING IN WAITING

———•◦•———

'*It is quite wonderful how much the King likes the Prince of Wales. He has good reason to do so, for the prince deserves all love. It is not only from love that the king takes the prince with him: he wishes to improve him.*'

Ferdinand, Duke de Estrada, to Queen Isabella, London, 10 August 1504.[1]

With just one healthy heir left alive, the old distressing doubts about the future of the Tudor dynasty crept back to dog Henry VII and haunt his every waking hour. He had fought off so many challenges to his possession of the English crown. Now, in the evening of his troubled reign, would his hopes and dreams come to naught?

The widower king had two clear courses of action open to him to finally banish his fears.

He could marry again and produce more sons, as an insurance against Prince Henry dying and thus snuffing out the precious and precarious Tudor succession. Time was moving rapidly against him: the average life expectancy of a male in England in the early sixteenth century was only about forty. The king was already in his mid-forties and not enjoying the rudest health.

Henry VII should also neutralise the outstanding Yorkist pretender, Edmund de la Pole, Sixth Earl of Suffolk,[2] and a 'cunning' nobleman who was 'bold, impetuous and readily roused to anger'.[3] Suffolk's elder brother John, Earl of Lincoln, was killed in open rebellion at the Battle of Stoke Field in 1487 and his cousin Edward, Earl of Warwick, had been executed twelve years later by Henry VII. Suffolk, resentful and aggrieved, posed a disquieting dormant threat to the Tudors as the thorny 'White Rose of York', around whom disaffected subjects might rally.

Suffolk had fled England in July 1499 after he killed a commoner in a mad moment of passion during a brawl and was accused of homicide.[4] But the earl had returned voluntarily, was fined £1,000 in exchange for a pardon and then attempted to claw his way back into royal favour. He witnessed the king's confirmation of the marriage treaty of Arthur and Katherine at Canterbury on 5 May 1500 and was due to take a starring role in the celebratory jousts that followed their carefully planned wedding in November 1501. Having heard that the Emperor Maximilian, King of the Romans, was no friend of Henry VII's, Suffolk again quit the shores of England that August, heavily in debt, but intent on seeking imperial assistance in reclaiming the throne for the Yorkist cause. The earl was accompanied in his flight by his younger brother Richard, but oddly left behind in London another sibling, William. The king 'was greatly disturbed [and] regretted that he had spared him on the first occasion and began to fear fresh upheavals', according to Vergil.[5]

A round-up of Yorkist sympathisers was not a comfortable option whilst the celebrations of the Prince of Wales' marriage were being so sumptuously staged in London to showcase the Tudor dynasty. So Henry VII, fighting back his eagerness to act, had to wait until the first Sunday in Lent, 13 February 1502, to arrest Suffolk's near relations and friends. Heading the list of the usual suspects was, naturally, William de la Pole. But they also included the courtier Sir William Courtenay, eldest son of the Earl of Devonshire, and Sir John Wyndham, who fought for Henry at Stoke Field and had been knighted afterwards for his loyalty. All were charged with complicity in Suffolk's treason and held in the Tower in the custody of the ambitious Welshman Sir Hugh Vaughan, who was responsible for the detention of royal prisoners there.[6]

Already imprisoned behind its walls was Sir James Tyrell, governor of the castle of Guisnes in the English territory (or 'pale') in the hinterland of Calais, who had unwisely sheltered Suffolk on his first panicky excursion abroad and had been tricked into returning to London. Tyrell was a man of evil repute: he was the knight who supposedly had been ordered by Richard III to murder the two princes in the Tower in 1483.[7] His death – and eternal silence – would be doubly expedient to Henry VII, who may have known more about the ramifications of the princes' disappearance than was politically safe. Tyrell and Wyndham were executed on 6 May – the former suspiciously not being allowed to speak on the Tower Hill scaffold – and the two Williams, de la Pole and Courtenay, were imprisoned at the king's pleasure.[8]

Suffolk himself, aside from being outlawed on 26 December 1502, was seemingly beyond Henry's vengeful reach in Aix-la-Chapelle (present-day Aachen in Germany), although the king managed to convince Pope Alexander VI to place the errant earl under the fearsome papal ban of anathema, which included all who supported his cause.[9] However, Maximilian proved less than a loyal and dependable ally to Suffolk. Instead of the pledged assistance to overthrow the Tudors, his bellicosity towards Henry VII had melted away at the first whiff of a generous bribe. The spendthrift and always penniless King of the Romans promised that July no longer to harbour any English rebels; a guarantee made in return for £10,000 of Henry's precious English gold. In modern spending terms, this is equivalent to £4.5 million – suggestive of just how much the king wanted Suffolk safely in his clutches.

Despite this generous enticement, the earl was left unmolested to plan his increasingly unlikely invasion of England, at the same time building up substantial debts. Just before Easter 1504, Suffolk and his followers left Aix, leaving his brother Richard as a hostage to his creditors. While en route to Friesland and the hoped-for protection of the irascible George 'the Bearded', Duke of Saxony, the earl was imprisoned in Hattem Castle, near Roermond (in today's Netherlands), by Charles of Egmont, Duke of Gueldres. Back in Westminster, an overjoyed English king began negotiations with Archduke Philip of Burgundy, who held sway over the Low Countries, to return the traitor Suffolk to his power.[10]

Henry VII meanwhile also turned his attention to finding himself a new bedmate. After the shameful, half-hearted suggestion of marrying his daughter-in-law Katherine, the king's prime choice was the recently widowed Queen Joan of Naples, the twenty-seven-year-old niece of Ferdinand of Spain.[11] He sent three trusty envoys to Valencia in 1505, armed with detailed, if not prurient, questions about her physical appearance and – being thrifty, if not sometimes niggardly – detailed instructions to assess her financial prospects. Even today, many of the twenty-four questions posed by Henry VII appear breathtakingly impertinent, if not injudicious, and the ambassadors' answers equally forthright:

> *Note well her eyes, brows, teeth and lips* – The eyes of the queen be of colour brown, somewhat greyish and her brows of a brown hair and very small like a wire of hair ...
>
> *Mark her breasts, whether they be big or small* – The queen's breasts be somewhat great and full [but] they were trussed ... high, which causes her grace to seem much the fuller.
>
> *Mark whether there appear any hair about her lips or not* – As far as we can perceive and see, the queen has no hair about her lips or mouth.
>
> *Approach as near to her mouth as they honestly may ... that they may feel the condition of her breath, whether it be sweet or not* – We could feel no savour of any spices ... and we think by her complexion and of her mouth that the queen is like to be of a sweet savour and well aired.
>
> *Inquire whether she be a great feeder or drinker* ... The queen eats well her meat twice a day and her grace drinks not often ... most commonly water and sometimes that water is boiled with cinnamon and sometimes she drinks hippocras,[12] but not often.[13]

If all this smacks of being something of a cattle market, this was what the royal marriage stakes were like in sixteenth-century Europe. As far as Joan was concerned, it was a case of so far, so good. The brown-haired queen was attractive, physically well endowed and happily entirely free of halitosis. Furthermore, she did not pig herself at mealtimes with food or even alcohol, so she might even retain her voluptuous figure. But was all this enough to capture the capricious fancy of the aging English king?

In potential royal wedlock, as in politics and the all-important state of his exchequer, Henry VII was as careful and cautious as ever. Despite

the favourable replies and enthusiasm of his envoys, he swiftly abandoned Joan as a potential wife[14] after he discovered that her marriage
jointure[15] in Naples, worth 30,000 ducats (about £14,000) had been
summarily confiscated. Moreover, Ferdinand had married Germaine de
Foix, the red-haired niece of the French king, Louis XII, in 1505, so his
erstwhile friend had become a trifle suspect.

Marriages were much on Henry VII's agenda. At long last, his delicate
eldest daughter Margaret, now aged just over thirteen, was judged
mature and fit enough to travel to Scotland and have her marriage to
James IV solemnised and then consummated. In preparation for her
new life, Henry ordered 'certain jewels, plate and other stuff for the
Queen of Scots as well as for the king's own use', paying out the very
large sum of £16,000 (more than £7 million at today's prices) on 23 June
1503.[16] Escorted by a huge retinue of English lords and ladies, led by
Thomas Howard, Earl of Surrey, the Lord Treasurer, Margaret left
Richmond Palace on 2 July for the slow, stately progress to Edinburgh,
via her grandmother's house at Collyweston. Prince Henry may have
been secretly pleased to see his elder sister depart out of his life: some
claimed he threw a raucous tantrum after his discovery that as Queen
of Scots, Margaret would enjoy precedence over him during court
ceremonies.

After crossing the Scottish border at Berwick, she was met by her
husband 'and the flower of Scotland' at the small village of Lamberton
Kirk and formally delivered up to James IV by the gorgeously dressed
Algernon Percy, Fifth Earl of Northumberland.[17] Margaret was married
on 8 August in the chapel of Holyrood House, Edinburgh, with Surrey
giving away the bride who was stunningly dressed in a gown of cloth of
gold.[18]

Her first letter written to Henry VII after her marriage betrays just a
hint of understandable homesickness. It also contains a flash of that
very same Tudor teenage temper shared by her brother over the attention
lavished on Surrey by her new bridegroom, who was paying scant regard
to her charms:

Sir, as for news I have none to send, but that my lord of Surrey is in [such] great favour with the King here that he cannot forbear the company of him [at] no time of the day . . .

For God's sake, Sir, hold me excused that I write not myself to your Grace, for I have no leisure this time, but with a wish I would I were with your Grace now, and many times more, when I would answer.[19]

Meanwhile, what of Prince Henry? With his father's fears for the succession still unabated, his life had changed markedly. Henry was now kept close to his father, above all for security reasons but also to learn the ways of kingship. In August 1504, the ingratiating Duke de Estrada reported:

The Prince of Wales is with the king. Formerly the king did not like to take the Prince . . . with him, in order not to interrupt his studies.

It is quite wonderful to see how much the king likes the Prince of Wales. He has good reason to do so, for the Prince deserves all love. But it is not only from love that the King takes the Prince with him: he wishes to improve him.

Certainly there could be no better school in the world than the society of such a father as Henry VII.

He is so wise and attentive to everything – nothing escapes his attention. There is no doubt the Prince has an excellent governor and steward in his father.

The ambassador ended this litany of sycophancy with the comment: 'If he lives ten years longer he will leave the Prince furnished with good habits and with immense riches and in as happy circumstances as man can be.'[20] Behind these fawning words that paint a picture of familial harmony lay indecision and uncertainty about Prince Henry's future. What was happening with his stuttering, syncopated progress towards married life with Katherine? Solemnisation in church of their nuptials was still firmly on hold until the missing half of her marriage portion arrived from Spain. Henry's formal dissent from the contract for the marriage was obviously a mere gambit, played out in his father's mystifying game of diplomatic chess. Therein lies something of a mystery.

A few months before Henry's repudiation of the marriage with Katherine was signed, a concerned letter was apparently dispatched to Rome, either by Henry VII or his heir, about Katherine's fervent piety and its sapping impact upon her physical wellbeing. Pope Julius II wrote that although the Spanish princess commendably sought a spiritual life of fasting, prayer, abstinence and pilgrimage, this was without her spouse's permission. He therefore granted his full authority to restrain her from 'excessive religious observances which are injurious to her health'. Such religious zeal, emphasised Julius, could harm her body, jeopardise the *maritalis consuetudo* (marital intimacy or intercourse) and imperil her ability to have children. As Christian tenets taught that procreation was one of the most important purposes of marriage, the Pope would allow the prince to forbid Katherine from taking such devout vows and she should now be encouraged to engage in less arduous acts of piety as her confessor might suggest.[21]

Although this interesting document is dated 20 October 1505, it is addressed to Arthur, Prince of Wales. Did the Vatican have that big a backlog in its correspondence? Arthur had been in his Worcester grave for more than three years when the letter went off to London. Or is this a case of a careless bureaucrat sending the letter to a prince whose name loomed large in a bulging and dusty docket entitled 'papal dispensations for marriage'?[22] Katherine herself denied her piety was damaging her body and blamed her poor health on tertian fever, a malignant type of malaria.[23]

Even as the Vatican official was misaddressing this document, Henry VII was hawking his son and heir around the European courts in a search for an eligible princess to become his wife. First there was sustained interest in the suitability of Eleanor, daughter of Archduke Philip of Burgundy, a match initially mooted in 1501. She was almost eight, perhaps a more acceptable age than Katherine, as her aunt, stranded high and dry in London, was now twenty. Considerable diplomatic progress towards this marriage had been achieved by 1507.[24]

Eleanor's brother Charles might also do very well for Mary, the youngest surviving Tudor child, and the king himself had become mildly interested in the Archduchess Margaret, another aunt of the Burgundian princess, as his own new wife. Some of Henry VII's council also suggested a French match – perhaps the prince should marry Margaret of Alençon?[25]

Archduke Philip now paid an unexpected and unintended visit to England. He had set sail on 6 January 1506 from the Low Countries with 3,000 German mercenaries, bound for Spain to claim the crown of Castile, as he was married to the mad Juana (elder sister to Katherine of Aragon), who had succeeded to the throne on the death of their mother Isabella. His fleet of Burgundian ships had safely transited the English Channel but then were dispersed by a 'mighty tempest of wind and foul weather'. Some vessels were lost and others remained 'in danger of shipwreck'.[26] In London, the huge brass eagle weather vane atop the tall needle spire of Old St Paul's was blown off in the same storm (which lasted from noon to midnight) and ended up 'three hundred paces away towards the east' in the churchyard, destroying, in its fall, a bookseller's sign on which a black eagle was painted. Some considered this an evil omen: 'Since Philip was the son of Maximilian, emperor elect of the Romans, who carried an eagle in his coat of arms, all were convinced' by this portent that the imperial family 'would shortly suffer a grievous disaster'.[27] Unknown to the superstitious Londoners, the majority of the archduke's fleet was only driven back eastwards by the tempest, some anchoring safely in the port of Falmouth, in Cornwall, but the royal ship and two other vessels ended up in Melcombe Regis (now swallowed up by Weymouth) in Dorset.

Philip 'was little accustomed to the ocean waves', which made him 'exhausted in both body and mind'. No doubt he was also a little green around the gills from prolonged bouts of *mal de mer*. He and his wife promptly boarded a small boat and landed safely on English soil on 16 January 'in order to recuperate'.[28] Initially the Dorset gentry feared that a foreign invasion was underway and began to muster local forces to repel it. Then the truth emerged and when reports of the archduke being literally washed up on the coast reached Westminster, Henry VII was elated at this God-given opportunity for him to lay his hands on the Earl of Suffolk.

A magnificently attired fourteen-year-old Prince Henry accompanied 'by five earls and diverse lords and knights' – a retinue totalling about five hundred – greeted Philip and his fellow orphans of the storm in Winchester and officially bade them welcome to the realm of England. Henry's crimson glaudekin (a long riding gown) and jacket of red velvet edged with black lambskin had been hurriedly made by sweating tailors for the occasion.[29] The next day the party rode on to Windsor and were chivalrously met by Henry VII and the Duke of Buckingham half a mile (0.81 km) outside the castle.[30] The king welcomed Philip in fluent French, 'with the greatest distinction, kindness and courtesy'. Juana, who had become obsessively possessive towards her husband,[31] joined the royal party shortly afterwards, eager to see her sister Katherine for what turned out to be a very short reunion. The princess later wrote of 'the very great pleasure it gave me to see you in this kingdom, and the distress which filled my heart, a few hours afterwards, on account of your sudden and hasty departure'[32] back to Falmouth and the postponed voyage to Spain. At least at Windsor Castle, Katherine had enjoyed a decent meal or two, rather than scraping along on her father-in-law's meagre allowance.

The weather was terribly cold – 'such a sore snow and a frost that men might go with carts over the [River] Thames'[33] – and Henry and the archduke got down to diplomatic negotiations in front of roaring log fires at Windsor and at Richmond. The king wanted Suffolk delivered up to him, but initially Philip denied that he was able to achieve this, 'and even if he was, he was unwilling to break his word and hand him over to his death'.[34] Henry was loath to promise to spare de la Pole, but 'upon the [archduke's] earnest request' agreed not to execute him in exchange for his return to England.

A treaty of perpetual friendship was renewed between Burgundy and England, and after Mass was said on 9 February at Windsor, Henry VII invested the archduke as a Knight of the Garter. Exchange is no robbery, and Philip in turn made Prince Henry – who read out the oath in French – a Knight of the Golden Fleece. Again, special clothes had been ordered for him for the occasion – a doublet of cloth of gold, with scarlet hose and another jacket of russet satin.[35]

Suffolk meanwhile had been transferred into the custody of Philip von

Lichtenstein at Namur (in today's southern Belgium) in October 1505. He now saw the writing on the wall. He independently sent messengers to London offering to come home if Henry VII would restore to him his sequestered lands and to royal favour. He pledged fealty to the king and after his death 'to my lord prince, the king's son' and sought freedom for his brother William and those imprisoned for his sake.[36] The earl was delivered into English hands on 16 March in Calais and by the end of April was in the Tower. Henry's promises looked totally worthless.

Prince Henry was impressed by the dashing Philip with something akin to hero worship. Later in his life he hung his portrait in one of his apartments at Greenwich which was 'called Philip's room after his name, which room I prefer to all the rest in my palace', he admitted.[37] Vergil described the archduke as being of 'medium height, handsome of face and heavily built. He was talented, generous and gentlemanly'[38] and something of a sportsman (he played tennis), as well as a chivalrous jouster nonpareil. Here was a role model in leadership, boldness and bravado that the heir to the English crown was to later emulate himself.

On 9 April 1506, the prince wrote in French to Philip in Spain, from Greenwich Palace. His father's secretary in the French tongue, John Meautis, may have helped him with the grammar, indeed may physically have written it – only the closing '*Vostre Humble cousin, Henry Prince de galles*' and the signature are in Henry's bold, angular handwriting. However, this earliest of Henry's letters to survive is surely his own composition and is succinct, if not a little gushing. He begins formally: 'Most high, most excellent and mighty prince' and then continues more casually 'I commend myself to you in the most affectionate and hearty manner that I can do'. Henry sought Philip's favour in assisting Pedro Manrique in his business in Spain. He was 'the chamberlain of my most dear and well-beloved consort the princess my wife' – a description that belies Henry's repudiation of the marriage less than a year before. Then the prince has a boyish request, hoping that the archduke

> will apprise me from time to time and let me know of your good health
> and prosperity which I particularly and with all my heart desire to be of
> long continuance as I would my own.

And for my part, whenever I can find a fitting messenger I am determined to do the like to you.

Moreover, on your intimating to me if there be anything here in which I can do you honour and pleasure, I will take pains to satisfy you in it with all my heart, by the good aid of Our Lord, whom I pray, right high, right excellent and mighty Prince, to give you good life and long.[39]

His good wishes were to no avail. On 25 September Philip died at Burgos in Spain, aged twenty-eight. Henry's striking hero was gone. The dark omen, provided by the falling weathercock, had been quickly fulfilled.

Erasmus, staying in Venice, wrote to Prince Henry with his condolences on the death of Philip.[40] On 17 January 1507, Henry replied in Latin in his own hand, and the elegance and style of his letter impressed and captivated the Dutch scholar. The prince headed his note with the pious cry 'Jesus is my Hope' and continues:

> I am much struck by your letter, most eloquent Erasmus, which is too elegant to appear composed on a sudden and so lucid and simple that it cannot be supposed to be premeditated by so dextrous an intellect . . .
>
> There is nothing I can compose in your praise which is worthy of that consummate erudition. I therefore pass over your praises, about which I think it better to be silent than to speak insufficiently.

He then wrote of his loss in Philip's death – and that of his mother, four years before – and asked Erasmus 'to signify us by letter any news you have, but let your news be of a pleasanter kind and may God bring to a good event whatever may happen worth telling'.

The scholar carried the prince's letter in his pocket for some time to show to his friends but suspected that Henry had been given some assistance in writing it. 'I knew the hand,' Erasmus wrote years later, 'but, to speak candidly, suspected a little at the time that he had had some help from others in the ideas and expressions.' However, Henry's companion and Latin scholar, William Lord Mountjoy, showed him examples of the prince's writing which dispelled these suspicions and the philosopher endorsed a copy with the note: 'the whole of the letter enclosed he wrote when a youth in his own hand.'[41] Erasmus went on to Bologna to superintend the studies of the two sons of Henry VII's Genoese physician Baptista Boerio. One of his pupils, Giovanni, inscribed two books written by ancient Greek orators and sent them as gifts to the Prince of Wales: a translation of Isocrates' *De Regno*, and a copy of Lucian's *Calumniæ non temere credendum*, a tract against believing lies and slanders too readily.[42] In later life, however, Henry was not to pay much attention to these important lessons.[43]

That hapless and benighted hostage to fortune, Katherine, Princess of Wales, meanwhile was still being kept in painful penury in Durham House. She begged Ferdinand in April 1506 to cover her debts 'not for extravagant things, but for food. The King of England will not pay for anything, though I have asked him with tears.' Henry, ever motivated by money, had retorted that the Spanish promises to pay the remaining half of the marriage portion of 100,000 scudos (about £25,000) had not been kept. Katherine was now

> in the greatest anguish. My people [are] ready to ask [for] alms and I myself [am] all but naked. I beg you to send me a confessor, as I cannot understand English and have been for six months near death.[44]

Prince Henry, unlike his father, was more solicitous. But she very rarely saw him and, as she acknowledged to her father, she still did not understand English, so any intimate communication between them would have been problematic.[45]

The Spanish envoy de Puebla visited Henry VII on the Wednesday of Holy Week in April 1507 and found him confined to his room 'with a very severe illness'. An attack of the quinsy – a throat infection with symptoms similar to tonsillitis – had 'prevented him for six days from eating and drinking. His life was despaired of, but now feeling better', the king agreed to see the Spaniard.

After 'many unpleasant conversations', de Puebla reported ruefully, Henry VII was at last persuaded to postpone payment of the marriage portion for five and a half months. In lieu of hard cash, he would generously accept gold and silver plate at face value, but gemstones and ornaments 'for much less' – at the price 'he could get for them if he sold them in London'. The ambassador begged his master not to value 'too highly the jewels' as Henry would 'resent it very much'.

Despite his illness the king wrote to Ferdinand, pointing out, less than subtly, that 'many other princesses have been offered in marriage to the Prince of Wales, with much greater marriage portions and even with a dowry twice as great as that of Princess Katherine'. However, Henry had not accepted these tempting offers because he loved and esteemed Ferdinand so much and therefore was willing to postpone the payment to 29 September, the Feast of St Michael the Archangel.[46]

A few days later de Puebla wrote enthusiastically to Ferdinand about the prospects of the English king marrying his daughter Juana, Queen of Castile, widowed by the death of Archduke Philip. 'There is no king in the world who would make so good a husband to the queen . . . as the King of England, whether she be sane or insane.' Ever enthusiastic, de Puebla believed 'she would soon recover her reason when wedded to such a husband as Henry' – perhaps his mania for the acquisition of cash would calm her troubled spirit?

> If the insanity of the queen should prove incurable, it would perhaps be inconvenient that she should live in England.
>
> The English seem little to mind . . . her insanity, especially since I have assured them that her derangement of mind would not prevent her from bearing children.[47]

While he pondered on the wisdom of marrying a mad wife, Henry VII betrothed his ten-year-old daughter Mary to Archduke Philip's son, Charles of Austria. Schooled by Katherine, she sang Spanish songs at the celebrations at court to mark the event.[48]

Ferdinand failed to meet the deadline for payment of the marriage portion but wrote to Katherine on 15 March 1507 promising to 'arrange matters . . . [so] that ere long she will be comfortable with her husband in her house'. He begged her to 'do everything to preserve the goodwill of Henry, the love of the Prince of Wales and the esteem of the people of England'. The king must be made to understand, added Ferdinand, that 'he has no better chance of securing the succession of his son than by marrying him to you'.[49]

Henry VII did *not* understand and continued to keep his daughter-in-law in straitened circumstances. The following month, Katherine told her father that she was obliged to sell off her plate to raise money and her 'officers and servants walk about in rags and live in misery'. She beseeched him to send her money.[50] In another letter, which followed hard on the heels of the earlier note, Katherine showed symptoms of desperation and emotional desolation. Her greatest complaint, she said, was 'the cruelty of permitting her so seldom to see the Prince of Wales, although he lived in the same house as her'. She had not seen him for four months and now Henry VII had told her 'very positively that he no longer regards himself and the Prince of Wales as bound by the marriage treaty because the marriage portion has not been paid'.[51] Katherine asked for a new ambassador to be sent to London as she had lost confidence in de Puebla, who was 'more a vassal of the King of England than a servant of your highness', she told Ferdinand.

To modern eyes, the king's behaviour towards Katherine seems heartless and cruel. After the death of Elizabeth of York, there was a dark change in Henry VII's character. He became dour, hard-faced and more rapacious, oppressing heavily the luckless people of England and Wales through taxes and the imposition of penal recognisances. Perhaps his callous treatment of the Spanish princess was part of the character of this new, unyielding monarch.

Aside from the loss of his beloved wife and eldest son, one factor behind this transformation in character might have been the death on 5 August 1503 of the righteous and just Sir Reginald Bray, Chancellor of the Duchy of Lancaster.[52] According to the Italian chronicler Polydore Vergil, when the king fell into error Bray 'was bold enough moderately to admonish and reprove him'.[53] That restraining hand was now gone and Henry felt free to squeeze his subjects until their very pips squeaked.

Paradoxically, as he grew older, Henry VII was also growing more pious. After his victory over the Yorkist rebels at Stoke Field in 1487, the king donated a votive statue of himself to the Shrine of Our Lady at Walsingham and throughout his reign he visited that of St Thomas Becket at Canterbury, as a humble pilgrim.[54] As early as 1499, the king was reported to be growing 'very devout'. The Spanish ambassador Don

Pedro de Ayala said he had heard 'a sermon every day during Lent and had continued his devotions during the rest of the day'.[55] Lenten fasting at court was scrupulously observed, which even the sanctimonious Katherine found harsh and oppressive. 'In the house of the King,' she told her father in March 1509, 'they would not give meat to any one, even if he were dying, and they look upon them who eat it as heretics.'[56] One of the king's favourite saints was St George, the patron of England. The French king Louis XII found a skeletal leg, said to be a relic of the saint, amongst the loot of his wars in northern Italy and sent it on to London as a gift for Henry. On St George's Day, 23 April 1505, the king took part in a procession and veneration of the relic in St Paul's Cathedral, where it remained on public display for pilgrims.[57]

The foundation stone of Henry's impressive new chapel at Westminster was laid in 1500 and the following year work began on his grand tomb, initially planned to be erected in St George's Chapel, Windsor, but later switched to Westminster. An indenture between the king and John Islip, Abbot of St Peter's Monastery,[58] describes in banal detail the daily prayers and Masses the monks should sing 'devoutly ... on their knees' for him, Elizabeth of York and his mother. New almshouses at Westminster would also shelter thirteen poor men, one 'an unbeneficed priest, a good grammarian aged over forty-five' (and 'the others having no wives') to pray 'for the king's good estate and afterwards his soul'.[59] A badge of a red Tudor rose beneath a crown would be embroidered below the left shoulder on their black gowns.

Henry VII founded six houses in 1499 for his favourite order of friars – the Observant branch of the Franciscan Order – including establishments at Southampton, Newcastle and Canterbury, and alongside his palace at Sheen. In addition, in 1505 he set up the Savoy Hospital, off The Strand in London, dedicated to the honour of 'the Blessed Jesus, the Virgin Mary and St John the Baptist' to feed and house one hundred poor people.[60]

His household accounts reveal a decline in the number of entertainments staged at court after 1504, particularly in the employment of fools or jesters. Perhaps, with all his family tragedies, responsibilities and advancing years, the king's appetite for a joke or a merry quip had faded away.[61] What is more, there are no 'disguisings' or early masques recorded after 1502 until Christmas 1507 when Master Wentworth wrote a 'disguising for a morris dance'.

His son expanded his own household, which still retained a strong feminine element: thirteen gentlewomen are listed, including Frideswide Puttenham, his former royal rocker, and Elizabeth Bayley, Jane Chace and Avice Skidmore, three ladies who had served in the nursery at Eltham Palace.[62] There were five Esquires of the Body, led by Edward Hungerford and Henry Guildford, cup-bearer, carver and waiter to the prince.[63] John Skelton, his tutor and chaplain, departed[64] and was replaced by a professional educator, John Holt of Chichester, West Sussex, tutor and friend of Thomas More, and the author of a schoolboy textbook on Latin grammar.[65] Holt died in 1504 and was succeeded by another schoolmaster in Latin, William Hone, who like Holt was a product of Magdalen College, Oxford. With Mountjoy also coaching him, Henry's proficiency in Latin is not surprising. He was fluent in French, understood Italian, and later on, probably from Katherine of Aragon, acquired some knowledge of Spanish. The prince also displayed 'a remarkable docility [facility] for mathematics'.[66]

Music was considered an important constituent of the new humanist education. Henry now had his own small troupe of trumpeters to greet his regal entrances and exits and himself became an expert performer on the lute, the organ and the keyboard virginals, as well as wind instruments (taught by 'Guillam', the 'schoolmaster at pipes'). Giles D'Ewes, who tutored Henry in the lute, also served as keeper of 'le prince's wardrobe' and later as his librarian, when he became king.[67] The prince was also an accomplished singer. This love of music was to stand him in good stead throughout his life and Henry became a composer of both sacred and secular music in his own right, although some of his scores were arrangements of existing melodies.[68]

In July 1504, the Prince of Wales finally moved to his father's court. That January, Henry Wyatt, master of the king's jewel house, listed the jewellery issued for thirteen-year-old Henry's use, including a cross set with five cut diamonds, valued at £13 6s 8d, or more than £6,000 at today's values. This inventory totalled forty-seven items by mid-1509, many of which were to remain in Henry's possession for years to come. A list of his jewellery in 1528 included 'diverse brooches and aglets [metal pendants] which were the king's when his grace was prince' and a jewelled collar from the same period.[69] Edmund Dudley, one of the king's notorious revenue collectors, fawningly gave the prince a ring with red and black enamel, decorated with a pointed diamond, but this was soon after lost by Henry in September 1507 at Langley, near Woodstock in Oxfordshire.[70]

Now he was of an age when he could enjoy more manly pursuits. As well as hunting and hawking, the prince became adept at wrestling, archery, casting the bar[71] and fighting on foot with the quarterstaff.[72] But his mind must have frequently returned to the thrilling spectacle of the joust after his creation as Duke of York in 1494, and the teenager yearned to emulate the panache of those chivalrous and noble challengers. In February 1505, a black satin arming doublet was purchased for the prince to wear beneath his armour, together with a pair of arming spurs and shoes. But the king, fearful about the succession to the throne and knowing too well the dangers of the tiltyard, limited his heir to mere practice sessions: 'running at the ring', where the rider's lance tip has to catch a suspended circle of metal. Difficult, but hardly dashing.

His grandmother, Lady Margaret Beaufort, was perhaps more indulgent than her son. In March 1506, she bought the Prince of Wales a horse costing £6 13s 4d, together with a shiny new saddle costing 10d, and harness, made of stool work bordered by black velvet and decorated with gilt flowers, priced at 10s. In 1508, she sent him a generous present after he had 'run at the ring'.[73]

Henry was also taught how to fight on foot in armour: his household included Thomas Simpson, the 'master of axes', who must have schooled him in the use of the short but deadly poll-axes in hand-to-hand combat.[74] One of the prince's new dashing companions, the wastrel Richard Grey, Earl of Kent, broke his arm teaching Henry how to fight on foot with swords in June 1508.[75] Another was Charles Brandon, the raffish son of Henry VII's standard bearer Sir William who was killed by Richard III himself at Bosworth. Brandon, in his early twenties, was something of a youthful roué; he had wed Margaret Mortimer before

1506 but this marriage was annulled a year later. In 1508 he married Anne Browne after she gave birth to his illegitimate daughter.

It is hardly surprising that the king so carefully protected his sole surviving heir. After the terror of the royal family in the blaze that destroyed Sheen at Christmas 1497, there was another narrow escape in July 1506 in the newly built palace at Richmond. Late one night, both Henry VII and his son were walking in a new wooden gallery near the royal bedrooms. At midnight, less than an hour later, the gallery dramatically and noisily collapsed.[76]

With divine intervention so obviously protecting him, the prince was very committed in his religious faith. A roll of prayers, written on a thin strip of parchment just over thirteen feet (4 m) long, used by Henry was purchased by the British Library in 2010 – for £485,000 (Plate 7). Two badges of Tudor roses and the ostrich plume of the Prince of Wales decorate the top of this 'bede' roll, together with the sheaf-of-arrows emblem of Katherine of Aragon. In the centre are a series of illustrations of the Holy Trinity, Christ's Passion and the Crucifixion with appropriate prayers in Latin alongside. Explanations in English detail the spiritual benefits of such devotion. Under the image of Christ being placed in the sepulchre is this generous promise, written in red ink:

> To all them that before this image of pity devoutly say five Paternosters, five Ave Maria[s] and one Credo, shall have 3,712 years and forty days of pardon granted by St Gregory and other holy men.

For praying to the portrayal of the Crucifixion, the supplicant was guaranteed that

> No evil spirit [shall] have power of you on land or on water, nor with thunder or lightning [will you] be hurt, nor die in deadly sin without confession, nor with fire burnt, nor water be drowned.
>
> And it shall break your enemy's power and increase your worldly goods and if a woman be in travail of child, lay this on her body and she shall be delivered without peril.

Munificent and comforting promises indeed and Henry obviously devoutly believed them. Under the image of Christ crucified, he wrote: 'William Thomas, I pray you pray for me, your loving master: Prince Henry.' Thomas, one of Arthur's servants, became Groom of Henry's Privy Chamber after his arrival at court, and must have become very close to the royal heir to be given this roll which had been specially written for Henry.[77]

The prince had grown into a strong-limbed youth, fit, hale and hearty. Doubtless he possessed all the frustrations and impatience of a teenager governed by an aging, often ill father, whilst sometimes living together in the same house, although in different apartments.

In contrast to that Spanish ambassador's gushing description of August 1504, perhaps in the final years of Henry VII's reign, father and son did not get on. Many years later in 1538, the prince's cousin Henry Pole, Lord Montague, was to claim rashly in a private conversation with his brother Sir Geoffrey that the king 'had no affection nor fancy unto' his heir. He paid for this with his head.[78]

A new Spanish ambassador, with a grand name and title – Gutierre Gomez de Fuensalida, Knight-Commander of Membrilla – replaced de Puebla in London in mid-1508, charged with rescuing Katherine's quiescent marriage.[79] Fuensalida tried to meet the Prince of Wales, but was denied access. He reported back on young Henry's seemingly sequestered life:

> He is never permitted to go out of the palace, except for exercise through a private door leading to the park.
>
> At these times he is surrounded by those persons especially appointed by the king as his tutors and companions and no one else, on his life, dared approach him.
>
> He takes his meals alone and spends most of his day in his own room, which has no other entrance than through the king's bedchamber.
>
> He is in complete subjection to his father and grandmother and never opens his mouth in public except to answer a question from one of them.[80]

It was, he wrote, more like the sheltered life of a young girl than that of a healthy young prince bulging with teenage testosterone. If this bleak picture of his disciplined and regimented life were not enough, Fuensalida alleged that the king once 'sought to kill' his heir during a quarrel and also attacked his younger daughter Mary after becoming angered by the contents of a mystery letter he had just received. Unfortunately no other details of this incident have come down to us.

Here, of course, the ambassador was probably reporting possibly unreliable gossip he picked up at court and elsewhere. As a newcomer on the diplomatic circuit, he had not yet had time to establish who his dependable sources were and who would tell him merely what he wanted to hear in exchange for a suitable reward. In addition, he needed an explanation to send to Spain for his failure to discuss the marriage with Katherine's intended husband. Yet his report of the prince's lifestyle has a ring of truth about it, given Henry's obsession with the security of his heir. Despite his association with the squanderer Earl of Kent and rakish Charles Brandon, it is likely that this close monitoring of his life ensured that Prince Henry regretfully retained his virginity.

His father's health began to break down from around 1497, probably with respiratory problems. The king was reported to be 'very ill' at his newly purchased hunting lodge at Wanstead, Essex, in 1503–4.[81] His eyesight was also beginning to fail about this time – a particularly irksome condition for a sovereign who liked perusing state papers, especially his own exchequer accounts. Various lotions, made from fennel, celandine and rose-water, were employed as eye-baths, but with little beneficial effect. The king was also losing weight despite a healthy appetite, although the bad state of his teeth – Vergil brusquely describes them as 'few, poor and blackish' – would not have helped his eating. His red hair had become thin and white.[82]

In 1504, a year after the death of his docile and reverent wife Elizabeth and two years after the demise of Arthur, Henry fell dangerously ill at Eltham Palace. His poor health inevitably led him to ponder deeply on matters religious. He vowed to appoint only devout men as bishops – the first being John Fisher, as Bishop of Rochester – but recovery (as it does) quickly put paid to his fears of mortality.[83]

There seems little doubt that Henry VII was suffering from a chronic tubercular infection, as he developed a bad cough in the spring, especially in the years 1507 and 1508.[84] His rich diet and consumption of alcohol may also have caused an excess of uric acid in his bloodstream, triggering a mild dose of painful gout in 1507, as later described by Bacon:

> The king ... began to be troubled with the gout. But the defluxion [phlegm] taking also in his breast, wasted his lungs so that thrice in a year (... especially in the spring) he had great fits and labours of the tissic [wheezy, or asthmatic problems]. Nevertheless, he continued to attend business with as great diligence as before in his health.[85]

His breath now smelt sour and stale because of the tuberculosis affecting his lungs. Henry VII recovered well from his attack in 1507, and in October that year, the Spanish ambassador reported him out every day riding, hunting deer and hawking in forests and parks. According to de Puebla:

> The king of England has never enjoyed, during the last twenty years, such perfect health and never been so strong and robust as now. It is wonderful to see how his long illness has given him twice as good a constitution as he had formerly.[86]

The ambassador was ever the optimist. Despite this recovery, Henry VII was ill again in February 1508, and after rallying was seriously ill again that July, with what his physicians called 'consumption' – in their terms, a severe wasting disease, in ours, pulmonary tuberculosis. On 17 August, the Venetian Senate heard reports from Milan that the king of England 'was very ill and *in extremis*'.[87] Yet again, Henry bounced back. Ferdinand wrote of his pleasure at hearing of his convalescence: 'The news of your illnesses has caused me much anxiety.'[88]

But the insidious disease was to finally claim him eight months later.

As was customary, Christmas was spent at Greenwich and Richmond, before the king moved on in mid-January to one of his smaller houses at Hanworth, Middlesex, six miles (9.66 km) away.

Quite suddenly, Henry VII felt the menacing, looming presence of Death very near and his conscience was troubling him.

On Ash Wednesday, 21 February 1509, the king called his confessor –

'a man of singular wisdom, learning and virtue' – to him. After making his confession 'with great repentance' he told the surprised and doubtless delighted confessor of three promises he had made to God. The first was 'a true reformation of all of them that were officers and ministers of his laws' and that 'justice from hence forward truly and indifferently might be executed in all causes'. Secondly, church appointments would now go to 'able men, such as were virtuous and well learned'. Finally, because of legal injustices committed in the past, he would 'grant a general pardon [to] all his people'.

Although he swore his confessor to secrecy, he told his closest servants that 'if it pleased God to send him a new life, they would find him, a new changed man'.[89]

Henry was not only terrified of death but possible damnation as well. When he sought absolution for his sins, 'he wept and sobbed by the space of three-quarters of an hour'. Two days later, now again at Richmond, the king received communion 'at midnight and again upon Easter Day with [such] reverence that all that were present were astonished'.[90]

Exhausted by these exertions, Henry VII retired to his Privy Chamber, amusing himself by gambling and, more piously, listening to priests singing psalms.[91] On 27 February John Fisher, Bishop of Rochester, and Thomas Wolsey, one of the king's chaplains, were paid for the 2,000 Masses said for his recovery in London. A further 2,000 were said by the Friar Observants. Henry was now growing ever more feeble, too weak even to take the Holy Sacrament. The king therefore asked for the 'monstrance', a gold receptacle holding the consecrated Host, to be brought to him. When it was handed to him by his confessor

> ... he, with beatings of his breast, did obeisance thereunto and kissed ...
> the foot of the monstrance so that the bystanders might scarcely contain
> themselves from tears and weeping.[92]

Outside the silent palace on the banks of the Thames, the new Venetian ambassador in London, Andrea Badoer – who arrived in late March, incognito, penniless and after a chapter of accidents[93] – wrote to the king of his intention to present his letters of credence. Henry 'expressed satisfaction and [said that] when better, he would give him audience'. On 29 March Badoer reported: 'The sick king is very ill and his life in danger.'[94]

Two days later Henry made his 13,000-word, thirty-seven-page will,[95] parts of which had been drawn up earlier over some time in readiness, but the final version is coloured by his recent penitential declarations[96] so the words of a desperate and frightened man cry out of the pages. He acknowledges that

> I am a sinful creature, in sin conceived and in sin have lived, knowing perfectly that of my merits I cannot attain to the life everlasting, but only by the merits of Thy blessed passion and of Thy infinite mercy and grace ... The most Blessed Mother, ever virgin, our Lady Saint Mary ... will now in my most extreme need of her infinite pity take my soul into her hands and present it unto her most dear Son, whereof sweetest Lady of Mercy, very Mother and Virgin, Well of Pity and surest refuge of all needful, most humbly, most entirely and most heartily I beseech thee.[97]

Henry VII took a long time to die – twenty-seven hours filled with pain and prayers.[98]

The final scene in his dramatic and violent life began late on the evening of Friday 20 April. Perceiving that 'he began utterly to fail' he called for his confessor to administer the last rites of the church. As the priest dabbed him with holy oil, the king 'offered every part of his body by order and as he might with weakness turned himself at every time and answered in the suffrages [intercessory prayers]'.

At some point on that last day, Prince Henry was summoned into his dying father's bedchamber. The king, propped up on heavy cushions, with difficulty 'gave him fatherly and godly exhortation, committing unto him the laborious governance of this realm'.[99] Prince Henry wrote afterwards that his father charged him 'on his death bed, among other good counsels, to fulfil the old treaty with Ferdinand and Isabella of Spain by taking their daughter Katherine in marriage'.[100]

During his last hours, Henry VII heard 'a Mass of the glorious Virgin, the mother of Christ, to whom always in his life he had a singular and special devotion'. A crucifix was frequently brought to him which 'he beheld with great reverence, lifting up his head as he might, holding up his hands before it and often embracing it in his arms ... kissing it, beating oft his breast'.[101]

This was a good end for a Christian prince.

We have a portrayal of this deathbed scene, drawn by Sir Thomas Wriothesley, Garter King of Arms (Plate 8). The king, still wearing his crown, lies in a great canopied bed surrounded by clerics and courtiers, all waiting for him to die. On his left is Richard Fox, Bishop of Winchester, and two tonsured priests. Then come members of the king's household, identified by their heraldry: George Lord Hastings; Richard Weston, Esquire of the Body and Groom of the Privy Chamber; Richard Clement, another Groom; Matthew Baker, another Esquire; two gentlemen ushers, John Sharpe and William Tyler; and Hugh Denys, the king's closest attendant. Then there is a mass of doctors, holding narrow-necked pots, either for administering medicine or to collect urine – in Tudor times, this was used to gauge symptoms of a patient's sickness, either by its colour, smell, or (horribly) by taste. Finally, standing next to the king and holding his wand of office, is William Fitzwilliam, another gentleman usher. He is shown closing the king's eyes.[102]

Henry VII drew his last shuddering breath at 11 pm on Saturday 21 April.

The first Tudor king had died after a reign of twenty-three years and eight months. He was aged fifty-two.

His son, destined to become the greatest king in England's long history, now waited in the shadows to win his own immortal power and glory.

5

VIVAT REX

-----•◆•-----

'Thanks be to God, our ... kingdom is in good obedience, peace and
tranquillity as it was in the time when the King, my late lord and father
was still alive.'

Henry VIII to Margaret of Savoy, Regent of the Netherlands, 27 June 1509.[1]

As Henry VII's body grew cold within his secret chamber in Richmond
Palace, outside the silent and darkened room his government was
thrown into feverish activity. Those who had witnessed his slow, agon-
izing journey to meet his Maker knew full well that the king's death
left his 'kingdom not without danger' as Fuensalida, the new Spanish
ambassador in London, shrewdly observed a few days later.[2] As far as
the residual Yorkist threat to the crown was concerned, Suffolk and his
brother William de la Pole were safely incarcerated in the Tower. Their
sibling Richard remained a fugitive in Europe, posing a distant hazard,
but a potential fresh claimant, Edward Stafford, the ambitious Third
Duke of Buckingham, was arrogantly enjoying life in England, holding
the greatest estates of any nobleman.[3]

It was therefore decided to keep Henry VII's death secret until
arrangements could be put in place for a smooth transition to the reign
of Henry VIII, now aged seventeen years and ten months. The new king
remained in his privy apartments at Richmond, presumably mourning
the loss of his father, while the behind-the-hand whispering went on all
around him.

A morbid and grotesque charade was played out in the echoing corridors of the palace to maintain the pretence that the old king still lived. Thomas Wriothesley, the Garter King of Arms and chief herald, maintained that the concealment was intended to allow time for his councillors to arrive at Richmond to discuss plans for the accession. But the embargo on the news being announced had a more sinister motive.

For forty-four tense hours, the façade of regal normality was kept up while partisan officials argued and haggled over their roles in the government of the youthful new monarch. Others covertly searched the palace for the treasure they knew had been stashed away by the old king in numerous 'secret places under his key'. A total of £180,000 (£93 million in today's money) in coins and gold was eventually discovered, secured and properly accounted for.[4] Meanwhile, the commonplace rituals of court life were observed as usual. Trumpeters heralded the arrival of tasty hot meals in the royal apartments, but with only the stiffening royal corpse inside, there was no one alive to eat them. At Mass on Sunday 22 April, the routine royal offering was made at the high altar in the name of Henry VII.[5]

The next morning, St George's Day, the heralds publicly cried 'largess' of Henry VII so that 'commoners should have less suspicion of his death'.[6] After dinner Richard Weston, Groom of the Privy Chamber – one of the faithful group who had watched the king breathe his last late on Saturday night – with a 'smiling countenance' asked the Lord Chancellor, Archbishop William Warham, to accompany him to speak to the king. When they emerged from the bedchamber a little later, they also had 'good countenance' on their faces, 'showing no great manner of mourning that men might perceive'.[7]

It was only then that the Privy Chamber courtiers revealed the king's death to his leading councillors and peers who had gathered, as usual, to celebrate the annual Feast of St George, England's patron saint, as Knights of the Garter. That night the new king attended evensong, probably in the church of the Friar Observants that abutted the western walls of the palace. Afterwards he went to supper. On both occasions he was still addressed as the Prince of Wales.

The court was then informed of Henry VII's death. Fuensalida adroitly picked up the news from a source inside Richmond Palace, accurately reporting that the king had died on Saturday night and the subsequent concealment of the event. Given his mission, it was no surprise that he also immediately enquired whether the king's death would have any impact on Katherine of Aragon's beleaguered and blighted marriage. The ambassador was disconcerted to be told by a courtier that this was now thought unlikely as 'from what they know of Henry it would burden his conscience to marry his brother's widow'.[8] Elsewhere in London, rumours of the king's death panicked foreign merchants into nervously packing up their expensive goods and hiding them in places of safety.[9]

The new king, having finished his sombre supper, must have had discussions with his father's veteran chief ministers late into the night. It was his first taste of the responsibilities of kingship. This eminent and distinguished group was led by Lord Chancellor Warham, who, during the previous reign, had been nicknamed 'the king's eye, the king's mouth and his right hand'.[10] The remainder consisted of Thomas Howard, Earl of Surrey (Lord Treasurer); Richard Fox, Bishop of Winchester (Lord Privy Seal); Charles Somerset, Lord Herbert (Lord Chamberlain); and George Talbot, Earl of Shrewsbury (Lord Steward of the Household). John de Vere, Earl of Oxford and Constable of the Tower, and Thomas Lord Darcy, Captain of the Royal Guard, were probably summoned when measures to protect the security of the realm came up for discussion.[11]

It is almost certain that Henry VIII's grandmother, Lady Margaret Beaufort, who had travelled to Richmond from her London home at Coldharbour to see her son shortly before his death, also took part in these closeted conversations. One of the decisions taken was that she would act as regent for the king until his eighteenth birthday on 28 June and she insisted that her grandson kept in post the old king's trusted ministers. Another, vengeful, decision was also taken (to be implemented very early the next morning), which was cynically designed to endear Henry VIII to his three million subjects.

On Tuesday 24 April the heralds – to raucous fanfares of trumpets – proclaimed the new king in the City of London: 'Henry the Eighth, by the Grace of God, King of England and France and Lord of Ireland'.

Upriver in Richmond, John Fisher, Bishop of Rochester, and Sir John Cutt, Under-Treasurer of the Exchequer, attended a reconvened meeting of the same ministerial group to begin planning Henry VII's extravagant obsequies. Precedents created by funerals of previous English kings were efficiently produced by the Garter King of Arms. These were carefully considered and some initial arrangements agreed.

After dinner his successor mounted up and quickly rode the twelve and a half miles (22 km) to the City of London amid the ragged cheers of groups of his subjects as the heavily guarded king and his escort clattered by.

This cavalcade headed straight for the Tower where the new sovereign took up residence in the royal suite on the top floor of the White Tower[12] and he was joined there shortly afterwards by the premier nobles of the realm, Buckingham and Algernon Percy, Earl of Northumberland. According to their servants' gamecock boasts, these strutting peers now expected to dominate and control the policies and decisions of their teenage monarch. Buckingham, they bragged ominously, saw himself in the powerful role of 'Lord Protector of England'.[13] Oxford, as constable, placed the Tower on high security alert and Henry wisely remained 'closely and secret' with his council within.[14] Lady Margaret travelled there shortly afterwards. Outside the walls of the fortress, the city fathers organised extra watches in each ward (or district) of London to snuff out disturbances and guard against sedition.

There is always a breathless, expectant pause immediately after the accession of a new ruler when their subjects or vassals wait to see their true mettle revealed. Henry VIII, guided by his councillors, acted swiftly and with an iron hand.

In fulfilment of the decision taken the previous night, Henry VII's two notorious councillors Sir Richard Empson and Edmund Dudley had been arrested early that morning and were brought to the Tower very soon after the king's arrival. Simultaneously, Buckingham's brother, Henry Lord Stafford, was also detained on suspicion of treason, possibly as a carefully calculated warning shot across the egotistical duke's bows, as Stafford was quietly released shortly after the coronation.[15]

Dudley, president of Henry VII's council, was charged that on 22

April he had conspired to 'hold, guide and govern the king and his council' by summoning a force of his tenants and retainers to his house in Candlewick Street Ward, London.[16] Empson, Chancellor of the Duchy of Lancaster, was accused of similar crimes.

It was a brilliant and stunning public relations *coup de maître*. 'By this action all the indignation of the people was appeased and everyone was grateful to the monarch for the punishment of the evil pair,' Vergil crowed.[17] Hall reported that their arrests brought 'rejoicing of many people which by them were grieved'. No wonder there was celebration in the streets of London. Empson and Dudley's 'unreasonable extortion, noble men grudged, mean men kicked, poor men lamented, preachers openly at Paul's Cross[18] and other places exclaimed, rebuked and detested'.[19] Lady Margaret was probably numbered amongst Empson and Dudley's countless enemies and took a leading role in the decision to detain them. Their rampant extortion and corruption during her son's reign may well have offended her moral prejudices.[20]

Smaller fry were also swept up in this dramatic and unexpected purge. Those who had perjured themselves in legal proceedings instituted by Empson and Dudley were taken into custody or fled to sanctuary in their nearest church or monastery. 'You could have seen a crowd of these creatures being led daily into London,' reported Vergil, 'a few of the perjured were led through the centre of the city and were punished with dishonour, who nearly all afterwards soon perished with shame at their exposure.' Most, however, were treated more leniently 'since they were considered less guilty'.[21]

Henry speedily moved on to his second populist action of the day, demonstrating that an iron hand can sometimes be concealed in a velvet glove. The pardon to offenders that a remorseful and penitent Henry VII had declared on 10 April had lapsed with his death. A more wide-reaching and generous general amnesty was now issued 'for all things except debt, to everyone who will sue to it from the Lord Chancellor' and covered all offences committed prior to Henry VIII's accession. 'No one is to make disturbances,' it warned, 'but any person wronged may seek remedy at the common law.'

There was an absolute pledge of fair justice for all, under Henry

VIII's law, for everyone, whether ranked high or low in the realm. The proclamation declared: 'All his officers and ministers of justice from henceforth do and administer justice and in every cause do and execute their offices freely, righteously and indifferently to every of his subjects afore the laws of his land [with] good conscience, equity and discretion.' Merchants, clothiers and artificers could also continue their occupations without fear of untrue accusations made against them 'by customs [officers], comptrollers or searchers', or by old laws never executed 'till now of late time'. The king also promised to right the wrongs suffered by those 'grievously vexed and troubled in times past'. Henry VIII's pardon was issued by the sovereign's 'good heart' and was 'much more ample, gracious and beneficial' than his father's proclamation of two weeks before.[22]

He had wiped the royal slate clean of all the greed and injustice of his father's reign and given the Tudor dynasty a fresh start.

The full text of the pardon was rushed into print by the king's licensed printer Richard Pynson and copies distributed, initially in London and then posted up in the marketplaces of England. This was the first use of the printing press as a propaganda weapon in the new reign and Henry VIII, familiar with the power of the printed word through his education, was to make plentiful use of it in the years to come as the principal method of representing himself and his policies to his subjects.[23]

Fuensalida reported that the king 'released many prisoners and arrested all those responsible for the bribery and tyranny of his father's reign. The people are very happy and few tears are shed for Henry VII. Instead, people are as joyful as if they had been released from prison.'[24]

The speed of implementation was bound to cause administrative problems. Five days later Henry sent Lord Chancellor Warham a list of those exempted from his general pardon, which included all those accused of treason, murder and other more serious crimes. Heading the list of seventy-seven names were the three de la Poles, Edmund, William and Richard, as well as William Courtenay and, of course, Empson and Dudley. The exemptions also listed less exalted miscreants like 'William Smith, late of the wardrobe'; 'Wigan, late footman'; 'Christopher Clapham, porter of Berwick'. At the bottom, Henry added, in his own hand, one more name to the list: 'Thomas Thomas of Southampton', whose felonies remain unknown. The king was getting a grip on the detail of the management of his realm.[25]

Henry VII's demise threw confusion and uncertainty into the smooth cogs of European diplomacy. Most directly affected was King Ferdinand in Spain who was fearful that Katherine's marriage was now in the greatest danger of never being solemnised or consummated. After hearing French rumours of the king's death, he sent off an urgent and desperate dispatch to Fuensalida in London:

> If the King of England is really dead, the French, as well as others, will enter into all kinds of intrigues to prevent the marriage of the new king with the Princess Katherine ...
>
> [Fuensalida] must ... by all the means in your power persuade the new king to marry the Princess without delay.
>
> The marriage is of great importance, not only with respect to the Princess, but also on general political grounds ...
>
> Go to the new king, give him the enclosed letter and explain to him at length everything contained in it, making use of the best arguments that occur to you and the sweetest words you can imagine.
>
> Tell the new King of England in my name that his age and position as king without heirs render it imperatively necessary to take a wife without delay and to beget children.

Ferdinand continued brazenly: 'Should you think it expedient to corrupt some of the most influential councillors of the King, you may offer them money.' He insisted: 'All your ingenuity and all your industry must be brought to bear on the one affair of the marriage. All other transactions are to be postponed.' Ferdinand added, almost as an afterthought: 'The dowry will be punctually paid' and the missing marriage portion would at last be provided.[26]

The Spanish king also dutifully sent his condolences to Henry VIII:

> I have heard with great sorrow the news of the death of King Henry, your father.
>
> The death of such a prince as he was is a great loss to his family and to

his friends. The only consolation is that he died a good Catholic. I have gained a son by losing a brother; I will consider you always as my son.

Raw political ambition lay behind this sanctimony. Ferdinand hoped fervently that Henry VIII had

ascended the throne unopposed. If that was not the case, and you need help, you have only to say so, and a powerful army, consisting of men-at-arms, infantry and artillery, ships and engines of war, will be sent without delay from Spain to your assistance.

I would even, if necessary, come in person to England at the head of a powerful army, and act in the same way as I would if the fate of my own dominions were at stake.[27]

A now galvanised, if not frenetic, Ferdinand also dashed off a letter in cipher to his daughter in London. She had become despairing of ever marrying her prince and was even now considering a life of chaste devotion to God within the walls of a convent. He promised Katherine that he had her welfare and 'especially the speedy conclusion of her marriage more at heart than anything else on earth'. The Spanish king had intended to send one of his prelates as special envoy to England to conduct negotiations but now thought it 'advisable not to change my ambassador, since such change would cause delay'.[28]

After all their procrastination in the final years of Henry VII's reign, the Spanish now at last had the missing marriage portion lined up for payment. Within two days of his letter to Katherine, Ferdinand reported his successful negotiation of the 100,000 scudos with bankers in Spain and was sending their bills of exchange drawn on merchants in London, amongst them Dominico Lomelyn, Francisco Grimaldi and Luigi de Vivaldo. He had also heard whispers that the English ambassador in Spain, John Stile, had 'sent unfavourable reports to England. I have spoken with him and have told him to write henceforth only good news.'[29]

In Venice, the Signory had yet more extreme problems: their Italian mainland territories were under fierce and successful attack by France.[30] They received news of the king's death from their expatriate traders in

London who claimed that Henry VIII had 'sworn that immediately after his coronation [he would] make war on the King of France'. 'Soon,' the merchants claimed excitedly, 'we shall hear that he has invaded France.'[31]

The Doge and Senate, clutching at these slender straws in the wind, instructed Andrea Badoer, their envoy in London, to urge Henry to launch 'an immediate attack on the King of France ... France being at present utterly ungarrisoned in the direction of England'.[32] The accelerating pace of the French advance amplified the anxiety of the Venetian government. They decided to appeal directly to Henry VIII's vanity: 'The King of France [is] so elate [proud] and haughty ... [he will] not only prepare to make himself emperor but to become monarch of all the world ... Therefore his majesty [of England] should forthwith take steps to thwart such plans,' urged a plainly rattled Doge.[33]

With a father to bury and a coronation to be planned, in their desperation they were hopelessly unrealistic to expect Henry to mount any kind of military adventure against the French – yet. Their ambassador could only comfort them with vague promises of military assistance in the future: 'This new king is magnificent,' he told the Venetian Signory, 'liberal and a great enemy of the French and will be [your] friend.'

Henry VIII inherited enormous riches from his father: the Venetians were told that the old king 'had accumulated so much gold that he is supposed to have more than well nigh all the kings of Christendom'.[34] But what of his greater inheritance: the kingdom of England and Wales and lordship of Ireland?[35] In 1509, his realm was a small damp country on the western fringe of Europe[36] – merely a sideshow in the cut and thrust of continental politics.

A Venetian diplomat of the early 1500s has left us a vibrant, vivid description of what Henry's England was really like and of the corporate personality of his people – ninety per cent of whom still worked in the fields of the countryside. In some aspects, the national character has not changed much in five hundred years.

The English are great lovers of themselves and of everything belonging to them.

They think that there are no other men than themselves and no other world but England. Whenever they see a handsome foreigner, they say that 'he looks like an Englishman' and that 'it is a great pity that he should not be an Englishman'.

When they partake of some delicacy with a foreigner they ask him 'whether such a thing is made in *their* country'?

The English enjoyed their food, remaining a long time at table, but were 'very sparing of wine when they drink it at their own expense' so that often 'three or four persons drink out of the same cup'. The English appetite for food – particularly meat – was both prodigious and notorious and amounted to almost a vice. (Years later, Stephen Gardiner, that devious and vicious Bishop of Winchester, argued strongly for pious Lenten fasting[37] to continue. 'Every country has its peculiar inclination to naughtiness,' the bishop wrote. 'England and Germany to the belly – the one in meat, the other in liquor.' The French vice, however, was always lechery: 'France a little beneath the belly; Italy to vanity and pleasures devised.' 'Let an English belly have a further advancement,' he warned, 'and nothing can stay it.')[38]

Few Englishmen kept wine in their own houses but when they planned to drink a great deal 'they go to the tavern and this is done not only by the men but also by ladies of distinction'. With no domestic production, most wine was imported from France, Germany and Spain, but there was 'an abundance of ale and beer' which was drunk in 'great quantities' at entertainments.[39]

No greater honour can be conferred, or received, than to invite others to eat with them or to be invited themselves.

They would sooner give five or six ducats [roughly £10–£12] to provide an entertainment for a person than a groat [four pence] to assist him in distress.

Some Englishmen wore fine clothes and were 'extremely polite in their language', which, despite being derived from 'the old German', was 'pleasing enough as they pronounce it'. When talking together, they politely removed their hats – an 'incredible courtesy' – and were generally 'quick at everything they apply their minds to', being particularly diligent in mercantile trade. In one London street, The Strand, 'there are fifty-two goldsmith's shops, so rich and full of silver vessels, great and small, that in all the shops of Milan, Rome, Venice and Florence together, I do not think the[re] would be found so many of the magnificence that is to be seen in London'.[40]

Another Venetian, attached to the city state's embassy in London, described in 1513 how all the London houses were built of wood – later the capital's nemesis in the Great Fire of 1666. The homes clearly stank:

> Over the floors they strew weeds called 'rushes' which resemble reeds and which grow in water. Every eight to ten days they put down a fresh layer.
>
> Aloft at the window sills, they put rosemary, sage and other herbs.

The women are

> very beautiful and good tempered: their usual vesture is a cloth petticoat over the shift lined with squirrel or some other fur.
>
> Over [this] they wear a long gown lined with some choice fur. The gentlewomen carry the train under their arm: the commonalty pin it behind or before or at one side.
>
> The head gear is of various caps of velvet with lappets [vertical bands of fabric] hanging down on their shoulders like two hoods. In front they have two others lined with silk.
>
> Their stockings are black and their shoes doubly soled of various colours.[41]

The English were very devout and attended Mass every day. They said 'many Paternosters in public, the women carrying long rosaries in their hands'. Those who could read Latin took the 'office of Our Lady[42] with them and with some companion recite it in the church, verse by verse, in a low voice, after the manner of churchmen'.

But when it came to war, the English were fearsome:

> They have a very high reputation in arms and from the great fear the French entertain of them, one believes it to be justly acquired.
>
> But I have it on the best information that when the war is raging most

furiously, they will seek for good eating and all their other comforts without thinking what harm might befall them.[43]

Rampant xenophobia percolated like venom through all levels of Tudor society. The English had a 'great antipathy towards foreigners and imagine they never come into their island but to make themselves masters of it and to usurp their goods' – folk memories of the Norman invasion of 1066, perhaps? The 50,000-strong population of London especially detested foreigners. Most believed that the alien merchants living in their city – the Germans of the Steelyard, the Spanish, Lombards, Burgundians and Venetians – damaged their trade and took bread from the mouths of honest, hardworking English citizens. Sometimes this hostility spilled over into riots and brutal violence against foreigners or their property, as in the extensive 'Evil May Day' riots by apprentices in 1517.

The second largest city was Norwich, with a population of 14,000, but it was in the process of rebuilding after a disastrous fire in 1506 in which a 'great part' was burnt.[44] Other major conurbations were Bristol and Newcastle, each with about 10,000 citizens. Across the Channel, the English clung on to a toe-hold on the continent of Europe with the heavily fortified town of Calais and its immediate hinterland – the last vestige of huge possessions in France, progressively lost during the Hundred Years' War of 1337–1453. To the north, the Venetians considered that Scotland was 'situated at the end of the world'.[45]

One Venetian diplomat believed that the scant love the English showed their neighbours applied at home as well: there were few sincere friendships as 'they do not trust each other to discuss either public or private affairs together'.

But what of romantic love? Were the English such cold fish in the sixteenth century?

> Although [they] are somewhat licentious, I have never noticed anyone, either at court or amongst the lower orders, to be in love.
>
> One must necessarily conclude either that the English are the most discreet lovers in the world or that they are *incapable of love* [emphasis added].

I say this of the men, for I understand it is quite the contrary with the women, who are very violent in their passions.

The English keep a very jealous guard over their wives, though anything may be compensated in the end by the power of money.

The want of affection in the English was also very strongly manifested in relationships with their children.

After having kept them at home until . . . the age of seven or nine years at the utmost, they put them out, both males and females, to hard service in the houses of other people. I believe they do it because they like to enjoy all their comforts themselves and that they would be better served by strangers than they would be by their own children.[46]

And what of the weather – that main topic of conversation since time immemorial?

The climate is very healthy . . . the cold in winter is much less severe than in Italy and the heat proportionately less in summer. This is owing to the rain which falls almost every day during the months of June, July and August. They never have any spring here.

Another foreign diplomat complained that it was always windy 'and however warm the weather the natives invariably wear furs'.

Men marvelled at the wonders of nature in a world free of pesticides and intensive farming methods. In Calais on Whit Sunday 1508 there was 'an innumerable swarm of white butterflies [as thick] as flakes of snow [so] that men shooting [outside the walls] could not see the town at four of the afternoon, they flew so high and thick'.[47]

This, then, was Henry's England, full of outlandish paradoxes and neuroses. His subjects, although pious Catholics, were pugnacious, aggressive, greedy, beer-swilling and unromantic – happy to accept hard cash in return for their silence if a lecherous Italian seduced their wives. Now he had to rule them. But before the coronation of Henry VIII could be staged, his father had to be buried.

Warrants for funeral expenses were issued on 11 May. These included purchases of black mourning cloth (from fifty-six merchants – the looms must have been working overtime), the chariot to carry the king's body and alms and wages to the three hundred and thirty poor people who were to carry torches in the funeral procession. Heading the endorsements indicating approval for payment was the signature 'Margaret R' – the king's grandmother.[48]

Henry VII's body had been embalmed and placed in a lead coffin before removal from his bedchamber to 'his oratory or secret closet' within Richmond, and then on to the palace chapel, facing the great hall in its middle courtyard. A twenty-four-hour vigil was mounted in shifts for three days by mourners drawn from the nobility, with three Masses being said over the coffin each day by a mitred prelate.[49] On 9 May it was reverently hoisted onto the wheeled chariot covered with black cloth. On top was placed a life-sized effigy of the dead king

> crowned and richly apparelled in his Parliament robes, bearing in his right hand a sceptre and in his left hand, a ball of gold, over whom there was hanging a rich cloth of gold, pitched upon four staves ... set at the corners ... of the chariot which was drawn by seven great coursers, trapped in black velvet with the arms of England ... on both sides.[50]

The plaster face of the effigy was a death mask attached to a wooden armature and deliberately painted to 'represent ... the pallor of death'. Its wig was made to resemble the king's own hair, of 'bright red human and grey hair'.[51]

The procession of 1,400 mourners set off along the southern bank of the Thames to St George's Fields, near Southwark, where it was met by the Mayor of London, most of England's peerage and the ambassadors of Spain, France, Portugal, Venice and Florence together with representatives of the 'Esterlings' – the affluent German merchants of the *Hansa* League. Within this multitude was Katherine of Aragon, equipped with a brand-new saddle, costing £25, and her Spanish household, right down to her 'laundry wife' and 'Hugh and Denis', her Grooms of the Stable. Elsewhere, listed amongst the king's many chaplains, was a 'Mr Wolsey'.

This augmented cortege then straggled across London Bridge and on to St Paul's Cathedral where, the following day after Mass, John Fisher,

Bishop of Rochester, delivered the funeral sermon. 'Not for any vain, transitory things will I praise the dead,' he began, 'which by the example of him all kings and princes may learn how sliding, how slippery, how failing' worldly goods were. Although Henry had as much of these

> as was possible . . . for any king to have, his political wisdom in governance . . . was singular; his wit always quick and ready, his reason pithy and substantial, his memory fresh and holding, his experience notable; his counsels fortunate and taken by wise deliberation; his person goodly and amiable . . . his mighty power was dreaded everywhere, not only within his realm but without also.
>
> [The king's] prosperity in battle against his enemies was marvellous; his dealing in time of perils and dangers was cold and sober with great hardness.
>
> If any treason was conspired against him, it came out wonderfully; his treasure and riches incomparable; his buildings most goodly.
>
> But what is this now to him but *fumus* [smoke] and *umbra* [shadow]; nor shall I praise him for it.[52]

Margaret Beaufort was so impressed by Fisher's hour-long homily that she asked for it to be printed and widely distributed – which it was, by Wynkyn de Worde, in a unique example of royal funerary publication in sixteenth-century England.[53]

At about one o'clock, the royal corpse began its last journey to Westminster for burial. Alms totalling £102 were distributed to the poor living between the two great churches in an attempt to persuade them to include the dead king in their prayers that day. More alms were distributed to prisoners in the Clink Prison in Southwark[54] and to thirty-nine miscreants freed from Newgate Gaol and other prisons in the City of London. After further requiems, Henry VII's wax effigy was taken into St Edward's Shrine and his coffin, with a cross of white satin laid on top, was lowered into the vault, to lie alongside that of his wife, Elizabeth of York. In the customary ritual of closure, the great officers of state snapped their white wands of office in half and threw the fragments down on top of the coffin. Thomas Wriothesley, Garter King of Arms, stepped forwards and shouted in a loud voice: *Le noble Roy,*

Henri le Septieme est mort ('the noble King Henry VII is dead') and –
after a momentary pause – *Vive le noble Roy Henri le Huitiesme* ('God
send the noble King Henry VIII long life!'). His cry echoed around the
great abbey church, amid the clouds of incense.[55] The funeral was over
and so was Henry VII's rapacious and turbulent reign. The mourners,
now with healthy appetites, 'departed to [Westminster] Palace where
they had a great and sumptuous feast'.[56]

The king is dead. Long live the king. As usual in this period, this
new king did not attend his father's funeral: the chief mourner was
Buckingham. Henry VIII had other matters to occupy his mind –
including the organisation of a tournament – and granting rewards to
those who had eased his passage into power, as well as to those who
enjoyed his special favour.

For example, Richard Weston – the Groom of the Privy Chamber
who wore that 'smiling countenance' during the charade of normality
at Richmond – was appointed Captain 'for life' of the Channel Islands
of Guernsey, Alderney, Sark and Herm. He was also given the lucrative
posts of Keeper of Hanworth Park and Steward of the Lordships of
Marlow, Buckinghamshire and Cookham, Stratfield Mortimer and Bray,
Berkshire.[57] Another Groom of the Chamber, William Tyler, was made
Ranger of Groveley Forest in Wiltshire,[58] and granted the 'corrodies' of
the Benedictine Abbey of Hyde, near Winchester, and the Franciscan
friars' house at Chichester, Sussex.[59] Less pleasant was the exemption
from the general pardon of Thomas Roberts, who had murdered Robert
ap Jankin, one of the gentlemen ushers to the late king, and John
ap Robert, 'the king's servant' in Usk, Monmouthshire, in the Welsh
Marches. Fifteen other 'murderers' involved in the same incident were
exempted from regal mercy, in a document signed by the king in three
places.[60]

Sir Henry Marney, who had been dubbed a Knight of the Bath with
Henry back in 1494, was now made Captain of the Guard and Vice-
Chamberlain of the Household on 12 May, in place of Thomas, Lord
Darcy.[61] Marney was then swiftly appointed Steward of the Duchy of
Cornwall and finally Chancellor of the Duchy of Lancaster, the latter
post left vacant by the imprisoned Empson. The appointment of the

1. Henry VII, painted *c.*1501. His claim to the throne of England was fragile and he faced a succession of claimants and pretenders throughout his reign. The insecurity of the Tudor dynasty was heightened when he lost his son and heir Arthur and a third son died in infancy. Only Henry was left.

2. Elizabeth of York – Henry VIII's beloved mother – painted c.1502, the year before her death. Years afterwards, he wrote about the wound inflicted upon him by her loss. This portrait was first recorded in the Royal Collection during his reign.

3. Lady Margaret Beaufort praying in the robes of a vowess, *c.*1500. Henry's pious grandmother acted as regent until his eighteenth birthday and her death, five days after his coronation, severed the last shackle of his sequestered childhood and youth.

4. Prince Arthur, painted *c.*1520. He wears a collar of red and white Tudor roses and a badge bearing the figure of St John the Baptist on his hat. However, some scholars have suggested that the portrait is of a young Henry.

5. Henry as a child. This drawing of a chubby toddler is inscribed '*le Roy henry d'angleterre*' although the style of his ostrich-plumed hat looks nearly four decades later and throws some doubt on the identification of the subject.

6. Bust of a laughing child, possibly Henry VIII, *c.*1498, by Guido Mazzoni. Probably commissioned by Henry VII after Mazzoni failed to win the commission to design and carve the King's tomb.

7. Prince Henry's bede roll which promised divine protection from a variety of perils, as well as shortening the agony of Purgatory. Henry gave the prayer roll to one of his servants, William Thomas, some time before 1509. Thomas was one of the two witnesses at Henry's quiet wedding to Katherine of Aragon at Greenwich on 11 June 1509.

8. Henry VII on his deathbed. This drawing by Sir Thomas Wriothesley, Garter King of Arms, shows the gentleman usher William Fitzwilliam closing the King's eyes. Ranged around the bed are Richard Fox, Bishop of Winchester, and one of the King's chief ministers; members of his household and three doctors holding long-necked bottles for urine – a vital method of evaluating symptoms in sixteenth-century medicine.

experienced old soldier Marney, at fifty-two hardly a young thruster, probably came through the influence of Lady Margaret Beaufort, as he was one of her favourites.[62]

George Talbot, Earl of Shrewsbury, already Lord Steward, was appointed one of the two Chamberlains of the Exchequer on 13 May.[63] John de Vere, Earl of Oxford, was made Lord Admiral of England, Ireland and Aquitaine two days later[64] and a raft of other preferments given to him earlier by Henry VII were confirmed – including the Keepership of the lions, lionesses and leopards in the royal menagerie within the Tower, at twelve pence a day, plus an allowance of an extra five pence for every beast. The firebrand Sir Edward Howard, a crony of Henry's, was appointed Royal Standard Bearer of England, with an annual payment of £40.[65]

On 19 May, Henry granted the royal house and manor of Woking in Surrey to his grandmother, which she had surrendered to his father in 1503 in exchange for an estate at Hunsdon in Hertfordshire. Large-scale improvements had been made to this moated house, attractively surrounded by verdant gardens and orchards, which had been one of Henry VII's favourite homes. Now the property was returned to its original owner by a dutiful grandson.

There remained the vexed question of Katherine of Aragon.

On 1 May, while Henry stayed within the security of the Tower, the king's council was closeted at Richmond. On their agenda were progress reports on the arrangements for Henry VII's funeral and the fulfilment of the provisions of the old king's lengthy will. The marriage issue was also raised, as the ministers were fully aware not only of the muddle of unfinished business and the importance of an alliance with Spain, but also the overarching need to secure the Tudor dynasty by the procreation of healthy, lusty male heirs.

A decision was taken during those discussions to resurrect the dormant, stultified marriage with the Spanish princess.

Two days later, Richard Fox, Lord Privy Seal, and the king's secretary, Thomas Ruthal (appointed Bishop of Durham earlier in 1509), summoned Fuensalida to a private meeting. The Spanish ambassador, despite Ferdinand's urgent instructions to secure the match, had already advised Katherine that her marriage was over – indeed he had begun to ship her few paltry possessions to Bruges in the Low Countries. He was unquestionably astonished at the counsellors' news. The Lord Privy Seal told him:

> You must remember now that the king is king and not prince. One must speak in a different way than when he was prince ... Until now, things were discussed with his father and now one must treat with him who is king.

Fox added that he intended to advise Henry to 'make up his mind to marry Katherine quickly', before people began to build obstacles. 'The king's council,' he added, 'were currently in favour of the marriage.'[66] Here was a strong hint that things could change again for the worse as far as Katherine was concerned. Fox was making a veiled allusion to Archbishop William Warham's strong belief that this would be a legally unsound marriage. The Lord Chancellor had not attended the Richmond Palace council meeting and throughout had opposed the marriage because of serious doubts about the validity of the six-year-old papal Bull of dispensation. He had also publicly disagreed with Fox about the issue.[67]

Henry, as we have seen, had been given his dying father's instructions to marry Katherine. Perhaps his grandmother added her formidable weight to the political arguments in favour of the match. We do not know whether his own doubts about marrying his elder brother's widow had surfaced in discussions with his ministers – or whether he had to be persuaded. In any event, willingly or not, he agreed of his own free will that the wedding should go ahead.

Despite his qualms about the wisdom of the affair, on 8 June Archbishop Warham issued a licence permitting the marriage to be solemnised in any church or chapel. The document, in just nine lines of elegant Latin, scrapped the legal prerequisite for three readings of the marriage banns and required them to be published only once.[68]

Ferdinand was cock-a-hoop at the news from London. On 18 May he wrote to Katherine expressing his thanks to God that the wedding would now go ahead. He told her he had always loved her more than any of his five other children and that she had always been 'a dutiful and obedient daughter ... Your marriage is a very grand and [a] very honourable one. Besides, there was no possibility in the whole world of marrying anyone but your husband.' Like all fathers before and since, great as his joy was, it would be greater when he heard that the ceremony had actually taken place. 'It would then be known in England what I am capable of doing for your sake and you will be much honoured in England.'

Ferdinand had finally agreed to pay the marriage portion entirely in coin and urged his daughter – who had fallen out with Fuensalida – to treat the ambassador with courtesy until after the wedding, when he would be recalled to Spain and a replacement appointed 'who will be obedient to her in all things'. Katherine, emboldened by the news of her forthcoming nuptials, must have shown some fiery Spanish spirit, for she was also urged to be polite to the banker Francisco de Grimaldi – 'as he is to pay her dowry'.[69]

The wedding took place just three days after Warham's licence was issued – on 11 June in the oratory of the Friar Observants' church, just outside Greenwich Palace, where Henry had been christened a few days after his birth. It was a private and very quiet affair, probably because of the speed with which it was arranged; Henry wanted his queen crowned with him at Westminster on Midsummer Day, in less than two weeks' time. Only two witnesses are known to have attended: George Talbot, Earl of Shrewsbury, the Lord Steward, and William Thomas, a Groom of the king's Privy Chamber and the servant mentioned in Henry's bede roll.[70] Katherine wore a dress of shimmering white satin and her reddish-gold hair hung long and loose, as befitted the virgin bride she firmly asserted herself to be.[71]

Ironically, it was Warham who officiated at the short, intimate ceremony. He demanded of Henry:

> Most illustrious Prince, is it your will to fulfil the treaty of marriage concluded by your father, the late King of England, and the parents of the Princess of Wales, the King and Queen of Spain, and, as the Pope has dispensed with this marriage, to take the Princess who is here present for your lawful wife?

The king answered firmly: 'I will.' Warham, in full pontificals and mitre, then turned to Katherine and asked her a similar question, beginning, 'Most illustrious Princess . . .' She, in turn, replied: 'I will.'[72]

They spent their wedding night in Greenwich Palace. Henry afterwards bragged that he found his wife a virgin, but in later years, after his taste in women had markedly changed, angrily claimed this had been 'spoken in jest, as a man, jesting and feasting, says many things which are not true'. But Katherine had many living witnesses who had heard him say it.[73]

She came to the marriage almost six years older than her bridegroom, at twenty-three, petite, pink-cheeked, somewhat plump but still beautiful. However, the years of fiscal and mental persecution by Henry VII and her continual hardship at Durham House had instilled an iron will inside that innocent and demure exterior. She also matched her husband's depth of learning – those lonely, isolated years had provided her with the opportunity to read widely, building on the foundations of her humanist education laid long before in Spain.

On 16 June, the king signed his receipt for 50,000 crowns (worth 4s 2d each), the last instalment of the marriage portion handed over to him by Fuensalida.[74] In turn, Henry settled on his wife a handsome jointure. Its eight pages of parchment detail more than £750 in income from annual rents, plus the gift of ninety-nine lordships and manors in at least eleven counties and other benefits, including the rights to 'drag mussels' in the River Thames at 'Tilbury Hope, Essex'.[75]

Planning for the joint coronation of Henry and Katherine was now in full swing. The king proclaimed 'that all who claim to do services on Coronation Day should be in the White Hall at Westminster Palace' by 20 June. A team of nobles, led by the Earl of Surrey, the Lord Treasurer of England, and the Earl of Oxford would determine whether their claims were justified. Henry ordered twenty-six 'honourable persons' to come to the Tower two days later to serve him at dinner in preparation for their creation as Knights of the Bath on 23 June. They included William Blount, Lord Mountjoy, his old companion in Latin studies; Sir Thomas Knyvet, one of his youthful jousting friends; Sir Henry

Clifford, who had been with him since he was made Duke of York; and Sir Thomas Boleyn, a rising star at court.[76]

It is traditional for the king to hold a solemn vigil before his coronation. For Henry's nocturnal watch, at the Tower on Friday 22 June, he wore a doublet of cloth of gold and damask satin under a long gown of purple velvet, furred with ermine.[77]

On Saturday 23 June at about four o'clock in the afternoon a glittering mounted procession trotted out of the Tower, en route to Westminster. The London thoroughfares had been sumptuously decorated for the coronation, the houses and shops hung with tapestry and cloth of arras, and on the south side of Cheapside, with costly cloth of gold. The cobbled streets were railed to keep the huge crowds back from the passage of the riders.

Determined to obtain a good view of proceedings, Lady Margaret Beaufort hired a house in Cheapside for the day, at a rent of 2s 10d, which overlooked the route taken by Henry and Katherine as they processed in triumph. Not for her the crush and stench of the unwashed hoi polloi Londoners in the streets below. She watched the pageant pass by below with Henry's younger sister Princess Mary from behind a latticed window. Moreover, Henry's proud grandmother had surprisingly cast off her everyday drab black and white vowess robes for the occasion, to wear – like her ladies – specially ordered dresses of tawny-brown silk and damask with black velvet bonnets.[78] Despite this frivolous exterior, dark forebodings lurked in Lady Margaret's saintly heart. Bishop Fisher recalled later that the coronation provided great joy to her 'yet she let not to say that some adversity would follow'.[79]

At the head of the dazzling cavalcade rode the newly created Knights of the Bath, wearing blue gowns. Edward Stafford, Duke of Buckingham, claimed his hereditary role of Constable of England and carried a small silver baton as mark of his office as he rode ahead of the king. The duke wore a long gown 'wrought of right costly needlework and ... about his neck a broad and flat close chain ... with great rubies and other stones of great value'.[80] Significantly, the Letters Patent conferring this office on Buckingham had stipulated: 'to be Great Constable on *23 June only*, namely the day preceding the Coronation'.[81] Henry, all too aware of the duke's vaunting ambition, had personally imposed strict limits on Buckingham's vanity and status.

The volume of noise in those narrow streets, overhung with houses, rose to a babbling, shrieking crescendo as the new king appeared amid his household, riding a horse trapped with gold damask and ermine, beneath a golden canopy held aloft by the Barons of the Cinque Ports, exercising a traditional right. Henry wore robes of crimson velvet trimmed with ermine over a gold jacket covered with a breathtaking array of sparkling diamonds, rubies, emeralds and pearls. Around his neck was a collar of huge violet-rose 'ballas rubies' from north Afghanistan.[82] Hall, an enthralled spectator in the crowds, was so beside himself with admiration that his descriptive powers began to fail him:

> The features of his body, his goodly personage, his amiable visage, princely countenance, with the noble qualities of his royal estate, to every man known, needs no rehearsal, considering that for lack of cunning, I cannot express the gifts of grace and of nature that God has endowed him with.[83]

Behind Henry straggled a long column of lords spiritual and temporal and many knights and esquires. Then came Sir Thomas Brandon, Master of the King's Horse, wearing a golden collar like his sovereign (but less showy) and a doublet embroidered with roses of fine gold. He led, by a silken rein, the king's spare charger, with a harness 'curiously wrought' in bullion by goldsmiths.

Katherine's procession followed. She sat in a litter 'born[e] by two white palfreys, trapped in white cloth of gold'. She was resplendent in embroidered white satin, 'her hair hanging down her back of very great length, beautiful and goodly to behold and on her head, a coronet[84] set with many rich orient stones' as Edward Hall enthusiastically reported.[85] Behind were chariots carrying her ladies and the wives of the peers of the realm, wearing gorgeously coloured silks.

Bringing up the rear were three hundred of the king's guard still wearing 'jackets of the old king's livery', some armed with bows and arrows, others with the harquebus (or hackbut), a muzzle-loading gun fired from the shoulder.

As Katherine's litter passed a tavern on the north side of Lombard Street displaying a board with a painted cardinal's hat hanging over its doorway

> such a sudden shower there came and fell with such force and thickness that the canopy borne over her was not sufficient to defend her from wetting of her mantle and fur of powdered ermines ... But she was ... conveyed under the hovel of a draper's stall till the showers were passed over which was not long.[86]

In the future, there would be some Londoners of long memory who remembered Katherine being drenched by that inopportune shower and pondered whether the location of the incident was an evil portent.

Henry and Katherine slept that night in the Painted Chamber of Westminster Palace beneath the huge mural, commissioned by Henry III, of the coronation of St Edward the Confessor in 1042.[87] The next morning, Sunday 24 June 1509, Henry and Katherine left the palace at about eight o'clock and walked through Westminster Hall into the abbey church, escorted by thirty-eight bishops and abbots.

The cloth merchants had been frantically busy, supplying 1,641 yards (1,500 m) of scarlet cloth and 2,040 yards (1,865 m) of red cloth, costing all together £1,307 11s 3½d, for everyone's coronation robes. Around 480 yards (440 m) of cloth in the Tudor livery were also used for the uniforms of one hundred and sixty personnel from the King's Bench and Marshalsea Prisons, who carried tipped staves at the ceremony and may have acted as ushers. The total bill for the silks and cloth amounted to £4,781 6s 3d. On top of this was the £1,749 8s 4d for the king and queen's own robes.

The abbey was packed not only with the great, the good and the merely curious but also with some of the hundreds of retainers who daily attended the royal couple in their separate households. Pip, the Keeper of the King's fool Merten (who received special clothes for the coronation), ended the long, long list of courtiers and servants in Henry's household and Privy Chamber.[88]

Amongst the invited spectators were two from Henry's childhood – 'Mrs Anne Luke, the king's nurse' and his old French master 'Giles D'Ewes and three of his fellows'.[89]

Lady Margaret watched, fondly and proudly, from her privileged seat in the choir as Archbishop Warham formally presented the new king to his subjects. A thousand voices replied with four deafening, resounding shouts of *Vivat, Vivat Rex* – 'Long live the King!'

The coronation oath sworn by Henry that Midsummer's Day included his pledge, made before Richard Fitzjames, Bishop of London, that

> With good will and devout soul, I promise ... I shall keep the privilege of the law canon and of holy church ... and I shall ... by God's grace defend you and every each of you, bishops and abbots, through my realm and all these churches to you and them committed; all these things ... I Henry, King of England promise and confirm to keep and observe, so help me God and by these holy evangelists by me bodily touched upon this holy altar.

The king stood up from Edward I's Coronation Chair[90] and moved to the abbey's high altar to make 'a solemn oath upon the sacrament laid upon the altar, in the sight of all the people'.[91] He was anointed with holy oil nine times – on the palms of his hands, his chest, back, on each shoulder and elbow and finally upon his head, each time with the sign of the cross. Henry was then handed the royal regalia of gold orb and sceptre and the crown of St Edward the Confessor was slowly and reverently lowered upon his head as he again sat resplendent in the great chair.[92]

Another record of the oath has him swearing to maintain the rights and liberties of 'holy church', and this has been amended, in Henry's own hand, to read 'of the holy church of England not prey to his jurisdiction and dignity royal'.[93] Some have claimed this was the oath administered on that august day, but it seems likely it was personally amended by the king in the 1530s, in a mischievous attempt to rewrite history when the religious break with Rome was underway.

Homage was paid to Henry by his nobility, led by the senior peer Buckingham, who knelt before his sovereign and pledged his loyalty and fealty:

> I Edward Stafford become your liegeman[94] of life and limb and of earthly
> worship and faith and truth I shall bear unto you, to live and die against
> all manner of folk, so God help me and his saints.

The duke's homage was followed by that of the four earls and twenty-
one barons present.[95]

It was then Katherine's turn. After all those bleak years of solitary
despair, fading or thwarted dreams, and the cruel treatment at the
grasping hands of her scheming father-in-law, her day of glory had
finally arrived. She was radiant, wearing a kirtle furred with miniver
(from the white stoat or ermine) and a mantle with a train of white
cloth of gold with gold and white tassels.[96] The archbishop gently placed
a crown of gold upon her head, the border set with sapphires and pearls,
and handed her a golden sceptre with the image of a tiny dove on top.[97]
She had become queen of England at last, although she could never
forget her bitter past.

With the ceremonial based firmly on precedent – the form used was
a variation of the coronation ritual used for Henry VII almost a quarter
of a century before – some things were bound to go awry. Edward Grey,
Baron Grey of Powys, was assigned the honour of leading the horses of
the queen's litter, a role fulfilled by his ancestors. But Edward was aged
just six. Viscounts were also detailed to carry the sceptre and ivory rod
in the queen's procession, but in 1509, there were no viscounts alive in
England.[98]

On the Tuesday following, there was a celebratory joust at Westminster with Sir Edward Howard leading the challengers in the contest
and Sir John Pechy (or Peche) heading the list of defenders. An anonymous London chronicler, who was present, described the start of the
extravagant spectacle:

> Two of the chief … challengers, enclosed in a mountain goodly and
> curiously garnished by a lion made of glittering gold, were conveyed out
> of Westminster Hall into the palace and so laid about the tilt [yard] till
> they came afore the king and queen standing and there the mountain
> opened and the two chief challengers rode forth, clean armed unto the
> tilt's end …

The defenders' entrance was also stunning:

> Sir John Pechy ... came in enclosed in a castle drawn with a lioness garnished with silver and upon the fore part of this castle was set a pomegranate [Katherine's personal badge] tree well and curiously wrought and so cunningly put it was to the people apparent as they had been very pomegranates that was hanged upon that tree.
>
> Upon the top of this castle stood a fane [banner] with the arms of St George there painted.
>
> The castle was drawn about the tilt and when it came against the king's tent, it was opened ... and out rode the said defender and made his obeisance to the king and queen.

On the second day there was a 'tourney', when the combatants fought on foot with swords, wielding a set number of blows. 'It was fearful to behold,' gasped the chronicler

> [and] continued with such eagerness that their number of strokes passed and the power of the marshals [was not] sufficient to part them till the king cried to his guard to help ... which was not done without great pain.[99]

All this was very jolly, but the celebrations and feasting had to stop some time. The sudden death of Henry's grandmother five days after the coronation put paid to the last vestiges of revelry. Lady Margaret had fallen ill at the beginning of the year. Her condition was serious enough for estimates of the cost of her funeral to be drawn up, and after recovering, she delegated some of her everyday affairs to Bishop Fisher and two others, all named executors.

After the coronation, she stayed at Cheyneygates, a lodging of the Abbot of Westminster within the monastery precincts,[100] where she suddenly became sick. Henry Parker, Baron Morley, who had served as her cup-bearer, suggested that consuming a roast cygnet was the cause of her malady.[101] Medicines certainly did not improve her condition and she died on 29 June.[102] Bishop Fisher reported that when the last rites were administered 'with all her heart and soul she raised her body ... and confessed assuredly that in that sacrament was contained Christ

Jesu, the Son of God that died for wretched sinners ... in whom wholly she put her trust and confidence'. Parker observed that she died at the very moment that the Host was raised in reverence.[103] Cardinal Reginald Pole, in later years Henry VIII's bête noire, claimed that Lady Margaret, 'with tears', entreated the young king on her deathbed to obey Bishop Fisher above all others, as she feared he would turn away from God's laws and Christian teaching.[104]

Lady Margaret was buried in Westminster Abbey on 9 July. Again Bishop Fisher, her chaplain, was chosen to deliver her funeral sermon. She was, he said,

> of marvellous gentleness unto all folk but especially to her own whom she trusted and loved right tenderly.
>
> Unkind she would not be to any creature, nor forgetful of any kindness or service done to her, which is no little part of nobleness.
>
> She was not vengeful, nor cruel, but ready anon to forget and to forgive injuries done to her ...
>
> All England for her death has cause for weeping. The poor creatures who were wont to receive her alms to whom she was always piteous and merciful. The students of both the universities to whom she was as a mother ... All good priests and clerks to whom she was a true defender.[105]

Henry celebrated his eighteenth birthday on 28 June. The death of his grandmother had snapped the last link with the overpowering constraints of his youth.

6

A GOLDEN WORLD

———•◦•———

'If you could see how nobly, how wisely the prince behaves, I am sure you will hasten to England. All England is in ecstasies. Extortion is put down – liberality is the order of the day.'

William Blount, Lord Mountjoy, to Erasmus, 27 May 1509.[1]

Married life enthralled Henry VIII – at least at this early stage in his reign. In the halcyon weeks that followed his crowning, he wrote enthusiastic letters to his father-in-law Ferdinand describing his joyful and enchanted life with Katherine. On 17 July 1509 he described their coronation: 'The multitude of the people who assisted was immense and their joy and applause most enthusiastic.'

These were happy, carefree salad days, spent in quest of boundless regal pleasure – whilst the king's ministers ran the country, as they had done for his father. Henry amused himself with 'jousts, birding [hawking], hunting and other innocent and honest pastimes, also in visiting different parts of my kingdom'. Lest Ferdinand should think him simply a frivolous young monarch, he hastened to add: 'I do not, on that account, neglect affairs of state.'[2]

A profound love for Katherine had blossomed unexpectedly in his teenage heart. Nine days later, Henry wrote again promising that the enduring bond between him and his bride was 'now so strict that all their interests are common. The love I bear Katherine is such that if I were *free* [the word is significant], I would choose her in preference to all others.'[3] He had conveniently forgotten Eleanor of Austria, his father's preferred imperial candidate for his wife, whom the king had now jilted following two years of marriage negotiations.

Henry was intent on pleasing his bride and devised elaborate entertainments to amuse her as well as purchasing presents, such as the 'eight fine pillows' delivered to 'our most dear wife' by the department of the Great Wardrobe in November.[4] The previous month, thirty shillings were paid for 'the queen's lavender'.

That fickle bowman Cupid was plainly active at the English court, for on 30 July Henry announced to Ferdinand that his long-time friend and mentor William Blount, Lord Mountjoy, 'whom I hold in high esteem, has married Inez de Venegas, one of the ladies of the queen. I think it very desirable that Spanish and English families should be united by [such] ties.'[5]

Katherine told her father that the chief cause of her love for her husband was that 'he is so true a son' to him. Henry had therefore 'put himself entirely in your hands'. Their kingdom was 'in great peace and entertains much love to the king, my lord and me' she added, and 'our time passes in continual festivities'. In a postscript, she begged Ferdinand to buy a special gift for her husband: 'my lord requests a jennet, a Neapolitan and a Sicilian horse' from Ferdinand 'by the first messenger'.[6]

In September, the Spanish king wrote of his enormous pleasure that Katherine 'and the king are well and prosperous and that they love one another so much'. He hoped fervently that their happiness would last 'as long as they live' and observed:

> To be well married is the greatest blessing in the world. A good marriage
> is not only an excellent thing in itself but also the source of all other kinds
> of happiness.
>
> God shows favour to good husbands and wives.

Her father had summoned home the unfortunate Fuensalida and had appointed Luis Caroz his successor in London. During the interregnum before the new envoy's arrival, Ferdinand instructed Henry that 'all my communications respecting the affairs pending between England and Spain will be made to the queen, your wife', who would act as his ambassador. He begged his son-in-law to 'give her implicit credit' or diplomatic credentials. Up to March 1510, when Caroz finally arrived in England, she frequently reported on developments at court in coded letters to Spain. If his wife's personal conflict of interests bothered the infatuated, lovesick Henry, he did not object.[7]

Indeed, he happily accepted paternal advice from Ferdinand about the problems of kingship and the perils of the perfidious French – all delivered via his wife. Katherine was requested to point out to Henry that

> ... secrecy and circumspection are always necessary in great enterprises.
>
> The King of England must therefore henceforth write in his letters nothing but such things as the French may read without danger.
>
> All other communications must be made by her and be written in her cipher or in the cipher of the [Spanish] ambassador.
>
> I have always observed and will, in future, always observe the same rule – namely, to write in common writing only what the French may see and to write all that is important in cipher.[8]

All this Henry took meekly like a lamb, even swearing eternal obedience to his fifty-seven-year-old father-in-law. He preferred an alliance with Spain over one with any other nation and would 'reject them all in order to preserve your friendship', he submissively told the Spanish king. Furthermore, he promised 'like a dutiful son, to obey all your behests, as I would obey the behests of my late father, if he were still alive'.[9]

Immediately on becoming queen, Katherine's household was increased to an establishment of one hundred and sixty courtiers and servants, governed by a Lord Chamberlain, the eighty-three-year-old Thomas Butler, Seventh Earl of Ormond, a grizzled veteran of the previous century's Wars of the Roses Battle of Tewkesbury. With seventy-two manors in England and further extensive land holdings in Ireland, he was one of the richest men in the realm.

Only eight of her retainers were still Spanish and these included one of her ladies, Maria de Salinas, 'whom the queen loved more than any other mortal'.[10] Her haughty and canny confessor, the Franciscan Friar Diego Fernández, played a dominant role in Katherine's daily spiritual and temporal life. Caroz, who occasionally felt the full force of Henry's exasperation, blamed the confessor for his low standing at court, claiming that the friar exerted 'undue influence' on the queen.

Amongst her Gentlewomen of the Bedchamber was Lady Elizabeth Boleyn, whose two daughters, Mary and Anne, were to have a calamitous impact on Katherine's health and happiness in the years ahead.

The queen afterwards became a patron of Juan Luis Vives,[11] a Spanish disciple of the humanist scholar Erasmus whom she brought to England as a doctor of laws at Corpus Christi College, Oxford. Years later, they talked earnestly about the capriciousness of destiny as they were rowed down the River Thames from the Bridgettine monastery at Syon in Middlesex back to Richmond Palace. The queen said she sought an uneventful, tranquil life but if she had to choose between adversity and prosperity, Katherine would always plump for the former as 'if the unfortunate lacked consolation, real loss of spiritual integrity usually visited the prosperous'. This creed was to comfort her during her later years of marriage.

Like his father, Henry was no slouch in his efforts to extend and thus protect the Tudor dynasty. By late autumn 1509, Katherine happily found herself pregnant, with Henry reporting to his father-in-law that 'the child in her womb is alive' and that he and his kingdom rejoiced at the news.[12] Ferdinand told his daughter in November of his joy at her impending motherhood:

> Your pregnancy is a great blessing since you and your husband and the English people have wished it so much. May God give you a good delivery. I will continually pray to the Almighty to grant my prayers until I am informed you have given birth to your child.

The Spanish king begged Katherine 'to be careful of her health' and firmly advised her to avoid all exertion and 'especially not write with your own hand. With the first child, it is requisite for women to take more care of themselves than is necessary in subsequent pregnancies.'[13]

For Henry, it was not all laddish pursuits in the tiltyard or the hunting field. He maintained a powerful intellectual curiosity derived from his classical education and it became his (sometimes irksome) habit to invite his friend Thomas More into his Privy Chamber and there some time in matters of astronomy, geometry, divinity and such other faculties and some time in his worldly affairs, to sit up and confer with him.

And other whiles would he in the night have him up into the leads [the palace roof], there to consider with him the diversities, courses, motions and operations of the stars and planets.[14]

During a conversation with Mountjoy that May, Henry admitted that he yearned to become more learned and wise. His old tutor said this was not really expected of monarchs, but instead, the king should foster the growth of knowledge by becoming a generous patron to philosophers. Henry exclaimed: 'Why, of course, for without them, life would hardly be life!' Mountjoy cheerfully recounted this conversation to Erasmus, who was still teaching in Rome, and urged him to come to England as soon as possible, even offering him £5 towards the expenses of the arduous journey across Europe. 'Avarice,' Mountjoy rhapsodised, 'has fled the country. Our king is not after gold, or gems, or precious metals, but virtue, glory [and] immortality.'[15]

It was an attractive, compelling prospect. The Dutch humanist duly came to England in high hopes of enjoying royal patronage – but despite his earlier affable correspondence with Henry the prince, he received no munificence from Henry the king. Instead, Erasmus stayed at the home of his close friend Thomas More amid the herbalist shops in Bucklersbury, off Cheapside in the City of London, and there suffered a sharp attack of lumbago. Eventually he was granted a professorial post at Cambridge by Bishop Fisher in August 1511 and a modest church benefice arranged by Warham at Aldington, south-east of Ashford, in Kent.

George Cavendish, later Gentleman Usher to Wolsey, recalled that the new king was seen as a 'natural, young, lusty and courageous prince [who was] entering into the flower of pleasant youth'. With his accession, England had entered 'a golden world'.[16]

More was impressed by the young Henry's extraordinary charisma and gracious presence. He reported to Fisher:

The king has a way of making every man feel that he is enjoying his special favour, just as the London wives pray before the image of Our Lady by the Tower, until each of them believes it is smiling upon her.[17]

With these personable talents, Henry VIII would have made a credible and successful politician.

More presented a *Coronation Suite* of five Latin poems to the king and queen, describing his sovereign as the 'glory of the age', with his succession inaugurating 'a new golden era'. Virtue and learning were to reign supreme; liberality was to expel avarice; darkness would give way to light. As for Katherine, he predicted that 'she will be the mother of kings as great as her ancestors'.[18] John Skelton, Henry's old Latin schoolmaster, also penned effusive verses in honour of the occasion, predicting that the king would be just and wise and protect England's common people.[19]

Touchingly, Henry did not overlook those who were important to him in his formative years. Anne Oxenbridge, 'late the king's nurse' who, after the death of her first husband, had married Walter Luke by 1504, was granted an annuity of £20 a year on 9 July.[20] The fifty shillings paid to a 'Mistress Oxenbridge' in September 1510 may be a slip of the clerk's pen and probably refers to the same lady. Spending money for her, perhaps?[21] In December 1519 there is also a payment of 6s 8d 'to the king's nurse for cheese'.

Elizabeth Denton, the former 'lady mistress' of the royal nursery at Eltham Palace, was also provided with a liberal annual pension of £50 for life. She was granted the Keepership of Coldharbour (Lady Margaret's London home), and a tun[22] of Gascon wine each year, delivered from the port of London by Sir Robert Southwell, Chief Butler of England.[23] Giles D'Ewes, Henry's French teacher, who also taught him to play the lute, was appointed that September as librarian at Richmond Palace on an annual salary of £10, payable from income from the customs of the port of Bristol.[24]

The loyal servants of the king's grandmother were also not forgotten by this grateful and considerate sovereign. The month after her death, eight were granted sinecure posts 'for services to the king's granddame', including her sergeant-at-arms, William Pool, who had moved across to Katherine's household to serve in the same capacity. He was made Bailiff of the town and Lordship of Holesworthy, North Devon.[25]

His father's faithful retainers were also rewarded: William Adbaston was granted a mill called 'Pole Milne, alias Shipton Milne in the manor of Langley, Oxfordshire', at an annual rent of fifteen shillings in thanks for his 'services to Henry VII and for his relief and succour in his old age'.[26] William Berryman, 'late yeoman for Henry VII's mouth [a food taster] in his kitchen', was given leases of a tavern called *le Rose super le Hope* and a brewery in the London parish of All Hallows, Staining, in return for his payment of the almost lyrical peppercorn rent of 'a red rose at Midsummer'.[27]

Henry signed Letters Patent allowing Lady Margaret's executors – amongst them Fox, Fisher and Sir Henry Marney – to acquire the site and possessions of the Priory of St John, Cambridge, 'now in a most impoverished and dilapidated condition' and instead found a college on its site 'for a master, fellows and scholars' to be called 'the College of St John the Evangelist, Cambridge'.[28]

His young, roistering friends were not left out of Henry's open-handed largess. Charles Brandon, his hero of the joust, was given the lucrative position of Chamberlain of the principality of North Wales in November 1509.

The king had also not forgotten his filial duties towards his parents, endorsing existing estimates to build their tomb within their new chapel in Westminster Abbey.[29] Eventually these plans were discarded and the Florentine sculptor Pietro Torrigiano, who signed a contract to build a monument in the chapel to Henry's grandmother in November 1511, was commissioned by the old king's executors in October 1512 to make the tomb of Henry VII and Elizabeth of York at a cost of £1,500.[30] It was one of the earliest Renaissance monuments in England.

Henry VIII's realm was not quite as tranquil as Katherine believed; danger and treasonous ambitions still lurked in the hearts of some of his higher-ranking nobility. His father's old fretful spectre of insecurity had returned to haunt his young successor.

In August the northern noble Thomas, First Lord Darcy,[31] warned Bishop Fox, the Privy Seal, of further treasonous statements by the servants of his neighbour, Sir Algernon Percy, Fifth Earl of Northumberland. In early June Darcy had replaced Northumberland as Warden General of the eastern Scottish Marches and as Captain of the frontier town of Berwick.[32] Now it seemed that the old disloyal whisperings by these 'knaves, craftsmen and beggars' about Buckingham and Northumberland's aspirations had not died away after the coronation. They claimed that:

> my lord of Buckingham should be protector of England and that their master [Northumberland] should rule all from north of the River Trent and have Berwick and the marches.
>
> Richard Tempest reported to me their saying, at coming into Craven [North Yorkshire] from London that 'if their lord had not rooms [appointments] in the north as his father had, it should not be long well'.
>
> Gilson, Ratcliffe and Tipping, 'servants to my said lord' in St Martin's in London in his place [house, said] that Sir Rhys ap Thomas [the Tudors' principal lieutenant in South Wales] was gone to the sea, fled of his country.[33]

Darcy cautioned that Fox was also the object of sinister treasonous mutterings:

> It is the saying of every market man that the Lord Privy Seal cannot bring himself to rule the king's grace [without] put[ting] out of favour the Earl of Surrey, the Earl of Shrewsbury, the Bishop of Durham [and others]. Now he will prove another way which is ... to bolster himself to rule with the Duke of Buckingham and the Earl of Northumberland. Doubtless, fast they curse and speak evil of my Lord Privy Seal beyond measure.

Darcy said Fox could show his two-page warning letter 'to the king's grace or otherwise'.[34]

Henry must have been well aware of this sedition. Away from his pleasure-seeking, he established ordinances on 25 July to improve the defences of the Tower in an attempt to provide a place of refuge – a final redoubt – for him in London in the event of an insurrection in the capital. These fresh standing orders instructed the Yeomen of the Guard and other soldiers stationed in the fortress 'not to be absent without leave' and stipulated that never more than one-third of the garrison should be away from the fortress at any time. Security at the Tower's gates was also tightened up.[35]

In November he also improved his personal protection. Henry VII had set up a group of fifty archers as a bodyguard – they exist today as the queen's Yeomen of the Guard – but his son wanted an additional force of peerless loyalty to call on in an emergency.

At the suggestion of William Compton (who was a page to Henry when he was Prince of Wales and was now the Groom of the Stool, fulfilling the king's most intimate personal needs), the king established a group of men-at-arms solely for his close security. This 'Retinue of Spears' was recruited from 'young men of noble blood' and formed a handy, quickly mobilised military force to safeguard the royal family.

Each 'Spear' was fully armed, clad in armour and equipped with four horses for himself and his page, together with another for his 'costrel' or shield-bearing servant who was armed with a lance. Each should bring 'two good archers, well-horsed and harnessed' to 'muster before the king at a month's notice'. None could depart from his duties without permission. This force, under the command of Henry Bourchier, Earl of Essex, and Sir John Pechy, its lieutenant, had to swear an oath of absolute allegiance to Henry:

> I shall be a true and faithful subject and servant to our sovereign lord King Henry the Eight and to his heirs, Kings of England, and diligently and truly give my attendance in the room of one of his Spears and I shall be retainer to no man, person or persons of what degree or condition, whosoever he be by oath, livery, badge, promise or otherwise but only to his grace without his special licence.[36]
>
> I shall not hereafter know or hear of anything that shall be hurtful or prejudicial to his most royal person, especially in treason, but I shall withstand it to the uttermost of my power and the same with all diligence to me possible, disclose to the King's Highness or the Captain of the Spears or his deputy, or such other of his council as I know will discover the same unto his Grace.[37]

Henry was testing his strength as king and his strutting Tudor arrogance was never far from the surface. In August, the Venetian ambassador, Andrea Badoer, watched gleefully as the new French envoy, the corpulent Abbot of Fécamp, was given very short shrift at Westminster. After being ushered into the royal presence, the abbot announced that he had come in response to Henry's letters to his master, Louis XII, 'requesting friendship and peace' and that he would now formally confirm that peace. Henry took immediate offence and

> turning to his attendants [he] exclaimed: 'Who wrote this letter? I ask peace of the King of France, who dare not look me in the face, still less make war on me?'

He stomped off angrily and would 'hear no more'. Later that day a display of 'tilting at the ring' was planned and, politely, the French ambassador had been invited to attend. Badoer reported that 'no place having been reserved for him upon a stage erected for guests, he departed in dudgeon. The king, however, had him recalled and caused a cushion to be given him and he sat down'. The Venetian summed up: 'In short, King Henry holds France in small account.'[38]

Possibly because of the plague that was raging in some parts of England, Henry kept Christmas isolated at Richmond, with forty shillings paid to the children of the Chapel Royal for singing *Gloria in Excelsis* and £10 to William Wynnesbury as 'Lord of Misrule', who presided over the full gamut of noisy revelry. The festivities continued until Twelfth Night (probably then the evening of 5 January), with a play staged in the great hall, but for the king, the merrymaking continued.

On 12 January 1510 he took part incognito in a private joust in Richmond Park together with Compton, who was also in disguise. This was the first time he had jousted as king and despite his efforts his presence was an open secret. There were 'many broken staves [lances] and great praise given to the two strangers, but especially to one, who was the king'.

Disaster followed.

Edward Neville,[39] one of Henry's cronies, ran a course against Compton and 'hurt him sore and [he] was likely to die'. There was panic amongst the spectators that the injured contestant was Henry, but when the visor of Compton's helmet was raised, 'one person that was there knew the king and cried "God save the king!" [and] with that all the people were astonished. Then the king discovered [revealed] himself to the great comfort of the people.'[40]

Unabashed by this accident, Henry decided to take on the persona of Robin Hood in a merry jape to entertain the heavily pregnant queen. After Christmas, the court returned to Westminster and one morning the king and eleven of his nobles, all disguised as Sherwood Forest outlaws, burst suddenly into the queen's chamber, dressed in

> short coats of Kentish kendal[41] with hoods on their heads and hose of the same. Everyone of them, his bow and arrows, and a sword and buckler[42] ... [like] Robin Hood's men.
>
> Whereof the queen, the ladies and all other[s] there were abashed ... for the strange sight [and] also for their sudden coming.
>
> After certain dances and pastime made, they departed.[43]

History does not record what Katherine thought of her husband's schoolboy prank; without question, her physicians would have advised against any sudden shocks in her condition.

Henry had summoned his first Parliament to be held at Westminster on 21 January – the first to be called for six years. On that day, all the lords assembled in the queen's great chamber and processed to the abbey church for God's blessings on their deliberations. The king was preceded by the sword of state and the cap of estate, borne respectively by Henry, Lord Stafford, and his brother Buckingham. Flanked by his sergeants-of-arms and four gentlemen ushers on either side, Henry represented the very image of majesty, his long train carried by Oxford and supported in the middle by Charles, Lord Herbert. After passing by his father's wooden and palled hearse, still standing in the abbey's choir, the king was delayed by the press of the crowd before he succeeded in passing through the gallery to the Parliament Chamber. Sitting on the throne and wearing the cap of estate, Henry listened approvingly as Warham, his Lord Chancellor, opened the Parliament with prayers and preached from the initial chapter of the first *Epistle General of St Peter* – 'Fear

God, honour the King' – which he used to underline the importance of temporal allegiance and the need for good laws.[44] The king attended Parliament again two days later and on 23 February.

Its business was routine – discussions on the revenues necessary to pay the expenses of the king's household and assigning money to fund the king's great wardrobe.

This income was very necessary: Henry VIII, freed of the shackles imposed by his father, was beginning to spend prodigiously. In the first two full months of his reign, May and June 1509, his household expenses (which included some incidentals from the coronation) totalled £3,414 1s 1d, compared with the £12,759 expended in a whole year by his father up to 29 September 1508.[45] The first manifestations of the king's later love for retail therapy – his purchases of nice trinkets and pretty objects in precious metals – began to appear in July and included £6 6s 8d for just over three ounces (372 g) of fine gold 'for the king's little chain', while Henry Worley, goldsmith, was paid forty-three shillings for 'garnishing of knives'. Katherine, after her years of penury, was also spending freely: the Under-Treasurer was authorised that month to pay her £1,000 for her debts. In October, a Frenchman was paid £223 at Croydon for jewels; the goldsmith John Munday £133 12s; and three Italian merchants, more than £584 for cloth of gold – the total for these three transactions amounting to £495,000 in today's purchasing power. Goldsmiths were also paid £333 6s 8d for the king's New Year gifts.

Parliamentary business also included some of the more prosaic aspects of Tudor society, such as a new law prohibiting coroners from charging fees for investigating obviously accidental deaths as 'their insistence ... often caused annoyance because bodies lie long unburied'.[46] Another Act was intended to stamp out perjury;[47] further legislation limited the export of coin, plate and jewels[48] and, ironically, the wearing of 'costly apparel'.[49] Finally, an Act provided legal redress to landowners who had been deprived of the titles to their property by the false inquisitions operated by Empson and Dudley in the years after 1504.[50] However, bills of attainder for the two councillors had been passed by the Commons but not by the House of Lords by the time Parliament was prorogued at the end of February.

Perhaps the king tried to make amends to Katherine for his earlier Robin Hood prank. On Shrove Tuesday – the last day before the dreary Lenten fast – Henry threw an elaborately arranged banquet in the queen's honour for the foreign ambassadors in the Parliament Chamber at Westminster. Amid polite applause, Henry personally led Katherine to his own regal seat beneath the golden cloth of estate canopy at the top table. The guests were 'marshalled by the king, who would not sit, but walked from place to place, making cheer to the queen and the strangers'.

Suddenly the king disappeared and then re-entered the banquet with Henry Bourchier, Earl of Essex. Both were dressed in the Turkish fashion, wearing long robes of baudekin (a rich figured silk) powdered with gold, and crimson velvet hats, and each armed with broad-bladed Middle-Eastern scimitar swords. The king's young friends followed, dressed in the Russian and Prussian styles, escorted by torchbearers in crimson satin, their faces blackened with soot to resemble Moors. All then took part in a 'mummery' – a silent play or dance to music. 'So the king made great cheer to the queen, ladies and the ambassadors,' reported Edward Hall.[51]

But Henry had not finished with the joys of dressing up. He disappeared again and in a short while, there came in

> drum and fife [players] apparelled in white damask [satin] and green bonnets [and] certain gentlemen followed with torches, apparelled in blue damask ... fashioned like an alb[52] and on their heads, hoods with ... tippets.[53]
>
> After them came a certain number ... whereof the king was one, apparelled all in one suit of short garments ... of blue and crimson velvet with long sleeves, all lined with cloth of gold.

Then followed ladies – one of whom was Princess Mary, Henry's younger sister – gorgeously attired, some wearing headdresses 'rounded ... like the Egyptians. Their faces, necks, arms and hands, covered with black ... so that the ladies seemed to be Negroes or Moors.' All danced 'a certain time' before 'they departed every one to his lodging'.[54] Henry had put on a good show – the silks alone cost him £133 7s 5d and the bill for the gold plate on the tables was a further £451 12s 2d.

At the end of April 1510, a chapter of the Order of the Garter was held at Greenwich. During the second office of vespers, 'the king in his stall and [the] other knights (including Buckingham and Northumberland) in theirs', Bishop Ruthal sought nominations for the vacant stalls (gaps in membership). He was acting registrar of the Order, as one had not been chosen. Henry promptly named his new almoner, Thomas Wolsey, to discharge the office thereafter.[55] Wolsey, his 'head full of subtle wit and policy', had caught the king's eye and was rapidly gaining in favour at court. That year Henry gave him Empson's house at Bridewell, off London's Fleet Street.[56]

Some time early in 1510 Katherine miscarried of a baby girl at Green-wich. The dates are confused – some reports suggest the miscarriage occurred on 31 January, but warrants dated February and March author-ised payments for preparations for the birth,[57] and it seems likely her miscarriage occurred much later in the spring, perhaps at the end of April.[58]

On 27 May Katherine told her father that she had been delivered of a still-born daughter, 'an event which in England is considered unlucky', and therefore she had not written sooner. She begged him 'not to be angry with her, for it has been the will of God'. Despite this tragedy, both she and her husband remained cheerful and Katherine '[thanked] God for a husband such as the King of England'.

The letter then contains a bizarre request from the queen. Whilst in the agony of labour, the queen vowed to present one of her most costly headdresses to St Peter the Martyr[59] (a favourite saint of the Franciscan friars). Katherine gave it to one of her longest-serving servants of the chamber, a niece of Pedro Morales (her treasurer),[60] to deliver to the prioress of the nunnery of the Virgin and St Francis, at Aldgate, on the eastern edge of the City of London.[61] But Morales retained both the queen's letter and the headdress and declared before a public notary that the latter belonged to his daughter. Katherine asked Ferdinand to reprimand her treasurer 'for such want of respect'.[62]

Fernández, the queen's confessor, reported that the queen had 'brought forth prematurely a daughter without any pain except that one knee pained her the night before'. The matter had been kept a closely guarded secret except for 'the king, my lord, two Spanish women, a physician and I'. Even Caroz, the Spanish ambassador, had been forbidden by Katherine to speak of the matter.[63]

The most startling news followed: 'The physician said that her highness remained pregnant of another child and it was believed and kept secret.' The queen tried to conceal it but

> ... her belly became swollen so much as never was seen in a pregnant woman.
>
> Her highness denies it to all the world and to the king but to me she has [said] she is since three months pregnant ...
>
> All the physicians know and affirm it and a Spanish woman who is in her private chamber told me the same thing from secret signs that they have.
>
> Her highness is very healthy and is the most beautiful creature in the world with the greatest gaiety and contentment that ever was.
>
> The king, my lord, adores her and her highness him.[64]

Then the swelling decreased – it was probably a post-natal infection of the womb – and Katherine's menstrual periods resumed. Although the pretence of a new pregnancy was maintained for a while, these were false hopes, born of wishful thinking.

Now the lie of a fresh pregnancy – if lie it was – had to be confronted. Caroz complained bitterly about those who suggested

> ... that a menstruating woman was pregnant and ... make her withdraw publicly for her delivery.
>
> The privy councillors of the king are very vexed and angry at this mistake – as they have said to me – although from courtesy they give the blame to the bedchamber women who gave the queen to understand that she was pregnant when she was not.
>
> I have asked them ... [that] they and the king should comfort and console the queen who might perhaps be sad and disconsolate as she had desired to gladden the king and the people with a prince.
>
> I know that many of the privy councillors and other persons are murmuring and they presume that since the queen is not pregnant, she is incapable of conceiving ...

I have spoken with the king as to what we are to say of the queen's confinement. They find the case so difficult that they do not know what to determine.[65]

Caroz was painfully aware of more bad news for Katherine, probably leaked to him by Francesca de Carceres, one of the queen's former attendants.[66]

While she was sequestered in Greenwich for her confinement, her husband's eye had begun to rove salaciously over the coquettish young women surrounding him at court.

Edward Stafford, Duke of Buckingham, had two sisters who served as ladies-in-waiting to the queen. Elizabeth, the elder, was married to Robert Radcliffe, Lord Fitzwalter, and twenty-seven-year-old Anne was the newly-wed wife of George, Lord Hastings.[67] 'The one of them,' Caroz reported to Miguel de Almazan, First Secretary of State to Ferdinand, 'is the favourite of the queen and the other ... is much liked by the king, *who went after her.*'[68] It is all too easy to speculate that Henry's affair with Anne lay behind the decision to create her younger brother, Henry Lord Stafford, Earl of Wiltshire on 3 February.[69]

Another rumour circulating at court was that William Compton, who had happily recovered from his jousting accident, was involved in an illicit relationship with Lady Hastings. It seems more likely that as Henry's close confidant, Compton's liaison was merely a smokescreen to conceal the king's own dalliance with the stunningly beautiful dark-haired girl. Unfortunately, her elder sister got wind of events and consulted both Buckingham and Anne's husband as to the proper course of action – perhaps Elizabeth Fitzwalter also sneakily told Katherine of her husband's infidelity. Caroz excitedly related its denouement:

Whilst the duke was in the private apartment of his sister who was suspected [of intriguing] with the king, Compton came there to talk with her.

[He] saw the duke, who intercepted him, quarrelled with him and the end of it was that he was severely reproached in many and very hard words.

144

Buckingham heatedly told the courtier: 'Women of the Stafford family are no game for Comptons,' and added tellingly: 'no, nor for Tudors either!' No doubt the duke's angry words were backed up with his fists – such was his reputation for violent anger. Caroz takes up the story again:

> The king was so offended at this that he reprimanded the duke angrily.
>
> The same night the duke left the palace and did not enter or return there for some days.
>
> At the same time, the husband of the lady went away, carried her off and placed her in a convent sixty miles [96.5 km] off that no one may see her.[70]

Henry was beside himself with fury – probably more than anything at almost getting caught in flagrante delicto – and immediately threw Elizabeth and her husband out of the palace precincts. He suspected there were some around him who had been spying on him on Katherine's behalf and 'the king would have liked to turn all of them out, only that it has appeared to him too great a scandal'.

It was Henry and Katherine's first major marital row, with her reputedly weeping and ranting at her husband.[71]

Caroz declared that 'almost all the court knew that the queen had been vexed with the king and the king with her and thus this storm went on between them'. She also frequently demonstrated her own fiery Iberian brand of ill-will towards Henry's favourite William Compton.

Fernández, the queen's confessor, steadfastly denied anything had happened and the ambassador branded him 'stubborn' and 'deranged'. Moreover, 'as the English ladies of this household, as well as the Spanish who are near the queen, are rather simple, I fear lest the queen should behave ill in this ado'.[72]

The sound and fury of that 'ado' may explain Henry's half-hearted, if not somewhat callous, letter to Ferdinand after his wife's miscarriage – written the same day as Katherine revealed to him her sad news. The king explained that he had not 'written of late because nothing has happened worth telling'. He and his queen 'are perfectly happy and his kingdom enjoys undisturbed tranquillity'. Henry wished 'like a good son' for more news from his 'good father' in Spain. It was composed sulkily, out of duty, almost as a pro forma communication written by a guilty son to a stern father-in-law.

Katherine's loss of her daughter came hard on the heels of a new treaty of alliance and friendship with France,[73] which some saw as a double blow to Spain's cause at the court of Henry VIII.

Caroz believed that the king's ministers were in the pay of France and he begged Henry to tell him 'which of them are the most trustworthy, because suspicions are rife in all quarters'. The king pondered for a moment and then replied: 'Do not speak with anyone except with the Bishop of Winchester [Richard Fox, Lord Privy Seal] about French affairs.'

The Spaniard asked the king: 'Do you confide in him?' and Henry replied, 'Yes, at my risk. Here in England they think he is a fox and such is his name.'

Caroz claimed that when the English learnt 'how arrogantly the French had behaved . . . and how they threatened and boasted on account of the treaty they had concluded with England, they were offended'. But Henry's ministers believed they had no choice but to sign the peace treaty with France 'because the king being young and not having a son, it would have been dangerous to engage in a war with France'. However, court gossip suggested that the king was against signing the treaty, but that

> some of his most intimate councillors insisted so much . . . that he at last gave way. The Duke of Buckingham and many others are mortal enemies of the French. It is due to their influence that the treaty was not concerted in a more offensive manner.

Caroz quickly sought a parallel alliance with Spain, asking Henry: 'Sire, why do we not conclude a closer union . . . ?' The king said he wished for nothing better and ordered 'three or four' councillors to be delegated to negotiate a new treaty.[74]

The envoy shrewdly observed that Henry 'does not like to occupy himself much with business'. It was always difficult to capture and hold his attention in dealing with important state papers, unless they concerned an issue that interested him. The king's preferred time for processing documents was during Mass, before the consecration of the

Host, and just before bed. Most were read out to him and decisions transacted by word of mouth. 'The king,' complained his counsellors, 'is young and does not care to occupy himself with anything but the pleasures of his age. All other affairs he neglects.'[75]

The ambassador enlarged on this theme in a second dispatch to Spain, written immediately afterwards:

> The king amuses himself almost every day of the week with running the ring, and with jousts and tournaments on foot, in which one single person fights with an appointed adversary.
>
> Two days in the week are consecrated to this kind of tournament, which is to continue till the Feast of St John. The combatants are clad in breastplates, and wear a particular kind of helmet. They use lances of fourteen hands'-breadth[s] long, with blunt iron points.
>
> They throw these lances at one another [sic] and fight afterwards with two-handed swords, each of the combatants dealing twelve strokes.
>
> They are separated from one another by a barrier which reaches up to the girdle, in order to prevent them from seizing one another and wrestling.

He added:

> There are many young men who excel in this kind of warfare, but the most conspicuous amongst them all, the most assiduous, and the most interested in the combats is the king himself, who never omits being present at them.[76]

There were other entertainments. May Day was a red-letter occasion in the court calendar. On 1 May 1510, Henry, 'being young and willing not to be idle, rose in the morning very early to fetch May or green boughs'. He had dressed himself 'all fresh and richly apparelled' and clothed his Privy Chamber officials in white satin and his guard in white sarsenet (a lightweight silk) especially for the occasion.

> And so went every man with his bow and arrow, shooting [in] the wood and so repaired again to the court, every man with a bough [twig] in his cap.

At [Henry's] returning, many hearing of his going 'a-Maying' were desirous to see him shoot, for at that time his grace shot as strong and as great a length as any of his guard.

Along came an archer boasting of his prowess and shot an arrow – 'a very good shot and well towards his mark, whereof not only his grace but all other persons greatly marvelled'.[77]

Henry had won back his happiness and marital bliss. Katherine swiftly became pregnant again and their progress along the Thames Valley that summer, beginning at Windsor, was unmarred by strife within the royal household.

The king exercised daily 'in shooting, singing, dancing [and] wrestling'. He also satisfied his love of music – playing the recorder, flute and virginals, and in writing songs and ballads. Being a pious man, he also composed two 'goodly Masses, every one of them in five parts, which were sung oftentimes in his chapel and afterwards in diverse other places'. The household stayed at the manor of Woking where there were more jousts and tournaments before they returned to Greenwich in October.

> The king, not minded to see young gentlemen inexpert in martial feats, caused a place to be prepared within the park of Greenwich for the queen and [her] ladies to stand and see the fight with battle-axes that should be done there.
>
> And the king himself armed fought with one Gyot, a gentleman of [Germany], a tall man and a good man [with] arms.
>
> [Afterwards] Gyot fought with Sir Edward Howard, which Gyot was by him stricken to the ground.

The next day, the royal party moved on to the Tower and fearing there had been bad blood between the combatants of the previous day, Henry donated two hundred marks (£123) for a cheerful banquet for them at the Fishmongers' Hall in London's Thames Street.[78]

While all this merriment was going on, the question remained of the fate of Henry VII's disgraced councillors, Edmund Dudley and Sir Richard Empson, imprisoned at the end of April the year before. Dudley was unaware of Parliament's failure to pass the bill of attainder against him in January and made an unsuccessful attempt to escape from the Tower.

Dudley was accused of attempting to seize Henry and his council by force and of calling on knights, gentlemen and other friends to come to London 'in warlike guise'. In his will, he complained of standing 'attainted of high treason by an untrue verdict lately passed against me in the Guildhall' on 18 July 1509.[79] In a petition to his late ministerial colleague Bishop Fox, he described himself as 'the most wretched and sorrowful creature, being a dead man by the king's laws' and appended a veritable litany of his extortion during the later years of Henry VII's reign. For example, there was the case of Robert Hawkins, a London haberdasher, who paid one hundred marks (£67) in January 1505 for a pardon for the death of a man 'upon [the] surmise of a lewd fellow'. Then there was Sir Henry Vernon, 'who was sore dealt with' – being fined £100 and £800 in recognisances for involvement in his son's abduction of a widow, Margaret Kebell, and his marriage to her against her will in July 1507.[80]

Dudley was beheaded on Tower Hill on 17 August 1510 and buried in the Church of the Blackfriars. His wealth at his death was estimated at £333 in cash and goods worth £5,000.[81] In November 1511 his widow Elizabeth married Arthur Plantagenet, the bastard son of Edward IV, who was created Viscount Lisle in 1523.

Empson was taken from the Tower to Northampton Castle[82] and, a lawyer to the last, he defended himself before a special court on 1 October 1509, accused of treason. Although the charge was probably false, he should have realised he was wasting his breath. He was beheaded at Tower Hill with Dudley and left only lands worth £200–£300 and goods worth £100.

Henry VIII had promised his subjects instant justice. Two scapegoats had been slaughtered to appease public opinion. It was time to redress their legal wrongs. In July 1509, commissions of *oyer et terminer*[83] were set up to inquire into the injustices perpetrated by Empson and Dudley. During the first year of the new reign, at least forty-five of these councillors' recognisances were cancelled and a further one hundred and thirty nullified over the following five years. Fifty-one of them specifically stated that the recognisances had been 'unjustly extorted'.[84]

Beyond the final bloody resolution of these domestic issues and Henry's constant jousting and revelry, there were grimmer signs that the king was preparing for war to further his burgeoning appetite for military glory. In October 1509, he authorised a warrant to pay £1,000 for metal to be used for 'making certain of our artillery and ordnance'[85] and that December, Venetian merchants in London reported ruefully that the price of Cornish tin had rocketed because Henry had bought 'a great quantity to make one hundred pieces of artillery'. Furthermore, the king 'wished to launch and arm four ships which he has been building in [South]ampton'.[86]

Early in the New Year, 1510, Thomas Spinelly, Henry's agent in the Low Countries, signed a covenant with the famous Flemish gunmaker Hans Poppenruyter of Malines to deliver forty-eight canon to fire lead or iron shot weighing between thirty-five and forty pounds (16–18 kg).[87] These were delivered between December that year and June 1512, each one marked with a name redolent of patriotism or heraldry: 'Rose', 'Portcullis', 'York', 'Elephant', 'Dragon', Lizard', 'Scorpion' or the more descriptive 'Smite'.[88]

Margaret, Duchess of Savoy and Regent of the Netherlands, pledged that the artillery would be made 'as cheap for the King of England as for the Prince of Castile' and had helpfully seized a consignment of artillery already completed for King James IV of Scotland. Spinelly asked that 8,000 or 10,000 tons of tin should be sent to him to make the gun metal, 'as the tin of England is better and cheaper than foreign tin'.[89]

During the following May, Henry made the first of several part-payments, totalling £400, to the London bowyers for their manufacture of 10,000 longbows and the following month paid £15 for Spanish gunpowder and saltpetre, the latter an ingredient in making that explosive. In November, the fletcher Walter Hyndy was paid £67 for arrowheads and bowstrings and £13 for checking 15,000 sheaves of arrows at the Tower.

Katherine's time was now approaching and at one-thirty on the morning of New Year's Day 1511, she gave birth to a healthy boy at Richmond.[90] Celebratory bonfires burnt brightly that night in the London streets, free wine was distributed to toast the prince's health and on the Tower's ramparts, cannon boomed out deafening salutes, the gunners enthusiastically firing a total of 207 pounds (94 kg) of gunpowder.[91]

Four days later, the child was christened in the Friar Observants' church adjoining the palace. Those attending – including the papal, French, Spanish and Venetian ambassadors – walked along a path from the palace's hall, twenty-four feet (7.32 m) wide, which had been strewn with rushes (it must have been wet weather) after being newly gravelled. Bishop Fox acted as deputy for one of the child's godfathers, King Louis XII of France (the other was Archbishop Warham), and the Countess of Surrey represented the godmother, Margaret, Duchess of Savoy. Louis was generous in his gifts to the infant: a salt weighing fifty-one ounces (1.45 kg) and a cup of just over forty-eight ounces (1.37 kg), both of fine gold, together with a chain valued at £30 given to the Lady Mistress of the Nursery and £10 in cash to the queen's nurse.[92]

The child was baptised Henry as he was dipped three times in the same silver font,[93] brought from Canterbury, as his father had been almost two decades before.

The king was beside himself with joy at the arrival of a son and heir. On 11 January he went on a pilgrimage to the Shrine of Our Lady of Walsingham in Norfolk and after offering up his profound thanks to God, made the remarkably modest offering of £1 13s 4d.

In contrast, a celebratory joust was organised at Westminster on 12/13 February which cost more than £4,000 (Plate 13). It was based on an obscure allegory, a challenge by a queen called 'Noble Renown', the ruler of a land called 'Noble Heart', who had heard of Prince Henry's birth, 'which [was] the most joy and comfort that might be to her and to the most renowned realm of England'. This fictitious queen, well aware of the value, virtues and noble expertise of Henry VIII, had sent four of her stalwart knights, 'Loyal Heart', 'Valiant Desire', 'Good Valour' and 'Joyous Learner', to England to demonstrate their skill at fighting. In reality, of course, these stranger knights were Henry himself, Sir Thomas Knyvet, Sir William Courtenay and Edward Neville respectively.[94]

Katherine and her ladies watched from a tiled gallery or grandstand as, on the opening day, an astonishing pageant on wheels, drawn by a mechanical golden lion and silver antelope, unfolded before their eyes. A forest, with 'trees and artificial boughs of hawthorn, oak, maples, hazel, birches [and] fern with beasts and birds' lay before them, complete with two foresters dressed in green satin, each carrying a bow and a hunting horn. A castle, made of gold paper, was amid this forest, containing a 'fair maiden' who occupied herself making a garland of silk roses to present to Queen Katherine.[95] Within the forest rode the king and his fellow challengers.

Henry excelled in the subsequent first day's jousting. He was clad in silver armour and rode a dark grey horse with gold stirrups, and trappings inscribed with the letter 'K' for 'Katherine' and the word 'Loyal' in golden letters. The king ran six courses, breaking four lances

> as well and as valiantly as any man of arms might break them and such as were broken on him, he received them as though he felt no dint of any stroke.
>
> There was many a fearful and timorous of heart for him, considering his excellency and his tenderness of age . . .
>
> After they had seen the courses run and his manful charging . . . he rejoiced the people's hearts . . . Then such as were in most fear, saw by his martial feats that by the aid of God, he was in no danger.

Henry then ran more courses and broke many lances and 'every man marvelled of his wonderful feats for none there was challenger, or defender, might attain to half the prowess he accomplished that day'.[96]

At the end of that day's jousting, the king could not resist a display of bravado. He decided to demonstrate his peerless horsemanship.

> No man could do better, nor sit more close nor faster, nor yet kept his stirrups more surely, for notwithstanding that the horse was very courageous and excellent in leaping, turning and exceeding flinging he moved no more upon him than he had held a soft and plain trot.

Henry rode up in front of the queen and 'leapt and coursed the horse up and down in wonderful manner'. Dramatically, he turned the horse and caused its back hooves to kick sharply against the wooden dividing wall of the tiltyard – the rap 'resound[ing] about the place as it had been

[a] shot of [a] gun'. The king then moved back in front of the queen's stand and gallantly made 'a lowly [bow]'. Soon afterwards, he was seen in Katherine's tent, 'kissing and hugging her in a most loving manner'.[97]

Despite all this praise for his prowess, Henry did not win the prize for the first day's contest – that prize went to Thomas Knyvet. The king was determined to do better on the second and last day.

This was opened by a fanciful entrance by Charles Brandon, the leader of the defenders. He rode into the lists enclosed in a tower, preceded by a jailer holding a huge key in his hand. His entrance was made in complete silence 'without [a] drum or noise of minstrelry'. After the tower was pushed in front of the queen, the jailer unlocked the gate and Brandon rode out, dressed as a 'recluse or religious person' wearing a pilgrim's hat and carrying a forked or notched pilgrim's staff that bore a letter for Katherine. This was a chivalrous request for permission to proceed with the tilt, which naturally the queen gave. Amongst his fellow contestants was Sir Thomas Boleyn, dressed as a pilgrim of St James of Compostella over his armour.

The joust that followed was won by Henry who ran twenty-eight courses, broke twelve lances and scored nine hits on the bodies of his opponents and a further one on the helmet of another.[98]

That evening the foreign ambassadors were entertained in the White Hall within the Palace of Westminster. At the conclusion, Henry allowed the envoys to take some of the eight hundred and eighty-seven 'H' and 'K' letters of gold sewn into his jacket, hose and bonnet as souvenirs of the evening. However

[the] common people, perceiving, ran to the king and stripped him to his hose and doublet and all his companions likewise. Sir Thomas Knyvet stood on a stage [but] for all his defence, he lost his apparel. The ladies likewise were spoiled.

The king's guard came suddenly and put the people back or else as it was supposed more inconvenience had ensued.

So the king with the queen and the ladies returned to his chamber where they had a great banquet and all these hurts were turned to laughing and game . . .

Richard Gibson, Sergeant of the Tents, who kept the accounts for the occasion, managed to recover some of the gold letters after 'long labour'. Some of those he missed were later sold by a poor shearman (woollen cloth-cutter) of London to a goldsmith for £3 14s 8d.[99]

There were some of more mature years who worried about the dangers of Henry's obsession with jousting. Hall reported that

> ... the ancient fathers much doubted [its wisdom], considering the tender youth of the king and diverse chances of horses and armour. It was openly spoken that steel was not so strong but it might be broken, nor no horse could be so sure of foot but he may fall. Yet, for all these doubts, the lusty prince continued in his challenges.[100]

Meanwhile, a sizeable household had been appointed for the baby prince. He had his own chaplains, yeomen and Grooms of his Chamber, a Gentleman of his Counting House – even his own Clerk of the Works, Walter Foster. More practically, Elizabeth Pointes was made his nurse.

They enjoyed very short-term appointments.

On 22 February 1511, after only fifty-three days of life, Prince Henry died, probably from what today we would diagnose as meningitis.

The king reimbursed Wolsey £35 13s 4d for his expenses 'about the interment and burial of my lord prince' at Westminster, and Sir Andrew Windsor was paid £759 6s ½d for the lavish funeral. In April, it was decided not to show Louis XII's letter of condolence to Henry or Katherine 'or say a word about it at present, as it would revive the king's grief'.[101]

He had taken to playing tennis and dice to distract his mind from sorrow, although

> to comfort the queen, he [dismissed] the matter and made no great mourning outwardly. The queen, like a natural woman, made much lamentation, [but] by the king's good persuasion and behaviour, her sorrow was mitigated, but not shortly.[102]

By that time, Henry's mind had moved on. His head was filled with the excitement of preparing for war.

7

THE PURSUIT OF
MILITARY GLORY

————•·•·•————

'As God gave Saul the power to slay 1,000 and David the strength to kill 10,000 enemies, so He has made me strong.'

Henry VIII to Pope Leo X in Rome, October 1513.[1]

It was time to stop pretending. For Henry VIII, the thrill and spectacle of the joust were simply a magnificent rehearsal for what he craved so much: the glory secured by military conquest and his own audacious and brave feats on the battlefield. Tournaments and jousts taught young men the benefits of élan and self-control plus the importance of the rituals of chivalry. Hunting trained them in the complexities of tactics, whilst testing their mettle in the chase. All were intended as knightly preparation for the chaos and slaughter of war.[2] The chronicler Polydore Vergil astutely observed that the king was 'not unmindful that it was his duty to seek fame by military skill'.[3]

In Henry's mind's eye was always the shining example set by one of his forebears and childhood heroes – another king called Henry who, against the odds, had decimated the French army at Agincourt almost exactly a century before.[4] It was predictable that the hopes and dreams of the dashing young monarch (Plate 10) would dwell on the recovery of his inheritance, that other kingdom across the English Channel, lost by the kings of England during the Hundred Years' War. The king was determined that both his dynasty and his destiny required an over-

155

whelming victory against the traditional enemy of France. In this, he was encouraged by his ambitious almoner, Thomas Wolsey.

There were frustrating problems to overcome before Henry could achieve this grand objective.

We have seen how many of his inherited councillors were pro-French, persuading and cajoling an unwilling Henry VIII to agree to a new treaty of alliance with Louis XII of France. Other ministers opposed any risky (and expensive) conflict against the battle-hardened French, believing that England should remain detached from distant, unimportant squabbles between the nations of mainland Europe.[5] Most vocal amongst them was the fiscally prudent Lord Treasurer Thomas Howard, Earl of Surrey, who discovered, to his immense chagrin, that his second son Edward had 'marvellously' angered and incited Henry over the Scots, France's long-time ally, so 'that his grace spends much money and is more disposed to war than peace'.[6] Surrey became increasingly anxious over the perils of England fighting a war simultaneously on two fronts – to the north with Scotland, and to the south and east with the French. He sought to dissuade the king from launching an invasion across the English Channel, but his arguments were dismissed 'in such manner and countenance ... [by Henry] that on the morrow he departed home'.[7] Surrey retired to his extensive estates in Norfolk and Suffolk in a deep sulk, his feelings red-raw at the realisation that he had been politically outmanoeuvred by the ubiquitous Wolsey, now increasingly enjoying the king's uninterrupted attention in the councils of state.

Henry VII may have left a bulging treasury to fund his son's insatiable appetite for martial adventure, but any military strategist worth his salt knows full well that intention is one thing, but possessing the capability to execute it is quite another. It takes a long time to build up sufficient military strength to embark on an expedition to hostile shores with any prospect of success.

It had been almost two decades since English troops last fought on the mainland of Europe, during Henry VII's brief campaign in northern France. His son possessed no standing army of trained or experienced soldiers, nor yet the full panoply of martial equipment with which to arm them. In November 1509 the king had published a royal proclamation warning those able to bear arms to be ready to fight[8] and had begun to buy up longbows and field artillery from suppliers at home and overseas. Henry needed to augment his forces to fulfil his bellicose bluster – particularly the English navy, which he wanted deployed as a floating bulwark to defend his realm and to aggressively control the narrow seas dividing it from mainland Europe.

A warlike Henry was therefore forced to wait impatiently to launch his chosen career as a European warrior-king. His limited resources then available dictated that it had to begin in a very modest manner.

Around 1,000 archers and 500 other troops under the veteran Sir Edward Poynings left the Kent port of Sandwich in June 1511 en route to the Low Countries. Their mission was to provide military assistance to the Emperor Maximilian in bringing to heel the errant Charles Egmont, Duke of Gueldres, a client of Louis XII who was subsidising his defiance of the Hapsburg Holy Roman Empire. The king's diplomatic objective was to wean the erratic emperor away from unwanted French influence and push him towards an alliance with her European rivals, such as England.[9]

A month earlier, Thomas, Lord Darcy, had been sent to Cadiz in Spain with another 1,000 men to form a small contingent in Ferdinand's campaign against the Moors in North Africa. The king impulsively wanted to go himself but his plan was vetoed by his cautious ministers, who were worried about the safety of the English throne given his lack of a son and heir. Darcy, appointed admiral and captain general of the expedition, was ordered to seek a subordinate command in the Spanish forces 'as the manner of war and ordering of the same in England is not like that against the Moors'.[10] An apprehensive French ambassador in London was speedily assured by silver-tongued officials that the English troops were to fight 'infidels only – for this king is in peace with all the princes of Christendom'.[11]

Archbishop Warham, Lord Chancellor since 1504, told Darcy before his departure 'on such a distant and dangerous journey' that the more painful his trials and tribulations would be, the more merit would accrue to his name.[12] Sadly, Darcy was to suffer all the pain but receive very little merit.

His expedition, largely funded out of his own pocket, swiftly descended into farce. When he and his troops arrived in Cadiz, they discovered that Ferdinand had already scrapped plans to fight the Moors in present-day Morocco because he feared an imminent French invasion of his own lands from the north. While they awaited more information from the Spanish king, some of the English soldiers went ashore and

> fell to drinking of hot wines and were scarce masters of themselves.
> Some ran to the stews [brothels], some broke hedges and spoiled orchards and vineyards and [ate] oranges before they were ripe and did many other outrageous deeds.

Darcy had to send his provost marshal ashore to restore order amongst the 'hot and wilful' yeoman archers, round them up and harry them back to their ships. The ill-discipline did not end there. Days later, an English soldier tried to buy a loaf of bread from a young girl – but she refused his proffered money. He followed her home and she screamed for help, fearing rape.

> The townsmen of Cadiz suddenly rang their common bell and all the town went into harness [armed themselves] and the few Englishmen that were on land went to their bows.
> The Spanish cast darts [threw spears] and sore annoyed and hurt the Englishmen and they likewise hurt and slew [many] Spaniards.

Darcy and his captains managed to halt the affray but not before an Englishman and 'diverse Spaniards' had been killed. Ferdinand's representatives and the townspeople had suffered enough of these disorderly allies with their unintelligible language and unchecked vandalism. They told Darcy: 'Sir, we pray you, since you know the king's pleasure ... that you, and all your people, will go with your ships away for we perceive you owe us some displeasure.' So Darcy returned to England, chastened and inglorious, after the shambles of a futile expedition that cost him dearly in reputation and in his own hard cash.[13]

Both this and Poynings' more successful foray into the Low Countries (where he captured several towns and castles) were mere tactical side-shows in the grand strategy now evolving in Europe against Louis XII.

The French king had summoned a breakaway General Council of the Catholic Church to meet in Pisa in May 1511, to discuss the removal of his former ally, Pope Julius II, now working actively against France. Julius himself sought to lure England into a multinational alliance to drive the French out of northern Italy, even offering Henry a curiously assorted cargo of bribes in August 1511 – a rose wrought in solid 24-carat gold, together with one hundred hard Parmesan cheeses and some barrels of wine – to win him over.[14]

Within two months, a Holy League against France was formed comprising the Papal States, Spain, Venice and (belatedly) the Holy Roman Empire. England did not join its ranks for a month or so – only because messengers were tardy in bringing authorisation to Henry's ambassador in Rome, Christopher Bainbridge, the rampantly Francophobe Archbishop of York, recently made a cardinal.

In London, Henry was incensed by Louis' plans to depose the Pope. He called together his Council which agreed unanimously on war with France. The king waxed angrily against 'the great sin of the King of France' in calling the divisive General Council at Pisa, which had 'lacerated the seamless garment of Christ' – Mother Church herself – and would 'wantonly destroy' its unity. He attacked those who were guilty of this 'most pernicious schism' as 'cruel, impious, criminal and unspeakable'.[15]

As far as Henry was concerned, he could now fight a holy war. More than twenty years later, a recklessly foolhardy Bishop of Durham, Cuthbert Tunstall, dared to remind the king how he had fought against Louis XII in defence of the papacy because he had 'assisted and nourished a schism'. Henry growled a tart riposte: 'We were but young and having little experience in the feats of the world.'[16]

The Treaty of Westminster of 17 November 1511 provided the diplomatic framework for mutual military assistance between two of the Holy League's allies, Ferdinand's Spain and Henry VIII's England. An Anglo–Spanish army would attack Aquitaine, a region of south-west

France bordering the Atlantic Ocean and the Pyrenees, and conquer it for Henry in his virtuous defence of Holy Church. There was another strategic objective. As well as regaining one of England's long-lost provinces in France, the invasion was intended as a diversionary stratagem – to lure French troops out of the Northern Italian theatre to defend their homeland, thus easing the military pressure on the papal and Venetian troops.

Battlefield glory beckoned irresistibly and preparations to ready the invasion forces stepped up in tempo during the winter of 1511 and well into the New Year.[17] By the spring of 1512, the English were as ready to fight as they would ever be and Thomas Wall, Lancaster Herald, arrived at Louis XII's court at the end of April to formally deliver Henry's declaration of war against France.

The king, furious to be again denied the chance of fighting himself, had to be content with merely inspecting his 12,000 troops under Thomas Grey, Second Marquis of Dorset, before their departure from Southampton in early June. The soldiers' enthusiasm for war had been 'marvellously encouraged' by the timely issue of a papal indulgence that promised every soldier a markedly reduced spell in Purgatory if he died gloriously in battle.[18] The English warships also pointedly bore the arms of Julius II, painted by John Brown, the king's painter. Henry told Cardinal Bainbridge in Rome that he believed that

> never had a finer army been seen, or one better disposed to die courageously in defence of the Church and the Pope, as the indulgence sent by him has roused them against his foes, whom they consider Turks, heretics and infidels.

The king considered that

> under God's favour our army will behave itself right gallantly and confound the malice and tyranny of those who, by fair means or foul, oppress the Church of God and favour the great schism, which will take effect unless Catholic princes resist it.

Henry solemnly pledged 'his whole power to attack the foes of the Church' so that 'they cannot escape defeat'.[19]

His cocksure optimism was echoed by the Venetian Lorenzo Pasqualigo in letters to his brothers which described the English soldiers as 'very fine men, well supplied with everything. In the Channel, there are thirty large ships armed by Englishmen which do not allow so much as a French fishing boat to put to sea without taking it.' In the war-fevered streets of jingoistic and xenophobic London, 'foreigners remain ... in great fear, but if they do give utterance, it is to abuse France, perhaps unwillingly, as if they were to do otherwise, their heads would be well broken'.[20]

As it transpired, these high hopes proved completely baseless.

Everything began to go wrong as soon as the fleet quit the shores of England. Shortly after the western cliffs of the Isle of Wight were left astern, the ships were dispersed, primarily because 'of the ungodly manners of the seamen, [in] robbing the king's victuals when the soldiers were seasick'.[21]

The force arrived on the north-west coast of Spain on 7 June and two days later took to the field, near Reinteria, within three miles (4.88 km) of Navarre. Dorset immediately fell out with the Spanish over the campaign's first objectives. He wanted to capture the French town of Bayonne and make it his forward base, from which he could advance further into Aquitaine. His allies rejected this plan and it soon became readily apparent that Ferdinand had been underhand in suggesting his son-in-law should send troops to Spain. His real purpose was to employ the English forces as a shield, a mere diversion, to cover his seizure of the independent kingdom of Navarre.[22]

There were also serious logistical problems, with Spanish promises of transport and ordnance largely unkept. 'The victuals have not been as they expected; the rain continual, to the annoyance of the soldiers, who lie nightly under the bushes,' complained the English envoy Dr William Knight to Wolsey back in England.[23]

Thomas, Lord Howard, one of the captains of the army, also bewailed the shortage of horses and provisions. He had been

in considerable peril these six days, being lodged in a field a mile [1.61 km] from Fuentarrabia,[24] an arrowshot from a town called Our Lady of

Vryne, where they are dying of sickness. Five Spaniards were buried this night [but there] are no English dead except Lord Brooke's servant.

My own company are healthy as yet. If the sickness comes, it will be hard to keep order.

I wish the king had never trusted [Ferdinand] more than they do, then they would never have been sent to this ungracious country where the people love a ducat better than all their kin.[25]

Shortage of victuals forced some to try unfamiliar sustenance:

The Englishmen ate of the garlic with all meats and drank hot wines in the hot weather and did eat all the hot fruits that they could get which caused their blood to boil in their bellies that there fell sick 3,000 of the flux[26] and thereof died 1,800 men.[27]

There were also clashes with the inhabitants of the town of Sancta Maria.

It so fortuned that a Spaniard gave evil language to [an] Englishman, who gave him such a buffet [blow] on the face, the town rose and set upon the Englishman ... who was slain.

The Almains [German mercenaries] that lay at the town's end [raised] the alarm, which hearing, the camp cried harness [to arms] every man ...

The soldiers in a rage ran to the town in such manner that the captains could not stay them and [they] slew and robbed the people without mercy.

Seven English soldiers were executed for looting and pillage. Unfortunately, no lessons were learnt from this incident and any last vestige of discipline within the army vanished like the wind blowing away cannon smoke. The English went on to burn the port of St-Jean-de-Luz, near the French border, and 'robbed and killed the inhabitants and so spoiled diverse other villages'.[28]

John Stile, English ambassador to Spain, reported in coded dispatches to Henry the growing discontent amongst the rude soldiery. They grumbled that because of the lack of food, 'they may not live with[in] your wages of sixpence a day' and wanted a two-pence increase, as 'their

THE PURSUIT OF MILITARY GLORY

clothing is wasted and worn and their money spent'. The attractions of Spain had palled: they now unilaterally planned to go back to England by Michaelmas (11 October) 'for no man will abide here'.[29] Knight confirmed that some had mutinied:

> The army is idle – a large band has refused to serve [any] longer under eight pence a day.
> The mutiny was pacified but one man suffered death . . .
> All this comes from inaction. Martial exercises are not kept up. The army is unlearned and has not seen the feats of war.
> Many are slain; others have died; some have deserted. They neglect their instructions.

The collapse in morale had infected even the army's war council – 'many of our council may suffer no counsel' was Knight's austere and punning complaint.[30]

Worse was to follow. On 28 August 1512, the army's leaders (without Dorset, as he was very ill) decided the troops should return home, although they were devoid of any battlefield victories, empty-handed of spoil or ransom and, indeed, had failed to achieve anything at all. Knight and one of the under-marshals, William Kingston, were deputed to travel on ahead with the unenviable task of 'excusing' their desertion to their king and country.

Some, such as Sir William Sandys, opposed this choice of envoys, claiming that Wolsey 'was the cause of all this mischief; that Knight was in his favour and if he went to England he would so represent matters to the king so as to cause their further abiding there'. Regardless, Knight and Kingston embarked at San Sebastian, but after suffering six days of violent storms out on the Atlantic were forced back into the Spanish port.

The army council reconvened at nearby Errenteria, where Knight pleaded with them not to bring the army home.

> Whereupon, like a noble man, my Lord Howard said . . . he would endure this winter war and gladly die for the honour of his master, the realm and himself, than contrary to the king's commandment, with rebuke and shame, return into England.

[But] one stole out of the chamber and told Lord Brooke's company that if the commonalty did not resist, they would all have to go into [France].

Great uproar ensued. Knight's life was threatened and 'things', he reported to Wolsey, 'are out of order' – meaning totally out of control.

Our enemies were men of long continuance in war, full of policy and privy to all our deeds [but] we [were] clean contrary [to this].

Discipline was so badly kept we might at any time have been crushed.

I heard Sir Henry Willoughby say that of 8,000 bows, not two hundred were sufficient.

It is no use blaming anybody as it would end in mutual recrimination.

Knight warned Wolsey: 'Be cautious. The great men of England say that you are the author of the war and its ill-success must be attributed to you.'[31]

It comes as no surprise that Henry was incandescent at his army's mass desertion. He sent their captains an urgent and 'stringent command to put yourselves under the orders of Ferdinand' and begged his father-in-law to stop his troops leaving the Spanish dominions 'at all hazards and to cut every man's throat who refused instant obedience'.[32]

It was too late. Having baked copious supplies of biscuit to sustain them on the voyage home, the English army struck camp and embarked, lock, stock and barrel, for England that November, its honour besmirched, its discipline despoiled. No glory, then, for Henry on this campaign. No triumphant recovery of the province of Aquitaine. No deeds of derring-do on the battlefield. Never before or since in history has an English army deserted en masse.

Even the devious Ferdinand was more generous than he could have been, given the circumstances. His letter to his ambassadors in London smacks of an uncomfortably critical end-of-term school report on his young son-in-law's military accomplishments, or rather his lack of them. The courtesy of his comments thinly masked a few sharp barbs that must have made Henry grind his teeth in anger and frustration.

The envoys were instructed to inform the king of England that his commander-in-chief (Dorset) was 'doubtless a very distinguished nobleman, but that it is to his behaviour from the first day he landed in Spain that is owed the failure of the splendid enterprise they had planned'. Henry should be aware that, if Dorset had not always opposed Ferdinand's plans, 'and if the two armies had entered Guyenne [in south-west France][33] without delay by way of Pamplona, the whole, or at least one-half of the duchy, would already be conquered'.

Stoically, the Spanish king continued:

The English are strong, stout-hearted, stand firm in battle and never think of taking flight.

They are very excellent men and only want experience. England has had no wars – the English do not know how to behave in a campaign. Unaccustomed as they are to warfare, they show a marked dislike to perform such labours as are inevitably entailed on soldiers.

They are inclined to self-indulgence and to idleness.

But their greatest fault is that in a combined action, they will never assist the [allied] troops, or act in concert with a commander of another nation.

It would be as well to practice [*sic*] a portion of the men in the evolutions of regular warfare.

After they had undergone military drill and acquired some useful combat experience, Ferdinand confidently predicted that 'the English troops would excel those of any other nation'. However, he considered Henry's army needed more soldiers armed with long pikes 'to give it greater efficiency in battle than it at present possesses'. Ferdinand added another helpful suggestion for improvement. Why not mix English archers with German pikemen? German 'infantry has deservedly acquired a high reputation' and would stiffen Henry's battalions. The Spanish king concluded his sobering assessment with a final, damning indictment on Albion's military prowess: thank you very much, but he needed no more English troops to help him against the French.[34]

Others were less charitable regarding Henry's militarily impotent adventure. Margaret of Savoy, the Regent of the Netherlands and daughter of the Emperor Maximilian, made Sir Edward Poynings squirm when she commented sarcastically: 'You see, Englishmen have so long abstained from war they lack experience from disuse. If the report be true, they are almost weary of it already.'[35]

Henry was only too painfully aware that his martial reputation and that of his force of arms had become something of a joke within the courts of Europe.

Like many rulers down the centuries, he sought to put a brave face on his misfortune by issuing a carefully sanitised version of the disaster for use overseas by his ambassadors. He instructed them to say that Ferdinand, hearing of the constant rain in those parts

> to the intolerable pains of the soldiers of our army, which in that barren country have persevered, lying in the fields continuously . . . without any breach or dissolution [of the military pact] had agreed to their return.[36]

His retribution inevitably followed. In London, the army's officers were summoned before Henry, his Council and the Spanish ambassadors on Friday 19 November. As they knelt before the king, who was sitting on a bench, Archbishop Warham demanded an explanation of their disgraceful conduct in Spain.

They proffered three excuses for their humiliating failure. Firstly, they had no provisions. Secondly, the soldiers had mutinied and demanded to come home. Lastly, the fiasco was all the fault of the Marquis of Dorset – 'who had been the cause of all that had happened'. Henry sent for Dorset to provide his version of events, as he told the captains 'that he wanted to know the truth in order to punish those who deserved punishment'.

The Privy Council eventually went into secret session and emerged with the decision that the English captains 'had done wrong and had compromised their honour as well as the honour of their country'. The Spanish were asked to name a well-deserved, severe punishment but, to the relief of the miscreants, politely declined to do so.[37]

After this fiasco, Henry looked to his burgeoning navy to re-establish England's battered pride and martial reputation.

French and Scottish pirates were running amok in the North Sea, capturing and ransoming English merchant ships, including the unfortunately named collier *Mary Buttocks*, whose home port was Hartlepool.[38] During June 1511 the king had received angry complaints about the Scottish privateer Andrew Barton seizing merchantmen at the eastern end of the English Channel. Henry ordered Barton's two ships, the *Lyon* and the *Jenett of Purwyn*, to be captured 'with all haste' and the privateer arrested as a common pirate.

The ships were eventually apprehended and Barton was brutally killed, together with many crewmen. The vessels were brought to London as prizes and the Scottish prisoners repatriated. James IV of Scotland – Henry's brother-in-law – protested furiously at this 'outrage', demanding the prosecution of Barton's 'murderers' and the ships' return. Henry responded mildly that justice had merely been done to a 'crafty pirate' and thief and he flatly ignored James' peremptory requests.[39]

The French, however, remained firmly in Henry's sights as his main quarry at sea as well as on land. Sir Edward Howard was appointed vice-admiral in April 1512 and ordered to control the English Channel between the French port of Brest and the Thames Estuary. Within weeks, he had captured sixty-six enemy ships and goaded the French into mobilising their navy.

In early August Howard sailed from Portsmouth, flying his flag aboard the newly commissioned *Mary Rose*,[40] at the head of twenty-five English warships. These included the aging but recently refitted *Regent*, 1,000 tons, commanded by Sir Thomas Knyvet, Howard's brother-in-law and one of Henry's jousting cronies. Their objective was Brest, the home base of the thirty-nine-strong French fleet.

On the morning of 10 August 1512 the enemy ships were stationed in the approaches to the port, south of Berthaume Bay, and were celebrating that day's Feast of St Lawrence[41] when the English unsportingly attacked. *Regent* came alongside the French carrack[42] *Marie la Cordelière*, 700 tons, and shackled herself to it by means of grappling irons and chains. The English boarded and as the furious fighting swept across the decks, Knyvet was cut in two by a cannon ball fired at close range and his second-in-command, Sir John Carew, mortally wounded by gunfire.[43] The French ship caught fire and a frenzied French gunner, deep in the bowels of the *Cordelière*, set fire to her gunpowder magazine, choosing mass death rather than the dishonour of capture. Both ships blew up, killing most of the *Regent*'s seven-hundred-strong crew and all 1,200 enemy sailors.[44]

Henry was stricken at the loss of one of his closest friends. Wolsey, in London, informed Bishop Fox of the loss of the English warship:

> At the reverence of God, keep these tidings secret to yourself, for there is no living man knows the same here, but only the king and I ... It is expedient for a while to keep the matter secret.
>
> To see how the king takes the matter and behaves himself, you would marvel ... [at] his wise and constant manner. I have not, on my faith, seen the like.
>
> All this with heavy heart and sorrowful pen, I make an end.[45]

Sir Edward Howard swore to avenge his brother-in-law, vowing to God 'he would never look the king in the face until he had revenged the death of [this] noble and valiant knight'.[46]

On 19 March 1513 Henry appointed him Lord High Admiral of England, Ireland and Aquitaine in succession to the Earl of Oxford (who had died nine days before) and paid him £66 for his services.

Howard was anxious not only to fulfil his oath but to provide the king with a swift, much needed victory. Within eight days, he sailed for the waters around Brest, running into fifteen enemy ships on 12 April. They 'fled like cowards' towards the port, which Howard then blockaded with his fleet.

French reinforcements – six shallow-draught, oared galleys – arrived in mid-April and put in at Conquet, fifteen miles (25 km) west of Brest, protected by powerful shore batteries. Anxious for action, an impatient Henry had penned an acerbic, taunting letter, commanding Howard 'to accomplish that which appertained to his duty'.

That caustic goad was the admiral's undoing. He planned a reckless assault in the face of superior firepower on 25 April. Because he could not deploy his large warships in the shallows near the shore, Howard decided to attack that morning using fifteen rowing barges, and accordingly transferred his flag to the eighty-ton *Swallow*, leaving his fleet to maintain their blockade further out to sea.

In the teeth of furious and deadly fire from guns and crossbows, Howard came about under the bows of the French flagship, hurled grappling irons over her sides and secured one of the ropes to *Swallow*'s capstan. He clambered aboard over the forecastle accompanied by sixteen of his men and threw himself into the melee on the decks of the French galley.

Disaster followed him. Either a French sailor severed the rope holding the two ships together with a boarding axe, or it was somehow let slip.

The *Swallow* drifted away on the tide, leaving the English commander marooned and grievously outnumbered on the enemy foredeck.

As the fighting and clamour raged about him, Howard faced imminent death and the dishonour of a failed mission. He lifted his admiral's gold whistle from around his neck and calmly threw it into the sea. Then he followed his badge of rank into the water – either by jumping, or falling in the press of hand-to-hand combat. Encumbered by his armour and probably wounded, he sank quickly beneath the waves.[47]

Howard's elder brother Thomas, Lord Howard, that veteran of the sorry debacle in north-west Spain, was appointed in his place as Lord High Admiral. Seeking to placate Henry's fury at the loss of both admiral and a naval victory, he wrote to the king from the *Mary Rose*, now safely at home in Plymouth:

> As to the actual feats of all such noblemen and gentlemen as were pr[esent when] my brother, the admiral, was drowned (whom Jesu pardon), I assure your [highness so] far ... as I can ... anyway understand, they handled themselves as ... men did to obtain their master's pleasure.
>
> It was the most dangerous enterprise [I have] ever heard of and the most manly handled.[48]

Howard promised to punish the two men 'who did their part very ill the day my brother was lost ... Cooke the queen's servant in a row[ing] boat [he was captain of *Swallow*] and Freeman my brother's household servant'.

The fleet was filled with sick, wounded and despondent men, their morale shot clean away. They were deserting in shoals. The new admiral, faced with Henry's insistent demands to return to the fray, admitted to Wolsey that he had never seen 'men in greater fear than all the masters and mariners be of the [French] galleys, insomuch that in a manner they were as lief [not unwilling] go into Purgatory [rather than] the Trade' – the English name for the sea approaches to Brest.[49]

In Edinburgh, James IV made an only half-serious offer of a truce to Henry, taking the opportunity to taunt him over the loss of Sir Edward Howard. He told his brother-in-law: 'We think more loss is to you of your late admiral who deceased to his great honour and laud than the advantage which might have been of the winning of all the French galleys and the equipment.' Days later, he decided to send a fleet of ships to reinforce France's naval might.[50]

Henry had earlier tried to disrupt the 'Auld Alliance' between France and Scotland. He suggested, rather disingenuously, to his elder sister Margaret, wife of the Scottish king, that he would, after four years, hand over her legacy bequeathed by their father – but only in return for a promise that the Scots would not invade England while he was away campaigning. Margaret contemptuously dismissed this unbrotherly offer:

> We cannot believe that [is] of your mind or your command that we are so [unfriendly] dealt with in our father's legacy ... Our husband knows it is withheld for his sake and will recompense us. We lack nothing – our husband is ever the longer the better to us.

The letter was signed: 'Your loving sister Margaret.'[51]

With the exception of Poynings' small-scale expedition to the Low Countries, all Henry's military adventures had ignominiously and very publicly failed. His dreams of battlefield glory had faded like spectres at dawn; his ambitions had turned to ashes.

At least he had acquired one item of matchless international kudos. On 20 March 1512 his ally Pope Julius II had stripped Louis XII of both his sobriquet of 'Most Christian King' and also his realm of France, which were immediately conferred on Henry. He and his heirs were invested with the title of King of France, with only the small catch that this should endure 'for as long as they shall remain in faith, devotion and obedience to the Holy Roman Church and Apostolic See'.[52] Henry was delighted – 'Most Christian King of England, France and Lord of Ireland' carried a superior ring and his claim to his outstanding inheritance now had the backing of papal authority.

He became even more resolute to secure his kingdom across the sea in more than just name. Although James IV had promised Ferdinand 'to be faithful to England' he attacked Berwick in September 1512 and English forces were sent northwards to deter further aggression. Katherine of Aragon told Cardinal Bainbridge that Henry 'has said openly he does not believe the Pope and the king her father will ever desert him, but if they were to do so, he himself would not desist from war until the schismatic king was removed'.[53]

Two months later Henry suggested to the Spanish ambassador that English troops should invade northern France while Ferdinand simultaneously assailed Aquitaine from across the Spanish border. Henry would again supply assistance to his father-in-law – but this time only by paying for 5,000 German mercenaries to serve alongside the Spanish troops. Diplomatic efforts were also intensified to persuade Maximilian to launch an offensive from his dominions in the north and east, including the staged payment of handsome subsidies in gold from Henry's exchequer.[54] Finally, Julius agreed to attack the French provinces of Provence and Dauphiné.[55]

All southern England became a vast armoury, ringing with the sound of hammer upon anvil as the blacksmiths and other craftsmen worked frantically to fulfil a mountain of orders for military equipment. The price of war was prodigious: gunpowder cost up to four pence per pound (0.45 kg), shoulder-fired handguns nine shillings each and a large brass cannon £35. Twelve huge pieces of field artillery – nicknamed the 'Twelve Apostles' for the figures embossed on their barrels – were cast in Flanders. Each fired an iron ball weighing twenty pounds (9.1 kg) and consumed the same weight of gunpowder each time they were fired.

Wolsey, the king's energetic almoner and now de facto Chief Minister, was at the heart of this frenzied activity. In May, Bishop Fox, the sidelined Lord Privy Seal, wrote to him from Southampton, concerned at his 'outrageous charge and labour'. He warned Wolsey of overwork, 'else you shall have a cold stomach, little sleep, pale visage and a thin belly'.[56]

Much of the warlike stores were purchased from foreign merchants – the almoner, for example, bought 2,000 light armours from Florence at sixteen shillings apiece for the infantry, which included visored helmets.[57] In January 1513, 3,000 harnesses were ordered at the same price from the London mercer Robert Bolt, for delivery at the Tower by 30 April.[58] Wolsey also authorised payment of £6 13s 4d 'in reward to a joiner which hath made certain secret engines [of war] for the King' – probably wooden catapults or slings like the medieval trebuchets, designed to batter the walls of fortified towns with stone missiles to create breaches through which the besiegers could attack.[59]

Henry's troops would go into battle wearing white tunics, proudly emblazoned with the red cross of St George, over their armour. Arrangements were made to purchase 'at reasonable price wheat, malt or oats and other victuals' to feed them and a proclamation banned export of grain, on pain of forfeiture to the crown, as well as unlicensed provisioning. As a means of economic warfare, the importation of Gascon wine into England was also prohibited that December.[60]

The soldiers of Henry's 'army royal' were again fortified by another papal indulgence from Julius, provided they serve for at least six months, but its coverage this time was extended to all those who provided cash to pay for the expedition or prayed for its success.[61] Unfortunately the Pope died from a fever in February 1513 and Giovanni de Medici was proclaimed his successor as Leo X the following month.

During those early months of 1513, fears of a French invasion of England were whipped up by Henry's government to create an aura of national danger. It was propaganda, pure and simple. Officially inspired rumours whispered of abortive French landings at undisclosed locations. A Venetian in London reported: 'Lately a number of French ships sailed to attempt a landing in England, which would have been difficult enough, but they were overtaken by a storm and all swamped.'[62] Now a proclamation declared that the king, with 'a tender zeal to the wealth, surety and defence of this, his realm of England and of his subjects . . .', had learnt 'that his ancient enemy the French king, continuing in his perverse and malicious purpose, has prepared and put in readiness a great and strong navy to invade and enter this ... realm'. Therefore, every man aged 'between sixty and sixteen [should] be ready in harness [armour] at one hour's warning to resort to such places as shall be assigned by the King's commissioners'.[63]

By May, final preparations for the invasion were underway and the vanguard of the army had crossed to Calais. The Milanese ambassador in Rome commented that Henry was 'so eager over the enterprise that no one can put it out of his head, unless it be God Almighty'.[64]

This time there were to be no mistakes. Henry was to lead his army himself, leaving his queen at home with full powers as regent of England in his absence.

He had one piece of business to transact before happily going off to war. Edmund de la Pole, Earl of Suffolk, had been safely shut up in the Tower of London since 1506 and now Henry had heard that his fugitive brother Richard had taken up arms with Louis XII. It is difficult to believe that the king thought Suffolk could get up to any mischief within the walls of that grim fortress. But the earl still represented a Yorkist threat, however dormant or suppressed. Better to be safe than sorry, so Henry had Suffolk quietly beheaded on 4 May.[65]

It was the first but by no means the last time that he had the blood of his nobility on his hands.

The king had assembled a mighty army more than 40,000 strong to fight the French. This was split into three divisions – the vanguard, the middle ward and the rearguard, the latter commanded by Henry himself. This contingent consisted of more than 9,000 men and included 1,000 archers mustered by the Spears (the royal bodyguard), six hundred of the king's own guard, and five hundred cavalry and pikemen paid for and commanded by the Duke of Buckingham.[66] Milanese diplomatic reports talked of this 'most formidable army' which Louis XII recognised could overwhelm his dispersed forces, so the French king decided only to 'defend the towns and abandon the country' near Calais.[67]

Henry's fleet transported the first two divisions across the Channel, but before he departed Dover, the king had one last military appointment to make. He feared that James IV of Scotland would attack England from the rear while he and his army were away in France. Therefore, he made Thomas Howard, Earl of Surrey, the aging veteran of many a border skirmish, General of the Northern Marches.

He took Surrey's hand and told him: 'My lord, I trust not the Scots, therefore I pray you not be negligent.' Surrey replied: 'I shall do my duty and your grace shall find me diligent and to fulfil your will shall be my gladness.'[68] The earl marched north at the end of July, gathering troops en route.

Henry was delayed at Dover, waiting for a favourable wind to carry him and his men across to France. He wrote to the diplomat William Knight, recounting how 30,000 Englishmen were now besieging the fortified town of Thérouanne, in the Île-de-France, ten miles (16 km) south-west of St Omer, and urging him to press Ferdinand to proceed with his own invasion, 'according to the treaty lately passed betwixt us and him'.[69]

One of the king's chaplains, John Taylor, stood on the walls of Calais at seven o'clock on the evening of Thursday 30 June 1513 to watch the twenty-two-year-old king's ships arrive. It was a stirring sight with a veritable forest of ships' masts, all flying brightly coloured banners and pennons, approaching from the north. The four-hundred-strong fleet made landfall a little to the west of the English-held town, which galvanised the French garrison of nearby Boulogne into a full alert, as they feared they were under attack. Their anxiety was understandable: the fleet was so large – 'such as Neptune never saw before' – and the gun salutes from the ships and the answering salvoes from the Calais ramparts were so loud 'you would have thought the world was coming to an end'.[70]

Henry came ashore wearing a decorated harness of light German armour beneath a white tunic of cloth of gold and a hat on which was pinned a 'rich brooch' bearing the image of St George. After hearing a Mass and a *Te Deum* sung in the town's cruciform church of St Nicholas, the king walked in procession to the Staple, or Prince's, Inn where he ate his supper and retired for the night.[71]

No doubt he had been immediately briefed on the latest military situation. There had been some minor setbacks. At the siege of Thér-ouanne, the defenders' cannon fire had 'done great hurt' in the sur-rounding English camp. One of the English commanders, Sir Edmund Carew,[72] had been killed by a cannon shot and was buried in the Resur-rection Chapel of St Nicholas Church four days before. The next day, 27 June, a food convoy of one hundred wagons heading for the besiegers' camp had been ambushed and two hundred of the English escort killed. Taylor recorded in his diary that the French

> had carried off their dead, whose number could not be ascertained, [and] had stripped the bodies and so mutilated their faces that it was difficult to tell which were English or which French.[73]

It was not long before Henry's sleep was disturbed. At about eleven o'clock, the town's bells rang out a warning of an attack. Three hundred French from the nearby fishing port of Wissant (called 'Whitesands' by the English) and Boulogne had infiltrated the English lines under cover of darkness. At low tide, they waded past Fort Risbank, built on a promontory just outside the harbour of Calais,[74] intent on burning the army's supply tents. Vigilant sentries had spotted them and they were driven off by archers at the harbour, watched approvingly by Henry from his vantage point on the walls of the town.[75] After waiting all his short life, this was his first exhilarating taste of military action.

Swift revenge was exacted. On 4 July, Wissant 'was almost entirely destroyed by fire' after its inhabitants plundered an English transport ship wrecked nearby and sent its crew as prisoners to Boulogne.

Henry tarried in Calais for three weeks with about a third of his army. Some complained this delay was symptomatic of an inexperienced general; it was the height of summer and a waste of the campaigning season. Moreover, his forces were divided and thus more vulnerable to French attack.[76] Henry, however, had to meet visiting Imperial ambas-sadors and in his vanity could not resist treating them to a spectacle of his skill at arms. John Taylor, his chaplain, described enthusiastically how the king was 'practising archery in a garden with the archers of his guard. He cleft the mark in the middle and surpassed them all, as he surpasses them in stature and personal graces.'[77]

The king's ordinances governing the conduct of his army in the field were published in Calais market so that 'no manner of person should pretend ignorance of them'. They demanded absolute obedience to him and his commanders on 'pain of hanging, drawing and quartering'. The same penalty would be imposed on any soldier who 'irreverently' touched the consecrated Host in a church and those who 'enforced [raped] any woman, religious or other' would be hanged. This was a holy war, after all. Gambling was banned, as was the keeping of bordellos, and those who quarrelled or 'reproach[ed]' comrades because of their country of origin ('be he French, English, Northern, Welsh or Irish or of any other country') risked imprisonment.[78]

At last, on 21 July, Henry left Calais in the midst of 28,000 men, 3,500 of whom surrounded the king as close protection. On either side of the army were two wings of archers and soldiers armed with bills[79] and at the front and rear of the straggling column were protective screens of field artillery.[80]

That night, the army huddled in damp tents, encamped near the small town of Fréthun, well fortified by nature with an impassable marsh on their left, and their artillery on the right. Taylor recorded: 'Such heavy rains fell in the afternoon and night, that the tents could scarcely protect them.' In conscious mimicry of Henry V's actions in the small hours before Agincourt, the 'King did not put off his clothes, but rode round at three in the morning comforting the watch – saying, "Well, comrades, now that we have suffered in the beginning, fortune promises us better things, God willing."'[81] Once again, it was 'a little touch of Harry in the night'.[82]

Back home, Katherine of Aragon was worrying about her husband. She wrote to Wolsey, who was accompanying the expedition, begging him to report frequently on Henry's health: 'As he draws near the enemy, I will never be at rest till I often have letters from you.' She was confident that the king would return 'with as great a victory as every prince had'.[83]

Henry, of course, was thoroughly enjoying every minute of the campaign. On the afternoon of 25 July, he entered enemy territory near Ardres and at dawn the following morning, the camp was wakened by an alarm, falsely warning of the approach of enemy forces. The king's

German mercenaries then 'mischievously burnt' some fortified houses and 'did not respect the churches'. Henry led a detachment of his guard in clearing the town of his rioting and pillaging troops and hanged three of the Germans that night.

More serious was the loss of the cannon named 'St John the Evangelist' – one of the brand-new 'Twelve Apostles' artillery – which toppled over into a pond. One hundred pioneers were sent to dig the three-ton cannon out and set to work, stupidly without posting sentries. They were surprised by a French raiding party who killed or wounded most of them, using guns or crossbows, and seized a bombard (or siege mortar) called 'the red gun'.[84] The old English weakness of military ill-discipline and poor training had raised its ugly head again. Later the cannon was dragged out of the water by a team of Flemish mares and safely returned to the English artillery lines.

A few days later, the army reached Tournehem with its castle. The army's passage was barred by the fast-flowing River Hem and when his officers hesitated to ford it, Henry impulsively led the way, wading into the waters and scrambling up the far bank.[85]

At last on 1 August the king reached Thérouanne. His columns of troops were welcomed by a violent rainstorm that turned the fields around the town into a sea of mire, forcing the soldiers to wade 'up to their knees in mud'. Henry now took charge of the siege operations.

Ten days later the Scottish herald, Sir William Cumming of Inverallochy, Lyon King of Arms, arrived in the English camp and delivered an ultimatum from his master, James IV. The Scottish king demanded that Henry

> desist from further invasion and utter destruction of our brother and cousin [Louis XII] to whom ... we are bounden and obliged for mutual defence, the one of the other, like as you and your confederates be obliged for mutual invasions and actual war; certifying you we will take part in defence of our brother ...
>
> And we will do what thing we trust may cause you to desist from pursuit of him.[86]

The king instantly discarded the normal courtesies of chivalry and diplomacy. Angrily, he rounded upon the startled herald, shouting:

> I am the very holder of Scotland – he holds it of me by homage! And he
> to summon me, [who is] here for my right and inheritance!
>
> Tell him there shall never [be a] Scot [to] cause me to turn my face.
>
> Where he says the French king to be his ally, it would be much better
> agreed and become him, being married to the King of England's sister,
> to count the King of England his ally.
>
> Tell him if he be so hardy [as] to invade my realm or cause to enter
> one foot of my ground I shall make him as weary of his part as ever was
> man that began any such business.[87]

Then, in more measured tones, Henry declared he could not 'easily
believe that his brother of Scotland would break his solemn oath [to
Ferdinand, not to invade] but if such was his intention, he doubted not
that he would repent it'.[88]

He wrote a letter to James the next day, pointing out that the Scots
alliance with Louis XII was 'especially dishonourable' but that he was
confident, with his friends, of being able to 'resist the malice of all the
schismatics and their adherents by the General Council excommunicate'.
Henry added ominously that James should note well the fate of the King
of Navarre, who after helping Louis was 'now a king without a realm'.[89]

On 15 August a riot broke out between the English troops and the
German mercenaries in the camp – embarrassingly just as the Emperor
Maximilian arrived for a meeting with the king. The disturbance escal-
ated rapidly into furious fighting and the Germans seized some of the
heavy siege guns and trained them threateningly on the English. In
response, some archers, 'greatly fumed with the matter', loosed off a few
arrows and the Germans regrouped into their traditional defensive wall
of pikes. Senior officers managed to restore order quickly: Maximilian
was impressed by their reaction and 'was glad to see the discreet hand-
ling' of the danger by these captains.[90]

That night came fulfilment of some of Henry's boyhood dreams for
battlefield renown.

The French planned to resupply the besieged city with sides of bacon
carried by horsemen, protected by a force of cavalry. It seems likely that

the English were forewarned by spies and they had time to stage a deadly trap. Ever thirsting for action, Henry decided 'at midnight to attack them in person [and] mounted [up], spear in hand, the emperor doing the same'.[91]

Dawn broke and the French had not appeared. Maximilian, courteously wearing the red cross of St George over his armour, suggested to Henry that some light guns be positioned on the crest of a small hill, near the village of Guinegatte, south of Thérouanne, protected by archers lining the hedges below. The king agreed and at four in the afternoon, after a long, boring and anxious wait, the trap was sprung.

The leading elements of the French cavalry were confronted suddenly by a strong force of English horsemen and pulled up in surprise, only to fall under fire from the guns and volleys of arrows from the archers. Fearing encirclement, they turned tail and almost immediately crashed into their comrades coming up behind. Chaos ensued and the panic-stricken French fled the field pell-mell, 'throwing away their spears, swords and maces' in their haste (Plate 14). They were pursued and hunted down by the English who captured nine standards and two hundred and fifty prisoners, led by Louis d'Orléans, Duc de Longueville, René de Clermont, Vice-Admiral of France, and Louis, Marquis of Rothelin. The speed of the French flight led to the contemptuous name – the Battle of the Spurs – given by the English to this brief clash.

That night Henry graciously dined with his noble captives, bidding them 'good greeting' and cladding Rothelin in an expensive gown of cloth of gold. A jarring note to all this magnanimous chivalry was sounded by the Frenchman, who refused to sit down to eat with his enemy, but the king was having none of that and told him brusquely: 'You are my prisoner and must do so.'[92]

Although the French force was routed, the fight was a far cry from a second Crécy or Agincourt, although Henry (who had taken no part in their pursuit) naturally hailed it as such. The queen also loyally waxed lyrical at her husband's feat of arms:

> The victory has been so great that I think none such has been seen before.
> All England has cause to thank God [for] it and I especially, seeing that

the king begins so well – which is to me, a great hope that the end shall be like.

I think with the company of the emperor and his good counsel, his grace shall not adventure himself so much as I was afraid of before.[93]

In truth, the Battle of the Spurs was little more than a skirmish but the final failure to resupply the embattled town led to its surrender at nine o'clock on the morning of 23 August. Over the next two weeks, Thérouanne's fortifications were systematically destroyed and its buildings burnt, save for the cathedral and the adjoining homes of the clergy.

Henry was jubilant at the town's capture. Cardinal Bainbridge in Rome – that walking embodiment of the adjective 'obsequious' – claimed his master's glory was truly 'immortal'.[94] The king convinced himself that the road to Paris now lay wide open to him and announced that he intended 'to have himself crowned King of France' there.[95]

Twenty-four hours earlier James IV, at the head of an army of 35,000 men, had crossed the River Tweed at Coldstream to invade and pillage northern England.

Henry decided to send his noble prisoner Longueville to Katherine 'as a present' to live in her household until he was ransomed, or a peace treaty signed with France. The homely queen, 'horribly busy' embroidering battle flags, was none too happy about this idea, as she was planning to lead reinforcements northwards towards the Scottish border. She told Wolsey 'there is no one to attend upon him except Lord Mountjoy who is going over to Calais'. Better that he be sent to the Tower, 'especially [with] the Scots so busy as they now be and I looking for my departing every hour'. She ended: 'Pray God to send us good luck against the Scots [such] as the King has had' in France.[96]

Maximilian meanwhile convinced his gullible English ally to besiege Tournai, a city on the borders of his dominions in the Low Countries, rather than attacking more logical strategic objectives such as Boulogne or Montreuil, which would have enhanced the defences of the English Pale around Calais.[97]

Henry arrived at Lille in early September – 'a place having much the appearance of an island in the middle of a marsh' according to the chaplain Taylor. The English king was paying a courtesy call on Margaret of Savoy and his arrival was greeted by its inhabitants in enthusiastically large numbers.

> Girls offered crowns, sceptres and garlands. Outlaws and malefactors with white rods in their hands sought pardon.
>
> Between the gate of the town and the palace, the way was lined with burning torches, although it was a bright day and there was scarce room for the riders to pass.

Maximilian sent Henry 'a great bull' as a present, although Taylor thought it was a strange gift, aside from its 'unwieldy size'.[98] The Milanese ambassador was completely overwhelmed by the splendour of it all:

> The most serene King of England entered this place, with about two hundred men-at-arms and his guards ... with great pomp.
>
> His majesty wore a white tunic over his armour and thirteen boys [?pages] went before him.
>
> The horses had trappings of solid silver and their cloths were of rich gold [on one side] and the other ... of black velvet, with numerous gold stripes and the fleur-de-lys of France.
>
> [Margaret of Savoy] went to meet him on the palace staircase and made him a deep reverence, while he bowed to the ground to her.

That night, the king boisterously danced with Margaret 'from the time the banquet finished until nearly day, in his shirt and without shoes'. Henry also gave her 'a beautiful diamond in a setting of great value'. Henry was 'wonderfully merry' and postponed a conversation with the Milanese ambassador Paulo de Laude to another time 'as he was in a hurry to go and dine and dance afterwards. In this he does wonders and leaps like a stag.'[99]

The flirtations continued. After dinner Charles Brandon knelt before Margaret and 'drew from [her] finger [a] ring and put it upon his'. He pledged himself her 'right humble servant' if she would 'do unto him all honour and pleasure'. Henry, it was reported, might have promoted the relationship between his old friend and Margaret. Afterwards the rumours of their possible marriage embarrassed the king who threatened death to those who spread this gossip, although in truth, it was probably Henry himself.[100]

A week later, Tournai was invested by the English and Imperial forces and siege works – gun emplacements and trenches – dug around its walls. It seemed a softer nut to crack than Thérouanne; the Milanese envoy reported that the besiegers 'walk close to the walls daily and the king himself does so occasionally for three hours and a half at a time'.[101]

Henry received news there from his wife of the crushing defeat of James IV and his army on 9 September at Flodden Field in Northumberland by the seventy-year-old Earl of Surrey and his 23,000-strong army.

> My lord Howard has sent me a letter by which you shall see at length the great victory that our Lord has sent your subjects in your absence.
>
> This battle is to your grace and all your realm the greatest honour that could be and more than [if] you should win all the crown of France.
>
> Thanks be to God for it and I am sure your grace [will not] forget to do this, which shall be cause to send you many such great victories, as I trust he shall do.
>
> I send your grace a bill found in a Frenchman's purse of such things as the French king sent to the King of Scots to make war against you.

Surprisingly warlike and bloodthirsty, Katherine dispatched James IV's torn and bloody tabard, bearing his arms, recovered from his mutilated body, to Henry as a proud trophy of war.

> Your grace shall see how I can keep my promise [to protect England], sending you for your banners a king's coat.
>
> I thought to send himself to you but our Englishmen's hearts would not suffer it.
>
> My Henry, my lord of Surrey ... would know your pleasure in the burying of the King of Scots' body.[102]

The queen then departed for the Shrine of Our Lady of Walsingham to offer up thanks for the victory, in which the Scots lost 12,000 killed, around half their number that fought that day. Almost every Scottish noble family had lost a father, son or brother.

Henry triumphantly passed on the news of Flodden to Maximilian Sforza, Duke of Milan. After the Battles of the Spurs and Flodden, his Tudor swagger was impossible to suppress, including playing down the importance of the Scots' initial gains:

> The King of Scots himself with a great army invaded our realm of England and first took a little old town belonging to the Bishop of Durham, already nearly in ruins and practically unfortified and ... almost deserted.
>
> He then advanced four miles (6.4 km) into our realm. There the noble lord, the Earl of Surrey, to whom we had committed the charge of repelling the Scots ... met them in a battle which was long and fiercely contested.
>
> With the Almighty ... aiding the better cause, our forces emerged victorious and killed a great number of the enemy ... and put the rest to flight, captured all their cannon and plundered the whole camp.

The king added a postscript: 'Since these were written, we have received news that the King of Scots himself was killed ... so he has paid a heavier penalty for his treachery than we would have wished.'[103]

Henry celebrated the news with a *feu de joie*, a carefully timed rippling salvo of 1,000 cannon, declaring: 'I will sing him a death knell with the sound of my guns.'

Surrey, the victor of Flodden, was rewarded by being 'honourably restored unto his right name of Duke of Norfolk' – his title lost after Bosworth when the Howards had fought for Richard III. His eldest son was created Earl of Surrey in his place.

Tournai surrendered after eight days' siege. The king wrote to Leo X, pointing out that the news of Flodden and the city's capitulation demonstrated clearly that 'God is fighting on behalf of the Holy Alliance'. He had intended to pursue the French army 'but they fled so rapidly that I despaired of overtaking them'.

Henry announced that he was returning to England 'now that winter is close at hand and the Scotch affairs are urgent'. He also planned to meet his Parliament, which had been summoned for 1 November.

The king promised Leo that he would return 'as soon as possible with a larger army and prosecute the war with all possible vigour'.

The court poet Bernard André penned some short Latin verses in praise of his 'invincible' master, invoking the 'deities of land and sea, whose duty is to guard England's crown'. For Henry, 'neither plunder nor bloodshed is the aim of his arms; instead is sought the return of dominions rightly due his sway'.[104]

But Henry did not return to France in full fighting fig for more than three decades to try again to claim that inheritance.

8

HOME AND ABROAD

─•◦•─

*'I am contented with what I have. I wish only to govern my own subjects.
Nevertheless, I will not allow anyone to have it in his power to govern
me – nor will I ever suffer it.'*

Henry VIII to Sebastian Giustinian, Venetian ambassador, June 1516.[1]

Henry fully intended to take another army back to France before June
1514. In the forefront of his thoughts was the unsettling knowledge that
he had failed to annihilate the military might of Louis XII, but instead
had merely captured a handful of French towns. One of them,
Thérouanne, he had deferentially relinquished to the Emperor
Maximilian and the other, Tournai, he briefly retained as an outpost of
the English possessions in northern France.[2]

The king therefore was no nearer to securing the throne of France
than he had been before the cripplingly expensive adventure across the
English Channel.[3] Moreover, Julius II's papal brief that named him
'Most Christian King' and so happily approved his claim on France had
mysteriously failed to arrive in England. Despite Henry's very best efforts
to lay his hands upon it, the document was hopelessly trapped in some
dusty corner of the Vatican's labyrinthine bureaucracy and, in fact, never
appeared again.

The king was nobody's fool. Howard's illustrious triumph at Flodden,
so devastating to the Scottish crown and nation, may have safely secured
England's northern borders but it unfortunately made his own inexperienced deeds on the battlefield, at the Battle – or rather skirmish –

of the Spurs, appear just a smidgen inglorious. They would certainly fail to be included in any history of famous victories, despite Henry's crowing hyperbole and his courtiers' fawning compliments.

At least England's military reputation had been restored at the European courts, creating the opportunity to cement alliances. As first fruit of the tactical successes in France, he had confirmed with the emperor that his younger sister Mary, now aged seventeen, should marry Maxmilian's grandson, Charles, Duke of Burgundy, at Calais by May, when he would be fourteen. After the lavish nuptial celebrations, emperor and king would don their armour, collect their fearsome trappings of war and again strike boldly at perfidious Gaul.[4]

Henry also received handsome gifts as tokens of friendship from lesser overseas potentates. In June 1514 the Marquis of Mantua sent him two fine horses named *Altobello* and *Goventore*. After riding them for six days, the king declared that he had never 'ridden a horse that pleased him more than *Goventore*'. He enquired what would please the marquis and was told he 'required nothing but the king's love'.[5]

But despite such minor tangible benefits from his foray into mainland Europe, none of Henry's ambitious schemes came to fruition, as he failed to take account of the treacherous shifting sands of European politics.

The new Pope, the vacillating and irresolute Leo X, decided to dissolve the Holy League and to seek peace with France. He sent his legate Gianpetro Caraffa to London to discuss the plan but Henry huffily refused to meet him. Leo, committed firmly to the sacred cause of Christian unity, wrote a smoothly worded appeal to the king in December 1513, pleading with him to 'eliminate all hatred' and to 'sow the seeds of peace'. As the holy purpose to which Henry took up arms 'had been secured' the Pope 'hoped he will listen to the proposals for an honourable peace'.[6] The same day he briefed the king's ministers, Warham, Ruthal and Fox, on his attempts to 'earnestly move Henry, King of England, to incline to peace'. Leo had not forgotten

that he took up arms for the liberty of the Church but as his adversary [Louis XII] has humbly come to the Apostolic See for pardon and he himself has gained both profit and glory, it is a Pope's office to prohibit slaughter and there are other enemies of the Faith [the Turks] to be repelled.[7]

He earnestly exhorted them to convince the king that universal peace should reign again amongst the European nations.[8]

Leo ramped up the pressure on Henry by sending him a costly sword and a *pileus* (the cap of maintenance)[9] given to European sovereigns by popes as a mark of their particular esteem.[10] The award was celebrated by a special high Mass at St Paul's on Sunday 21 May. The king, wearing a chequered gown of purple satin and gold, knelt at the high altar as the long sword, with a gilded guard and scabbard, was buckled around his waist. The foot-high (30.5 cm) cap 'of purple satin, resembling the crown of the caps worn by the Albanian light cavalry' was placed on his head, 'which by reason of its length covered his whole face'.[11] The subsequent stately procession proved a little perilous as the king felt his way around the interior of the cathedral.

It may be that the king's pointed snub to the Papal Legate was not merely immature tantrum. Around December 1513 Henry contracted smallpox, a disease rife in sixteenth-century England. The attack was severe: foreign reports suggested his physicians 'were afraid [for] his life ... [but] he is risen from his bed, fierce against France'.[12] Erasmus had planned to give a gift to Wolsey (now appointed Bishop of Lincoln) while in London in January, but postponed his plans 'deeming it unsafe there in consequence of the plague'. He reported: 'The king was ill when I was there, that is at Richmond [Palace] but the doctor said he had escaped all danger.'[13] Happily, Henry was spared any pockmarks on his face, often a telltale sign of the disease.

Princess Mary was meanwhile pining for her young bridegroom-to-be, who was reported to be a sickly boy with a solemn disposition verging on the melancholy.[14] Gerard de Pleine, the President of the Council of Flanders, met her in London in June 1514 and described his impressions to Margaret of Savoy:

> She is one of the most beautiful young women in the world. I think
> I never saw a more charming creature.

She is very graceful. Her deportment in dancing and in conversation is as pleasing as you could desire.

There is nothing gloomy or melancholy about her.

It is certain ... that she is much attached to Prince Charles of whom she has a very bad picture and is said to wish to see it ten times a day.

Never a day passes that she does not express a wish to see him.

I had imagined that she would have been very tall but she is of middling height and ... a much better match in age and person for the prince than I had heard.[15]

But this match was not to be. Louis XII's wife, Anne of Brittany, died on 9 January 1514 and the fifty-one-year-old French king made unexpected secret overtures to take Mary as his new wife.

Sporadic fighting between England and France continued. The following month the French attacked the south coast of England and burnt Brighton to the ground (leaving only the parish church of St Nicholas standing) before they were driven off by hastily mustered archers.[16] In retaliation, Henry sent a punitive expedition to Normandy under the newly created Earl of Surrey to burn and ravage the countryside near Cherbourg.[17] French troops also attacked Guisnes in the Pale of Calais and threatened to besiege it, 'but the English sallied forth and repulsed them with much slaughter'.[18]

Surprisingly, the French king's proposal was not rebuffed, primarily because Ferdinand of Spain was about to sign a unilateral peace treaty with France and Maximilian had pulled out of the Holy League.[19] Thus deceitfully deserted by his allies, Henry at first considered fighting on alone against France but then began to woo the Swiss as potential fellow combatants. Wolsey and Bishop Fox, however, urged a new peace treaty with the French king: Henry instructed Wolsey that he required 100,000 crowns as an annual 'tribute' paid 'for withholding my inheritance' – the throne of France – and that peace should 'no longer continue than the payment of the money'.[20]

Under the subsequent treaty, signed on 7 August 1514, Louis agreed to pay a million gold crowns (£250,000) to Henry in ten annual instalments. The final clause was an agreement that Mary should marry Louis XII.[21]

In Rome, the English ambassador Cardinal Bainbridge, Archbishop of York, died suddenly on 14 July, having probably been poisoned by his chaplain Renaldo da Modena, who was indignant after being punched by his violent master. Henry formally requested Pope Leo to make Wolsey a cardinal in his place: 'His merits are such that we esteem him above our dearest friends and we can do nothing of the least importance without him,' he wrote. Furthermore, 'no one laboured and sweated' for the Anglo–French peace more than Wolsey.[22]

Louis was not an attractive catch for Mary. He was toothless, syphilitic and gout-ridden, suffered from a scorbutic skin condition like scurvy and displayed symptoms of premature senility. Some roguish reports even suggested he had contracted elephantiasis[23] or leprosy. He was scarcely the first choice of lover in any teenage girl's dream of wedded bliss.

The only glimmer of hope was that he was unlikely to live long. After much cajoling, a reluctant princess eventually told her brother that she would marry Louis only on condition that she had complete freedom to choose her next husband after he died. She already had Charles Brandon, created Duke of Suffolk in 1514, in her sights. On 30 July, she solemnly renounced her proposed marriage with Charles of Burgundy at a short formal ceremony at the royal manor of Wanstead, Essex, witnessed by Wolsey, Norfolk and Suffolk himself.[24]

The proxy wedding was held on 13 August at Greenwich, with the French hostage, the Duc de Longueville, acting as Louis XII's representative. The symbolic consummation followed with Mary, after having undressed, climbing into bed in the 'presence of many witnesses'. Another French prisoner, the Marquis de Rothelin, wearing a doublet and garish red hose (but with one leg naked) crept under the covers and touched her body with his bare leg.[25] The marriage was declared duly consummated amid polite applause from the bystanders. Mary's real wedding night would be much less entertaining.

The king paid out nearly £1,000 for her trousseau, more than half of which went on embroidery, including the £233 paid to a jeweller for the glittering gilt spangles sewn on Mary's dresses.[26]

Henry and Katherine saw his unenthusiastic sister off at Dover on 30 September 1514 but her voyage to France became an uncomfortable chapter of accidents. The Earl of Surrey, as Lord Admiral, was detailed to shepherd the wedding party safely across the English Channel but stormy weather delayed them for four days of *mal de mer* and abject misery.[27] Mary's ship was separated from the flotilla and ran jarringly aground on a sandbank outside Boulogne, forcing her to be rowed ashore in a small boat through the raging surf. Finally, Sir Christopher Garnish, staggering through the waves, had to carry her in his arms onto the beach.[28] A true Tudor, she was vocal in her angry protests at the danger and damage to her dignity. Amongst her ladies was Mary Boleyn (daughter of Katherine of Aragon's lady-in-waiting and the diplomat Sir Thomas Boleyn), who was chosen to join the entourage because of her fluent French.

The bride's first glimpse of her husband at Abbeville was unedifying. Clearly entertaining lascivious thoughts, the French king was 'licking his lips and gulping his spittle'. His outfit was ludicrous, more befitting a younger man. The wedding was postponed for a few weeks because drooling Louis suffered a bad attack of gout, but finally their nuptials were celebrated in Abbeville Cathedral on 9 October. After the wedding night, the groom boasted vaingloriously that he had 'performed marvels' although his cousin and heir apparent Francis, Duke of Angoulême, unkindly gossiped 'that unless I have been told lies ... the king and queen cannot possibly have a child'.[29] Most of her English servants were promptly sacked, much to Mary's chagrin, although Mary Boleyn remained a lady of her chamber.

Henry sent Suffolk to Paris on a secret mission to discuss plans to wreak his personal revenge on the Spanish king for violating his alliance with England and his cavalier treatment of him. Henry sought a military pact with Louis to expel Ferdinand from the kingdom of Navarre and assistance in pressing a barely plausible claim on Castile, of which Queen Katherine, the king insisted, was the legitimate heir.

Before the duke departed, Henry extracted a solemn promise from

him at Eltham Palace in front of Wolsey that he would make no attempt
to seduce or make love to Mary while he was in France.[30]

In London, Ferdinand's ambassador Luis Caroz was feeling the effects
of Henry's wrath, being treated like 'a bull at whom everyone throws
darts' – a graphic Spanish simile. The king's behaviour was now 'most
offensive and discourteous' and 'if God does not change [his] mind, he
will really carry out what he intends – to do as much harm [to Ferdinand]
as he can'. If the father-in-law did not 'bridle this colt' it would be
impossible to control him, Caroz warned gloomily.

Katherine of Aragon's surprising role as Ferdinand's own envoy at
Henry's court had long since ended. It seems likely she was unaware of
her husband's thirst for vengeance on her father and with the continuing
absence of a male heir, she probably would have been more worried
about the fragility of her marriage. The Spanish ambassador bewailed
the fact that her confessor, Friar Diego Fernández, had urged her that
she

> ought to forget Spain and everything Spanish in order to gain the love of
> the king and of the English. She had become so much accustomed to this
> idea that she will not change her behaviour unless some person . . . near
> her tells her what she ought to do in order to be useful to the king her
> father.[31]

Perhaps she had heard of the rumours circulating in Rome that Henry
planned to repudiate her and put her away in a distant nunnery.[32]

Suffolk, supposedly in France to attend Mary's coronation, caught up
with the newly-weds at Beauvais on 25 October. He found Louis lying
down, with Mary sitting shyly by the royal bedside. The French king
embraced him 'and held me a good while and said I was heartily welcome'. The duke said Henry 'recommended himself to his entirely
beloved brother and thanked him for the great honour and [love] that
he showed to the queen, his sister'. Louis in turn reported that no queen
had ever 'behaved herself more wisely and honourably' and had 'a loving
manner'.[33]

Suffolk handed over his secret letter and after due consideration, the
French king promised he 'was most willing to render all the services he

has in his power'. But with Louis, there was always a sting in the tail: in return for his help against Spain, he required an English loan of 200,000 crowns and military assistance to seize the duchy of Milan the following March.[34]

Mary was crowned Queen of France in St Denis just over a month later. Three days of celebratory jousts followed when Mary 'stood so that all men might see her and wonder at her beauty' but her husband was 'feeble and lay on a couch for weakness'.[35]

On 1 January 1515, Louis XII died, some whispered, from eighty-three days of over-exertion on the marriage bed with his teenage bride. With the demise of this tired old roué died also any hopes Henry had for French military support in punishing Spain.

At the very hour of his death, Mary announced that she was not pregnant, so Louis was immediately succeeded by his son-in-law, the twenty-year-old Francis, Duke of Angoulême. He was 'inexpressibly handsome and generous ... he rises at eleven, hears Mass, then remains for two or three hours with his mother and afterwards visited his sweet-hearts or [goes] out hunting'.

The young widow sat in her quarters, 'dressed all in black, with a white kerchief on her head and under her chin like a nun. [She] is never still [and] moves her head.'[36] Patently her agitation suggested that she had other things on her mind than mourning a depraved, diseased husband.

Mary now felt liberated to marry Suffolk – given Henry's earlier promise of her freedom of choice – but both inevitably feared Henry's angry reaction. In March the duke wrote to Wolsey for help.

> The queen would never let me [be] in rest till I had granted her to be married.
>
> And so, to be plain with you I have married her [secretly] and have lain with her in so much [as] I fear ... that she is with child.

Suffolk acknowledged he would 'rather be dead' than have Henry 'discontented'.[37] Writing 'with sorrowful heart', Wolsey replied that although Suffolk wanted to keep his letter secret, he had shown it to Henry.

The king would not believe it [and] took [the news] grievously and displeasantly – not merely for [your] presumption but for breaking your promise made . . . at Eltham. [He] would not believe your promise would be broken had you been torn with wild horses.

Cursed be the blind affection and counsel that has brought you here!

Wolsey added an ominous warning: 'You are in the greatest danger that ever man was in.'[38]

Nothing ventured, nothing gained. Suffolk took his courage in both hands and wrote a pleading and contrite letter to his old friend and monarch. He begged forgiveness 'for my offence in this marriage' and prayed 'for the passion of God that it may not turn your heart against me'.

I will make good against all the world [to] die for it that ever I . . . did anything, saving the love and marriage of the queen that should be to your displeasure, [I p]ray God let me die as shameful a death as ever did man.[39]

Mary also wrote to her brother, begging him to remember his pledge to her. Since Louis was dead and because of Suffolk's great virtues – 'to whom I have always been of good mind, as you well know' – Mary had married him 'without any request or labour on his part'. She was now so 'bound to him that for no earthly cause can I change'.[40]

Suffolk was frightened for his life and suspected that most of Henry's Council – with the exception of Wolsey – wanted him executed. He felt hard done by – he had helped them all in the past but 'now in this little trouble they are ready to destroy me' he told the king. But the duke emphasised he was willing to undergo any punishment decreed by Henry.[41]

After keeping the lovers agonisingly on tenterhooks, the king eventually granted them his royal prerogative of mercy that May – in return for repaying him £24,000 for the expenses of her wedding to Louis and handing over all her plate and jewels.[42] On 11 March 1516 a son was born to Suffolk and his royal wife, and at the christening the king and Wolsey were godfathers and Katherine of Aragon the godmother. The child was baptised 'Henry'.[43]

Louis was not the only European monarch to join his maker. Ferdinand died on 23 January 1516 and was succeeded as joint ruler of Castile and Aragon by his grandson Charles and his mother, the mad Juana, who was promptly locked away in a remote Spanish castle. After his paternal grandfather Maximilian died in January 1519, Charles became the Holy Roman Emperor with extensive domains in central, western and southern Europe, together with the Spanish colonies in the Americas.

Charles visited England briefly in late May 1520, breaking his voyage from Spain back to the duchy of Burgundy. He landed at Dover and with Henry went on to Canterbury, where, for the first time, he met his aunt Katherine of Aragon in the archbishop's palace.[44] It was only a brief visit as Henry himself was en route to meet Francis I of France – annoyingly still the 'Most Christian King' – for another summit arranged between Guisnes and Ardres, which was to become known as 'The Field of the Cloth of Gold'.

Both sovereigns tried to outdo each other in the magnificence and splendour of their entourages. Instead of fighting on the battlefield, it was a war of culture between the two traditional enemies. More than 5,000 courtiers and their attendants formed the English contingent. Wolsey had organised the erection of a huge temporary square palace for Henry, built of timber and canvas on brick foundations, at the designated meeting place, the Val d'Or. The sides of this valley had been laboriously excavated so that neither nation could enjoy the superiority of being raised above the other. The site today is marked by a granite stele on the busy D231 road near Balinghem, ten miles (16 km) south-east of Calais.

It was not all talk. The meeting opened with almost two weeks of jousting and sport. Henry managed to sprain his wrist and so ran few courses while Francis, who 'shivered spears like reeds', suffered a black eye and had to wear a black patch over the injury. On one day of bad weather there was wrestling – including a bout between the two kings, arranged as they were drinking in a pavilion. Henry, to his great fury, was hurled to the floor by Francis using a *touche de Bretagne* – a Breton throw.[45] He jumped up from the floor, calling for a rematch, but was refused with icy Gallic politeness. At least he had excelled at archery alongside twenty-four of his royal guard.

The formal diplomatic extravaganza ended on Saturday 23 June, when Wolsey celebrated Mass in the presence of the English and French kings and queens. The theme was inevitably peace and a foundation stone was laid on the site for a church, to be called 'Our Lady of Friendship', endowed by both monarchs.[46] At the start of the service, a firework, fashioned as a dragon, was floated over the camp at the height of a bowshot by the English.[47]

This great Renaissance occasion failed to eradicate one traditional national character trait, at least amongst some of the English. On the way home, Lord Leonard Grey, brother of the Marquis of Dorset, scornfully told a friend: 'If I had a drop of French blood in my body I would cut myself open to get rid of it,' and the other replied, 'And so would I.' So much for *entente cordiale*. The king had them arrested.

Although Henry enjoyed a fascination for both foreign intrigue and naval power, he was curiously lacking in enthusiasm for exploration and exploitation of the new worlds across the Atlantic. In 1517, John Rastell, a lawyer and printer (and brother-in-law to Thomas More), planned a voyage of colonisation to 'this new land found lately . . . called America'. Henry provided him with letters of commendation addressed to any indigenous potentates he might come across, but funding came from two London Merchants, with More acting as a guarantor.[48]

Rastell departed Gravesend on 1 March 1517 with two ships, one named the *Barbara*, but having reached Waterford on the coast of south-east Ireland, the crew decided that piracy was a more attractive option than distant, unfriendly coasts and abruptly put him ashore. They sailed on to Bordeaux and sold off his stolen cargo of flour, salt and tallow.[49]

In early 1521 the London guilds were invited to fund a five-strong flotilla of ships to seek the elusive North-West Passage through the Arctic wastes to the riches of Cathay (China) and the East Indies. A royal ship was to accompany these intrepid vessels in a plan endorsed by both Henry and Wolsey, but merchants were loath to risk their money on this venture into the far unknown. They were instantly summoned into the royal presence and told to stump up the cash – 'His grace would have no "nay" therein but spoke sharply to the mayor to see [the expedition] put in execution to the best of his power.'[50] Several ships were funded but the flotilla never sailed.

The North-West Passage continued to fascinate adventurous Englishmen. In 1541 Roger Barlow, the renowned explorer of the River Plate (between today's Argentina and Uruguay) considered that 'the shortest route, the northern, has been reserved by Divine Providence for England'. In 1527 the Bristol merchant Robert Thorne, whose father claimed to be the first to discover Newfoundland in 1494,[51] tried to convince Dr Edward Lee, Henry's ambassador at Charles V's court, of the immense wealth of the East, which was just lying there, waiting to be picked up. The islands, now known as the Philippines, were

> fertile of cloves, nutmegs, mace and cinnamon ... and abound with diamonds, balasses,[52] granates[53] and other stones and pearls. For we see where nature gives anything, she is no niggard.

In his nineteen-page letter Thorne tried to explain, interminably, how courses were plotted at sea: 'Your lord[ship] knows that the cosmographers have divided the earth by 360 degrees in latitude and as many in longitude under which is comprehended the roundness of the earth.'[54] Poor Dr Lee! The still fresh concept of the earth being round was difficult enough, without the mathematical complexities of maritime navigation.

Ever the enthusiast, Thorne immediately proposed an expedition to the North Pole to Henry, urging that the North-West Passage could outflank the Spanish and Portuguese by cutting down the sailing time to the Far East.[55] Although the merchant bought a ship for the voyage, there is no record of any response from the king.

The same year, 1527, the crown did support an English attempt to find the Passage. The leader, John Rut,[56] was a king's man and one of his two ships, the three-masted *Mary Guilford*, 160 tons,[57] was a royal vessel.[58] On 10 June he departed Plymouth but lost his other ship, the *Samson*, in heavy Atlantic storms. Braving icebergs, he reached the coast of Labrador. Anchored in the harbour of St John, Newfoundland, Rut wrote to Henry on 3 August 1527 – the earliest surviving letter written from North America:

All the company are in good health. The *Mary Guilford* with all her [crew are safe] thanks be to God.

Went northward till we came to [latitude] 53° where we found many islands of ice and deep water [where] we found no sounding [and] dared go no further for fear of ice . . .

Went southward . . . [and] landed at Cape de Bas, a good harbour with many small islands and a great fresh river going up far into the mainland. The land is wilderness, mountains and woods and no habitation or people. In the woods we found the footing [tracks] of diverse great beasts but we saw none, not in ten leagues.[59]

In the harbour, they found eleven boats from Normandy and one from Brittany, together with two Portuguese barques, all fishing the nearby cod grounds.[60]

Rut then sailed south to Florida and into the Caribbean, reaching the Spanish town of Santa Domingo on the island of Hispaniola (the present-day Dominican Republic) in November. Faced with deep suspicion, and perhaps encouraged by a mortar shot fired across his stern, Rut hastily departed within twenty-four hours. The Spanish report on the incident said:

They had sailed [as] far north as fifty and some degrees where certain persons died of cold; the pilot had died and one of the vessels lost.

The ship being so anchored . . . that from the fortress of this city there was fired at it a small lombard loaded with a stone which passed close to the ship which at once cleared on a course for Castile.

The ship was well equipped for war with much heavy brass artillery in two tiers [and] that she was ready for action.[61]

Despite all the romance and adventure of this voyage, its ultimate failure to find the passage to China may have convinced the king that his true destiny lay in Europe. He still wanted the throne of France.

We have vivid descriptions dating from this period of Henry VIII in his proud, swaggering prime – the living embodiment of imperial splendour.

A harness of engraved silver armour especially made for him in 1515 indicates he was at least 6 ft 1 in. (1.84 m) in height, with broad shoulders and a trim waist measurement of 35½ in. (0.9 m). As such, he was taller than most of those around him.[62] Sebastian Giustinian, who left London as the Venetian ambassador in August 1519, painted a detailed word picture of the then twenty-eight-year-old Henry (Plate 11). The king was:

> much handsomer than any other sovereign in Christendom – a great deal handsomer than the King of France.
>
> He is very fair and his whole frame admirably proportioned.
>
> Hearing that King Francis wore a beard, he allowed his own to grow and as it was reddish, he ... got a beard that looked like gold.[63]

The beard at this stage in Henry's life did not survive long as Katherine of Aragon objected strongly to it, apparently nagging her husband daily until his barber shaved it off (Plate 12).[64] During the first half of his reign, Henry's hair was bobbed, but later it was cropped closer to his head.

> [He is] very religious, hearing three Masses daily when he hunted and sometimes five on other days, besides hearing vespers and compline daily in the queen's chamber.[65]
>
> He is extremely fond of hunting and never takes the diversion without tiring eight or ten horses which he causes to be stationed along the line of country he means to take.

In August 1520 while on progress, Henry rose daily at four or five o'clock 'and hunts to nine or ten at night. He spares no pains to convert the sport of hunting into martyrdom' complained one weary courtier.[66]

Giustinian described how the king loved playing tennis, 'at which game it was the prettiest thing in the world to see him play – his fair skin glowing through a shirt of the finest texture'.[67] In 1527 he hurt his foot during one energetic match, probably at the Palace of Westminster, and the next month was forced to wear a black velvet slipper to ease the pain still troubling him.[68]

Like his father, he had a passion for gambling, placing wagers on the outcomes of jousts, tennis and archery contests, as well as betting on games of dice, playing cards and chess. He 'gambled with the French hostages to the amount occasionally ... of from 6,000 to 8,000 ducats

[£2,750–£3,680] in a day', according to the Venetian envoy.[69] Dice or cards normally occupied him during late evening sessions after court masques or plays and often went on into the small hours. Large sums changed hands: in 1511 'crafty persons', knowing Henry's love of gambling, 'brought in Frenchmen and Lombards to make wagers with him and so he lost much money but when he perceived their craft he eschewed their company and let them go'.[70]

Henry had plenty of money to fund these excesses. Giustinian believed him to be very rich:

> His father left him ten millions of ready money in gold, of which he is supposed to have spent one half in the war against France.
>
> His revenues amounted to about 350,000 ducats annually [£165,000, or £66.5 million at current prices] ... [and] his majesty's expenses might be estimated at 100,000 ducats ... [including] 16,000 for the wardrobe, for he is the best dressed sovereign in the world. His robes are very rich and superb and he put on new clothes every holiday.[71]

Henry certainly knew how to dress to impress: 'His fingers were one mass of rings and around his neck he wore a gold collar from which hung a diamond as big as a walnut,' gasped one diplomatic visitor.[72]

Lorenzo Pasqualigo, another Venetian, echoed Giustinian's enthusiastic praise for Henry's good looks. He watched Henry taking part in a St George's Day procession in Richmond in 1515:

> The king is the handsomest potentate I ever set eyes on. [He is] above the usual height with an extremely fine calf to his leg, his complexion very fair and bright with auburn hair combed straight and short in the French fashion and a round face so very beautiful that it would become a pretty woman.[73]

The Venetian had seen Francis I in Paris, and Henry, three years his senior, was curious about his brother king. Dressed (yet again) in a Robin Hood costume for the bucolic May Day festivities at Shooter's Hill, near Greenwich, Henry asked Pasqualigo about his rival monarch's physical attributes:

'Is the King of France as tall as I am?' I told him there was little difference. 'Is he as stout?' I told him he was not.

'What sort of legs has he?' I replied: 'Spare.'

Whereupon he opened the front of his doublet and placing his hand on his thigh said, 'Look here. I have a good calf to my leg.'[74]

The king maintained his love of music, frequently playing for hours on a variety of instruments and continuing to compose his own music: 'After dinner, he took to dancing and playing on every musical instrument,' reported a diplomat after enjoying a splendid evening at the court. Nicolo Sagudino, Giustinian's secretary, no mean musician himself, attended a soirée at Greenwich Palace in June 1515 when

> Two musicians ... in the king's service played the organ but very badly. They kept bad time, their touch was feeble and their execution not very good.
>
> The prelates who were present said the king would certainly desire to hear me as his majesty practises on these instruments day and night.[75]

Henry decided to hire a maestro and lured Friar Dionysius Memo, the organist of St Mark's Cathedral in Venice, to London in September 1516 and made him his head musician and chaplain. Giustinian told the Signory in Venice:

> [Memo] brought a most excellent instrument with him at great expense.
>
> The king ... sent for him after dinner and made him play before his lords and all his *virtuosi*.
>
> He played to the incredible admiration of everybody, especially the king.[76]

The king was also both predatory and ruthless in hiring sweet-singing choristers from other colleges and chapels to augment the choir of his own Chapel Royal. Henry was jealous of the quality of plainsong sung in Wolsey's chapel at York Place, his opulent London palace, as Richard Pace, his secretary, warned the cardinal in March 1518:

> My lord, if it were not for the personal love that the king bears your grace, surely he would have out of your chapel, not children only but also men.

His grace has plainly shown unto [William] Cornish[77] that your grace's chapel is better than his and proved the same by this reason – that if any manner of new song should be brought into both the chapels to be sung *ex improviso* then the song should be better and more surely handled by your chapel than by his grace's.[78]

Henry was always scrupulous in putting on a good show, knowing full well that pomp and circumstance symbolised England's growing importance on the European political stage. In June 1517, Francesco Chieregato, the Apostolic Nuncio in England, was impressed by the king's appearance, dressed in white damask 'in the Turkish fashion with a robe embroidered with roses made of rubies and diamonds in accordance with his emblems'.

After hearing Mass the royal party went on to the joust where forty gentlemen, members of the Spears' bodyguard, opened proceedings, dressed in silk livery and wearing gold chains formed by the initials 'H' and 'K'. These chains were 'of five fingers' breadth [and] upwards of 2,000 ducats [were] melted [down] to make each'. They all rode white horses, also decorated with the gold initials, which 'cost the king a mint of money as during the last four months all the London goldsmiths have wrought nothing but these trappings'. The bridles and girths and the pommels of the saddles were made of pure silver.

Henry was drawn that day against Suffolk:

They bore themselves so bravely that the spectators fancied themselves witnessing a joust between Hector and Achilles.

The king appeared on a tall white horse trapped from head to foot with little bells . . . and on his head a very large feather quite full of jewels.

[He] presented himself before the queen and the ladies, making a thousand jumps in the air and after tiring one horse, he entered the tent and mounted another of those ridden by the pages, doing this constantly and reappearing in the lists until the end of the joust.

Afterwards, there was a buffet set out, thirty feet in length and twenty feet high (9.14 m by 6.01 m), 'with silver gilt vases and vases of gold, worth vast treasure. All the small platters used for the table service and the goblets were of pure gold.' The meal took seven hours to serve and consume:

> The removal and replacing of dishes the whole time was incessant, the hall in every direction full of fresh viands on their way to table.
>
> Every imaginable sort of meat known in the kingdom was served and fish in like manner, even down to prawn pasties but the jellies of some twenty sorts surpassed everything.
>
> They were made in the shape of castles and animals of various descriptions as beautiful and as admirable as can be imagined.

The Nuncio ended this breathless paean of praise to the opulence and glamour of Henry's court with a valediction – which would have come as music to Henry's ears:

> The wealth and civilisation of the world are here and those who call the English barbarians appear to me to render themselves such.
>
> I here perceived very elegant manners, extreme decorum and very great politeness.
>
> There is this most invincible king, whose acquirements and qualities are so many and excellent that I consider him to excel all who ever wore a crown.
>
> Blessed and happy may this country call itself in having as its lord so worthy and eminent a sovereign.[79]

Henry's court was a magnificent, well-ordered institution. Two of his Privy Chamber Gentlemen always slept on a pallet inside the royal bedchamber and all had to be ready for service at seven o'clock in the morning to help him dress – 'in [a] reverent, discreet and sober manner'. None were allowed to touch the king's sacred person without his special command. Regulations ordained that members of the Privy Chamber were

> to be friendly to each other and keep secret all things done there; not to enquire in the king's absence where he is going or talk about his pastimes and if anyone uses unfitting language [about] the king, it is to be immediately reported.

They must not exploit their position for special pleading on behalf of others: 'the nearer they are to his person the more humble they must show themselves.' One groom, called Peter Malvesey, was recruited especially for 'tennis play' – Henry's coach, perhaps?

Penney, the royal barber, attended Henry

at his rising, having in readiness his water, clothes [towels], basin, knives, combs, scissors, to trim his head and beard. He must take care to keep his own person and apparel clean and not to go in company with vile persons or misguided women on pain of losing his place and being further punished at the king's pleasure.

The Privy Chamber should be kept

pure and clean and free from great resort of people who disturb the king's retirement [therefore] no one is to be allowed to enter besides those he himself calls for, except the ministers deputed to attend.

The knight marshal and his officers were ordered to exclude 'boys and vile persons and punish vagabonds and beggars' who were always hanging around the court looking for handouts of food. No one at court was allowed 'to have greyhounds or other dogs, except for a few spaniels for ladies'.[80]

Henry needed to be protected from distractions because he had now become an author. In late 1517 the German priest Martin Luther had attacked the church's system of indulgences, claiming that avoidance of God's punishment of sin could not be bought merely by cash. Both Pope Leo X and Charles V demanded the retraction of his views and Luther's refusal resulted in his excommunication and banishment as an outlaw. None knew it, but it was the beginning of the Reformation.

In England a pious Henry immediately wrote a refutation of Luther's opinions and these emerged in 1521 as the opening three chapters of his book *Assertio Septem Sacramentorum* (the 'Defence of the Seven Sacraments'). That April, his secretary Richard Pace wrote to Wolsey, mentioning that the king was much occupied '*in scribendo contra Lutherum*' (writing against Luther) 'as I do conjecture'.[81] He was aided in his work by some of his clerics and Thomas More helpfully marshalled the royal arguments 'as a sorter-out and placer of the principal matters therein'.[82] More himself did not fail to mince his words about Luther, graphically describing him in his own writings as 'an ape, an arse, a drunkard, a lousy little friar, a piece of scurf, a pestilential buffoon, a dishonest liar'.[83]

Leo X concurrently ordered Wolsey to burn all Luther's books in England and prohibit their reading.[84] There was an evocative public incineration of the heretic's works at Paul's Cross alongside the London Cathedral on 12 May and John Fisher, Bishop of Rochester, preached a sermon, railing against Luther's errors.[85]

A copy of Henry's book was specially bound in cloth of gold and presented to the Pope in October 1521. The king had personally inscribed dedicatory verses (dutifully supplied by Wolsey) on its endpaper and his Latin Secretary Richard Pace, aware they were 'written with a very small pen ... and I knew the Pope to be of a very dull sight, I would have read the verses aloud [but] his Holiness took the book from me and read the verses promptly, commending them singularly'.[86] Six weeks later, by papal Bull, Leo at last granted Henry his coveted recognition – *Fidei Defensor*, 'Defender of the Faith'[87] – but refused to add the words *Gloriosus* ('famous') or *Fidelissimus* ('ever faithful') that several cardinals had suggested.[88] The title was intended for the personal use of the king, but it became inextricably attached to the English crown by Parliamentary Act in 1543.[89]

Despite the slightly grudging award, the king was delighted. One later tradition of uncertain veracity has it that his fool, or jester, found Henry 'transported with an unusual joy' because 'the Pope had honoured him with a style more eminent than any of his ancestors'. The fool boldly answered: 'O good Harry, let you and I defend one another and let the faith alone to defend itself.'[90]

Wolsey's star was now in the ascendancy at Henry's court and he handled all England's business. Giustinian in 1519 described him as 'about forty-six years old, very handsome, learned, extremely eloquent, of vast ability and indefatigable'. Honours and preferments were heaped upon his grey-haired head: Archbishop of York in September 1514; cardinal in September 1515; and in May 1518, he was appointed Papal Legate to England. On Christmas Eve 1515, Henry appointed him Lord Chancellor in succession to Warham.

The Venetian ambassador recalled that on his arrival in London Wolsey used to say to him:

> His Majesty will do so and so ... Subsequently, by degrees, he forgot himself and commenced saying, 'We shall do so and so.' He then reached such a pitch that he used to say: 'I shall do so and so.'[91]

No one obtained audience with Wolsey until the third or fourth attempt – and then had to walk through eight rooms at his palace at York Place before reaching the audience chamber.

The cardinal's household numbered almost five hundred, and one of them, George Cavendish, described this prince of the church's daily procession to Westminster Hall to hear legal cases in the Chancery Court:

> [He] would issue out, apparelled all in red, in the habit of a cardinal which was either of fine scarlet or else of crimson satin ... the best he could get for money. Upon his head, a round pillon.[92]
>
> He also had a tippet [cape] of fine sable around his neck, holding in his hand a very fair orange [with] the substance within taken out, wherein was vinegar and other confections against the pestilent airs, the which he most commonly smelt unto, passing among the press [of people] or ... when he was pestered with suitors.

His procession was led by a page bearing the Great Seal of England and another his red cardinal's hat[93] and these were followed by tall priests carrying two large silver crosses, one symbolising Wolsey's role as Archbishop of York and the other, a double cross like that of Lorraine, his position as Papal Legate. Two pillars of heavy silver, again carried by priests, came next, together with the cardinal's pursuivant of arms, with a 'great mace of silver gilt'. Wolsey himself was humbly mounted on a mule, but this was richly trapped out in crimson velvet with gilt stirrups, and he was surrounded by his own guards, armed with gilded poleaxes and whose uniforms bore the initials 'T. C.' for '*Thomas Cardinalis*' embroidered in gold.[94]

After Leo X died on 1 December 1521 Wolsey may have entertained some hopes of succeeding him as the second English Pope[95] – indeed, the king urged him to stand as a candidate. In the conclave of cardinals, he only received five votes, all in the fifth scrutiny on 3 January 1522. In the event sixty-three-year-old Adrian VI[96] was elected but he died on 14 September 1523. Wolsey may have been relieved when Clement VII succeeded to the papacy, preferring the domination he enjoyed over English affairs to the byzantine intrigues and conspiracies of the Vatican.[97]

Henry liked able men about him. For years he pestered Wolsey to recruit Thomas More into royal service. He stepped up his efforts after the lawyer had appeared on behalf of Leo X in a Court of Star Chamber case concerning a papal cargo of the chemical alum (used to preserve fruit and vegetables) which had been illegally confiscated by Suffolk in 1514.[98] More's friend Erasmus acknowledged that the king 'could not rest until he had dragged [him] to his court – dragged is the word for no man tried more strenuously to gain admission to court than he did to escape from it'.[99]

More admitted in a letter, now lost, that he came to Henry's court 'with the greatest unwillingness ... as the king himself often throws in my face'. He was appointed Master of the Court of Requests – the hearer of 'poor men's [legal] suits' – in 1518 and a month later joined the Privy Council.[100] Henry warned More that 'in all his doings and affairs touching the king, he should first respect and regard God and afterwards the king, his master'. He was knighted in 1521.

In May 1519 the court was purged of some of the noisiest and most badly behaved of Henry's cronies – his close friends of the joust and those endless late-night gambling sessions. Six Gentlemen of the Privy Chamber – the one-eyed Francis Bryan, Nicholas Carew, Edward Neville, Arthur Pole, Henry Norris and William Coffin – were dismissed for being too 'familiar and homely' with Henry and 'not meet to be suffered for the king's honour'.

The underlying cause was not just the scale of Henry's mounting gambling debts. Although some blamed Wolsey for the purge, it seems more likely that the group's behaviour had offended some of the more conservative elements at court. Some of them had returned from a boisterous diplomatic mission to France in the autumn of 1518 during which they had

> ridden disguised through Paris throwing eggs, stones and other foolish trifles at the people ...
>
> And when these young people came again into England, they were all French in eating, drinking and apparel and yes, in French vices and brags so that all the [nobles] in England were by them laughed at.[101]

There was a more serious – and more important – casualty to come.

The proud and powerful Sir Edward Stafford, Third Duke of Buckingham, was riding for a fall with his sovereign. Up to now, he had been a regular partner in energetic games of tennis against the younger Henry (£14 was lost in a wager with the king in 1519) and had sumptuously entertained him at his home in Penshurst, Kent, in August 1518.

But Henry had deliberately isolated him from any political power. The duke may have been a member of the king's Council, but he attended meetings only infrequently.[102] By 1520, Buckingham was falling out of royal favour because of jealousy over his wealth,[103] his huge estates and concerns over his status, based on his connections by marriage[104] and, most importantly of all, his ancestry.

Henry could never completely put out of his mind the duke's dormant but compelling claim to the throne of England, which descended from Thomas of Woodstock, seventh and youngest son of Edward III. In the event of Henry having no surviving male heir, that claim would threaten the Tudor dynasty – in such a circumstance, the Venetian ambassador considered the 'very popular' duke 'might easily obtain the crown'.[105] Doubtless the king also recalled those ominous rumours about Buckingham's unbridled ambitions that circulated at his accession, and his public embarrassment about his affair with the duke's younger sister.

Perhaps the duke was aware of this antipathy and may have taken steps to demonstrate his loyalty. Probably in 1517, he had excused himself from competing in a joust against the king because of the risk 'of running against his person, for I would liever [rather] by his commandment go to Rome than do so'.[106]

Hot-tempered Buckingham had also made an enemy of Wolsey, whom he, like so many of England's old nobility, regarded as a low-born upstart who not only exerted far too much influence over Henry but had his chubby fingers in too many state and church pies. The duke was truly galled to have to be 'subservient to so base and uncivil a fellow'. He also believed him to be hostile to the aristocracy, claiming: 'My lord Cardinal is so sore with noble men, that they would be all ... his top [superiors] if the king's grace were displeased with him ... He would undo all noble men if he could.'[107]

At court, the duke was furious to see Wolsey – that 'vile and impor-tunate' man – impudently wash his hands in the water used by the king in his ritualised ablutions before dining. He snatched up the basin and angrily tipped its contents over Wolsey. The drenched minister swore a furious oath that he would shortly 'sit upon [Buckingham's] skirts' – or take him down a peg or two. The following morning Buckingham turned up at court, cheekily wearing a short doublet, explaining to the king that this garment would prevent Wolsey from extorting his revenge.[108]

There was genial laughter at this merry quip, but the cardinal never forgot a slight and could bear grudges for a season or two. Wolsey secretly warned Buckingham in 1520 that although he knew the duke was accustomed to rail (complain) against himself, the duke should be careful how 'he did use himself towards his highness'.

Late in 1520 or early 1521, Henry wrote secretly to Wolsey regarding fresh suspicions he entertained about Buckingham and some of his fellow noblemen. The king could not trust his clerks or messengers on this sensitive issue, so despite finding 'writing somewhat tedious and painful', he took the rare step of penning the short note himself 'as none other but you and I' should be aware of its contents. The king instructed his minister to

> make good watch ... on the Duke of Buckingham, on my lord of North-umberland, on my lord of Derby, on my lord of Wiltshire [Buckingham's brother] and on others which you think suspect to see what they do with this news.

No more to you at this time but *sapienti pauca* [these few words are judicious].

Written with the hand of your loving master.[109]

What this mysterious 'news' constituted is unfortunately unknown to us – but there were rumours of a plot to assassinate Wolsey in 1518 and Buckingham may have been considered a ringleader. Above all, there were his aspirations for the crown. When the duke sought Henry's permission to visit his own properties in the Welsh Marches in late 1520, his application was peremptorily refused, because of fears that he would raise a rebellion from among his tenantry and retainers.

The duke was deeply patriotic with an irrational, jingoistic hatred of the French; he greatly resented his personal expense in attending the Field of the Cloth of Gold. He was also fervently religious, founding a college in August 1514 at Thornbury, south Gloucestershire, where from 1511 he began building an impressive fortified house[110] set within a park of a thousand acres (404.69 hectares) for his deer.

In 1520, Buckingham told his Chancellor Robert Gilbert that he had been such a great sinner he was sure he lacked grace. While he may have hoped for forgiveness from his Maker, he was to receive no mercy from Henry.

While contemporary chroniclers believed Wolsey conducted a vindictive campaign against the duke[111] there is little documentary evidence for this. But the king now took a high level of interest in the duke's activities, so much so that in November 1520, Buckingham was worried that a member of his own household was 'misreporting' him to Henry.

This campaign of covert surveillance and assiduous collection of information about the duke at last bore its bitter, poisonous fruit.

On 8 April 1521, Henry summoned the duke, who was at Thornbury, to come without delay to Greenwich Palace. Buckingham, with his customary ducal largess, generously rewarded the royal messenger with a mark (13s 4d) and obediently departed for London. He was blissfully unaware that his small entourage was being followed at a distance by a group of Henry's courtiers and sergeants-at-arms, under the command of one of the king's praetorians, Sir William Compton.

Buckingham paused only to visit devoutly the Shrine of Our Lady of Eyton, near Reading, and then lodged in a hostelry at Windsor for the night. While in the building, he identified one of those shadowing his progress as Thomas Ward, a gentleman harbinger at Henry's court. Habitually forthright and direct, the duke demanded to know why he was there – but Ward would only answer that he was engaged on the king's business. Buckingham guessed his true mission in one heart-stopping moment of acuity, followed instantly by the awful logic that his life was now forfeit. Ashen-faced, he 'perceived that he could not escape. Much was he in spirit troubled that as he was at his breakfast his meat would not down.' Anyone would suffer a loss of appetite confronted with the sure knowledge that their journey would end in the Tower of London and that their chances of survival were minimal.

The duke, however, was made of stern stuff. He presented a brave face and rode on to Tothill Fields,[112] alongside Westminster, where he boarded his barge on 16 April for the last stage of his planned journey to Greenwich Palace. Minutes later he passed Wolsey's palace, York Place, and ordered his boatmen to put him ashore there, intending to confront the cardinal face to face in perhaps his last opportunity to tell him what he really thought of him. However, he was politely informed the minister was 'diseased' and could not see him. Buckingham must have felt the black clouds of Nemesis gathering around him, but he still left Wolsey's cooks a twenty-shilling tip.

> Well, said the duke, yet will I drink of my lord's wine [before] I pass. Then a gentleman of my lord's [Wolsey] brought the duke with much reverence into the cellar, where the duke drank.
>
> When he saw and perceived no cheer to him was made, he changed colour and so departed to his barge, saying to his servants, I marvel where my chancellor is, that he comes not to me.[113]

Naïve Buckingham! Gilbert, his chancellor, was already locked up in the Tower.

As the duke was rowed in stately fashion downriver towards London Bridge, his barge was intercepted by another boat, packed with one hundred of the king's Yeomen of the Guard. Their captain, Sir Henry

Marney, leapt aboard and arrested the duke in the king's name. Prisoner and escort landed at nearby Hay Wharf and marched the short distance along Thames Street to the gates of the Tower. As well as Gilbert, the duke's confessor John Delacourt and a Carthusian monk called Nicholas Hopkins were already in custody. His attendants on the barge were ordered to go to the duke's London home, the Manor of the Rose in the parish of St Lawrence Poultney.[114]

The same day the king's secretary Richard Pace wrote to Wolsey to postpone a planned visit by Thomas Ruthal, Bishop of Durham, as 'the king would not suffer him so to do, but commanded him to tarry here [at Greenwich] for the examination of certain things of Buckingham's servants'. Ruthal had sent on a letter, written on Henry's orders, to those looking after Buckingham's house.[115] (The letter has not survived, but knowing the king's habits on such occasions, it probably contained orders for them to inventory and value the duke's possessions.)

The charges were quickly drawn up and his trial by seventeen peers, presided over by his old friend Thomas Howard, Second Duke of Norfolk, began at eight o'clock on the morning of Monday 13 May at Westminster.[116] The executioner's axe – the blade turned away – was carried before Buckingham as he was brought into court to stand at the bar, between Sir Thomas Lovell, Constable of the Tower, and Sir Richard Cholmeley, its deputy lieutenant. The clerk of the court opened proceedings:

> Sir Edward, Duke of Buckingham, hold up your hand.
>
> You are indicted of high treason in that you traitorously have conspired and imagined as far as in thee lay, to shorten the life of our sovereign lord the king.[117]
>
> Of this treason how will you acquit yourself?

Buckingham answered formally: 'By my peers.'[118] Then the charges against him were read, and the duke snapped: 'It is false and untrue and [was] conspired and forged to bring me to my death and that I will prove.'[119]

Wolsey had lined up Gilbert, Delacourt and Charles Knyvet (a distant relation whom Buckingham had earlier sacked as his surveyor) as witnesses against their master over the next three days. There was much talk of Nicholas Hopkins, a monk from the Carthusian priory at Hinton, Somerset, who was notorious for his cryptic prophecies which held the duke spellbound. The monk several times predicted that Buckingham 'would have all and that he should endeavour to obtain the love of the community'; that 'the king would have no male issue of his body'; and that 'if anything but good should happen to the king … the duke was next in succession to the crown of England'.

Buckingham had given generously to the Carthusians and warned his chaplain to keep these predictions secret under seal of confession, saying prophetically 'that if the king knew of it, I will be altogether destroyed'.[120]

Knyvet testified that the duke planned

what his father intended to do to Richard III at Salisbury when he made suit to come to the king's presence, having upon him secretly a knife, so that when kneeling before the king he would have risen suddenly and stabbed him.

In saying this, the duke put his hand treasonably upon his dagger and said that if he were so ill-treated he would do his best to execute his purpose.

This he swore by the blood of our Lord.

There was more damning testimony. Knyvet heard of Hopkins' predictions and warned that the monk might be deluded by the devil 'and [that] it was evil to meddle with such things':

The duke said it could not do him harm and feloniously rejoiced in the words of the monk, adding that if it had happened well with the king when he was last sick, the duke would have cut off the heads of my lord cardinal, Sir Thomas Lovell and others, also that he would rather die than be ordered as he was.

Later Buckingham was walking in the gallery of his house at Bletchingly, Surrey, with his son-in-law Sir George Neville, Lord Abergavenny. He declared that if the king should die, he 'meant to have the rule in England, whoever would say the contrary'. If Abergavenny had opposed this, Buckingham 'would fight with him in that quarrel and strike him on the head with his sword. This he affirmed with great oaths.'[121]

Gilbert's deposition claimed that the duke believed the Tudor family lay under a curse because of Henry VII's execution of the Earl of Warwick, back in 1499, and God would punish them 'by not suffering the king's issue to prosper, as appeared by the death of his son [Prince Henry] and that his daughters prosper not and that he had no issue male'.

> The chancellor had heard Buckingham say several times that Wolsey was an [id]olater, taking counsel from a spirit how he might contin[ue to have th]e king's favour and that he was the king's bawd, showing him [what w]omen were most wholesome and best of complexion and that his life was so abominable that God would not allow it to continue.

Furthermore, he had heard the duke complain 'he had done as good service as any man and was not rewarded and that the king gave fees and offices to boys, rather than noblemen'.[122]

The witnesses were then carted off to the Tower without Buckingham being able to cross-examine them, but Norfolk told the prisoner at the bar:

> The king ... has commanded that you shall have his laws ministered with favour and right to you.
> If you have anything to say, you shall be heard.[123]

Buckingham certainly did and his angry words tumbled out for more than an hour, refuting the charges with surprising eloquence.[124] He alleged that of all men, Norfolk's own heir, the Earl of Surrey, his son-in-law, 'hated him the most and had hurt him the most to the king's majesty'.[125]

Although the jury of peers debated 'a great while', the verdict, delivered on 16 May, was a foregone conclusion.

The king clearly considered Buckingham guilty and we have some curious evidence to support that statement. On the reverse of an earlier private letter from Rome to Richard Pace, Henry's secretary had jotted down some obscure memoranda to himself. At the top is this sentence, written in Latin: 'The king is convinced that Buckingham will be found guilty and be condemned by the lords and for this matter and for the affairs of Ireland, a Parliament will be summoned.' Other notes follow – the duke's confessor and the monk Hopkins had been sent to the Tower; 'Arthur Pole [Buckingham's cousin] has been expelled [from] the court'; and finally 'as to the Countess of Salisbury [whose daughter Henry Stafford, the duke's son married], nothing has yet been decided on account of her noble birth and many virtues'.[126]

When the peers returned, each was asked by Norfolk: 'What say you of Sir Edward, Duke of Buckingham, touching these high treasons?' Beginning with the junior baron, each one solemnly placed his right hand on his breast and replied: 'I say that he is guilty.' Every time, Norfolk scribbled each peer's verdict on a small piece of parchment in his narrow, cramped handwriting: *Dicit quod et culpabilis* – 'Asserted guilty'.[127]

Buckingham was brought back into court from a nearby house called Paradise where he had awaited the verdict. Norfolk sat silent, agitated and sweating profusely. He seemed to compose himself, bowed low to the court and stared hard at the prisoner. Then, breathing deeply, he declared: 'Sir Edward, you have heard how you are indicted of high treason. You pleaded not guilty, putting yourself to the judgement of your peers [who] have found you guilty.' Norfolk suddenly burst into torrents of tears, sobbing uncontrollably. It was some time before he could bring himself to pronounce on his friend Buckingham the sentence reserved for traitors –

> to be hanged, cut down alive, your members to be cut off and cast into the fire, your bowels burnt before you, your head smitten off and your body quartered and divided at the king's will. And God have mercy on your soul. Amen.[128]

The axe was turned so that its edge faced him. Buckingham denied he was a traitor. 'I was never one, but my lords, I nothing malign [you] for that you have done to me but the eternal God forgive you my death and I do.' He was then led away to a barge. Lovell wanted him to sit on the cushions and carpet provided, but the duke refused, saying, 'When I went to Westminster I was Duke of Buckingham, now I am but ... the most caitiff [wretched prisoner] of the world.' They landed at the Temple stairs and Buckingham was led through the city amid crowds who 'wept and lamented'.[129]

At about eleven the following morning Buckingham was escorted out of the Tower by the Sheriffs of London, Sir John Skevington and John Kyme, and led to the public scaffold on Tower Hill. Buckingham climbed the steps with resolution and asked the crowd to pray for him, 'trusting to die the king's true man, whom, through his own negligence and lack of grace, he had offended'. Darkly, he warned his fellow nobles to beware his fate.

Henry had commuted the sentence to simple beheading, as an act of mercy. It still took three blows to sever his head. Six Augustinian friars picked up Buckingham's bloodstained body and head, placed them in a crudely made wooden coffin and carried it off to the Church of the Austin Friars for burial.

The king spent that day at Greenwich. As he sat in a chair in his gallery in the palace, recuperating from a bout of malaria, Wolsey urged him to send 'letters of consolation and credence' to Buckingham's widow and son. Henry refused to answer and a few days later Wolsey repeated his request, adding: 'If you think them convenient to pass, I remit that to you.' We do not know whether they were ever sent and Henry left Greenwich shortly afterwards on a pilgrimage to the Shrine of Master John Shorn at North Marston, Buckinghamshire, to give thanks for his recovery.[130]

Wolsey provided details of the case to English ambassadors abroad:

> The king has for some time known the duke to be ill-disposed and recently he has been detected in treason against the king's person and succession, especially against the princess with whose alliance in France he was much displeased. These things being proved and at last confessed by himself, he has been executed according to his demerits.[131]

As befits all traitors, Buckingham was attainted and his goods and lands confiscated by the crown under an Act of Parliament dated 31 July 1523.[132] Some properties, however, were returned to the duke's son, Henry Stafford, Earl of Wiltshire, shortly afterwards but he was not restored to his full titles until 1547. The prophetic monk was exiled from his religious house at Hinton and was to be 'sent to some other place of their religion to be punished for his offences'.[133] He is believed to have died in the Tower, broken-hearted at the fate of his patron.

There remained one last immediate living threat to the Tudor crown.

Richard de la Pole, youngest brother of the Earl of Lincoln, executed in 1487 by Henry VIII, and of the Earl of Suffolk, beheaded by Henry VIII in 1513, had been traitorously serving the interests of France in his attempts to claim the English throne for the Yorkists.

In 1514, he had been given command of 12,000 German mercenaries to defend Brittany but this was a cover for an invasion attempt that never left St Malo. Another abortive invasion was planned in 1523 and two years later, Pole found himself fighting for Francis I of France outside the walls of the city of Pavia in central Lombardy. The Imperial forces of Charles V inflicted a crushing defeat on the French and Pole was killed by German *Landsknechte* as his troops were slaughtered around him.[134]

In London Henry was told of the massacre and the capture of the French king. He enquired of the messenger: 'And Richard de la Pole?' The messenger replied: 'The White Rose is dead in battle ... I saw him dead with all the others.'

The king cried out in delight: 'God have mercy upon his soul! All the enemies of England are gone.'[135] And he ordered more wine for the courier.

9

THE KING'S
'SCRUPULOUS CONSCIENCE'

'If it be determined ... that our marriage was against God's law and clearly void then I shall not only sorrow the departing from so good a lady and loving companion but much more ... bewail my unfortunate chance that I have so long lived in adultery to God's great displeasure and have no true heir of my body to inherit this realm.'

Henry VIII's speech to the Lord Mayor and Aldermen of London, Bridewell, 8 November 1528.[1]

Between January 1510 and July 1518, Katherine of Aragon became pregnant six times. We have seen how she initially miscarried of a girl child and then on New Year's Day 1511 delivered a boy, christened Henry, who lived just fifty-three days. There are unsubstantiated reports of a live birth in September 1513 shortly after the victory at Flodden but if these are true, the male child must have died within hours.[2] Another boy was stillborn in November/December 1514 when Katherine was distraught at Henry's angry reproaches over her father's 'ill faith' and treachery.[3]

But at four in the morning of Monday 18 February 1516 at Greenwich, a daughter was delivered who survived the perils of primitive Tudor post-natal care. Six days later, the king declared confidently to the Venetian ambassador Sebastian Giustinian: 'We are both young. If it was a daughter this time, by the grace of God, the sons will follow.'[4]

The baby was named Mary – after Henry's younger sister – on

Wednesday 20 February in a christening in a temporary wooden structure, hung with Arras tapestries, erected outside the door of the Franciscan Observant Friars' church adjoining Greenwich Palace. Wolsey was chosen godfather as Henry did not want to single out one of the European heads of state for the role and thus offend the others.[5]

A physical manifestation of Henry's conviction that he would eventually have a son was included in the heraldic arms set in the façade of the gatehouse of a grand new mansion the king was building at Beaulieu, near Boreham, in Essex.[6] The emblems above the Tudor dragon and greyhound are Henry's red rose and Katherine's pomegranate, shown with its seeds bursting out, itself a representation of her fecundity. But one pomegranate has a Tudor rose emerging from it – symbolising the hoped-for birth of a male heir.[7]

Fourteen months later, the queen was pregnant yet again. On 1 July 1518, the king wrote to Wolsey from Woodstock in Oxfordshire:

> I trust the queen my wife be with child. I am ... loath to repair London-wards because about this time is partly of her dangerous times and because of that I would [move] her as little as I may now.
>
> My lord, I write this to [you] not as an assured thing but as a thing wherein I have great hope and likelihoods.[8]

When the king returned to the hunting lodge four days later, his Latin secretary Pace reported that 'the queen welcomed him with a big belly'.[9] In October Giustinian told the Doge: 'The queen is near her delivery which is anxiously looked for.'[10] But on 10 November, Katherine was delivered of a dead daughter, one month off her full term, 'to the vexation of as many who know it', according to Giustinian, as 'the entire nation looked for a prince'.[11]

Henry's hopes of a crop of robust Tudor sons with Katherine were never fulfilled. If they had been, England's subsequent political and religious history would have developed along very different paths.

There has been speculation that the queen's tragic record of one miscarriage and four stillbirths was due to Henry having had a balanced translocation of his chromosomes. His sperm cells might have had extra – or missing – genetic material, which can sometimes cause miscarriages. After almost five centuries nothing can be asserted with any certainty, and even with modern medical investigation it is frequently difficult to identify precisely why recurrent miscarriages or spontaneous abortions occur. Potential causes are legion but the queen's natal problems could have been caused simply by viral infection or nutritional imbalances. Given the lack of hygiene and the unhealthy diets of the period, she may have suffered from Listeriosis, which can trigger spontaneous abortion or stillbirth, a disease caused by the bacterium *Listeria monocytogenes*, found in stream water and some food. This also manifests itself as meningitis or pneumonia in newborns, which possibly killed the two boys that Katherine delivered in 1511 and 1513.[12] Her unhappy travails are hardly startling given the prevalent infant mortality rate, which was almost two hundred in 1,000 during the Tudor era.[13]

Regular pregnancies had taken a huge physical toll on the queen. In October 1519 an ungallant Giustinian described Katherine (whom he seldom saw) as 'not handsome, though she had a very beautiful complexion. She is religious and as virtuous as words can express.'[14] Other Venetian envoys were still less gracious – reporting that Henry 'has an old deformed wife while he himself is young and handsome'.[15]

The queen was now aged thirty-three and in Tudor times this was an advanced age for childbirth. She was growing stout (Plate 15) and as she approached the menopause, any chance of safeguarding Henry's uncertain dynasty looked increasingly slender. In his desperation, the king promised God that he would crusade against the infidel Turks if he could have a male heir born in wedlock.

What redoubled the king's frustration and disappointment was his success in siring a bastard son with Elizabeth (or Bessie) Blount, the eighteen-year-old blonde daughter of Sir John Blount, a member of his Spears bodyguard. She came to court as one of Katherine's maids of honour[16] (a misnomer if ever there was one) probably through the influence of her cousin and Henry's childhood mentor William Blount, Lord Mountjoy, appointed Chamberlain to the queen in 1512, or the family's earlier links with Prince Arthur's court at Ludlow. Elizabeth's vivacity and her talents for dancing and singing caught Henry's eye, as well as her singular beauty. She was also well educated and is known to have possessed a copy of the poet John Gower's *Confessio Amantis* ('The Lover's Confession') written in *c*.1386–93 at the request of Richard II.[17] Suffolk, away in France on secret diplomatic duties in October 1514, knowingly asked Henry to pass on his best wishes to 'Mistress Blount',[18] who probably became the king's mistress about this time.[19] One can envisage the leer on Suffolk's face as he penned the words.

In Rome, there was scurrilous talk of the king being merely 'a young-ling, [who] cares for nothing but girls and hunting and wastes his father's patrimony'.[20] Later, Thomas Howard, Third Duke of Norfolk, praised the queen's 'great modesty and patience' over the king 'being continually inclined to *amours*'.[21] Henry was often promiscuous during the last stages of Katherine's pregnancies (when vigorous, energetic intercourse could endanger the foetus) and her last in 1518 was no exception. Elizabeth Blount's condition dictated that her last appearance at court came on 3 October 1518. Her child was born on 15 June, far away from prying, pruient eyes, at the Augustinian priory of St Lawrence at Blackmore, near Ingatestone, Essex, in a residence alongside the churchyard named 'Jericho' – an epithet for a 'house of pleasure' reputedly utilised by the king.[22] The child, named Henry Fitzroy, was taken into regal care and later provided with his own household. Bessie was safely married off to Gilbert Talboys in 1522 and provided with a generous dowry of lands and property in Lincolnshire and Yorkshire by a Parliamentary Act approved compliantly by both houses.[23] She continued to receive tokens of royal favour between June 1522 and January 1539 and in 1531 a New Year's gift from Henry consisted of a silver-gilt cup weighing thirty-five ounces (992 g).

Years later, a critic of Wolsey's ministry commented sarcastically:

> We have begun to encourage the young gentlewomen of the realm to be our concubines by the well marrying of Bessie Blount whom we would yet by sleight have married much better than she is and for that purpose changed her name.[24]

But Henry was not the great libertine with an insatiable debauched appetite that some fiction writers would have us believe. Most of his adventures were mere flirtatious dalliances rather than serious affairs;

more romantic courtly love than heavy-breathing lust.

In the European royal lechery stakes, he runs out a poor finisher behind his brother monarchs. Francis I of France maintained a string of constantly changing 'sweethearts' as well as two official mistresses at his court. The dark-haired Françoise de Foix, Comtesse de Chateaubriand, held the king's affections from 1519 but was supplanted seven years later by the blonde Anne de Pisseleu d'Heilly, Duchess d'Estampes, who wielded formidable political power in Renaissance France. Francis had also sampled the delights of Mary Boleyn soon after she arrived in Paris in the bridal entourage of Mary Tudor in 1514, brutally labelling her in March 1536 as *per una grandissima ribalda et infame sopre tutte*, 'a singular great whore and more notorious than all the others' – and this in a court infamous across Europe for its wantonness and immorality.[25] The Emperor Charles V also maintained a stable of mistresses, including Johanna Maria van der Gheynst, who bore him a daughter, and Barbara Blomberg, who had his son. Thus *La chéri du Roi*, 'the darling of the king', had a recognised and not entirely dishonourable position in sixteenth-century royal courts.

Henry now at least knew he was physically capable of producing a male heir and he must often have pondered over what seemed like a curse on his marriage with Katherine.

His elder sister Margaret had married that 'young witless fool' Archibald Douglas, Sixth Earl of Angus, after her first husband James IV of Scotland was killed at Flodden. In 1519 she decided to desert Angus after being parted from him for six months[26] and Henry was priggishly aghast at her dissolute behaviour. He sent Margaret a stern letter remonstrating about the separation and her 'suspicious living' and sent an Observant Friar, Henry Chadworth, to correct and amend her morals.[27] In 1526 when she began divorce proceedings in a Papal Court so she could marry the dashing young courtier Henry Stewart, the king lectured her on her 'inevitable damnation'. He warned Margaret that her very soul was endangered unless 'as in conscience you are bound under peril of God's everlasting indignation' she relinquished 'the adulterous company with him that is not nor may not be of right your husband'.[28]

Henry was therefore a king with a complex, almost schizophrenic character, obsessed about the future of his dynasty. Aside from his tantrums and his later descent into ruthless, despotic cruelty, the most singular aberration in his personality was breathtaking hypocrisy. He was happy to behave promiscuously when Katherine was in the advanced stages of pregnancy, but conversely, he was prudishly censorious of any immorality amongst those close to him, like his friend William Compton, cited in an ecclesiastical court in 1527 for living in open adultery with a married woman – no less than Henry's former paramour, Anne Hastings.[29] In 1536 he clapped his twenty-one-year-old niece Lady Margaret Douglas[30] in the Tower after she secretly married Lord Thomas Howard, youngest half-brother to the Third Duke of Norfolk. Her would-be groom followed her into the fortress where he died the following year. Lady Margaret was later pardoned – 'considering that copulation had not taken place', but was dispatched to the spartan discipline of the Bridgettine nunnery at Syon Abbey in Isleworth, Middlesex, to improve her spiritual health.[31]

Mary Boleyn had returned to England from France in April 1515 and secured a place in Katherine of Aragon's household, probably through the influence of her diplomat father Sir Thomas Boleyn. (Katherine was evidently a poor judge of morality in her ladies.) She married William Carey, an Esquire of the Body in Henry's Privy Chamber,[32] on Saturday 4 February 1520, when she was in her early twenties. Henry was the guest of honour and gave the couple a less than generous wedding present of 6s 8d. A series of grants to Carey from early in 1522 to 1526 (some of the properties formerly owned by Buckingham) suggests that Henry had taken his wife to his bed and her cuckolded husband was being amply rewarded for both his silence and his discretion. One of the last royal gifts was Carey's appointment as Keeper of the manor, garden and tower of Greenwich Palace.[33] One account reveals that Henry 'in his barge [went] from Westminster to Greenwich to visit a fair lady whom the king loved who was lodged in the tower in the park' – probably Mary Boleyn.[34] Not that the king was always so discreet: a ship was brazenly named after his mistress in September 1523.

Mary had two children, a daughter called Catherine born in about 1524 and a son significantly named Henry, born on 4 March 1526. On the premise that Henry's psyche demanded chastity from his sexual partners[35] it has been suggested that both children were his.[36] Years later in April 1535, when Mary's sister Anne was queen, John Hale, the elderly, ailing vicar of Isleworth, recalled having 'young Master Carey' pointed out to him as 'our sovereign lord, the king's son by ... the queen's sister, whom the queen may not suffer to be in court'.[37] John Leek, a priest at nearby Syon Abbey, also claimed that Henry had 'meddled' with Lady Elizabeth Boleyn, Mary and Anne's mother.[38] This must have been commonplace gossip, as in 1533, in one of those little dramatic tableaux so redolent of Henry's reign, Sir George Throgmorton was unwise enough to tell the king: '"I fear if you did marry ... Anne you [would] have meddled both with the mother and sister." And his grace said: "Never with the mother!" And [Thomas Cromwell] standing by, said: "Nor with the sister either – and therefore put that out of your head."'[39]

Carey died of the sweating sickness on 23 June 1528 and the king granted Anne Boleyn the wardship of Mary's son Henry immediately afterwards, warning her that her sister was in 'extreme necessity' and it was her father's duty to support her.[40] If this sounds callous, it was – but Henry was now wooing Anne and felt it was high time to tidy up his relationships with the Boleyn family.[41]

The king had abandoned any hope of having further children by Katherine by the early 1520s, despite the efforts of physicians brought specially from Spain. Although he continued to treat her with the respect appropriate to her station as queen consort, he probably stopped sleeping regularly with her in 1524, after fifteen years of marriage. His ambassadors at the Imperial court referred obliquely to this realisation when they wrote to him in July 1525 that the nine-year-old Princess Mary was

> your only child at this time in whom your highness puts the hope of propagation of any posterity of your body, seeing the queen's grace has been long without child.
>
> Albeit God may send her more children, yet she is past that age in which women most commonly are wont to be fruitful and have children.[42]

This impression was publicly (some might say shamelessly) confirmed on Sunday 18 June 1525 when Henry's six-year-old bastard was created Duke of Richmond (Henry VII was Earl of Richmond before he seized the throne) at a grotesque ceremony at the newly built Bridewell Palace on the western edge of London.[43] Henry, surrounded by Wolsey, Norfolk, Suffolk and other nobles of the realm, stood beneath a canopy of estate in the presence chamber as the little boy was ushered into the room by his ladies. The king tenderly wrapped the ducal robes around the child and looped the sword belt over his shoulder.[44] Other titles were showered by a doting father upon his innocent, tousled head: Earl of Nottingham, Duke of Somerset and, perhaps in conscious mimicry of the king's own childhood, Lord Warden of the Cinque Ports, Lord Lieutenant of Ireland and Vice-Regent of the North. Properties yielding an annual income of £4,845 were also bestowed on Fitzroy. Subsequently Wolsey dutifully enquired about the health of the 'entirely beloved son, the Lord Henry Fitzroy'.[45] On the same day Sir Thomas Boleyn was created Viscount Rochford.

Henry's illegitimate son had his own extensive household at Durham House – Katherine's lonely home in those bitter years between Arthur's death and her marriage to the king – and later moved to a Yorkshire castle, Sheriff Hutton, in his purely nominal roles as Lord President of the Council of the North and Warden of the Scottish Marches. His young life was minutely organised with set menus carefully drawn up and his wardrobe inventoried. For example, from Easter to Michaelmas each year, the menu for dinner included, as a first course: beef and mutton, geese, roast capons and roast veal. For the second, there were half a lamb or kid, roast chickens, pigeons, wildfowl and a 'tart or baked [mince]meat'. For drink, there were four gallons of ale and two pitchers of wine. Cost: not to exceed 17s 1d.[46]

The renowned Greek scholar Richard Croke[47] and John Palsgrave, author of the first French grammar in English, were appointed tutors to Henry Fitzroy. A letter from the boy to Wolsey dated 4 March ?1526, was probably one of his writing exercises. The easily read note, written under dictation in the fashionable Italianate italics, pledges laboriously:

I shall, God willing, endeavour myself and apply my time for that learning
... whereby I may be more able to do unto the king's highness such service
hereafter which shall be consis[tent] with his most gracious pleasure.[48]

In 1528, the nine year old wrote to Henry asking for his own armour 'for
exercise in arms, according to my learning in Julius Caesar in which
I hope to prosper' and sought Wolsey's support for his request.[49]

It is gratifying that the boy's mother received reports on his scholastic
progress, even when one, from Palsgrave, also bemoaned the tutor's
poverty and misfortune. He informed Elizabeth Talboys in July 1529 that
'my lord of Richmond is of as good a nature, as much inclined to all
manner virtuous and honourable ... as any babe living'. The king had
told him on his appointment: 'I deliver unto you my worldly jewel. You
... Palsgrave [must] bring him up in virtue and learning.'[50] His mother
sent gifts to her son: an inventory of his possessions in 1531 recorded a
doublet and two horses given by Elizabeth.

All this fuss and public hoopla about the king's bastard was naturally
bitter gall to Katherine of Aragon. The Venetian ambassador commented:

> The queen resents the earldom and dukedom conferred on the king's
> natural son and remains dissatisfied, at the instigation, it is said, of three
> of her Spanish ladies, her chief counsellors.
>
> So the king has dismissed them [from] the court – a strong measure
> but the queen was obliged to submit and to have patience.[51]

She truly had great need of the quality of fortitude.

Katherine bore bravely the public stigmata of failure – it was the
queen's first duty, after all, to produce male heirs – and she knew full
well that her barrenness was the talk of the European courts. After
enjoying the glamour of those heady glory days early in her husband's
reign, she had been returned to a forlorn existence, isolated from public
affairs, bereft of her husband's affections and parted from him for long
periods of the court's year. If she possessed the sin of pride, events had
cruelly conspired to irrevocably and grievously injure her self-esteem
and belief.

Katherine was prematurely old, her short stature accentuating her new dumpiness, and she fell sick frequently. The queen had a soft, sweet voice which retained a strong Spanish accent. She had developed considerable resilience, tenacity and above all displayed a serene dignity, derived from generations of her pride of caste.[52] She still spent her time making (or mending) Henry's shirts, carefully embroidering the collars with fine black needlework. Much of her considerable reservoir of love was poured out on her sole surviving progeny, Princess Mary, a fair child with red-gold ringlets, who suffered frequent headaches, probably because of a sinus condition. The queen had taught her Latin and the little girl was also fluent in French, Italian and Spanish.

But even the daily delight of seeing her daughter was now denied Katherine. Mother and child had to be separated by the imperatives of state. Henry summarily sent Mary, as Princess of Wales, to Ludlow Castle to preside over her principality and the border country, as had Katherine's first husband Arthur. Margaret Pole, Countess of Salisbury, was appointed governess in her small embryo court. In October 1525, the queen wrote to Mary of her distress at their separation: 'The long absence of the king and you troubles me. My health is meetly [moderately] good.' She urged her daughter to continue her Latin studies and requested samples of her work to be sent: 'It shall be a great comfort to me to see you keep your Latin and [your] fair writing ... your loving mother.'[53]

Juan Luis Vives, the Spanish humanist scholar who enjoyed the queen's patronage, wrote a book, *De institutione feminæ Christianæ* ('The Education of a Christian Woman'), especially for Mary, containing more than two hundred maxims to protect a child's mind from dangerous worldly distractions and to preserve her 'more securely and safely than any spearman or bowman'.[54]

Katherine's isolation was not even palliated by contact with her nephew, the Emperor Charles V. In November 1526 she wrote to reproach him for ignoring her:

Most High and Powerful Lord – I cannot imagine what may be the cause of your Highness having been so angry, and having so forgotten me, that for upwards of two years I have had no letters [from Spain].

I am sure I deserve not this treatment, for such are my affection and readiness for your Highness' service that I deserved a better reward.

I cannot help doing what I consider my duty – writing whenever an opportunity offers itself, and by all those who go to Spain from these parts, begging to know ... what is the state of your precious health?[55]

Although he still had only a male heir born out of wedlock, Henry tried hard to put his qualms about his dynasty behind him. He embarked on the furious pursuit of pure pleasure in the early 1520s, hunting his way across southern England and leaving politics, diplomacy and the boring daily grind of running England to Wolsey and his Council. It was as if he had completely withdrawn from public life. As one of his courtiers reported: 'I received a packet of letters addressed to the king, which I took to his majesty immediately, but as he was going to have a shot at a stag, he asked me to keep them until the evening.'[56] Outbreaks of the plague also kept Henry on the move from house to house as he had a morbid fear of the disease. Lorenzo Orio, the new Venetian ambassador, reported in January 1526:

On account of the plague the king is moving about the island with a few of his attendants, as two of them died of the plague in his dwelling.

He leaves everything in charge of Cardinal Wolsey, who keeps a great court, and has comedies and tragedies performed.[57]

Those close to the king remained his old friends and cronies – William Compton, the one-eyed Francis Bryan, Nicholas Carew and Henry Norris. In July 1525 Henry promoted Sir Thomas More to the Chancellorship of the Duchy of Lancaster on the death of Sir Richard Wingfield. The king admired More's wit, conversation, learning and modesty.

And for the pleasure he took in his company, would his grace suddenly ... come to [More's] house at Chelsea to be merry with him.

Whither on a time, unlooked for, he came to dinner [with him] and after dinner, in a fair garden of his, walked with him by the space of an hour, holding his arm about his neck.

The young lawyer William Roper,[58] who had married Margaret, one of More's daughters by his first wife, in 1521,[59] rejoiced at the king's happiness and his close friendship with his father-in-law. But More warned of the quicksilver fickleness of Henry's favour:

> I thank our Lord I find his grace my very good lord indeed and I believe he singularly favours me as any subject with[in this] realm.
>
> Howbeit son Roper, I may tell you I have no cause to be proud thereof, for if my head [could] win him a castle in France ... it should not fail to go.[60]

His words were unhappily prophetic. A new salacious power that was to touch their lives and damage all of them – the queen, More and countless others – had now come to court.

Mary Boleyn's younger sister Anne made her debut at a court pageant on 1 March 1522 – Shrove Tuesday – staged in honour of Imperial ambassadors visiting London. She was probably aged around twenty-three.

The extravagant masque, at Wolsey's palace at York Place, was based on the theme of courtly love. Workmen had laboured twelve days to erect a large wooden castle, complete with battlements and three towers. Its green tinfoil decoration provided the name of this mock fortress: 'Chateau Vert'. Eight masked ladies were perched in the towers, dressed in white satin and wearing Milan bonnets trimmed with Venetian gold, representing the feminine virtues of Honour, Kindness, Perseverance, Bounty, Beauty, Pity, Constancy and Mercy. Considering her new role in Henry's life, it is not surprising that Mary Boleyn took the leading role of 'Beauty'. Anne played 'Perseverance'.[61] Every tower bore a banner with embroidered emblems symbolising the agonies of unrequited love: three broken hearts, a female hand gripping a man's heart and another lady's hand turning a man's heart upside down.

The allegorical roles of the opposite male attributes were led by Henry, again not unexpectedly acting as 'Amorousness'. He and his seven fellow thespians wore caps and coats of cloth of gold and tinsel and cloaks of blue satin.

Defending the ladies were eight boy choristers from the Chapel Royal,

9. Katherine of Aragon aged about twenty, *c*.1504–5. Eyes cast down, demure Katherine endured frequent periods of illness and abject poverty in the lonely years at Durham House, near Charing Cross, after the death of her young husband Arthur in 1502.

10. Henry aged about twenty-two, painted *c.*1513 – the earliest known portrait of him as King. A Venetian ambassador described him at this time as having 'a round face so very beautiful that it would become a pretty woman'.

11. Henry VIII, painted *c.*1520 at the peak of his power with everything to look forward to – military glory, prowess in the tiltyard, but where were his lusty Tudor heirs?

12. Miniature of Henry VIII, painted *c.*1525–7 by Lucas Horenbout. One of a group of six miniatures of the King painted by this artist in this period for diplomatic gifts. Half show Henry clean-shaven and the remainder with a beard: Katherine of Aragon did not like the King with a beard and insisted that he shaved it off.

13. Henry VIII jousting at the tournament to celebrate the birth of a son and heir. But his joy was short-lived: Prince Henry lived just fifty-three days before dying, probably from meningitis.

14. Battle of the Spurs, 1513. A rare taste of military success for Henry, even though it was more of a skirmish than a full-blown battle. This painting was recorded in the Royal Collection during Henry's reign and portrays English military prowess and glory.

REGIN
THER
EIVS +

A · KA
INA ·
· VXOR

ihs

15. Katherine of Aragon, painted *c*.1525, by Lucas Horenbout. The Queen was now becoming stout, her short stature emphasising her dumpiness. Regular pregnancies had taken a huge physical toll on her.

16. Anne Boleyn, painted by an unknown artist in *c*.1533–6. To modern tastes, no great beauty, but her black almond eyes were bewitching – her enemies claimed she was a sorceress who used her evil powers of magic to seduce the King.

17. Love messages written by Henry and Anne Boleyn during Mass in a Parisian *Book of Hours* c.1528. Below Christ as 'the Man of Sorrows', the King wrote in French: 'If you remember my love in your prayers as strongly as I worship you, I shall hardly be forgotten, for I am yours. Henry R. Forever'. Anne wrote a couplet in English in reply, artfully using this page with the Annunciation: 'By daily proof you shall me find/To be to you both loving and kind'.

dressed bizarrely as Indian women, representing the supposed feminine vices – Disdain, Jealousy, Scorn, Malebouche (a sharp tongue) and the like. They were invited to surrender the castle but when Disdain and Scorn piped up their staunch refusal in their treble voices, the courtiers playfully assaulted the fortress, throwing oranges, dates and 'other fruits made for pleasure' at its occupants, who stoutly defended themselves with streams of rosewater and by hurling sweetmeats at the assailants. At the climactic moment, the boy choristers clumsily retreated in their dresses, but not without three losing their hats, for which Richard Gibson, the master of the revels, had to ruefully pay 11d each.[62]

The ladies were made winsome prisoners and then both groups of gorgeously attired actors 'danced together very pleasantly' which 'much pleased' the envoys. 'When they [had] danced their fill' they removed their masks to reveal their identities and all went into a costly banquet.[63]

Anne had returned from a spell at the French court. To modern tastes, she would not be considered a great beauty: short rather than tall, with a sallow (if not swarthy) complexion, a 'bosom not much raised', a wide, sly mouth and a long neck (Plate 16). She was proud of her long brown hair and her black flashing almond eyes were compelling, if not bewitching. Anne aroused strong emotions and some were uncomplimentary about her appearance. Nicholas Sander, the Elizabethan recusant, claimed later that

> she had a projecting tooth under the upper lip and on her right hand, six fingers.
>
> There was a large wen [goitre] under her chin and ... to hide its ugliness she wore a high-[necked] dress covering her throat.[64]

Therein lies the genesis of Anne Boleyn's abominable sixth finger on her left hand, indicating to the superstitious that she was a witch or a sorceress with evil magical powers which she deployed against the king. In truth, she did have a small growth on one finger, as testified to by George Wyatt:

> There was found on the side of her nail upon one of her fingers some little show of a nail which yet was so small by the report of those that have seen her ... and was usually by her hidden.[65]

Anne Boleyn now briefly recedes from the limelight to a dim, barely seen role at Henry's court until 1527. Katherine fatally accepted her as one of her maids of honour. Her uncle, the Third Duke of Norfolk, had urged a politically expedient marriage between Anne and James Butler, one of the disorderly Irish nobility, but the Boleyns showed no great enthusiasm for this match. She had a brief affair with Henry Percy, heir to the earldom of Northumberland, and then amorously toyed with the poet Thomas Wyatt the Elder, who lived quite close to the Boleyn seat at Hever Castle, Kent, and moved in the same circles at court.

How Henry fell lock, stock and barrel for her some time in 1526 is unclear. There is one unsubstantiated story, with its elements of courtly love and obscure symbolism, that smacks of some veracity. One of Anne's attendants, Anne Gainsford, recounted how Wyatt had filched a small jewel from her mistress to wear around his neck on a ribbon. About the same time, the king also took 'from her a ring and that [he] wore upon his little finger'. Several days later Henry was playing bowls with Wyatt and other courtiers and claimed his throw had hit the jack. He pointed with his little finger wearing the ring, saying, 'Wyatt, I tell you that it's mine!' The poet pulled out Anne's jewel and used its ribbon to measure the distance between jack and wood, declaring: 'If it may like [please] your majesty to give me leave to measure it, I hope it will be mine.' The king was immediately angered, snapping, 'It may be so, but then am I deceived' – with ominous emphasis on the last word. He strode off to confront Anne, who hastily explained she had played no part in Wyatt's theft.[66]

Around eighteen months after the ennoblement of his illegitimate son, Henry must have decided to seek a decree of nullity on his marriage from Pope Clement VII.[67] He had briefly considered declaring Fitzroy his heir instead of Princess Mary, but had discarded this as a risk too far politically. The idea of Mary governing England after his death was also unacceptable to a patriarchal Tudor who understood only too well the lessons of English history.[68]

The king was still young and frenetically active and convinced himself that with another wife, the longed-for male heirs would soon fill the royal nursery. The alternatives were just too ghastly to contemplate –

Mary married off to a European ally with a subsequent union between England and a foreign crown, or worse still, a return to the anarchy of divisive civil war, such as the thirty-two bloody years of the Wars of the Roses, which were still fresh in the nation's memory.

There were also painful reminders of his own mortality. On 10 March 1524 Henry survived a perilous jousting accident as he ran against Charles Brandon, Duke of Suffolk. The king was proudly wearing new armour 'made of his own devise and fashion' but he thundered down the tiltyard vaingloriously with the visor of his helmet still up, leaving his face unprotected. Spectators cried out warningly: 'Hold! Hold!' but the horses ran on, their riders' lances menacingly levelled. Edward Hall was probably a witness:

> What sorrow it was to the people when they saw the splinters of the duke's spear strike on the king's headpiece.
>
> The duke struck the king on the brow right under the defence of the headpiece on the very skull ... [it] broke all to shivers ... all the king's headpiece was full of splinters.

Henry was lucky not to have his neck broken or his skull fractured. With typical Tudor bravado, he ran six more courses to show he was unharmed, even though his face was painfully bruised. But thereafter, he suffered headaches which became more severe in 1527–8, suggesting that he had sustained a cerebral injury.[69]

During the royal progress of that year, Henry was also confined to bed at Canterbury with 'a sore leg' – thought to be a varicose ulcer on the left leg. This was probably caused by the constrictive garter he fashionably wore below the knee, or alternatively was the result of a traumatic injury received while jousting. Thomas Vicary, a local surgeon, managed to heal the ulcer quickly and relatively painlessly.[70]

In 1525 Henry had another narrow escape while hawking near Hitchin in Hertfordshire. The king, showing off as usual, athletically vaulted over a water-filled ditch using a pole, but it suddenly broke 'so that if Edmond Moody, a footman, had not leapt into the water and lifted up his head which was fast in the clay, he [would] have drowned'.[71]

Three years later the fourth pandemic of sweating sickness struck

England – infecting 40,000 people in London alone and killing more than 2,000 of them.[72] Wolsey and the Duke of Norfolk both contracted the disease and recovered, but five members of the royal household went down with it, including the king's apothecary. Three courtiers very close to Henry died – William Compton, William Carey and Francis Poyntz. The king fled from Greenwich to Eltham and then on to the more remote of his palaces to escape the ravages of 'the sweat'. Anne Boleyn was dispatched to a quarantined existence at Hever, with Henry assuring her that 'few women or none have this malady'.[73] She and her brother George did contract a mild dose and the king thoughtfully sent William Butts, his second-best physician, to successfully treat her.[74]

God 'of His Goodness' may have preserved the king again but would death claim him before he had his son and heir? A divorce and a new wife, in Henry's eyes, grew more urgent each day.

A manuscript in the royal library provided a potentially persuasive argument to support an annulment. It is a thirteenth-century copy of the biblical Book of Leviticus produced by the monks of St Augustine's Priory in Canterbury. On folio 159 verso are the lines from chapter twenty, verse twenty-one, in Latin:

> If a man shall take his brother's wife, it is an unclean thing. He hath
> uncovered his brother's nakedness; they shall be childless.

Alongside, in the margin, is a 'manicule' or 'pilcrow', a tiny hand with a long pointing index finger, freely sketched in ink to emphasise the importance of the passage.[75] Here was the veiled reason for his lack of sons at last revealed – he had married his brother's wife clean against the law of God and His Holy Church. The king's 'scrupulous conscience', usually rarely troubled, was immediately assailed by the awful realisation that all along he had been living in mortal sin with Katherine.

Many were convinced it was Wolsey who had planted this idea in the king's mind, using John Longland, Bishop of Lincoln, to impart it during the secrecy of the royal confession.[76] For example, the new Spanish ambassador Iñigo de Mendoza claimed that 'as the finishing stroke to all his iniquities, the cardinal is scheming to bring about the queen's divorce'[77] But Wolsey, perhaps thinner skinned than he appeared, always refuted this and later asked Henry to declare publicly 'whether I have been the chief inventor or first mover of this matter unto your majesty for I am greatly suspected of all men herein'. The king replied: 'My lord cardinal I can well excuse herein ... You have been rather against me in attempting or setting forth thereof.'[78] On another occasion Wolsey said that when he heard of the divorce, he knelt humbly before the king 'in his Privy Chamber ... the space of an hour or two, to persuade him from his will and appetite but I could never bring to pass to dissuade him therefrom'.[79] Longland, for his part, maintained it was the king who raised the subject 'and never left urging him until he had won him to give his consent'.[80]

So it was all Henry's idea, and when he wanted something, nothing would deter him from grasping it. Those chilling words from Leviticus were a revelation from God Himself and the fact that he had fallen for another woman was irrelevant – merely forming the means to the all-important end of securing his dynasty.

In February 1527 the College of Cardinals in Rome wrote to Wolsey warmly complimenting him on his encouragement of Henry to defend Holy Church. It was a glowing testimonial:

> Placed as you are at such a distance and in the very corner of Christendom, in piety and affection to the Church you are superior to many who are much nearer.
>
> So long as Henry rules and has such an adviser, the ship of the Church will ride safely through the storm.[81]

Pride, they say, comes before a fall. As far as both the Vatican and Wolsey were concerned, one of the greatest falls in history was swiftly heading their way.

Like most major catastrophes, a number of small factors conspired to increase the tempo of a headlong flight to disaster.

Two months after the cardinals had heaped their praise on him, an unenthusiastic Wolsey sent his officials to Winchester to interrogate Bishop Richard Fox on the events of 1501 to 1505. The seventy-eight-year-old former minister was decrepit, completely blind and his memory lacked clarity. For two days they badgered and hectored him on whether Katherine's marriage to Arthur had been consummated and whether Henry had truly wanted to marry his brother's widow. The poor old man was stammering and hesitant in his replies to their progressively more vexed questions. The officials reported:

> He cannot speak of his own knowledge but he thinks that Henry desired the marriage and that he loved Katherine for her excellent qualities ... He does not remember that Henry, when he arrived at the age of puberty, expressly consented to, or dissented from the marriage ... but he thinks a protestation was made ... still to be found with Master Ryden, clerk of the council.

Fox, as wily as ever, refused to sign his deposition, but one of his interrogators, the lawyer Richard Wolman, signed it for him.[82]

This was not an auspicious start. Wolsey had no choice but to convene his legatine court at York Place on 17 May to covertly examine the validity of Henry's marriage to Katherine. William Warham, the seventy-seven-year-old Archbishop of Canterbury, who had voiced doubts about the marriage in 1509, acted as assessor. In his dotage, he lived in mortal terror of the king: '*Indignatio Principis mors est*,' he warned Katherine, 'the wrath of the king is death'[83] – precisely the phrase that Norfolk would later employ, in 1534, in his private conversation with Sir Thomas More.

As legate of the Holy See, it was Wolsey's duty to correct offences against the marriage laws. This, however, was no ordinary marriage and the offence no ordinary infringement. Henry sat at Wolsey's right hand, fidgeting and impatient to win the desired result. He had not dared to tell his queen of the proceedings, conducted wholly in Latin.

The cardinal began by reciting the facts of the marriage. The validity of Pope Julius's dispensation allowing Henry to wed his dead brother's wife was questioned. The king felt serious 'scruples of conscience' on the matter and, dreading God's vengeance which inevitably was wreaked upon those who disobey Him, wanted the legality of his marriage put to legatine judgement.[84] The king appointed Wolman as his counsel.

The court never pronounced. There was a fatal weakening in Wolsey's resolve: he realised that, given the notoriety of the case and its inter-national ramifications, his judgement could easily be quashed in Rome. Furthermore, it would be impossible to grant the divorce by stealth. Seeking security in numbers, he asked the most learned theologians in England – amongst them John Fisher, Bishop of Rochester, Longland, Bishop of Lincoln, and Cuthbert Tunstall, Bishop of London – for their opinions on the issue. Fisher replied robustly that there was no sound reason why the marriage should have been prohibited and 'considering the fullness of authority given by our Lord to the Pope, who can deny that the latter may give a dispensation for any serious cause?'[85] Not helpful.

It was therefore no cut-and-dried case. Furthermore, news of an unexpected problem stunned London on 1 June. Rome had been sacked by Imperial troops during one of those endless wars on Italian soil and Pope Clement VII and his cardinals had fled for safety into the Castello St Angelo, overlooking the River Tiber. One observer wrote:

> What Goths, what Vandals, what Turks were ever like this army of the Emperor in the sacrilege they have committed? They strewed on the ground the sacred body of Christ [consecrated hosts], trod under foot the relics of the saints to steal their ornaments. No church or monastery was spared. They violated nuns amid the cries of their mother [superiors].[86]

It would hardly be business as usual in the Vatican.

On 22 June Henry finally summoned up enough courage to admit to his queen that he planned to divorce her on the grounds that they had been living in mortal sin for eighteen years. This being the opinion of the churchmen he had consulted, he said, she should now name the English nunnery to which she would retire gracefully, while yet retaining her dignity.

It was a forlorn hope, to expect her to go quietly. Katherine burst into floods of tears 'and being too much agitated to reply' Henry tried to console her by weakly promising 'that all should be done for the best' before fleeing her apartments, thoroughly chastened. The Spanish envoy Mendoza heard more about the confrontation:

The king begged her to keep secrecy upon what he had told her. Not that the people of England are ignorant of the king's intentions, for the affair is [as] notorious as if it had been proclaimed by the public crier, but they cannot believe that he will ever carry so wicked a purpose into effect.

Katherine wanted her nephew Charles V to make 'every possible effort ... with the Pope to deprive the cardinal of his legatine powers' – a shrewd move, since Pope Clement VII was virtually in the Emperor's pocket. Mendoza coloured his dispatch with some wishful thinking:

There is so much feeling expressed here about the queen's divorce ... that should 6,000 or 7,000 men land on the coast of Cornwall to espouse [her] cause, 40,000 Englishmen would at once join them ...

A cold douche of realism then quenched his righteous indignation and he added the cautionary ' ... though popular favour often fails when put to the test'.[87]

Henry, with a strange sense of detachment from the hornet's nest he had disturbed, then went off hunting in Hertfordshire and Essex, entertaining a large party at his house at Beaulieu. Sir William Fitz-william, Treasurer of the Household, wrote despairingly to Wolsey:

The king is keeping a very great and expensive house for here are lodged the Duke of Norfolk and his wife, the Duke of Suffolk, the Marquis of Exeter, the Earls of Oxford, Essex and Rutland, Viscounts Fitzwalter and Rochford ... and others.

I and the other officers intended to reduce the expenses this summer but I do not see how this can be done.

The king is merry and in good health and hunts daily.[88]

Wolsey counselled his master to handle the queen 'both gently and docilely'[89] before he scurried majestically off through France to a con-vocation of refugee cardinals in Avignon in an abortive attempt to reorganise church governance, as Clement was *hors de combat*. As he rode, he was 'hourly musing' on Henry's 'great and secret affair' and on how to free the king from his 'pensive and dolorous life' for the 'continuance of your health and the surety of your realm and succession'.

Pausing breathlessly at Abbeville only to dash off a letter to the king, he wrote that

> I consider the Pope's consent must be gained in case the queen should decline my jurisdiction or the approbation of the cardinals be had.
>
> For the first, the Pope's deliverance will be necessary, for the other the convocation of the cardinals in France.
>
> If the Pope were delivered, I doubt not he would be easily induced to do everything to your good satisfaction and purpose.[90]

Meanwhile, Henry's affair with Anne was gathering momentum. Seventeen of his love letters to her survive, beginning with one preserved in the Vatican Library, probably dating from January 1527 and written in French, with a few crossings-out. The king was delighted by her New Year's gift of a bespoke trinket – a tiny model of a ship crewed by a single girl – given possibly to heal a lover's tiff. Henry wrote wistfully:

> The proofs of your affection are such . . . that they constrain me ever truly to honour, love and serve you . . .
>
> Praying you also that if ever I have in any way done you offence that you will give me the same absolution that you ask, ensuring you that henceforth my heart shall dedicate to you alone, greatly desirous that so my body could be as well, as God can bring to pass if it pleases Him.[91]

This now had gone much further than courtly love.

But Henry was unsure of where he stood with Anne Boleyn. An early letter prayed her to

> expressly certify me of your whole mind concerning the love between us two. I must ensure me of this answer having been now above one whole year struck with the dart of love, not being assured either of failure or of finding place in your heart . . .
>
> Which last point has kept me for some little time from calling you my mistress, since if you do not love me in a way which is beyond common affection, that name in no way belongs to you, for it denotes a singular love, far removed from the common.[92]

The king was not at this stage offering marriage – rather the status of official royal mistress, copying the French royal fashion.[93] But that would not solve his problems of a male heir; he already had one royal bastard in his form book.

Then, amid showers of expensive jewellery lavished on the dark-haired girl, marriage with her became Henry's all-consuming ambition. A ring set with emeralds was given to Anne during Henry's stay at Beaulieu that August. This was the first of many such costly trinkets during the following months: 'a diamond in a brooch of Our Lady of Boulogne'; 'nineteen diamonds for her head'; two bracelets set with ten diamonds and eight pearls; 'two diamonds on two hearts for her head' and so on.[94]

In another billet-doux to Anne, Henry complained that the brief time spent parted from her felt 'like a whole fortnight' and that his letter was shorter than usual 'because of a pain in my head'. He ended his sickly-sweet note: 'Wishing myself specially in an evening in my sweetheart's arms, whose pretty dubbys [breasts] I trust shortly to cusse [kiss]'.[95]

Henry scribbled a message in French to Anne on a page portraying Christ as the 'Man of Sorrows' in his prayer book during Mass in the Chapel Royal: 'If you remember my love in your prayers as strongly as I worship you I shall hardly be forgotten for I am yours. Henry R. Forever.' Anne replied in a hastily written English couplet: 'By daily proof you shall me find/To be to you both loving and kind.' Calculatingly, perhaps, her notes were written below an illustration of the Annunciation when the angel Gabriel told the Virgin Mary she would have a son (Plate 17).[96]

Some time in the late summer of 1527 the king ignored Wolsey's advice and sent the experienced diplomat William Knight to Rome on a mission with three secret objectives. Firstly, he was to obtain papal annulment of the marriage to Katherine and secondly, absolution of Henry's sin in living with her as man and wife. The third objective was yet more controversial and damning as, implicitly, Henry was acknowledging his earlier adultery and his desire to marry Anne Boleyn as soon as possible. Ironically, to achieve that, papal dispensation was required for this second marriage as Anne was 'a woman related to himself in the first degree of affinity' as the sister of his former bedmate Mary Boleyn. No surprise then that the contents of the letter that Knight was to hand over to Clement VII were kept secret, 'which no man doth know but they ... will never disclose it to any man living for any craft [subterfuge] the Cardinal or any other can find'.[97]

The fact that this was done behind Wolsey's back while he was away in France must signal Henry's avid desire for Anne. The cardinal quickly got wind of the plan and of rumours at court that the king believed he was dragging his heels over the divorce. He wrote an excruciatingly subservient letter to Henry from Compiegne on his way back to England:

I shall never be found but as your most humble, loyal and faithful obedient servant ... [enduring] the travails and pains which I daily and hourly sustain without any regard to the continuance of my life and health which is only preserved by the assured trust of your gracious love and favour ... I intend to depart hence ... continuing my journey towards your highness with such diligence as my old and [cracked] body may endure.

There was never lover more desirous of the sight of his lady than I am of your most noble and royal person.[98]

By the time Wolsey arrived back at court, he found the king with Anne and willing to allow him into his presence only with her approval.[99] It was an early portent of the shape of things to come.

Clement VII had now escaped his enforced confinement, but he was still caught on the prongs of a painful regal pitchfork: should he grant Henry, his 'Defender of the Faith', all he desired, based on the grounds of an imperfect dispensation by his predecessor, or reject the divorce and so placate Katherine's nephew, the all-powerful Emperor Charles V? As usual, prevarication was the papal answer. Despite intense rival diplomatic activity by both English and Imperial agents, the Vatican flaccidly proposed a legatine commission to examine the validity of Henry's marriage, appointing the gout-ridden Cardinal Lorenzo Campeggio to limp his way across Europe to preside, with Wolsey, over proceedings in London. Campeggio was the official 'protector' of England in the Vatican and was the absentee Bishop of Salisbury. He was a heavy, sluggish and tired man with a long straggling beard, but his appearance hid a clever expert in canonical law.[100] Henry soon offered him the lucrative bishopric of Durham as an incentive for making the right decision. Campeggio, however, had three secret strategies from the Pope to pursue: firstly to persuade the king to drop the idea of divorce; secondly to persuade the queen to enter a nunnery; and thirdly, to proceed as slowly as possible.[101]

It was glaringly apparent that Katherine enjoyed vocal popular support as a spurned queen and on Sunday 8 November 1528, Henry summoned his counsellors and leading London citizens to Bridewell to hear his sanitised version of events.

> Although it has pleased almighty God to send us a fair daughter ... begotten to our great comfort and joy, yet it has been told to us by diverse great clerks that she is neither a lawful daughter nor her mother our lawful wife but that we have lived together abominably and detestably in open adultery.
>
> Think you, my lords, that these words touch not my body and soul, think you that these doings do not daily and hourly trouble my conscience and vex my spirits?

Katherine was a woman

> of most gentleness, of most humility and buxomness, yes, and of all good qualities ... she is without comparison as I this twenty years almost have had the true experiment. If I were to marry again, if the marriage might be good, I would choose her above all other women.
>
> But if it be determined by judgement that our marriage was against God's law and clearly void, then I shall not only sorrow the departing from so good a lady and loving companion, but much more lament and bewail my unfortunate chance that I have so long lived in adultery to God's great displeasure, and have no true heir of my body to inherit this realm.
>
> These be the sores that vex my mind. These be the pangs that trouble my conscience. For these griefs I seek a remedy.

The king failed to win their sympathy, still less their support. The chronicler Hall reported that some of Henry's audience sighed and said nothing. Others were sorry to hear the king so troubled in his conscience. Others that favoured the queen much sorrowed that this matter was now opened and so every man spoke as his heart served him.[102]

Campeggio had finally reached London in October 1528. Anne Boleyn had been installed in a fine suite of rooms in Greenwich Palace conveniently adjoining the king's own apartments. But Henry, for the sake of appearances, resumed eating with Katherine at table and sometimes shared her bed. She made 'such cheer as she has always done in her greatest triumphs; nor to see them together could anyone have told there was anything the matter', according to the French ambassador, Jean du Bellay.[103] By 2 December Henry had tired of such polite niceties and Katherine had been ignominiously packed off to Hampton Court.[104]

He resorted to a blatantly populist move to distract attention from the divorce, issuing a commission the following day to investigate how many aliens were trading in London. Only ten alien households for each trade were permitted and the remainder had to close down their businesses, work under Englishmen or quit the realm. The French ambassador estimated this would remove 15,000 foreigners from London but his Spanish counterpart believed that up to twice this number would be deported.[105]

As the matter dragged on, month after month, Clement VII's secretary in Rome, Giovanni Sanga, told Campeggio of the Pope's utter frustration and weariness over the king's marriage:

> Would to God the cardinal [Wolsey] had allowed the matter to take its course [at his legatine court in 1527] because if the king had come to decision without the Pope's authority, whether wrongly or rightly, it would have been without blame or prejudice to His Holiness.

Sanga added:

> It would greatly please the Pope if the queen could be induced to enter some religion [nunnery].
>
> Although this course would be portentous and unusual, he could more

readily entertain the idea, as it would involve the injury of only one person.[106]

But Katherine was not going to be shunted off into a convent merely to please the Pope. At stake was the justice of the queen's cause before God, her own pride, the legitimacy of her daughter Mary and her rightful position as the king's lawful heir.

Campeggio, amid this maelstrom of intrigue and conspiracy, suffered 'infinite agitation of mind' as well as a crippling attack of the gout in his knee. The weather, even that of an English summer, was too cold for his Italian blood and he complained of 'having to wear winter clothes and use fires as if it were winter'. He also feared pestilence: 'The plague continued vigorously and there is some fear of the sweating sickness.' It says something of Henry's grim determination to seal an annulment that he overcame his normally rampant phobia about the plague to press his case.

Wolsey visited Campeggio one day at dawn while he was still in bed to discuss events and then at nine o'clock Katherine arrived to make her confession, asserting firmly that she came to Henry an 'intact and uncorrupted maid'. The queen intended 'to live and die in the estate of matrimony to which God had called her' and 'although she should be torn limb from limb, [nothing] should induce her to alter this resolution'.[107]

As the volume of paper accumulated, delay followed delay, much to Henry's vexation.[108] At last he lost patience and on 30 May 1529 authorised Wolsey and Campeggio to proceed with the public trial of his marriage with Katherine. The two cardinals rejected Katherine's appeal to Rome and summoned her to appear before them.[109]

The chosen location was the first-floor parliament chamber above the inner cloister of the Dominican friary commonly known as Blackfriars, on the western edge of the City of London. It was linked with the Bridewell Palace by a gallery across the River Fleet. At the southern end of the 110 ft (33.53 m) long room, a table and two chairs for the papal commissioners were set up on a dais. On the right was a cloth of gold canopy above Henry's throne with a corresponding one for the queen facing it on the left.[110] In front were benches for lawyers and the bishops.

On the morning of Monday 21 June the full court assembled. Henry and Katherine entered from Bridewell amid loud cheers from a large crowd of her supporters and in a vain attempt to silence their shouts, an enraged Henry ordered his guards to ensure 'that nobody should again be admitted to the place'.[111]

Proceedings began with the usher's cry of: 'King Harry of England, come into court,' and Henry rose from his throne with a brisk, peremptory, 'Here, my lords!' The usher then asked the same of the queen but, instead of the formal answer, she stood up and walked slowly around the bishops and knelt at her husband's feet. Her barely suppressed emotion brought back her Spanish accent:

> Sir! I beseech you for all the love that has been between us and for the love of God, let me have justice and right.
>
> Take [on] me some pity and compassion for I am a poor woman and a stranger born out of your dominion. I have no assured friend and much less indifferent counsel.
>
> I flee to you as ... the head of justice in this realm.

Henry sat silent and stony-faced as his discarded wife's words rang around the hushed chamber. Katherine continued her eloquent attack on his hopes and dreams of a divorce:

> Alas Sir! Wherein have I offended you or what occasion of displeasure?
>
> Have I designed [plotted] against your will and pleasure, intending (as I perceive) to put me from you?
>
> I have been to you a true, humble and obedient wife, ever conformable to your will and pleasure ... always well pleased and contented with all things wherein you had delight or dalliance ...
>
> I loved all those whom you loved only for your sake, whether I had cause or not and whether they were my friends or enemies.
>
> This twenty years I have been your true wife and by me you have had diverse children, although it has pleased God to call them out of this world, which has been no default in me.

Katherine moved on to the main plank of her argument:

When you had me at the first, I take God to be my judge, I was a true maid without touch of man and ... I put [this] to your conscience.[112]

The queen paused. She had told the Spanish ambassador that Henry had often boasted that she had come to him a virgin and that she believed he would never deny it. Katherine had now posed the question very publicly and dared him to give his answer.

It never came. The king sat stunned, immobile on his throne, as the seconds ticked by amid an expectant silence in the huge chamber.[113]

Katherine continued with a steady voice:

I most humbly require you, in the way of charity and for the love of God, to spare me the extremity of this new court ... and if you will not extend to me so much indifferent favour, your pleasure will then be fulfilled and to God I commit my cause.

She rose up from her knees, made a low, dignified curtsey to the king, turned on her heel and moved sedately down the room on the arm of her Receiver General, Griffith Richard.

Henry was later to be warned by Anne Boleyn about arguing with Katherine. 'Whenever you disputed with the queen,' she told him tartly, 'she is sure to have the upper hand.'[114] This occasion was no different. The king angrily ordered the usher to summon her back and Richard whispered to his mistress: 'Madam, you are called again.' Katherine looked straight ahead as she continued her departure. 'On, on,' she insisted, 'it makes no matter, for it is no indifferent court for me, therefore I will not tarry.' She then went back to her lodgings in nearby Baynard's Castle.

The process became bogged down with technicalities, and with constant behind-the-scenes meetings and showers of paper. Campeggio was at its very vortex. He wrote to his friend Giacomo Salviati, the Pope's second secretary, in cipher:

I find myself in such trouble and anxiety that if your Lordship saw me in bed with a cruel attack of gout in seven places, accompanied with fever ... brought on by the pain and surrounded by fifteen [lawyers] with two piles of books to show me all they conclude is according to law and nothing else can or ought to be done, I am sure you will have compassion upon me . . .

I am obliged to have myself carried to the place where the trial is held, God knows with what discomfort to me and danger in moving, in ascending and descending staircases and landing from the vessel [from the Thames].

I pray God I may not have to remain for ever in England.[115]

He admitted: 'I understand the desire of his Holiness to be that we should not go on to pronounce judgement and that I should keep on procrastinating as long as I can.' After one inconclusive meeting, Henry pathetically pleaded with Campeggio and his secretary in Latin: 'Be good friends to me and have pity on me.'

Unknown to the king, Clement VII, yielding to Imperial pressure, had already annulled the legatine commission and Campeggio, watched by an incredulous Henry from a gallery next to the door of the court-room, adjourned its proceedings on 23 July for a lengthy vacation to follow the normal summer practice of courts in Rome. It could not re-sit until October at the earliest, but in practice, the matter of the divorce had been referred back to Rome. The king, black-faced with anger, stormed back to Bridewell, but Suffolk, down in the hall, slammed his fist on a table and exclaimed: 'By the Mass! Now I see that the old saying is true! It was never merry in England while we had cardinals amongst us.'

Wolsey had promised to deliver a papal annulment to his master on a golden plate, but Vatican bureaucracy, procrastination and duplicity had failed him. The warning signs of royal disfavour and displeasure were there for all to see. The French ambassador du Bellay said that 'the cardinal is in the greatest pain . . . the Dukes of Norfolk and Suffolk and the others lead the king to believe that he has not furthered the marriage as much as he could have done if he wished it'. Anne Boleyn's cousin, Francis Bryan, who was openly using 'fair means or foul' to carry out his mission in Rome, told Henry: 'Whosoever has made your grace believe that he [the Pope] would do for you in this case, has not, I think, done your grace the best service.'[116]

Wolsey's downfall followed in October. A Venetian merchant in London wrote that the cardinal

> has at length found fortune irate and hostile beyond measure, in such ways that she [Anne Boleyn] has brought him to ruin.
>
> He has lost the royal favour and incurred his majesty's utmost indignation, his supreme authority being converted into bondage and calamity.
>
> He has been forbidden to act as legate, and has lost the chancellorship, the bishopric of Winchester, the abbacy of St Alban's and all his other revenues and properties, with the exception of the archbishopric of York.[117]

A strict watch was mounted at all ports to prevent Wolsey from smuggling his immense wealth out of the realm, which Henry coveted for himself.

Unfortunately, a battered and weary Campeggio, gratefully heading back to Rome, was caught up in the paranoia. Tediously, he had been stopped at road blocks en route to the coast and at Dover he found that a lack of shipping was being used as a transparent excuse to detain him in England.[118]

Finally, his luggage was seized by customs officials at Dover. His long beard bristling, he angrily refused to surrender the keys to his trunks and so the locks were forced. As they gleefully picked over his dirty washing, Campeggio, beside himself with rage at this insufferable affront to his legatine dignity, snapped: 'You do me great injustice to suppose that the cardinal [Wolsey] could corrupt a man like myself – who has been proof against the king's innumerable presents.'[119]

Of course, what the searchers had been instructed to look out for was Campeggio's secret commission from the Pope – plus any copies of his secret correspondence. According to the partisan Edward Hall, they were sadly disappointed as only 'a few letters [were] found ... in many chests were old hosen [close-fitting breeches], old coats and such vile stuff as no honest man would carry'.[120]

A less-than-contrite Henry responded to the cardinal's remonstrances. The king's patience had been worn thin by the old Italian's intransigence. A pungently worded one-page letter in Latin brushed aside Campeggio's irate complaints of 'disrespect shown to the pontifical dignity and the violation of . . . legatine authority'. Henry added, somewhat disingenuously:

> I . . . wonder that your wisdom should exaggerate such minute offences and take such dire offence – as though it were in *my* power to anticipate the temerity of the mob, or the excessive officiousness of others in the discharge of their duty.

The king relished the cardinal's discomfort and could not resist a last opportunity to cut him down in size:

> As to your legateship, no wrong has been done by me or mine, seeing that your authority only extended to the termination of my cause and when that was revoked by papal inhibition, it . . . expired.
>
> Neither I nor my subjects acknowledge that you have any other authority.
>
> I wonder that you are so ignorant of the laws of this kingdom that you were not afraid to make use of the title of legate when it became defunct, seeing that you are a bishop here[121] and so bound by the most solemn obligation to observe and respect my royal dignity, jurisdiction [and] prerogative.

Henry, with reluctant bad grace, attempted to smooth the cardinal's ruffled dignity:

> As to the business of the porters, long before your return to Italy they had received orders to allow no one to pass on any legal suspicion, even with our letters patent, without diligent examination of their baggage.
>
> As we had no intention that this should prove an annoyance to you, nor hinder your journey, or cause you any loss, we request that you take this in good part.
>
> We regret that greater caution and prudence was not shown by the officers in discharge of their duty. As it was done in fulfilment of their oath, we trust you will not consider them deserving of punishment.
>
> You will do us wrong if you think the worse for this fact.[122]

This was as much of an apology as Campeggio was ever to get. After two weeks in Dover, he finally arrived on French soil on 26 October 1529, still seething. One can only hope that at least he was free from the pain from his gout.[123]

Henry found it impossible to forgive Katherine for her telling *coup de théâtre* at Blackfriars. On St Andrew's Day, 30 November, the royal couple dined together and the queen taxed him about her 'long suffering the pains of Purgatory on earth'. She was 'very badly treated by his refusing to dine with and visit her in her apartments', she grumbled. Henry snapped back that 'she had no cause to complain of bad treatment, for she was mistress in her own household, where she could do what she pleased'. As for not eating with her, 'he was so much engaged with business, owing to the cardinal having left the affairs of government in a state of great confusion that he had enough to do to work day and night to put them to rights again'. What was more, he did not sleep with her because he was not her legitimate husband. If the Pope did not declare their marriage null and void, Henry 'would denounce the Pope as a heretic and marry whom he pleased'.[124]

Much against his will, Thomas More succeeded Wolsey as Chancellor and the disgraced cardinal was banished north to York. Sensing the blood of a kill, his enemies closed in and he was arrested for treason as he sat down to dinner in his palace at Cawood on Friday 4 November. He died on the way back to London at the Augustinian abbey of St Mary's, Leicester, on 29 November, probably from dysentery, although there were some who believed 'he killed himself with purgatives'.[125] He was aged about sixty.

Henry did not immediately give up on his efforts to secure a papal annulment. On 13 July 1530, the peers of England sent an address to Clement VII, praying him to consent to the king's desires and avoid the 'evils which arose from delaying the divorce'. The parchment, with eighty-five red wax seals attached, remains in the secret archives of the Vatican to this day.[126]

This was also to no avail. Even Katherine despaired at Rome's failure to come to a decision, any decision, just or unjust. 'God knows what I suffer from these people; enough to kill ten men, much more a shattered woman who has done no harm,' she plaintively told her nephew Charles V in mid-October 1531.[127]

Henry was ever the man of action. The title 'God's Deputy on Earth' complemented his self-vision of imperial majesty. Exasperated with popes, cardinals and bishops, the Defender of the Faith now moved to sever all links with Rome and to take his first steps towards independence of the church in England – with him as its Supreme Head. This was adroitly achieved via a series of legal measures steered through Parliament by his capable and cunning new adviser Thomas Cromwell, who had his own aspirations for change in the Church in England.[128]

The king also had a new champion in Thomas Cranmer, who became Archbishop of Canterbury in succession to Warham, who had died in August 1532. Cranmer's support for the 'King's Great Matter' was impeccable: he had been private chaplain to Anne Boleyn's father, now elevated to the earldom of Wiltshire and Ormond.

On 1 September 1532 Anne herself was raised to the peerage when she was created Marchioness of Pembroke with a munificent annuity of £1,000. Henry then took her on to glittering meetings with Francis I of France in Boulogne and Calais, where she wore a scintillating array of jewellery heartlessly confiscated from Katherine of Aragon.

The king's paramour remained deeply unpopular in England. Cromwell's legion of informers reported reams of public slander, both sacred and profane, about her in the noisy taverns and marketplaces of England. The Lancashire parson James Harrison promised: 'I will [have] none for queen but Queen Katherine! Who the devil made Nan Boleyn, that whore, queen?'[129] The Colchester monk John Frances declared that when Henry had met Francis I, Anne had 'followed his arse as the dog follows his master's arse'.[130]

It was shortly afterwards that Anne welcomed Henry into her bed for the first time. About the middle of January 1533, she found she was pregnant and a jubilant Henry secretly and bigamously married her on the 25th in a chamber above the Holbein Gate in his Palace of Westminster.

Her condition dictated that some speed was necessary to contain public scandal. Cranmer convened his ecclesiastical court at Dunstable,

Bedfordshire, near Ampthill, where Katherine and her now tiny household had been exiled by the king. She resolutely refused to appear. At ten o'clock on the morning of 23 May 1533, the archbishop declared her marriage 'to be against the laws of God' and 'divorced the king's highness from the noble lady Katherine'.[131]

At last Henry was free of his barren wife. His mistress was expecting their first child, and God willing, it would be a son.

Anne was ostentatiously crowned by Cranmer in Westminster Abbey on Whit Sunday, 1 June 1533, in a spectacular ceremony that cost Henry an estimated 100,000 gold ducats, plus another 200,000 obsequiously donated by the City of London[132] – equivalent to more than £55 million at today's values. By anyone's standards, a high price for an heir.

Sir Thomas More, who had resigned as Lord Chancellor in May 1532, was conspicuous by his absence.

Despite her amply cut flowing robes, Anne's pregnancy was obvious. Henry's corps of physicians was unanimous that the child would be a boy. Like his father before him, the king also consulted astrologers who confidently predicted the desired outcome.

Circular letters announcing the birth of a male heir had been carefully written out for immediate dispatch to the great and good once Anne had delivered both Henry and England's hope for the future.

At four o'clock in the afternoon of Sunday 7 September 1533, at Greenwich Palace, Queen Anne gave birth to a baby girl. She was called Elizabeth after Henry's beloved mother.

Within that silent, unhappy palace, a clerk sighed, picked up his pen and painstakingly began to squeeze an extra two 'S's at the end of the word 'prince', on the first of a pile of those circular letters.[133]

Henry's dreams remained unfulfilled. His Tudor dynasty remained just a heartbeat away from oblivion.

Epilogue

Henry's breach with Rome and his supremacy over matters religious set the bloody tone for the remainder of his almost four decades on the throne of England. Many were to die as a consequence of his dynastic ambitions in a series of executions that made the scaffolds in the cities of England a butcher's block of stinking gore and entrails.

Among the first to die was his grandmother's favourite, John Fisher, Bishop of Rochester, who had strenuously opposed the annulment of the king's marriage and refused to swear an oath under the Act of Supremacy which gave Henry control of the church in England. After months of cruel imprisonment, the aged and infirm prelate was executed on 22 June 1535 on Tower Hill.

His journey to the scaffold, carried in a chair – he was too old and weak to walk – was hastened by the unfortunate decision by the new pope, Paul III, to make him a cardinal. Although prevarication had been honed to a fine skill, timing was not the Vatican's forte. The king angrily declared that he would 'send [Fisher's] head to Rome for the cardinal's hat'.

Then it was the turn of the king's friend Sir Thomas More to face Henry's rough justice. Royal promises of his immunity over the issue of the marriage proved mere hot air and his resignation as Lord Chancellor on 16 May 1532 did not save him. He had been condemned to perpetual imprisonment for cleverly avoiding taking the Oath of Succession that recognised Anne Boleyn as the king's lawful wife and their children as the legitimate heirs to the throne. Anyone refusing to take the oath was guilty of treason and More, as a revered national figure, was just too important to escape retribution. He was beheaded with one blow of the axe on the morning of 6 July 1535 after a perjured trial.

Katherine died, lonely and neglected, at Kimbolton Castle, Huntingdonshire, probably from cancer of the heart, on 7 January 1536. She had last seen Henry and her daughter Mary late in the summer of 1531.

Anne Boleyn did not live up to her personal motto: 'The Most Happy'. After she suffered several miscarriages, Henry became weary of a wife whom he increasingly saw as a peevish and arrogant tartar and alleged that she had tricked him into marriage 'by means of sortileges [sorcery] and charms and that owing to that, he would hold it . . . nullified'.

His chief minister, Thomas Cromwell was the ideal man to free him of such a termagant wife. After he scrabbled around finding dubious evidence, she was accused of adultery with five of the king's courtiers as well as plotting Henry's death. One alleged accomplice was her brother George, Viscount Rochford, who was charged with committing incest with the queen. At her trial at the Tower, witnessed by 2,000 awestruck and enthralled spectators, a slip of paper was produced recording Anne's damning description of her husband's poor performance in bed: '*Que le Roy n'estait habile en cas de soi copuler avec femme, et qu'il n'avait ni vertu ni puissance*' – 'The king was not skilful when copulating with a woman and he had not virtue or power'. If nothing else, this was enough to condemn her.

Rochford and his fellow courtiers were executed on 17 May 1536 and two days later Anne was beheaded by a single sweep of a long two-handed sword wielded by a French executioner especially brought over from St Omer at a fee of £24.

Henry Fitzroy, Duke of Richmond, the king's illegitimate son by Bessie Blount, married Mary Howard, daughter of the Third Duke of Norfolk. The marriage was never consummated and he died, probably from tuberculosis, on the morning of 23 July 1536 in St James' Palace. He was just seventeen.

Henry still harboured fears about the threat of the Yorkist nobility and in November 1538 Thomas Cromwell swept up the surviving distant members of the White Rose faction – who coincidentally were also numbered amongst his countless bitter enemies.

Henry Courtenay, Marquis of Exeter, Henry Lord Montague, Sir Edward Neville and Princess Mary's old governess, Margaret Pole,

Countess of Salisbury, were all arrested. The first three were executed on 9 December at Tower Hill. The sixty-seven-year-old countess was imprisoned in the Tower and eventually was led to the scaffold on 27 May 1541. She refused to lay her head on the block saying, 'So should traitors do [but] I am none neither.' The executioner was a ham-fisted, inexperienced youth who limply told her that this was 'the fashion'. He repeatedly hacked her grey-haired head and shoulders before he could bloodily finish the job. Montague's heir Henry disappeared within the Tower and died some time after September 1542. Exeter's twelve-year-old son Edward was held there until Mary ascended the throne in 1553 when he was eventually freed.

On 30 May 1536, Henry married Jane Seymour, one of Anne's ladies in another secret wedding, this time in the Queen's Closet at Westminster.

At two o'clock in the morning of Friday 12 October 1537, Henry's elusive dream of a male heir was at last transformed into happy reality. After a harrowing thirty hours in labour, Jane Seymour gave birth to a boy, named Edward, at Hampton Court. But she died twelve days later, aged twenty-eight, probably from puerperal fever and septicaemia.

Analysis of Henry's symptoms and the changes in his appearance as shown in portraits, suggests that from the late 1530s Henry probably suffered from Cushing's syndrome, a rare endocrine abnormality that causes gross obesity in the body's trunk and increased fat around the neck, as well as weakening of the bones and diabetes. In some cases – and Henry was possibly one – the condition turns the victim into a paranoid psychotic. In his last years he could barely walk and was carried around his palaces in a kind of sedan chair, called 'the king's tram'.

The king had three more wives – Anne of Cleves, Catherine Howard and the matronly Katherine Parr – but by then was probably incapable of procreating.

Henry died speechless, alone and friendless in the great carved walnut bed within his secret apartments in Westminster Palace at around two o'clock in the morning of Friday 28 January 1547.

As with his father, his death was kept a close secret for three days with road blocks set up around London and England was sealed off from Europe by closure of the ports.

The king's legitimate male heir, nine-year-old Edward, was proclaimed king on 31 January, as the cannon boomed out their salutes from the ramparts of the Tower and from ships moored on the Thames. The Tudor dynasty had been secured – for the moment anyway.

CHRONOLOGY

1457 **28 January** Henry Tudor (later Henry VII) born in Pembroke Castle to fourteen-year-old Margaret, widow of Edmund Tudor, First Earl of Richmond, who had died from the plague three months before whilst imprisoned by the Yorkists in Carmarthen Castle, south Wales.

1471 **2 June** Henry flees to Brittany and fourteen years of exile after the defeat of the Lancastrian cause at the Battles of Barnet and Tewkesbury.

1483 **June** Edward V and Richard Duke of York, young sons of Edward IV, disappear after entering Tower of London. They are believed to have been murdered on the orders of Richard, Duke of Gloucester, 'Lord Protector of the realm', later Richard III.

1485 **7 August** Henry Tudor lands at Milford Haven in South Wales with 3,000 French mercenaries and English and Welsh supporters to claim the crown of England.

1485 **22 August** Henry defeats and kills Richard III at Bosworth Field, Leicestershire, becoming Henry VII, the first monarch of the Tudor dynasty.

1485 **30 October** Henry crowned king at Westminster.
He imprisons ten-year-old Edward Plantagenet, Earl of Warwick, in the Tower, because of his potential claims to the crown.
First outbreak of sweating sickness in London.

1485 **9 November** First Parliament of Henry VII's reign opens at Westminster.

1485 **16 December** Katherine of Aragon born at Alcala de Henares, Spain.

1486 **18 January** Henry VII marries Elizabeth of York, daughter of Edward IV and sister of the 'Princes in the Tower'.

1486 **20 September** Arthur, first child of Henry VII and Elizabeth of York, born at Winchester.

1487 **24 May** Lambert Simnel, ten-year-old pretender to the throne of England, crowned king in Dublin Cathedral.

1487 **16 June** Rebel Yorkist forces supporting Simnel's claim and John de la Pole, Earl of Lincoln, defeated at Stoke Field, Nottinghamshire. Lincoln is killed but Simnel spared and employed in royal kitchens.

1487 **25 November** Elizabeth of York crowned queen consort at Westminster Abbey.

1489 **29 November** Margaret, second child of Henry VII and Elizabeth of York, born.

1489 **30 November** Arthur created Prince of Wales and Earl of Chester at Westminster.

1491 **28 June** Prince Henry (later Henry VIII) born at Greenwich Palace.

1491 **November** Perkin Warbeck, pretender to the throne, arrives in Cork in south-west Ireland.

1493 **5 April** Prince Henry made Lord Warden of the Cinque Ports and Constable of Dover Castle.

1493 **August** Warbeck attends funeral in Vienna of Holy Roman Emperor Frederick III and is recognised as 'King Richard IV of England' by Maximilian I, King of the Romans.

1494 **12 September** Prince Henry appointed Lord Deputy of Ireland.

1494 **31 October** Prince Henry dubbed a Knight of the Bath.

1494 **1 November** Prince Henry created Duke of York.

1495 **16 February** Sir William Stanley, step-uncle of Henry VII and his supporter at Bosworth, executed for treason.

1495 **17 May** Henry Duke of York made a Knight of the Garter.

1495 **3 July** Troops from Warbeck's invasion fleet land at Deal and one hundred and fifty are killed and a further one hundred and sixty taken prisoner.

1496 **18 March** Mary born to Henry VII and Elizabeth of York at Sheen Palace, Surrey.

1496 **September** Warbeck, with Scottish assistance, leads 1,400 men in a small scale invasion across the border into Northumberland.

1496 **21 September** Prince Henry's first public duty – witnessing a royal grant of a charter to the abbot and convent at Glastonbury, Somerset.

1497 **17 June** Battle of Blackheath in present-day south-east London: Cornish rebels defeated by royalist forces. Prince Henry and his mother are in the Tower of London for safety.

1497 **18 July** Treaty of marriage between Katherine of Aragon and Prince Arthur stipulating that she would come to England when Arthur was aged fourteen and that her dowry of 200,000 crowns would be paid in instalments.

1497 **7 September** Perkin Warbeck lands in Cornwall and collects an army of Cornish discontents; attacks Exeter and marches on Taunton.

1497 **5 October** Perkin Warbeck surrenders at Beaulieu Abbey, Hampshire.

1497 **21 December** Fire destroys royal apartments at Sheen Palace, Surrey.

1499 **July** Edmund de la Pole, Earl of Suffolk, potential Yorkist claimant to the throne, flees England but later returns voluntarily.

1499 **summer** Dutch humanist scholar Desiderius Erasmus visits Prince Henry and his sisters at Eltham Palace.

1499 **23 November** Perkin Warbeck executed at Tyburn.

1499 **28 November** Edward Plantagenet, Earl of Warwick, beheaded for treason at Tower Hill.

1501 **August** Edmund de la Pole, Earl of Suffolk, again flees England with his younger brother Richard.

1501 **12 November** Katherine of Aragon makes her formal entry into London, escorted by Henry Duke of York – his first sight of her.

1501 **14 November** Prince Arthur, aged fifteen, and Katherine of Aragon, aged sixteen, married at St Paul's Cathedral, London. Prince Henry gives away the bride.

1502 **2 April** Arthur dies at Ludlow Castle, Shropshire.

1503 **11 February** Death of Queen Elizabeth following the birth of a daughter on 2 February. The baby subsequently dies on or around **14 February**.

1503 **18 February** Henry Duke of York created Prince of Wales.

1503 **25 June** Prince Henry and Katherine of Aragon formally betrothed by Bishop of Salisbury.

1504 **autumn** Sir Richard Empson and Edmund Dudley empowered to act as bond agents for Henry VII.

1504 **November** Pope Julius II sends his dispensation allowing Henry to marry his brother's widow.

1505 **27 June** Prince Henry, on his father's instructions, makes a secret protest against his marriage with Katherine of Aragon at Richmond Palace, Surrey.

1506 **January** Archduke Philip of Burgundy arrives in England after his fleet is dispersed by storms in the English Channel.

1506 **24 April** Edmund de la Pole, Earl of Suffolk, is imprisoned in Tower of London.

1509 **21 April** Henry VII dies in Richmond Palace, aged fifty-two, from tuberculosis. His death remains secret for two days.

1509 **24 April** Public proclamation of the accession of Henry VIII, under the regency of his grandmother, Lady Margaret Beaufort, until his eighteenth birthday.
Arrests of Empson and Dudley.

1509 **11 June** Henry VIII and Katherine of Aragon married by Archbishop William Warham at the church of Friars Observant adjoining Greenwich Palace.

1509 **24 June** Coronation of Henry VIII and his queen consort at Westminster Abbey.

1509 **29 June** Death of Henry VIII's grandmother, Lady Margaret Beaufort, at Westminster.

1509 **November** 'Retinue of Spears' set up as personal bodyguard for Henry VIII.

1510 **21 January** First Parliament of Henry VIII's reign.

1510 **17 August** Executions of Empson and Dudley.

1511 **1 January** Birth of a son, christened Henry, to Henry and Katherine of Aragon at Richmond. The child lives only fifty-three days, dying on 22 February.

1511 **May** Abortive English expedition to assist Ferdinand of Spain's campaign against the Moors in North Africa.

1511 **June** 1,500 English troops depart Sandwich for Low Countries expedition under Sir Edward Poynings.

1511 **17 November** Treaty of Westminster provides framework for military assistance between countries of the 'Holy League'.

1512 Wolsey becomes Henry's de facto chief Minister.

1512 **June–November** Disastrous English expedition to Fuentarrabia in Spain.

1512 **10 August** Loss of the English warship *Regent*, commanded by Sir Thomas Knyvet, off Brest.

1513 **25 April** Lord High Admiral Sir Edward Howard killed in reckless naval action off Conquet.

1513 **4 May** Edmund de la Pole, Earl of Suffolk, beheaded inside Tower of London.

1513 **July** Henry invades northern France, leaving Katherine as regent of England.

1513 **16 August** 'Battle of Spurs' at Guinegatte when French supply force is routed.

1513 **23 August** French town of Thérouanne surrenders.

1513 **9 September** English army, under Thomas Howard, Earl of Surrey, defeats Scots at Flodden Field, Northumberland. James IV of Scotland and 12,000 of his army killed.

1513 **23 September** French city of Tournai falls to Henry.

1513 **December** Henry VIII contracts smallpox.

1514   **9 October** Henry's younger sister Mary marries Louis XII of France in Abbeville.

1515   **1 January** Louis XII of France dies. Accession of Francis I.

1515   **February** Charles Brandon, Duke of Suffolk, secretly marries Mary in Paris.

1515   **24 December** Wolsey appointed Lord Chancellor in succession to Archbishop William Warham.

1516   **23 January** Ferdinand of Spain dies in Spain and is succeeded, as joint rulers, by his grandson Charles and his mother, the mad Juana, who is locked up in a Spanish castle.

1516   **18 February** Birth of Mary at Greenwich, sole surviving offspring of Henry VIII and Katherine of Aragon.

1518   Thomas More enters royal service as Master of the Court of Requests.

1518   **May** Wolsey made Papal Legate.

1519   **12 January** Maximilian I dies and Charles V of Spain is elected Holy Roman Emperor.

1519   **May** Royal household purged.

1519   **15 June** Birth of Henry Fitzroy, illegitimate son of Henry VIII and his mistress, Elizabeth Blount.

1520   **May** Visit of Emperor Charles V to England.

1520   **7–24 June** Field of Cloth of Gold meeting between Henry VIII and Francis I of France.

1521   **17 May** Execution on Tower Hill of Edward Stafford, Duke of Buckingham.

1521   **24 November** Title of 'Defender of the Faith' granted to Henry VIII by Pope Leo X.

1522   Mary Boleyn becomes Henry VIII's mistress.

1522   **1 March** Anne Boleyn makes first appearance at court.

1523   **August** Charles Brandon, Duke of Suffolk, leads a 10,000-strong English army in a second invasion of northern France but bad weather disrupts his advance on Paris and he retreats to Flanders.

1524   Henry stops sleeping regularly with his wife Katherine of Aragon.

1524   **10 March** Henry is injured whilst jousting against Charles Brandon, Duke of Suffolk.

1525   Henry nearly drowns in a hunting accident near Hitchen, Hertfordshire.

1525   **24 February** Richard de la Pole killed fighting on the French side at Battle of Pavia in Italy.

1525 **18 June** Henry VIII's bastard son, Henry Fitzroy, created Duke of Richmond at Bridewell.

1525 **July** Sir Thomas More appointed Chancellor of the Duchy of Lancaster.

1525 **October** Princess Mary separated from her mother and sent to Ludlow Castle.

1527 **17 May** Wolsey's legatine court sits to try Henry's marriage but fails to make a pronouncement on its validity.

1527 **May** Sack of Rome by German mercenaries serving with Imperial forces in Italy.

1527 **22 June** Henry VIII tells his wife he plans to divorce her as they have been 'living in mortal sin' for eighteen years.

1527 **3 August** John Rut writes to Henry VIII from St John's harbour, Newfoundland – the earliest surviving letter from North America.

1528 **May** Fourth pandemic of sweating sickness in England.

1529 **21 June–23 July** Legatine court sits at Blackfriars on the marriage of Henry VIII and Katherine of Aragon but is adjourned without making a judgement.

1529 **18 October** Wolsey delivers Great Seal of England to Dukes of Norfolk and Suffolk at York Place.

1529 **26 October** Sir Thomas More takes oath of fidelity as Lord Chancellor in Westminster Hall.

1530 **4 November** Wolsey arrested on treason charges and dies (**29 November**) at Leicester, probably from dysentery.

1531 **8 March** Convocation of bishops recognises Henry VIII as Head of the Church of England 'as far as the law of God allows'.

1531 **July** Henry separates from Katherine of Aragon.

1532 **16 May** Sir Thomas More resigns as Lord Chancellor.

1533 **25 January** Henry secretly (and bigamously) marries the pregnant Anne Boleyn in a chamber above the Holbein Gate in the Palace of Westminster.

1533 **23 May** Thomas Cranmer, Archbishop of Canterbury, divorces Henry VIII from Katherine at an ecclesiastical court at Dunstable, Bedfordshire.

1533 **1 June** Anne is crowned queen by Cranmer at Westminster Abbey.

1533 **7 September** A baby daughter, subsequently christened Elizabeth, is born to Anne at Greenwich Palace.

DRAMATIS PERSONÆ

Richard III (1452–85). Eighth and youngest child of Richard Plantagenet, Duke of York, who was killed at Battle of Wakefield, 30 December 1460. Created Duke of Gloucester at age of eight. In 1472 he married the Prince of Wales' widow, Anne, younger daughter of Richard Neville, Earl of Warwick, 'the Kingmaker'. Edward IV died on 9 April 1483 and Richard was appointed Lord Protector to the heir to the throne, twelve-year-old Edward V, who disappeared after entering the Tower of London with his younger brother Richard, Duke of York. Seized power and was crowned 6 July 1483 in Westminster Abbey. His army was defeated and he was killed at the Battle of Bosworth on 22 August 1485 by invading forces commanded by *Henry VII*. Richard was the last reigning English monarch to be killed in battle.

Henry VII (1457–1509). Born to *Margaret Beaufort*, wife of Edmund Tudor, First Earl of Richmond, who died from the plague three months before in Carmarthen Castle, south Wales, where he was imprisoned by Yorkists. Exiled in 1471 after the defeat of the Lancastrian cause in the Wars of the Roses and spent fourteen years under the protection of Francis II, Duke of Brittany. Snatched the throne of England after his defeat of *Richard III* at Bosworth, 22 August 1485. Crowned as first Tudor monarch at Westminster that October and married *Elizabeth of York*, daughter of Edward IV and Elizabeth Woodville, in 1486.

Lady Margaret Beaufort, Countess of Richmond (1443–1509). Daughter of John Beaufort, First Duke of Somerset. She was aged twelve when she married Edmund Tudor, First Earl of Richmond on 1 November 1455. She gave birth to their only child, later *Henry VII*, on 28 January 1457, three months after the death of her husband whilst incarcerated. On 3 January 1462 Margaret married her cousin, Henry Stafford, son of Humphrey Stafford, First Duke of Buckingham, who had died in 1471. In June 1473 she married for the third time to Thomas Stanley, Second Baron Stanley, who with his brother *William*, decisively changed sides at Bosworth to hand victory to *Henry VII*. Now known as 'the King's Mother', Margaret was not only was the richest woman in England but also one of the most pious. In 1499, after securing her husband's permission, she took a vow of chastity and lived apart from Stanley. In 1505 she refounded the impoverished Godshouse in Cambridge as Christ's College and six years later her executors founded St John's College in the same university. After being regent to *Henry VIII* for a few weeks after his accession, she died at Westminster on 29 June 1509.

Elizabeth of York (1466–1503). Eldest child of Edward IV (died 1483) and his queen Elizabeth Woodville. This marriage was declared invalid by Richard III's *Titulus Regius* in 1483, making the couple's children illegitimate and ineligible for the succession to the crown. After *Henry VII* snatched the throne at Bosworth, the *Titulus Regius* was repealed and he married Elizabeth on 18 January 1486. She was crowned queen consort on 25 November 1487. The couple had eight children: *Arthur*, Prince of Wales; a boy reputedly named Edward who died shortly after birth; *Margaret*, later queen consort of Scotland; Henry, later *Henry VIII;* Elizabeth (died 1495); *Mary*, later queen consort of France; Edmund, Duke of Somerset (died 1500) and Katherine (died a few days after her birth, 1503). Elizabeth herself died after delivering her last child.

Arthur Tudor, Prince of Wales (1486–1502). First child of *Henry VII* and *Elizabeth of York*, born a month prematurely at Winchester. Created Prince of Wales and Earl of Chester at the age of three. Married *Katherine of Aragon* on 14 November 1501 in St Paul's Cathedral and the couple moved to Ludlow Castle, Shropshire in Arthur's role as Prince of Wales and president of the Council of Wales and the Marches. Died, probably of tuberculosis, on 2 April 1502 and buried in Worcester Cathedral.

Henry VIII (1491–1547): Second son of *Henry VII* and *Elizabeth of York*. After his father's death, his accession to the throne was proclaimed on 24 April 1509. Only a daughter, *Princess Mary*, survived as issue of his marriage with *Katherine of Aragon*, whom he sought to divorce because of his claim that their union was against the law of God and the church. At least one illegitimate child: *Henry Fitzroy*, born to Henry's mistress, *Elizabeth Blount* on 15 June 1519. Awarded the title 'Defender of the Faith' by Pope Leo X but later became Supreme Head of the Church of England after his break with Rome. Married his mistress *Anne Boleyn* who was beheaded for adultery and incest (one child – *Elizabeth*); Jane Seymour (one child – *Edward*) and Catherine Howard (beheaded), Anne of Cleves (annulled) and Katherine Parr who outlived him.

Katherine of Aragon (1485–1536). Henry's first queen. Youngest surviving child of *Ferdinand of Aragon* and *Isabella of Castile* and aunt to *Charles V* of Spain, the Holy Roman Emperor. Married Henry's elder brother, *Arthur*, on 14 November 1501 but left a widow after his death on 2 April 1502. Married Henry on 11 June 1509 and had six pregnancies but only *Princess Mary* survived birth.

Died at Kimbolton Castle, Huntingdonshire, of cancer of the heart, 7 January 1536.

Anne Boleyn (*c.*1501–36) second daughter of Sir Thomas Boleyn, Earl of Wiltshire and Ormond and second wife of *Henry VIII*, secretly marrying the king on 25 January 1533. Gave birth to *Elizabeth*, her only child, on 7 September 1533 at Greenwich. Arrested on charges of adultery and incest and executed at the Tower, 19 May 1536.

Princess Mary, later Queen Mary I (1516–58). Only surviving child of *Henry VIII* and his first wife *Katherine of Aragon*. Proclaimed queen on 19 July 1553. Re-introduced Catholicism to England. Married Philip, son of *Charles V* of Spain at Winchester, 25 July 1554. Died, childless, from ovarian or stomach cancer, St James' Palace, London, 17 November 1558.

Princess Elizabeth, later Elizabeth I (1533–1603). Daughter of *Henry VIII* and his second wife *Anne Boleyn*. Succeeded *Mary I* as queen 17 November 1558. Secured Protestantism as state religion. Died, unmarried, from pneumonia and dental sepsis, Richmond, 24 March 1603.

Prince Edward later Edward VI (1537–53). Legitimate son of *Henry VIII* and his third wife Jane Seymour. Proclaimed king 31 January 1547 at the Tower of London. Died of tuberculosis, complicated by measles and sundry unorthodox medicines, Greenwich Palace, 6 July 1553.

Henry Fitzroy, Duke of Richmond (1519–36). Bastard son of *Henry VIII* and *Elizabeth Blount*, a maid of honour to *Katherine of Aragon*. Created Duke of Richmond at Bridewell on 18 June 1525. Under care of Thomas Howard, Third Duke of Norfolk. Married, on 26 November 1533, Mary Howard, daughter of Norfolk. Died 23 July 1536 of a pulmonary infection. The marriage was never consummated.

Margaret Tudor, queen consort of Scotland (1489–1541). Elder daughter of *Henry VII* and *Elizabeth of York*. Married *James IV* of Scotland in Edinburgh on 8 August 1503 and was crowned in March 1504. In 1512 she gave birth to a son who succeeded as James V after his father was killed at Flodden in 1513. The following year, Margaret bore a posthumous son, Alexander, Duke of Ross, who died in 1515. She married Archibald Douglas, Sixth Earl of Angus, on 6 August 1514 and lost the regency and guardianship of her sons by James IV. After divorcing Douglas in 1527, Margaret married Henry Stewart, created Lord Methven, and died at Methven Castle on 18 October 1541.

Mary Tudor, queen consort of France (1496–1533). Second daughter of *Henry VII* and *Elizabeth of York* and *Henry VIII*'s younger sister. In 1508 she was betrothed to Charles of Castile, afterwards *Charles V* but the marriage plans were scrapped and instead, she married the aging *Louis XII* of France on 9 October 1514 and was crowned queen of France in November. He died on 1 January 1515 and Mary secretly married *Charles Brandon*, Duke of Suffolk, much to *Henry VIII*'s anger. After the couple agreed to pay back Mary's dowry and hand over her plate and jewels, the king's indignation was mollified and their marriage was publicly solemnised at Greenwich in May 1515. They had four children: Henry, who died young; Frances, later the wife of Henry Grey, Marquis of Northampton and mother of Lady Jane Grey, Eleanor, and a second son, also called Henry who died about the age of twelve. Mary died at Westhorpe, Suffolk and was buried in the abbey at Bury St Edmund's but after the Dissolution of the Monasteries, her body was moved into the parish church there.

PRETENDERS TO THE CROWN OF ENGLAND

Edward Plantagenet, Seventeenth Earl of Warwick (1475–99). Son of George, First Duke of Clarence, and younger brother of Margaret Pole, Countess of Salisbury (governess to *Princess Mary* but executed by *Henry VIII* on 27 May 1541 when she was aged sixty-seven). After the death of Richard III's son Edward in 1484, Warwick was named heir to the throne, but this was overtaken by the later declaration of *John de la Pole, Earl of Lincoln* as his heir. After *Henry VIII* seized the throne at Bosworth, Warwick was imprisoned in the Tower as a dangerous potential claimant. Contemporaries described him as simple-minded, 'not able to tell a goose from a capon'. The last of the male Plantagenet line, he was executed on 28 November 1499 at Tower Hill.

Lambert Simnel (*c.*1477–*c.*1525). Son of an Oxford joiner or organ-maker. Because of his physical resemblance to the ten-year-old *Edward Plantagenet, Earl of Warwick*, Richard Simons, an Oxford-trained priest, took the boy to Ireland, claiming that he was the true Warwick. He was crowned in Christ Church Cathedral, Dublin on 24 May 1487 as 'Richard IV' and with Irish troops mustered by Gerald Fitzgerald, Earl of Kildare, and German mercenaries under another pretender, *John de la Pole, Earl of Lincoln*, the rebel force landed in Cumbria that June. They were defeated by royalist forces at Stoke Field on 16 June, but Simnel was spared and sent to the royal kitchens as a scullion and turnspit, later progressing to the post of falconer.

John de la Pole, First Earl of Lincoln (1464–87). Eldest son of John de la Pole, Second Duke of Suffolk and Elizabeth Plantagenet. Served *Richard III* as Lieutenant in Ireland and president of the Council of the North in England.

After Bosworth, he was reconciled with *Henry VIII* but tried to seize power, allying himself with the pretender, *Lambert Simnel*. Killed at the Battle of Stoke Field on 16 June 1487. His younger brother *Edmund de la Pole, Sixth Earl of Suffolk*, became the leading Yorkist claimant but was executed by *Henry VIII* on 4 May 1513. Their brother *Richard* continued the de la Pole claim until his death at the Battle of Pavia on 24 February 1525.

Edmund de la Pole, Sixth Earl of Suffolk (?1472–1513). Second son of John de la Pole, Second Duke of Suffolk, and younger brother to *John*, First Earl of Lincoln, and elder brother to *Richard de la Pole*. In 1499, he was indicted for murder and fled England in July but was persuaded to return. Having heard that the *Emperor Maximilian* was no friend of *Henry VIII*'s he went to the continent again in August 1501 with his brother *Richard*. Three years later he was attainted and Archduke *Philip* of Burgundy agreed to return him to England and he was imprisoned in the Tower on 24 April 1506. He was beheaded on *Henry VIII*'s orders on 4 May 1513, before the king left for the invasion of France.

Richard de la Pole (d.1525). Fifth son of John de la Pole (1442–91), Second Duke of Suffolk, and younger brother to *John* and *Edmund*. Fled England with his brother and remained at Aix-la-Chapelle in 1504 as surety for Edmund's mounting debts. He escaped and when *Louis XII* was fighting English forces in France, he recognised Richard's claims to the throne and appointed him a commander in the French army. In 1514 he was given 12,000 German mercenaries for an invasion attempt which was stymied by a peace treaty. Under Francis I, he also planned a further invasion in 1523 but this also proved abortive. He was killed fighting for the French at the Battle of Pavia in February 1525.

Perkin Warbeck (c.1474–99). Born in Tournai, the son of a French official John de Werbecque (or Osbek), comptroller of the city, but claimed to be Richard, Duke of York, one of the missing 'Princes in the Tower'. Landed in Ireland in November 1491 in the hopes of winning support and was later recognised by *Margaret of York*, protector of Burgundy, sister to Edward IV. Funded by Burgundian cash, he landed at Deal on 3 July 1495 but some of his troops were killed or captured and he ended up at the court of James IV of Scotland who gave him shelter. There he married James' cousin, Lady Catherine Gordon, and launched an abortive invasion of England across the Scottish border. The remnants of his fleet landed in Cornwall in September 1497 and Warbeck rallied 8,000 Cornish malcontents to his cause. After vainly attacking Exeter he fled his forces at the approach of the royalist army and surrendered at

Beaulieu Abbey on 5 October 1497. He was hanged at Tyburn on 23 November 1499 after reading out a confession.

Edward Stafford, Third Duke of Buckingham (1478–1521). Eldest son of Henry Stafford, the Second Duke, who was attainted and executed for treason by *Richard III* in 1483. On *Henry VII's* accession, the attainder was reversed and the custody of Edward's lands and his wardship was given to *Lady Margaret Beaufort*, the new king's mother. Despite his aspirations for the throne, Buckingham was sworn a Privy Councillor on 20 November 1510. He was a captain in the English army in France in June–October 1513 and attended the Field of the Cloth of Gold in June 1520. He became an enemy of *Wolsey* and the subject of deep suspicion by *Henry VIII*. He was tried by his peers for treason and beheaded on Tower Hill on 17 May 1521.

MISTRESSES OF HENRY VIII

Anne Hastings, *née* **Stafford** (*c.*1483–1544). Youngest daughter of Henry Stafford, Second Duke of Buckingham and sister to *Edward Stafford*. Married George Hastings, later Earl of Huntingdon, in December 1509 and had eight children. She had an affair with *Henry VIII* in 1510 and was sent to a convent by her husband. Anne later lived with *Sir William Compton*. Her husband also died in 1544, leaving debts of £9,466, mostly incurred by his expensive life at court.

Elizabeth ('Bessie') Blount (*c.*1500–?41). Second daughter of Sir John Blount of Kinlet, Shropshire. Appointed maid of honour to *Katherine of Aragon. Henry VIII's* mistress from 1514 to 1519, when she gave birth to his illegitimate son, *Henry Fitzroy.* In 1522 she married Gilbert Talboys and was given a generous income by act of Parliament from the properties owned by his mad father, who died in 1517. She had three children by him. Talboys died in April 1530 and some time after 1533 she married her Lincolnshire neighbour, Edward Clinton, Ninth Baron Clinton and Saye (1512–85) and had three daughters. Anne was appointed a lady-in-waiting to Anne of Cleves but left court because of her ill-health and died of tuberculosis probably in 1541.

Mary Carey, *née* **Boleyn** (?1499–1543). Elder daughter of Thomas Boleyn and his wife Elizabeth, daughter of Thomas Howard, Second Duke of Norfolk, and sister to *Anne Boleyn* and George, whose career at court began as a royal page. She attended *Mary Tudor* for her marriage to *Louis XII* in 1514 and stayed on at the French court where she was notorious for her immorality. She secured a place in *Katherine of Aragon's* household and in February 1520 married a Gentleman of the Privy Chamber, William Carey, producing a son and daughter. Mary was *Henry VIII*'s mistress from 1522 to the mid-1520s. Carey died of the sweat in 1528 and she secretly married Sir William Stafford (?1512–56), a member of the Calais garrison, in 1534. Her marriage was exposed when she became pregnant and her sister banished her from court. Mary's daughter Katherine was appointed maid of honour to the ill-fated Anne of Cleves in November 1539.

Anne Boleyn – *see English Royalty.*

TUDOR GOVERNMENT

Richard Fox (1448–1528). Accompanied *Henry VII* in his invasion and was present at Bosworth Field in 1485. Became secretary to the king and appointed Keeper of the Privy Seal in February 1487 and Bishop of Exeter. Baptised Prince Henry at Greenwich, 1491. Bishop of Winchester 1501. Continued as Lord Privy Seal under *Henry VIII* and promoted *Thomas Wolsey* in the king's favour who, by 1513, had overtaken Fox in importance. Three years later the bishop resigned as Lord Privy Seal and retired from politics. By 1518, he was almost blind.

William Warham (?1450–1532). Appointed to the Mastership of the Rolls in February 1494 and Keeper of the Great Seal in August 1502. Consecrated as Bishop of London the following month and appointed Lord Chancellor in January 1504. He was enthroned as Archbishop of Canterbury in March 1505. He never enjoyed cordial relations with *Henry VIII* and was probably dismissed as Chancellor in December 1515, although Thomas More believed he was very pleased to leave politics.

Sir Richard Empson (*c.*1450–1510). Appointed Attorney-General to the Duchy of Lancaster in 1478 but lost this position under *Richard III*. He was reappointed by *Henry VII* and was chosen Speaker of the House of Commons in 1491. In 1505 he was appointed Chancellor of the Duchy of Lancaster and, with *Edmund Dudley*, was responsible for the king's policy of extortion. Arrested at the accession, Empson was executed with Dudley for treason on 17 August 1510.

Edmund Dudley (?1462–1510). Appointed Speaker of the House of Commons in 1504 and two years later, President of the Council. With *Sir Richard Empson*, was responsible for *Henry VII*'s policy of extortion through the imposition of bonds guaranteeing good behaviour. Like Empson, Dudley was arrested at the accession and executed for treason on 17 August 1510.

Thomas Wolsey (?1473–1530). Son of Robert Wulcy, an Ipswich, Suffolk, butcher, innkeeper and cattle-dealer. Appointed chaplain to *Henry VII* in 1507 and in

February 1509, royal almoner and dean of Lincoln. Created Bishop of Lincoln in 1514 and Archbishop of York in September of same year. Cardinal (September 1515) and succeeded *William Warham* as Lord Chancellor on Christmas Eve 1515. Papal Legate May 1518. Indicted under Statute of Praemunire, 9 October 1529 and property confiscated. Died 29 November 1530 at Leicester after being arrested for treason.

Sir Thomas More (1478–1535). Son of a prominent judge, Sir John More. Helped *Henry VIII* to write his book on the Seven Sacraments against Martin Luther. Speaker of the House of Commons, 1523 and Chancellor of the Duchy of Lancaster, 1525. Lord Chancellor after fall of *Thomas Wolsey*. Refused to take Oath of Succession. Executed 6 July 1535 after perjured trial on treason charges.

Thomas Cromwell later **Earl of Essex** (?1485–1540). Son of a Putney, south-west London, innkeeper, blacksmith and fuller. Legal adviser to Cardinal *Thomas Wolsey*; lawyer and money-lender. Later, Lord Privy Seal and Vice-Regent for religious affairs. Earl of Essex and Lord High Chamberlain of England. Beheaded for treason, 28 July 1540 on Tower Hill.

THE ROYAL HOUSEHOLD

Sir William Stanley (*c.*1435–95). Younger brother of Thomas Stanley, later First Earl of Derby. The intervention of the two brothers at Bosworth secured the crown for *Henry VII* and William was appointed Lord Chamberlain. According to the historian Polydore Vergil, Stanley 'was more mindful of the favours he had given than those he had received'. In 1495, he was convicted of treason and executed for his vocal support of *Perkin Warbeck*, the pretender to the English throne.

Sir William Compton (?1482–1528). Son and heir to Edmund Compton of Compton, Warwickshire. Page to Prince Henry after 1501. After *Henry VIII's* accession, their close friendship continued with Compton being appointed Groom of the Stool in 1510. He continued in royal service until 1526 and was frequently charged with the most sensitive and discreet missions by the king – including acting as go-between in Henry's affair with *Anne Hastings* and the arrest of *Buckingham*. Compton was knighted after the capture of Tournai in 1513 and was dispatched by Wolsey to the Scottish borders a decade later. In 1526 he was appointed usher of the receipts in the exchequer and obtained a licence that entitled him to wear his hat in the king's presence. Around 1519 he became involved with *Anne Hastings* and was cited in an ecclesiastical court for living with her in adultery. He died of the sweating sickness in 1528, leaving provisions in his will for Anne.

Charles Brandon, Duke of Suffolk (*c.*1484–1545). Son of Sir William Brandon, *Henry VII*'s standard bearer at Bosworth, where he was killed by *Richard III*. Brought up at *Henry VII*'s court and became a great favourite of *Henry VIII* through his skills at jousting and was appointed Master of the Horse in 1513. Before February 1506 he married Margaret Mortimer, *née* Neville. but the match was annulled the following year. In 1508 he married Anne Browne (died 1511), daughter of Sir Anthony Browne, Standard Bearer of England. On 15 May 1513 Brandon was created Viscount Lisle, having entered into a marriage contract with his ward, Elizabeth Grey, Viscountess Lisle in her own right, but she refused to marry him when she came of age. That year he was marshal of the English army invading France and he was created Duke of Suffolk in 1514. In late February the following year he secretly married *Mary Tudor*, queen dowager of France, creating a rift with *Henry VIII* but this was healed after the couple's payment of her dowry and surrender of Mary's plate and jewels. In 1528 he secured a papal Bull from *Clement VII* assuring the legitimacy of his marriage with Mary, as Margaret Mortimer was still living. After Mary's death in 1533, he married, for the fourth time, his ward Catherine Willoughby and by her had two sons, both of whom died of sweating sickness in 1551. Brandon commanded an unsuccessful English invasion of France in 1523 and commanded the army which again attacked France in 1544. He died at Guildford in Surrey on 24 August 1545 and was buried, at Henry's expense, in St George's Chapel, Windsor.

FOREIGN RULERS

Margaret of York, protector of Burgundy (1446–1503). Daughter of Richard Plantagenet, Third Duke of York, and sister to Edward IV and *Richard III*. She was the third wife of Charles the Bold, Duke of Burgundy, who was killed in battle in 1477. Margaret subsequently ruled as dowager duchess as the marriage was childless and her stepdaughter Mary, who had married *Maximilian I* on 18 August 1477, died after a hunting accident in 1482.

Margaret of Austria, also called **Margaret of Savoy** (1480–1530). Daughter of *Maximilian* I and regent of the Netherlands 1507–15 and again in 1519–30. In 1497, she married John, Prince of Asturias, son and heir of *Ferdinand II of Aragon* and *Isabella of Castile*. However, John died six months later and she returned to the Low Countries early in 1500. A year later she married Philibert II, Duke of Savoy, who died in 1504. Both marriages were childless. She appointed her nephew *Charles V* her sole heir.

Philip of Burgundy (1478–1506). Son of *Maximilian I* who inherited the largest part of Burgundy from his mother and briefly succeeded to the crown of Castile as the husband of Queen Juana. *Charles V* was the second of their six children. Philip died, probably from typhoid fever, at Burgos on 25 September 1506 and his wife reputedly refused to allow his body to be buried, or to be parted from it, for a time.

Ferdinand II of Aragon, (1452–1516). Son of John II of Aragon by his second wife, Juana Enríquez. Married *Isabella*, half-sister and heiress of Henry IV of Castile in October 1469. Ferdinand succeeded his father as King of Aragon in 1479, ruling this and Castile with his wife. They conquered the kingdom of Granada, the last Moorish state in the Iberian peninsula, and fought a number of campaigns against the French in Italy. *Katherine of Aragon* was the youngest of four daughters. After the death of Isabella he ruled Castile in the name of his mad daughter Juana and married Germaine de Foix, niece of *Louis XII* of France, in October 1505.

Isabella of Castile, Queen of Castile and León (1451–1504). Daughter of John II of Castile and Isabella of Portugal. Her marriage to her second cousin Ferdinand was contested but Pope Sixtus IV granted them a dispensation.

Louis XII, King of France (1462–1515). Son of Charles duc d'Orléans and Marie of Cleves. As the four children of his cousin Charles VIII died in infancy, Louis succeeded to the French throne on his death in 1498. He married first Joan of France, the daughter of his second cousin, Louis XI, but this was nullified on his accession so he could marry Charles' queen, Anne of Brittany. On her death in 1514, he married *Mary Tudor*, younger sister of *Henry VIII*. Less than three months afterwards he died.

Francis I, King of France (1494–1547). After death of Anne of Brittany's son in 1512, styled 'Dauphin of France'. Son-in-law of *Louis XII*. Crowned at Rheims 1515. In 1520, Edward Hall described him as 'stately of countenance, merry of cheer, brown coloured, great eyes, high nosed, big lipped, fair breasted and shoulders, small legs and long feet'. Died at Château Rambouillet, 30 miles (48 km) south-west of Paris and succeeded by his son Henry II.

Maximilian I of Austria (1459–1519). King of the Romans from 1493 but elected as Holy Roman Emperor in 1508. He governed the dukedom of Burgundy via his first wife, Mary (stepdaughter of *Margaret of York*) who died in a riding accident in 1482. Married Anne of Brittany by proxy in December 1490 but the contract was dissolved by the Pope two years later and she married Charles VIII of France. He finally married Bianca Maria Sforza in 1493 bringing him suzerainty over the duchy of Milan. He was notoriously frugal and Pope Julius

II described him dismissively as 'light and inconstant, always begging for other men's money which he wastes in chamois hunting'.

Charles V, King of Spain and Holy Roman Emperor (1500–58). Son of Philip of Burgundy and his wife, the mad Juana, daughter of *Ferdinand* and *Isabella*. As such, he was nephew of *Katherine of Aragon*, first wife of *Henry VIII*. Acceded to Spanish throne in 1516. Abdicated in favour of son Philip (husband of *Mary I* of England) 1556. Retreated to monastery of Yuste, dying two years later.

James IV of **Scotland** (1472–1513). Supported *Perkin Warbeck*, pretender to English crown, 1496. Married *Margaret*, daughter of *Henry VII*, 1503. Signed a treaty of mutual military assistance with *Louis XII* of France against *Henry VIII* and invaded Northumberland whilst Henry was in northern France. Defeated by Thomas Howard, Earl of Surrey, at Flodden Field on 9 September 1513 and was killed.

THE VATICAN

Innocent VIII (1432–92) was Pope from 1484 until his death. He granted the dispensation to Henry VII for his marriage to Elizabeth of York to 'end the long and grievous variance, contentions and debates' between England's warring factions. The Bull also underlined Henry Tudor's legal claim to the throne.

Julius II (1443–1513) succeeded Pius III in 1503 after a conclave lasting a few hours – the shortest in the history of the papacy. He was Pope until he died of a fever in 1513. On 22 January 1506 he founded the Swiss Guard as a security force to protect the pontiff. In November 1504 Julius issued the required dispensation allowing the marriage of Henry VIII with his brother's widow, *Katherine of Aragon* – the validity of which was later challenged by Henry. In 1511 he promoted the 'Holy League' of *Ferdinand, Maximilian, Henry VIII* and the Venetians against France.

Leo X (1475–1521) occupied St Peter's throne from 1513 until his death after an attack of malaria. He excommunicated the religious reformer Martin Luther for heresy on 3 January 1521 and awarded *Henry VIII* the honorific title of *Defensor Fidei* – 'Defender of the Faith' – on 24 November the same year for his book *Defence of the Seven Sacraments* which attacked Luther's teachings. The title was intended for the king's personal use but became inextricably attached to the crown of England.

Clement VII (1478–1534) succeeded the short-lived Adrian VI as Pope in November 1523 and saw Rome sacked by unpaid mutinying Imperial troops in May 1527. He fled to the castle of St Angelo and was held prisoner there for seven months, eventually escaping to Orvieto disguised as a pedlar. Clement returned to Rome in July 1529 and was confronted by *Henry VIII's* demands for the annulment of his marriage to *Katherine of Aragon*. Papal prevarication resulted in the passing of the Act of Supremacy by the English Parliament in 1534 that established an independent Church of England. Clement launched a sentence of excommunication against Henry and declared Cranmer's decree of divorce invalid. He died in September 1534 after inadvertently eating a lethally poisonous 'death cap' mushroom, *amanita phalloides.*

Paul III (1468–1549) was Pope from 1534 until 1549. He offered a cardinal's hat to John Fisher, Bishop of Rochester, and after his execution told Francis I of France that *Henry VIII* 'had exceeded his ancestors in wickedness'. Paul was compelled 'by the unanimous solicitation of the cardinals to declare Henry deprived of his kingdom and his royal dignity'.

Cardinal Lorenzo Campeggio (1474–1539) began in the legal profession in Bologna and Pavia. After his wife died in 1510 he went into the church, becoming a cardinal in 1517. He was made protector of England in the Roman *curia* and *Henry VIII* gave him the bishopric of Salisbury. After his abortive legatine hearings (with *Wolsey*) of the annulment of Henry's marriage, Campeggio was deprived of the protectorate and the see of Salisbury.

NOTES

PROLOGUE: THE UNCERTAIN CROWN

1 *LP Henry VII*, p.239. As Prince Arthur was dead by 1503, this is a reference to Prince Henry.

2 *PROME*, vol. 15, p.93 and *Crowland Chronicle Continuations*, pp.194–5.

3 Cavill, p.23.

4 From *King Henry IV, Part II*, 3. 1. 30.

5 Henry VII defeated the last remnants of the Yorkist party at Stoke Field, Nottinghamshire, on 16 June 1487, and Cornish rebels at Blackheath, south-east of London, on 17 June 1497. Henry VIII faced rebellion in Lincolnshire in October 1536 and the more dangerous widespread 'Pilgrimage of Grace' insurrection throughout the North of England in January 1537. His son Edward VI eventually put down rebellions in the West, Norfolk and the South Midlands in 1549, but only with the assistance of German mercenaries and not without great difficulty. Henry's daughter Mary I was threatened by rebels in 1554 who opposed her marriage to Philip of Spain. They fought their way up to the western gates of the City of London before being defeated. Finally, Elizabeth ordered repressive measures to punish those who took part in the abortive rising by the Earls of Northumberland and Westmorland in November 1569 and faced regular conspiracies against her by Catholic supporters of Mary, Queen of Scots, who had a viable claim to the throne of England through her direct descent from Henry VIII's elder sister, Margaret.

6 Margaret was the daughter of John Beaufort, First Duke of Somerset (1403–44), who apparently killed himself after being banished from the royal court. His father was John de Beaufort, First Earl of Somerset (*c*.1371–1409), who was the eldest of the four children of John of Gaunt and Katherine Swynford. Therefore, she was John of Gaunt's great-granddaughter.

7 In Welsh, *Owain ap Maredudd ap Tewdwr*.

8 Hall, p.421.

9 Monuments to some of those who died on the losing side at Bosworth or during its aftermath display an unsurprising coyness about their part in the battle. For example, at Morley, Derbyshire, the monumental brass to John Sacheverell who was killed fighting for Richard III was only erected in *c*.1525, forty years after the battle. At Ashby St Legers, Northamptonshire, the monument to William Catesby ('the Cat' in the famous doggerel rhyme about Richard and his chief advisers) gives his date of death as 20 August 1485, *two days before the battle*. In fact, he was executed in Leicester three days afterwards. The brass was laid down under instructions in the

will of his son George in c.1507. See Simon Payling's 'Rise and Fall of the Fifteenth-Century Catesbys' in *The Catesby Family and the Brasses at Ashby St Legers*, Jerome Bertram (ed.), London, 2006, pp.12–13.

10 *Paston Letters*, vol. 6, p.82.

11 *PROME*, vol. 15, p.97. The Act, 1 Henry VII cap.1, laid down 'by authority of this present Parliament that the inheritance of the crowns of the realms of England and of France . . . be, rest, remain and abide in the most royal person of our now sovereign lord King Harry the VIIth and in the heirs of his body lawfully coming perpetual with the grace of God so to endure and in none other' (*RP*, vol. 6, p.270).

12 This was on the grounds of Edward IV's pre-marriage contract with Eleanor Butler (d.1468), daughter of John Talbot, First Earl of Shrewsbury.

13 *PROME*, vol. 15, pp.133–4; *RP*, vol. 6, pp.288–9. See also Cavill, p.30. The new Act required the surrender of all copies of the *Titulus Regius* and their destruction by the following Easter on pain of imprisonment or fine at the king's will. It declared that 'the said Bill, Act and Record, be annulled and utterly destroyed and that it be ordained by the same authority that the same Act and Record be taken out of the Roll of Parliament and be cancelled and burnt and be put into perpetual oblivion'. However, the text remains in the Parliament Roll of 1484 (see *PROME*, vol. 15, pp.13–18). The remainder of the Parliament was spent reversing the attainders on the king's friends and imposing new ones on the nobility who had supported Richard. See Anglo, 'Spectacle', p.18.

14 The betrothal had been agreed during Richard III's short reign, by Edward's queen, Elizabeth Woodville, and Henry's mother, Lady Margaret Beaufort.

15 He was already appointed Chancellor of the Exchequer.

16 *RP*, vol. 6, p.278 and 'Materials', vol. 1, pp.209–10.

17 Leland, vol. 4, pp.196, 198. See also: Chrimes, p.66 and Cavill, pp.31–2. It was confirmed by Pope Innocent VIII on 2 March 1486 and it is obvious that the pontiff was wholly ignorant that the marriage had already taken place on 18 January.

18 The Bull was reprinted in 1494, two years later by Wynkyn de Worde and again in 1497. See Anglo, *Spectacle*, p.19.

19 He died on 30 March at his house at Knole, near Sevenoaks, Kent, and was buried in Canterbury Cathedral. He was thought too infirm to take the full role of the Archbishop of Canterbury during Henry's coronation, other than anointing the new king and placing the crown upon his head, and Thomas Kempe, Bishop of London, conducted that service.

20 'Memorials', p.39.

21 Hall, p.425.

22 BL Cotton MS *Cleopatra E III*, fol.123.

23 BL Royal MS 2A XVIII, f.30v. Margaret Beaufort's 240-page *Book of Hours*, which she used to jot down memorable events, was probably drawn up for John Beaufort, First Duke of Somerset, before 1399.

24 Madden, p.279. St Eustace, a legendary second-century Christian martyr, has now been removed from the Catholic calendar of saints.

25 On 30 May 1488 a grant of a £40 annuity was made to Stephen Bereworth, doctor of

medicine, 'in consideration of the grantee's cordial affection and good service to the king and in reward for his medical attendance upon Prince Arthur, the king's first-born son'. Was Arthur a sickly infant? See 'Materials', vol. 2, p.319.

26 BL Lansdowne MS 978, f.26.

27 See, for example, David Starkey, 'King Henry and King Arthur' in *Arthurian Literature*, J. P. Carley and F. Riddy (eds.), vol. 16 (1998), pp.171–96 and 177–8, and Starkey, *Henry – Virtuous Prince*, pp.41–2.

28 Bacon, pp.18–19.

29 Hall, p.428.

30 See Anglo, *Images*, p.51.

31 Such as Bernard André's sycophantic attempt to perceive the image of the ancient king in the appearance of the child. See Sydney Anglo, 'The *British History* in Early Tudor Propaganda', *Bulletin of the John Rylands Library*, vol. 44, (1961), pp.29–30.

32 Jasper, Earl of Pembroke and First Duke of Bedford, married Catherine Woodville, sister of Edward IV's queen, Elizabeth Woodville, on 7 November 1485. She was the widow of Henry Stafford, Second Duke of Buckingham, executed by Richard III at Salisbury on 2 November 1483 after his abortive rebellion.

33 'Plumpton Correspondence', p.50. On 14 October 1486 a rabbit warren and lands in Much Marcle and Stretton, Herefordshire, were granted to Thomas Acton after being seized by the king because of the rebellion of Thomas Hunteley 'and his adherence to the rebels of Wales' (*CFR*, pp.60–1).

34 See Luckett, pp.166–8.

35 Edward Plantagenet (1475–99) was the elder son of the fatally ambitious George, First Duke of Clarence (1449–78), brother of both Edward IV and Richard III, who was accused of treason by the former and secretly executed in the Tower of London on or around 18 February 1478. Tradition has it that he was drowned in a butt of Malmsey wine, and a body, believed to be that of Clarence, was subsequently exhumed. It had not been decapitated. See Michael Hicks, *False, Fleeting, Perjur'd: George Clarence, Duke of Clarence*, Bangor, 1992, pp.184–6.

36 Bennett, p.63.

37 In 1996 Gordon Smith suggested that Simnel might have been Edward V, the elder of the two princes who disappeared in the Tower – or claimed to be him (see 'Lambert Simnel and the King from Dublin', *The Ricardian*, vol. 10, pp.498–536). Tradition has it that the Simnel cake – a light fruitcake with marzipan, eaten during Lent – was named after this youthful imposter, but the term appears in medieval English literature and so pre-dates him.

38 Leland, vol. 4, p.212, and Starkey, *Henry – Virtuous Prince*, p.55.

39 Oxford led Henry's vanguard at Bosworth. Perhaps the king's experience during that battle, when he and his bodyguard had to fight off a furious, frenzied mounted attack by Richard III and his household knights, persuaded Henry to direct the battle from behind the front lines. See Hutchinson, *House of Treason*, p.xvi.

40 A vault opened at Lovell's home at Minster Lovell, near Witney, Oxfordshire, in 1728, contained a man's skeleton seated at a table, which has been assumed to be the missing viscount (Brooks, p.273).

41 For a fuller discussion of the rebellion, see Bennett, *passim.*

42 BL Royal MS 2A XVIII, f.30v.

43 Leland, vol. 4, p.216. The coronation was attended by fifteen bishops, seventeen abbots, two dukes, twelve earls, two viscounts, twenty barons, three duchesses, four countesses, seven baronesses, thirty-one knight bannerets and one hundred and fifty knights, plus their wives and other gentlewomen.

44 Halsted, p.177.

45 At the banquet that followed in Westminster Hall, Henry and Lady Margaret watched proceedings from a stage erected on the left wall of the building, 'richly beset with cloth of arras, that they might see privily at their pleasure the noble feast' (Leland, vol. 4, p.227).

46 Ibid., p.236.

CHAPTER 1: IN MY BROTHER'S SHADOW

1 Thomas & Thornley, p.254. A 'courser' was a large war horse.

2 Leland, vol. 4, pp.179–83.

3 See 'Ryalle Book', pp.304–6 and 333–8.

4 A coarse twill of linen and cotton.

5 Leland, vol. 4, pp.179–80.

6 BL Royal MS 2A. XVIII, f.30v. Henry's birth is recorded, using the Roman calendar under '*IV Kalendar Julii*'. Lady Margaret recorded the precise hour of the birth of both Arthur and his sister Margaret – but not that of Henry. In the manuscript of the *Great Chronicle of London*, Henry's birth was inserted some time after the event and was recorded under the wrong year. See Starkey, *Henry – Virtuous Prince*, p.373. Lady Margaret's imprecision was normal in the late fifteenth century. John More, the lawyer father of Thomas More, noted the date of his son's birth on a page in his copy of Geoffrey of Monmouth's *Historia Regnum Britanniæ* as 1477, amended it to 1478 and then changed it back. It was probably 7 February 1478 (see Ackroyd, p.4).

7 Construction of the church began in 1482, and three years later Henry VII founded the convent of Observant Friars there with a warden and twelve brethren from this reformed Franciscan Order (see William Page (ed.), *Victoria History of Kent*, vol. 2, London, 1926, p.194). Images in painted glass of saints and of Henry VII, Lady Margaret Beaufort and Elizabeth of York were inserted in its windows (see BL Egerton MS 2,341).

8 In January 1485, Richard III stopped Fox's appointment to the vicarage of Stepney, north of London, because he was associated with the 'great rebel, Henry ap Tudor'. Thirty-eight years later, Fox recalled his baptism of Henry (*LP Henry VIII*, vol. 4, p.2,588).

9 Starkey, *Henry – Virtuous Prince*, pp.11–12 and Doran, p.19.

10 TNA E 404/81/1 – 31 December 1491.

11 The Launcelyn arms were *Gules, a fleur-de-lis argent*. Her grandfather John was Justice of the Peace for Bedfordshire in 1423 (see William Page (ed.), *Victoria History of Bedfordshire*, vol. 3, London, 1912, p.238).

12 Charles Cooper, p.35.

13 Frideswide may have been one of the five daughters of George Puttenham of Penn, Buckinghamshire, knighted in 1501.

14 The Tudors were always generous to their nursery staff. Katherine Gibbs, former wet nurse to Prince Arthur, was granted an annuity of £20 'from Christmas last' on 28 April 1490 (*CPR Henry VII*, vol. 1, p.306). Shortly after her royal duties ended, Anne, widow of Geoffrey Oxenbridge, was granted the office of Bailiff of the town of Winchelsea, subject to a rent of £20 to the king, 'beyond the £10 a year that the king gave the said Anne for her service, to hold so long as she shall continue the said payment' (*CPR Henry VII*, vol. 2, p.11). On 5 March 1504 she and her second husband, Walter Luke, were granted an annuity of 100 shillings for life, paid out of the customs of Winchelsea 'of boats fishing on the sea called "snares" [a type of fishing line] anchorage and ... other small customs of woods, herring, barley, ale, salt, peas, cheese, timber and feather beds' (ibid., p.345). Luke was also commissioned in July 1505 along with four others to investigate land ownership in Bedfordshire (ibid., p.422). He was later knighted and appointed a Justice of the Court of King's Bench. Anne died on 9 September 1538 and Luke six years later. The couple have a Purbeck marble tomb, with brass plates depicting them both kneeling at prayer desks, in the chancel of All Saints Church, Cople. The inscription proudly declares that Anne was 'nurse unto his ... majesty'. The brass is illustrated in William Lack, H. Martin Stuchfield and Philip Whittemore's *Monumental Brasses of Bedfordshire*, London, 1992, p.25.

15 The use of swaddling or 'swathing' bands went out of fashion in the seventeenth century, but apparently is now reviving, as some believe that restricting a baby's movement lowers the risk of sudden infant death syndrome (see Alison Sim, *The Tudor Housewife*, Quebec, 1998, p.26). There are a number of monuments to children who died very soon after their birth depicting them in their swaddling bands, such as at Rougham, Norfolk, 1510; Stoke d'Abernon, Surrey, 1516; Chesham Bois, Buckinghamshire, c.1520; and Cranbrook, Kent, of the same date. Anne Asteley (d.1512), at Blicking, Norfolk, holds two children in swaddling bands, one in each arm – a double tragedy. These are known as 'chrisom' monuments after the name of the child's white baptism robe which was utilised as a shroud if he or she died within a month of birth.

16 'Ryalle Book', p.337; Leland, vol. 4, p.302.

17 Leland, vol. 4, pp.301–2.

18 Starkey, *Henry – Virtuous Prince*, p.63.

19 TNA E 404/81/3 – 17 September 1493.

20 She was the eldest daughter of John Jermingham and his wife Agnes (daughter of Sir John Darell), of Somerleyton, near Lowestoft, Suffolk. The couple had seven children, including three other daughters who all became nuns and were alive in 1473. Elizabeth married a John Denton and in 1517 became governess to Princess Mary, daughter of Henry VIII and his first wife Katherine of Aragon. She died a year later.

21 See Flügel, *Men and Their Motives*, p.277 and 'On the Character ...', pp.124ff. Two of

Henry's wives had been married or declared for close relatives – his first wife Katherine of Aragon had previously married his brother Arthur, and his last, Katherine Parr, planned to marry his brother-in-law, Thomas Seymour. See Hutchinson, *Last Days*, p.59.

22 Bentley, p.95.

23 On 29 May 1494, the king paid five shillings for 'a hat for my lord Harry'; Bentley, p.98.

24 The portrait, inscribed 'le Roy henry d'angleterre' beneath the sketch, is in Bibliothèque de Méjanes MS 442 Res MS 20. There are doubts about its authenticity, particularly regarding the dress and style of hat, which look more appropriate to the fashion of *c.*1515–25. See Doran, p.17 and Hayward, p.89.

25 Tudor kitchen staff worked either naked or wore clothes smothered in grease. See Peter Brears, 'Food and Drink at Henry's Court', in Rimer et al., p.85.

26 Edward IV had six illegitimate children by at least three mistresses, in addition to the ten legitimate offspring, of which only seven survived him.

27 Warbeck's later confession said he was the son of John Osbek, Comptroller of Tournai. See S. J. Gunn, 'Perkin Warbeck', *ODNB*, vol. 57, pp.246–8.

28 Her crown, made in 1461, was adorned with enamelled white roses for the House of York set between pearls. It remains the only surviving medieval royal English crown and is held in the treasury of Aachen Cathedral in Germany. The remainder of the medieval English crown jewels were broken up after the seventeenth-century English Civil War.

29 The purple-red colour of mulberry, from the Old French *morée*.

30 Wroe, p.141.

31 Frederick III died at Linz aged 77 during a botched attempt to amputate his left leg.

32 Wroe, pp.134–6.

33 Bernard André, *De Vita atque gestis Henrici Septimi Historia*, in 'Memorials', pp.49–52.

34 Henry wrote to Sir George Talbot, Fourth Earl of Shrewsbury, giving news of 'the feigned lad called Perkin Warbeck [who was] born at Tournai in Picardy'. See Ellis, 'Original Letters', 1st ser., vol. 1, p.20.

35 Bacon, pp.134–5. Stanley had earlier been disappointed by Henry VII in his claim to the Earldom of Chester: his 'suit did not only end in denial but in a distaste' according to Bacon. Prince Arthur was created Earl of Chester on 30 November 1489.

36 *CPR Henry VII*, vol. 1, pp.407 and 438–9. Arthur was empowered to 'array men-at-arms, archers and other fensible [militia] men' in these counties 'for the defence of his person and the resistance of ill-doers ... and for putting the laws in execution'.

37 The town of Droitwich, Worcestershire, bought bows and arrows to arm newly recruited soldiers 'sent when my lord prince went into Wales' (Worcestershire Record Office, 261.4/BA1006/31b/319).

38 J. B. Smith, 'Crown and Community in the Principality of North Wales in the Reign of Henry Tudor', *Welsh History Review*, vol. 3 (1966), pp.163–71.

39 *CPR Henry VII*, vol. 1, p.423.

40 Sir Edward Poynings succeeded Henry as Lord Warden in 1509. Later holders included the Duke of Wellington (1829–52), Sir Winston Churchill (1941–65) and Queen Elizabeth the Queen Mother (1978–2002). The post is currently held by Admiral the Lord Boyce, former Chief of the Naval Staff and later Chief of the Defence Staff, who was appointed in July 2004. The ports were required to supply fifty-seven ships and their crews for fifteen days' service each year, either as warships or royal transports.

41 Poynings (1459–1521), soldier-administrator, led an expedition to subdue the Irish and impose English-style justice upon them. An Act (10 Henry VII cap. 9), which came to be known as Poynings' Law, ensured that no parliament could be held in Ireland without the king's prior consent. Only bills earlier approved by the Privy Council in London could be considered. His illegitimate son Thomas was also a loyal Tudor courtier.

42 *LP Henry VII*, vol. 2, p.374.

43 TNA E 404/81/4; BL Cotton MS Julius B. XII, ff.91–110. Failure to attend incurred a fine.

44 With some prurience, one suspects use was made of the disposable earthenware urinals of the type we know were employed by members of Henry VIII's Privy Council later in the sixteenth century so that their calls of nature did not interrupt proceedings. They were supplied at three pence each, according to his apothecary's accounts. See Hutchinson, *Last Days*, p.207.

45 'Dinner' in the Tudor period was eaten around ten o'clock in the morning.

46 BL Cotton MS Julius B. XII, ff.91–110.

47 Thomas Grey, Lord Harrington, was the son and heir of Thomas Grey, First Marquis of Dorset, a stepson of Edward IV. Dorset was imprisoned during the Lambert Simnel uprising in 1487 and was required to make his heir a ward of Henry VII, together with proving guarantees of his loyalty to the Tudor crown. See T. B. Pugh, 'Henry VII and the English Nobility' in *The Tudor Nobility*, G. W. Bernard (ed.), Manchester, 1992, pp.49–110.

48 Jocelyn Perkins, *Most Honourable Order of the Bath*, 2nd ed., London, 1920, p.7.

49 The two-storey chapel was completed in 1348 but was destroyed in the great fire of 1834. The lower storey, which was reserved for use by members of the royal household, survives as the Chapel of St Mary Undercroft. After 1547, in the reign of Henry VIII's son Edward VI, the chapel was deconsecrated and became the debating chamber of the House of Commons, with the Speaker's chair positioned on the old altar steps.

50 On 31 October 1494, Northumberland received a payment of £2 6s 8d for the robes of a Knight of the Bath, worn during the ceremony. See Bentley, p.99.

51 The last time this ritual was employed was during Charles II's coronation in April 1661. It is perhaps somewhat apposite that the Order's chapel is now the Henry VII Chapel in Westminster Abbey. Its Grand Master is Charles, Prince of Wales, who was appointed in May 1975 by Queen Elizabeth II.

52 Westminster Hall was completed in 1097 and at the time was the largest hall in England, if not in Europe. It measures 250 feet in length and 67 feet in width

(73 m by 20 m) and has a fourteenth-century raftered roof.

53 BL Cotton MS Julius B. XII, ff.91–110. Henry did not wear his spurs for very long. Within an hour or so, the king's master cook claimed them as his fee for services rendered during the long ceremony.

54 Ibid., ff. 92v–93.

55 The priest, Thomas Lyng, wrote to Sir John Paston (who was knighted at the Battle of Stoke) in Norfolk, describing the scene in Westminster Hall: 'The king and queen went crowned on Hallowmass Day last and my Lord of Shrewsbury bore my Lord Harry in his arms and ten bishops with mitres on their heads, going before the king that day round about Westminster Hall with many other estates [nobles].' He probably confused a couple of abbots for bishops as only eight bishops took part in the proceedings. See *Paston Letters*, vol. 6, p.152.

56 *LP Henry VII*, vol. 1, pp.393–4.

57 Vergil, pp.73–5; Thomas & Thornley, p.256.

58 Thomas & Thornley, p.257.

59 Henry's Privy Purse paid out £15 19s for Stanley's burial in the Bridgettine Church at Syon, near Isleworth, Middlesex, on 27 February 1495. Eleven days earlier, the accounts recorded a £10 payment to 'Sir William Stanley at his execution' – probably the traditional *guerdon* (or reward) to the headsman, given in the hope of a clean, speedy end. Bentley, p.101.

60 The £500 was delivered to Clifford by Sir Reginald Bray, one of Henry's ministers, on 20 January 1495 (Bentley, p.100). He used the money piously – an attack of conscience perhaps? – to build a new aisle onto his local parish church at Aspenden, Hertfordshire.

61 He died in 1508 and was buried in an expensive tomb in the church at Aspenden. Its south porch, erected between 1508 and 1526, was endowed by his widow, Elizabeth, and bears Clifford's arms and those of her first husband, Sir Ralph Jocelyn.

62 Hall, p.472.

63 Bacon, p.142.

64 Warbeck asked James IV to 'benignly bend' his ears to 'hear the tragedy of a young man that by right ought to hold in his hand the ball of a kingdom but by fortune is made himself a ball, tossed from misery to misery and place to place' (see Bacon, p.148).

65 During the border wars between England and Scotland during the Middle Ages, Berwick had changed hands thirteen times. It had been recaptured by Richard, Duke of Gloucester, later Richard III, in 1482.

66 After crossing the border, Warbeck issued a proclamation promising the people of England that he did not 'intend their hurt and damage or to make war upon them, otherwise to deliver our self and them from tyranny and oppression. For, Our mortal enemy Henry Tudor, a false usurper of the crown of England (which to Us by natural and lineal right appertaineth) ... has not only deprived Us of Our kingdom, but likewise by all foul and wicked means sought to betray Us and bereave Us of Our life' (Bacon, pp.154–60).

67 Warbeck complained passionately to James IV about his soldiers' destruction of

property in Northumberland and their return 'heavy and laden with spoil', declaring that 'no crown was so dear to his mind as that he desired to purchase it with the blood and ruin of his country'. The Scottish king, an old campaigner, replied skittishly that he doubted if 'he was careful for that which was not his and that he [would not] be too good a steward for his enemy' (Bacon, p.160).

68 *LP Henry VII*, vol. 2, p.57.

69 A fabric woven from goats' hair and silk.

70 Hayward, p.90.

71 TNA E. 404/82 – warrant for the payment of funeral expenses, 26 October 1495. There is a description of the funeral in BL Egerton MS 2,642, f.185v.

72 The monument had a brass inscription around the edge of the cover-stone and another rectangular one beneath the feet of the effigy. These are now lost – probably torn off during the 'cleansing' of Westminster Abbey in 1548 under religious reforms introduced by the government of Elizabeth's nephew, Edward VI.

73 *CPR Henry VII*, vol. 2, p.72.

74 Scarisbrick, *Henry VIII*, p.4.

75 Hall, p.479.

76 Hall, ibid. Joseph, of St Keverne, was sentenced to death for his part in the insurrection and while he was being drawn on a sheep hurdle to the place of execution, 'he said that for this mischievous and facinorous [extremely wicked] act, he should have a name perpetual and the same permanent and immortal'. Today, of course, people go on television talent shows in the same hope.

77 Bacon, p.182.

78 Bentley, p.114.

79 Walsingham has been a place of pilgrimage since 1061 when a Saxon noblewoman, Richeldis de Faverchies, wife of the local lord of the manor, had three visions of the Virgin Mary who requested the replication of the holy house of the Annunciation in Nazareth in this Norfolk village. The medieval shrine was destroyed during the reign of Henry VIII in 1538. An Anglican shrine was re-established in the village of Little Walsingham in 1931 and is today visited annually by more than 300,000 pilgrims, 10,000 of them residential. There is also a Catholic shrine, founded in 1934.

80 Warbeck was arrested by John Godfrey, Mayor of Southampton, and his henchmen. He was paid the large sum of £482 16s 8d for expenses and rewards 'for business concerning Piers Osbeck' (Wroe, p.317).

81 Hall, p.485. She was treated generously by Elizabeth of York and remarried three times during the reign of Henry VIII: first to James Strangeways, a Gentleman of the Privy Chamber; then to Matthew Craddock; and finally in 1531 to Christopher Ashton. Catherine died in 1537 and was buried at Fyfield, Berkshire. Henry paid out £7 13s 4d to Robert Southwell for horses, saddles 'and other necessaries bought for the conveying of my lady Catherine Huntley' (Bentley, p.115).

82 Hall, p.486.

83 *CSP Spain*, vol. 1, p.185.

84 Polydore Vergil asks why this 'unhappy boy should have been committed to prison, not for any fault of his own but only because of his family's offences; why he was

retained so long in prison and what, lastly, the worthy youth could have done in prison which could merit his death – all these things could obviously not be comprehended by many'. But the answer was tragically clear: 'Truly the wretched lot of the Yorkist house was such that Earl Edward had to perish in this fashion in order that there should be no surviving male heir to his family'(see Vergil, p.119).

85 Arthurson, p.209.

86 Also involved in the brawl were Suffolk's Yorkist companions, William Courtenay, Sir Thomas Neville and William Brandon. Henry VII had halted the common-law proceedings against Suffolk to win some political advantage over these vulnerable Yorkist supporters (Cunningham, *ODNB*, vol. 44, p.697).

87 *CSP Spain*, vol. 1, p.206.

88 As a foreigner he could not be accused of treason and therefore was not hanged, drawn and quartered – the penalty for traitors. The site of the scaffold at Tyburn is today's Marble Arch in London and the location is named after the Tyburn Stream, which flows into the River Thames near Vauxhall Bridge. Executions there ended in 1783.

89 'Greyfriars Chronicle', p.26. Henry paid a total of £12 18s 2d for Warwick's burial at Bisham Abbey in Berkshire.

90 *CSP Spain*, vol. 1, p.213.

91 *CSP Milan*, p.322.

92 He was baptised in the Greyfriars Church at Greenwich on 24 February. John Davy was paid 6s 8d to ride to Canterbury to collect the special silver font and the prior given a £2 reward for supplying it (Bentley, p.120).

CHAPTER 2: THE SPARE HEIR

1 Nichols, *Epistles of Erasmus*, vol. 1, p.201.

2 RCIN 73197. It has been variously described in catalogues as 'head of a laughing child' and 'bust of a German dwarf'.

3 Attributed in 1925 by the art historian Sir Lionel Cust (1859–1929), when Surveyor of the King's Pictures and Works of Art. By 1494, Henry VII began to plan his tomb, originally intended to be erected in the Lady chapel of St George's Chapel, Windsor, but four years later his planned burial site was switched to Westminster; see Condon, 'God Save the King' in Tatton-Brown & Mortimer, *Westminster Abbey*, p.60.

4 Bentley, *Excerpta Historica*, p.105.

5 Starkey, *Henry – Virtuous Prince*, pp.118–19.

6 Herbert, *Life and Raigne of King Henry the eighth*, p.2.

7 Corpus Christi College MS 432. See Doran, *Man and Monarch . . .*, pp.30–1. It is now known as the *Récits d'un ménestrel de Reims*, and was presented to Henry by Skelton in 1511.

8 Nelson, *John Skelton . . .*, p.15 and Gunn and Monkton, *Arthur Tudor*, p.8. Some of Arthur's books were in English, including a translation of Virgil's *Aeneid*, published in 1498 by William Caxton and dedicated to 'my coming natural and sovereign lord'. See: W. J. B. Crotch (ed.), *The Prologues and Epilogues of William Caxton*, EETS original publication 176 (London, 1928), p.110.

9 Now held by Emmanuel College, Cambridge; MS 5.3.11. The picture of Arthur is at f.1. See Carley, *Books of Henry VIII . . .*, p.49. The illuminated initial is illustrated on p.51.

10 A mountain in Greece, formerly sacred to the Muses, which was often confused by sixteenth-century writers with the springs of Aganippe and Hippocrene which rose in it.

11 Scattergood (ed.), *John Skelton . . .*, p.132.

12 Salter, 'Skelton's *Speculum Principis*', pp.25–37. The surviving copy of this moral treatise, which dates from Henry's accession, is in BL Add. MS 26,787 as a small octavo book, with some text lost at the beginning. It was formerly in the library of Lincoln Cathedral.

13 Pollard, *Henry VII*, p.15.

14 More was called to the bar and admitted to Lincoln's Inn in 1496. He became a barrister in 1501.

15 Nichols, *Epistles of Erasmus*, vol. 1, p.26 and pp.201–2, originally contained in Erasmus' *Catalogue of Lucubrations*, an account of his early attempts at poetry. Henry's note to Erasmus has not survived.

16 It was printed and published in 1500 with a dedication to Henry.

17 BL Egerton MS 1,651, f.1.

18 Bentley, *Excerpta Historica*, p.116.

19 Hayward, *Dress at the Court of Henry VIII*, p.90.

20 TNA E 36/219 f.8v and 12v. In 1498–9, Henry VII spent a total of £134 8s 6½d on clothing for the royal children. See Hayward, p.90.

21 A recent study of the 1505 portrait of Henry VII suggests that the traditional view that it represents a mean and crafty king results 'from a misinterpretation of the artist's intentions'. See Frederick Hepburn, 'The 1505 Portrait of Henry VII', *Antiquaries Jnl*, vol. 88 (2008), pp.245–6.

22 Vergil, *Anglica Historia*, p.145.

23 Pollard, *Reign of Henry VII*, vol. 1, p.204.

24 Edmund died at the bishop of Ely's house at Hatfield, Hertfordshire. His body was brought to London on 22 June and 'conveyed honourably through Fleet Street with many noble personages, the Duke of Buckingham [one of his godfathers] being the chief mourner' for burial that day in Westminster Abbey; Pollard, *Henry VII*, vol. 1, pp.215–16. Edmund's funeral bill was £242 11s 8d.

25 *CSP Spain*, vol. 1, pp.177–8. The old English nursery rhyme *Sing a Song of Sixpence* is traditionally supposed to portray Henry and his queen, Elizabeth of York: 'The king was in his counting house / 'Counting out his money / 'The queen was in the parlour / 'Eating bread and honey . . . /'

26 TNA E 101/413/2/3, ff.1–4.

27 Letter to Ferdinand and Isabella, 26 March 1499; *CSP Spain*, vol. 1, pp.206–7.

28 Horowitz, 'Henry Tudor's Treasure' *HR*, vol. 82 (2009), pp.562–3. This was not a one-off payment: on 25 February that year, another payment in 240,000 pennies was made, with a loan, paid in 480,000 pennies, made two days later. See Horowitz, ibid., fn. p.563.

29 Attainder involved forfeiture of estate and/or deprivation of rank or title for treason.

30 See J. R. Lander, 'Bonds, coercion and fear', p. 339.

31 He was threatened with fines of £5 per retainer – totalling £70,500 – for illegally maintaining liveried servants and supporters. Henry VII tried to curb the 'private armies' of retainers held by the nobility, outlawing them by laws of 1487 and 1504, although the latter legislation introduced a form of licensing system. See A. Cameron, 'Giving of Livery and Retaining in Henry VII's Reign', *Culture, Theory and Critique*, vol. 18 (1974), pp.17–35.

32 Chrimes, *Henry VII*, fn. p.215. Grey was a spendthrift and ended up heavily in debt, mainly through gambling. He was forced to alienate his property, much of which ended up in Henry VII's possession.

33 A groat was worth four pennies.

34 Vergil, *Anglica Historia*, pp.127–9. Dudley and Empson received a percentage for the cash they collected as a 'success fee'.

35 See: G. R. Elton, 'Henry VII: Rapacity and Remorse', *HJ*, vol. 1 (1958) pp.21–39; and the contra-argument proposed by J. R. Cooper, 'Henry VII's Last Years Reconsidered', ibid., vol. 2 (1959), pp.103–29 and Elton, 'Henry VII; A Restatement', ibid., vol. 4 (1961), pp.1–29.

36 See C. J. Harrison, 'Petition of Edmund Dudley' *HR*, vol. 87 (1972), pp.82–99 and Chrimes, *Henry VII*, pp.309–11. Recognisances owed to Henry VII averaged one hundred and one per year in the period 1501–9, sixteen times higher than in Edward IV's reign and five times more than under Richard III (Horowitz, 'Henry Tudor's Treasure' op. cit., p.574).

37 Bacon, p.230.

38 Horowitz, 'Henry Tudor's Treasure', op. cit., p.577.

39 'Greyfriars Chronicle', pp.26–7. There had been two royal residences on the site before Henry's rebuilding. The first was demolished by Richard II in 1395 and the second was built by Henry V, beginning in 1414 and completed by Henry VI. Richmond Palace fell into decay in the seventeenth century and large portions were demolished. The remains were divided into tenements around 1720. Little remains above ground today other than the fifteenth-century 'Old Gate'; the eighteenth-century 'Old Gate House'; the Trumpeters' House (previously the guard house and now a private residence), built 1708; the Wardrobe (formerly the stables, and now private homes) of the early eighteenth century, but incorporating re-used Tudor brick; and finally 'The Old Palace', again eighteenth-century and another private residence.

40 Thomas & Thornley, *Great Chronicle*, p.286. Henry VII paid £20 'for rewards given to them that found the king's jewels' after the fire. Bentley, *Excerpta Historica*, p.115.

41 Jones & Underwood, *The King's Mother*, p.76. A visitor in 1501 described the new three-storey palace buildings: 'On the walls and sides of the hall between the windows be pictures of the noble kings of this realm in their harness [armour] and robes of gold ... On the right side of the chapel is a goodly ... privy closet for the king ... on the other side ... the like closets for the queen's grace and the princes, my lady

the king's mother with other estates and gentlewomen.' See: G. Kipling (ed.), *Receyt of the Ladie Kateryne*, pp.71–3.

42 Baynard's Castle was originally built by William the Conqueror to guard London's river approach from the west. It was destroyed by fire in 1423 but rebuilt by Humphrey, Duke of Gloucester, and became a royal palace. It was almost completely destroyed in the Great Fire of London in September 1666, save for one tower which remained in use until 1720. The rest of the palace site was given over to buildings and wharves. Archaeological excavations in 1972–4 discovered foundations of walls and one tower.

43 Greenwich was the favourite palace of Elizabeth of York and she took a major role in planning the new buildings. Robert Vertue, who controlled construction work from 1499 to 1504, was paid for the 'new platt [plans] of Greenwich which was devised by the queen' (BL Add. MS 59,899, f.24). See: Thurley, *Royal Palaces*, p.35.

44 Bacon, op. cit., p.243. See also S. Gunn, 'Courtiers', p.24. The animal, of the *Ateles* family of monkeys, must have come from central America and was probably a gift from the Spanish.

45 Bentley, *Excerpta Historica*, p.98.

46 *CSP Milan*, vol. 1, p.375.

47 *CSP Spain*, vol. 1, p.439.

48 TNA E 101/414/6 f.25v. In a letter to his mother, Henry VII refers to his deteriorating eyesight: 'Verily madam my sight is nothing so perfect as it has been. I know well it will impair daily. Wherefore I trust that you will not be displeased though I write not so often with my own hand, for on my faith I have been three days [before] I could make an end to this letter'; Ellis, *Original Letters . . .* vol. 1, 1st ser, p.46.

49 Bentley, *Excerpta Historica*, pp.102 and 133.

50 TNA E 404/86/1 f.28. See also S. Gunn, 'Courtiers', p.26.

51 BL Add. MS 7,099, f.129. Keyley was a witness to a notarial instrument at Lichfield, Staffordshire, on 17 March 1495. See BL Stowe Charters 625. See also R. Edwards, 'King Richard's tomb at Leicester' *The Ricardian*, vol. 3 (1975), pp.8–9.

52 Bentley, *Excerpta Historica*, p.105. The tomb was destroyed after the Greyfriars surrendered on 10 November 1538 during the Dissolution of the Monasteries. The body of Richard III was removed and local tradition suggests that it was thrown into the nearby River Soar. There is no evidence to support this legend, but in 1862, a skeleton was found on the bed of the river near Bow Bridge. The cranium was damaged by what looked like sword blows, and it was immediately assumed the remains were that of the deposed king. The skull was taken into the safe-keeping of the Goddard family of Newton Harcourt, Leicestershire, where it remains.

53 For example, in 1495, fourteen shillings was paid on 8 March to Hugh Dennis, Groom of the Close Stool, 'for the king's loss at tennis' and twelve days later '£1 to my lord marquis [probably Thomas Grey, Marquis of Dorset] at [the archery] buttes'. Bentley, *Excerpta Historica*, pp. 101–2.

54 Wroe, p.155.

55 This game, described as 'cleke' in the accounts, was popular from the sixteenth century through to the eighteenth.

56 Anglo, 'Court Festivals', p.14.

57 Bentley, *Excerpta Historica*, p.126.

58 The house at Collyweston was largely demolished in 1720, although a description of 1741 talks of the shattered remains of the great hall, a tower, a dungeon [*sic*] and the kitchen (*Associated Architectural Societies' Reports and Papers*, vol. 28 (1905), pp. 569–74). The site today (National Monuments Record SX 90 SE 6) is marked by a range of earthworks, still over eleven feet (3.5 m.) high, garden terraces, two fish-ponds fed by natural springs and low fragmentary boundary banks to what was the park (Map grid reference: SK 9945 0287).

59 Jones & Underwood, *The King's Mother*, p.154. By 1506, the house had its own chapel and vestry, a library, great hall, parlour and Margaret's own rooms, including a chamber of presence and accommodation for her household. It had its own jewel house and even its own prison.

60 Jones & Underwood, *The King's Mother*, p.81.

61 Coldharbour is first mentioned as being used by William de Hereford, goldsmith and mayor of London in 1287. It was the London home of the dukes of Exeter in the fifteenth century and was granted by Richard III to the College of Heralds in 1483. Henry VII cancelled this grant early in his reign and spent £88 in reparations to the building before giving it to his mother in March 1487. On 4 July 1509, his son Henry VIII granted Coldharbour to George Talbot, Earl of Shrewsbury, for life. The building was destroyed in the Great Fire of London in 1666 but the foundations and the footings of its stairs survived until 1843. Up to the end of the nineteenth-century, its name was preserved in Coldharbour Lane. The site is now occupied by an office block at 89 Upper Thames Street (Kingsford, pp.94–5, 97 and 99).

62 BL Harley 7,039, f.34.

63 BL Cotton MS, *Vespasian F XIII*, f.60, reprinted in Ellis, *Original Letters ...* vol. 1, 1st ser, pp.46–8 and Pollard, *Reign of Henry VII ...*, vol. 1, p.217.

64 Pollard, *Reign of Henry VII ...*, vol. 1, p.219.

65 On 27 June 2009, the college celebrated the 500th anniversary of the death of its foundress.

66 Halsted, *Life of Margaret Beaufort*, p.221.

67 Prayers for the dead, sick and poor.

68 Cooper, *Memorials of Margaret Beaufort*, p.75. Giovanni de' Gigli, Bishop of Wor-cester, presented Lady Margaret with a slim volume, written in Italy, of the lives of the Saints. On the flyleaf (f.20), is a ten-line mournful poem written by the bishop who died the following year. See BL Add. MS 33,772.

69 Halsted, *Life of Margaret Beaufort*, p.196.

70 Jones & Underwood, *The King's Mother*, pp.157–8.

71 In April 1496 Lady Margaret wrote to the Earl of Ormond, the queen's chamberlain, to thank him for the gift of a pair of French gloves which were 'right good, save they were too much [too big] for my hand ... Blessed be God, the king, the queen and all our sweet children be in good health. The queen has been a little crazed [sick or infirm] but she is now well, God be thanked.' Halsted, *Life of Margaret Beaufort*, p.190.

72 *CSP Spain*, vol. 1, p.164.

73 Dr Roderigo de Puebla said in July 1498 that it was 'scandalous' that Don Pedro Ayala had delayed his departure from London and there was no hope of him leaving 'if his officers and servants were not implicated in so many street fights and scuffles. A short time ago, Don Pedro himself received a blow from a brick on his arm in a fight of his servants. Last week the servants ... attacked some Englishmen, one of whom has since died. [I] went to see the corpse buried. The police [*sic*] arrested one ... if the king had not interceded the man would most probably have been hanged. Afterwards the chaplain of Don Pedro, a Scotchman, was arrested for killing an Englishman and sent back to Scotland' (*CSP Spain*, vol. 1, p.155).

De Puebla was himself accused by Friar Thomas de Matienzo, sub-prior of Santa Cruz, of living 'meanly ... in the house of a mason who keeps dishonest women. His landlord robs men who come to his house and the ambassador protects him in his dishonest trade against the [authorities]' (*CSP Spain*, vol. 1, p. 166). Furthermore, another diplomat claimed he was 'avaricious and a notorious usurer, an enemy of truth, full of lies, a calumniator of all honest men, vain glorious and ostentatious ... When the court is staying in the country, he dines every day in the palace of the king and begs wine and bread for his supper and for his servants ... It would require all the paper in London to describe the character of the man' (*CSP Spain*, vol. 1, p. 167). De Puebla certainly had a reputation for scrounging free meals. In 1498, an unnamed courtier wondered aloud why the envoy had turned up unexpectedly at court. 'To eat' another exclaimed and Henry VII laughed at the riposte. Gunn, 'Courtiers', p.39.

74 *CSP Spain*, vol. 1, p.156.

75 Such as the two stilted letters written by Arthur from Ludlow Castle in October and November 1499. See BL Egerton MS 616, article 5.

76 *CSP Spain*, vol. 1, pp.246–7.

77 Letter from Henry VII to the Archbishop of Santiago, 25 September 1501 (*CSP Spain*, vol. 1, pp.261–2).

78 *CSP Spain*, vol. 1, p.262.

79 *CSP Spain*, vol. 1, p.263.

80 Kipling, *Receyt of the Ladie Kateryne*, p.7 and Strickland, *Queens of England*, vol. 2, pp.101–2.

81 *CSP Spain*, vol. 1, p.264 and p.265.

82 A ribbed cloth made of silk, wool, mohair or camel hair.

83 Hayward, *Dress at the Court of Henry VIII*, p.90.

84 Strickland, *Queens of England*, vol. 2, p.103.

85 *LP Henry VII*, p.411.

86 Hall, *Chronicles*, p.493.

87 'More Correspondence', p.4.

88 *LP Henry VII*, p.413. The cost of the wedding and for escorting Katherine from Exeter to London amounted to £10,512 18s 1¼d. BL Royal MS 14 B XXXIX.

89 Kipling, *Receyt of the Ladie Kateryne*, p.43.

90 Thomas & Thornley, *Great Chronicle*, p.31; Kipling, *Receyt of the Ladie Kateryne*, pp.57–8.
91 Strickland, *Queens of England*, vol. 2, p.106.

CHAPTER 3: PRINCE OF WALES

1 *CSP Spain*, vol. 1, p.439.
2 There had been four days of wrangling within the royal household over whether or not Katherine should go with Arthur to Wales, with the princess's confessor Alexsandro Geraldini firmly opposed to the move. Henry VII, however, urged the bridegroom to persuade her 'to say that she preferred rather to go than to stay'. This she refused to do and 'the king, making a show of great sorrow' according to the Spanish ambassador Don Pedro de Ayala, decided himself on her departure to Ludlow. The envoy complained that Henry had given 'nothing at all' to furnish the newly-weds' apartments in the castle, 'nor any table service – nor does he intend to give, but, on the contrary, he has ordered that they must live together and take their meals together'. With unintentional irony, de Ayala reported in another section of his dispatch that the king was 'afraid to be thought a miser' (*CSP Spain*, Supplement to vols. 1 and 2, pp.1–5). John Wint was paid ten shillings for carriage of Katherine's baggage from Plymouth to Ludlow Castle on 18 February 1502 (Bentley, p.127).
3 *CSP Spain*, vol. 1, p.167.
4 Ibid., p.176.
5 Leland, vol. 4, p.261.
6 Ibid., p.260.
7 PPE Elizabeth of York, p.2. Goor had been given half a mark for performing in front of Henry VII in August 1501 and 3s 4d again the following February. On each occasion, he was named only as 'the Duke of York's fool' (Southworth, pp.63–4). On 26 October 1501 John Goor was granted a coat 'with our son's colours', four pairs of shoes, two shirts and two pairs of hose (TNA E 101/415/7 no.76). The queen had her own fool or jester, called William, who was looked after by William Worthy.
8 The corporation of New Romney, one of the Cinque Ports, recorded payments in 1505 and 1508 to the 'minstrels of the lord Prince' (*Fifth Report of the Royal Historical Manuscripts Commission*, London, 1876, pt. 1, pp.549 and 552).
9 PPE Elizabeth of York, p.52.
10 TNA E 101/415/7 nos. 15 and 83.
11 Kipling, p.79.
12 BL Egerton MS 2,642, f.174v.
13 Hayward, p.88.
14 It was set up in the private chapel of the Abbot of Waltham at Copt Hall, near Epping, Essex, before being removed during the Dissolution of the Monasteries. In 1758 the window was purchased for four hundred guineas by the parishioners of St Margaret Westminster and inserted in the east window of the church, where it remains today. See Walter Thornbury, *Old and New London*, vol. 3, London, 1878, pp.569–70 and *Transactions of St Paul's Ecclesiological Society*, vol. 2 (1888–90), pp.108–9.

15 The Tudors may have had a predisposition for contracting tuberculosis (MacNalty, p.25). Henry VII was to die from tuberculosis, as did Henry VIII's illegitimate son Henry Fitzroy, Duke of Richmond, on 23 July 1536, and Edward VI, on 6 July 1553 – although the latter's condition was complicated by an attack of measles and the unspeakable medicines administered secretly by a wise woman who probably did for him.

16 Clifford Brewer, p.109.

17 Shortly after Henry's triumphal arrival in London on 28 August 1485, following his victory at Bosworth, there was a serious epidemic of the sweating sickness in the capital, which caused great mortality.

18 Caius, fol.9.

19 Taviner et al., p.96. See also G. Thwaites, M. Taviner and V. Grant, 'The English Sweating Sickness', *New England Journal of Medicine*, vol. 336 (1997), pp.580–2.

20 See Paul Slack, *The Impact of the Plague in Tudor and Stuart England*, London, 1985, pp.65 and 75. The inhabitants of Worcester were forbidden from making pious offerings at Arthur's funeral there 'because of the sickness that reigned amongst them' (see Leland, vol. 5, p.380).

21 In 1499, 20,000 died from bubonic plague in London (Vergil, p.119), although Hall (p.401) estimates the death toll then was 30,000. Henry VII and Elizabeth of York fled to Calais to avoid the disease and stayed there for about a month.

22 BL Cotton MS Vitellius B xii, f.85.

23 Bacon, p.205.

24 Hall, p.494. Although Katherine would have learnt a few words and phrases in English, the couple's lingua franca would have been Latin – hardly the most romantic language in the world (Strickland, *Queens of England*, vol. 2, p.109).

25 Shrove Tuesday fell on 8 February in 1502.

26 BL Cotton Appendix xxvii, f.145.

27 J. S. Brewer, vol. 2, p.303.

28 Kipling, p.80.

29 'Towardly' – willing to learn and promising.

30 Kipling, p.81.

31 Katherine is said to have 'foretold the wretched outcome of the marriage'. The storm that buffeted her ship en route to England convinced her and her entourage that 'the tempest portended some calamity' (Vergil, p.125).

32 Kipling, p.82.

33 A long delay between a royal death and the funeral was customary at this time, to allow arrangements for the complicated ceremonial to be made (see BL Egerton MS 2,642, f.174v).

34 BL Add. MS 45,131, ff.37–41; Leland, vol. 5, p.377.

35 Gunn & Monkton, p.167 and Sandford, p.476. A re-enactment of the funeral was staged in Worcester in May 2002. This took a total of 666 days to organise, compared with the twenty-one for that in 1502 (see Gunn & Monkton, pp.167–79).

36 It originally had a brass marginal inscription, probably ripped off during the reign of Edward VI. A painted inscription, free of any precatory prayer, replaced this later

in the sixteenth century, which was recorded by the royalist officer Richard Symonds in 1644 during his military service in the English Civil War: 'Here lyeth buryed Prince Arthur the first begotten son of the right renowned king henry the seventhe, which Noble Prynce departed oute of this transitori lyfe in the Castle of Ludlowe in the seventeenth yere of his fathers rayne and in the yere of our Lord God on [*sic*] thousand five hundred and two' (BL Harley MS 965 f.41v and Sandford, p.477).

37 TNA LC 2/1/1 ff.4r–4v.

38 *CSP Spain*, vol. 1, p.267. Ferdinand and Isabella to Ferdinand, Duke de Estrada, Toledo, 10 May 1502.

39 Ibid., pp.267–8. Ferdinand and Isabella to de Puebla, Toledo, 12 May 1502.

40 A London tailor, John Cope, was paid five shillings for providing the cloth and lining and covering Katherine's litter (PPE Elizabeth of York, p.103).

41 He was paid 8d for his pains (PPE Elizabeth of York, p.14).

42 *CPR Henry VII*, vol. 2, p.258.

43 Henry Roper, Page of the Queen's Beds, was paid 16d for two days' work preparing her lodgings at the Tower (PPE Elizabeth of York, p.98).

44 PPE Elizabeth of York, p.78.

45 The Bruton girdle later fell into the grasping hands of Thomas Cromwell, Henry VIII's Chief Minister during the Dissolution of the Monasteries. His visitor Dr Richard Layton wrote to him on 24 August 1535: 'I send also Our Lady's girdle of Bruton, red silk, and Mary Magdalene's girdle, covered with white, sent to women "travailing" which last the Empress Matilda, founder of Ferley, gave them, as saith the holy father of Ferley' (see BL Cotton MS *Cleopatra E IV*, f.249).

46 Some claim that the executions of Warbeck and Warwick followed one of Parron's prognostications. The first Privy Purse payment to Parron was on 6 February 1498: 'To Master William Parron, an astronomer, £1' (Bentley, p.121).

47 Ironically, before Parron worked for Henry VII he was employed by Edward Frank, a notorious Yorkist conspirator, between his release from the Tower in November 1487 and his re-arrest for treason two years later. Parron claimed to have warned Frank to behave himself and predicted his 'bad end', which was fulfilled by his execution in 1490 (Carlin, p.861).

48 The sixty-three-page *Liber de optimo fato nobilissimi domini Henrici Eboraci ducis ac optimorum ipsius parentum* (BL Royal MS 12 B. VI) has a prefatory letter of sympathy on the death of Prince Arthur. The initial letter on f.2 contains a small miniature of Henry VII enthroned with the royal arms in the border of the page. Another astrological work by Parron, *De astroruim ui fatali . . .* , dedicated to Henry VII, is in the Bodleian Library, Oxford (Selden MS Supra 77), with a miniature of the king and his court on f.4. See Armstrong, pp.451–3 and Hilary Carey, *Courting Disaster: Astrology at the English Court and University*, Basingstoke & London, 1992, p.219. Astrology loomed large in Henry VII's court: a monk at the house of Bonhommes at Edlington, Wiltshire, wrote a treatise on the portents of the marriage between Arthur and Katherine in 1501 (BL Add. MS 4,822).

49 Pollard, *Henry VII*, vol. 1, p.231. This was Candlemas Day. A doe deer had been sent especially for the queen's dinner that day (PPE Elizabeth of York, p.97).

50 PPE Elizabeth of York, pp.96–7.

51 Her unnamed dry nurse was also paid £3 6s 8d in reward (Bentley, p.130).

52 It was bought from Robert Lanston at the rate of twelve pence the yard (PPE Elizabeth of York, p.94).

53 Henry may also have had an illegitimate son, born during his exile in Brittany. The bastard was reputedly Roland de Velville, born in 1474, who was knighted in 1497 and became Constable of Beaumaris Castle on Anglesey, off North Wales, in 1509. If he was the king's illegitimate son, he was generously provided for. Henry VII lent him money in 1492 because he could not afford to arm and equip himself to take part in the English invasion of France (TNA E 404/86/3). His standard of living appears to have depended on royal annuities of £46 13s 4d granted in 1493 and three years later. Chamber accounts suggest he was involved in falconry while at court (Gunn, 'Courtiers', p.36). Roland de Velville died on 25 June 1535. See also S. B. Chrimes, 'Sir Roland de Velville', Welsh History Review, vol. 3 (1967), pp.287–9 and W. R. Robinson, 'Sir Roland de Velville and the Tudor Dynasty: A Reassessment', Welsh History Review, vol. 15 (1991), pp.351–67.

54 Cavendish, pp.52–3.

55 Crawford, p.156; Antiquarian Repertory, vol. 4, p.655.

56 BL Add. MS 45,131, ff.41v–47v. There is a drawing of her funeral procession on ff.41v–42r. See also BL Stowe MS 583 ff.27–33v (with further pen-and-ink drawings of the procession) and Sandford, p.470.

57 Chapter 19, verse 21. Fitzjames took the service because the newly appointed Archbishop of Canterbury, Henry Deane, died unexpectedly on 15 February.

58 Antiquarian Repertory, vol. 4, p.662. After the funeral, a 'great dole' of groats (four-penny pieces) was given to every man and woman watching in the abbey, and alms provided to 'bed-ridden folks, lazars [diseased people] blind folks and others', and every community of Friars Observant was given five marks (£3 6s 8d) together with twenty heraldic escutcheons used in Elizabeth's funeral.

59 Wroe, p.453. His later career is unknown but he died in or after 1503 (Carlin, p.862).

60 R. S. Sylvester, King Richard III, vol. 2, pp.119–23.

61 Byrne, pp.4–5.

62 Hayward, p.90.

63 LP Henry VII, vol. 1, p.167.

64 See Chrimes, p.287 and Busch, p.378, fn.4.

65 Queen Isabella to Ferdinand, Duke de Estrada, 11 April 1503 (CSP Spain, vol. 1, pp.295–6).

66 The Spanish ratified the treaty on 24 September 1503 (see BL Add. MS 48,000, ff.590–594v.

67 Thomas & Thornley, p.323. Audley was also Chancellor of the Order of the Garter.

68 My italics. The treaty stipulated that the Spanish and English sovereigns promised to 'employ all their influence with the Court of Rome, in order to obtain the dispensation necessary for the marriage ... The Papal dispensation was required because Princess Katharine had on a former occasion contracted a marriage with the late Prince Arthur, brother of the present Prince of Wales, whereby she became

related to Henry, Prince of Wales, in the first degree of affinity, and because her marriage with Prince Arthur was solemnised according to the rites of the Catholic Church, and afterwards consummated' (*CSP Spain*, vol. 1, p.306).

69 *CSP Spain*, vol. 1, p.309; Ferdinand of Spain to Francisco de Rojas, Barcelona, 23 August 1503.

70 Ibid., p.322.

71 Sherborne died in 1526. He forged a papal Bull to appoint himself to the see of St David's in 1505 and became Bishop of Chichester three years later.

72 *CSP Spain*, vol. 1, p.328.

73 Duke de Estrada to Queen Isabella, London, 10 August 1504 (*CSP Spain*, vol. 1, p.330).

74 Henry VII to Julius II, Westminster, 28 November 1504 (*CSP Spain*, vol. 1, p.342).

75 Addressed 'To the most illustrious Lady Katherine, Princess of Wales, my most beloved daughter', Isle of Sheppey, Kent, 4 August 1504 (*CSP Spain*, vol. 1, p.328).

76 London, 10 August 1504 (*CSP Spain*, vol. 1, pp. 326–7).

77 The failure to draw blood from Katherine probably was not because the surgeon failed to find a suitable vein to cut into; de Estrada says he was her household physician who 'generally bleeds very well'. Why did he not use leeches?

78 Durham House was a large complex with a number of courts and its own chapel close to Charing Cross. Battlemented walls and a tower fronted the river. On its western and northern perimeters there was a narrow lane giving access to a landing stage on the Thames. See Wheatley, p.155.

79 *CSP Spain*, vol. 1, p.331.

80 Ibid., pp.349–50.

81 He succeeded the traitor Sir William Stanley as Lord Chamberlain in 1495.

82 Strickland, *Queens of England*, vol. 2, p.118. The repudiation was described in a two-page document in Latin – BL Cotton MS *Vitellius D XII*, which was probably destroyed by fire on 23 October 1731 at Ashburnham House, Westminster, where the Cotton MSS were being temporarily housed – but not before it was seen by early antiquaries. This version is taken from Burnet, vol. 2, pp.vi–vii.

CHAPTER 4: KING IN WAITING

1 *CSP Spain*, vol. 1, pp.329–30.

2 De la Pole was the son of John, second Duke of Suffolk, by Elizabeth Plantagenet, younger sister of Edward IV When his father died in 1491, Henry VII forced him to forego the title of duke, which rankled.

3 Vergil, p.123.

4 See Hanham, pp.239–50.

5 Vergil, p.125.

6 In May 1492, Vaughan – then a Gentleman Usher of the King's Chamber – had tried to take part in a court joust at Sheen, but the heralds organising the event said he was 'not of a respectable descent'. He did take part, killing Sir James Parker in the first course by his lance piercing Parker's helmet visor and 'forcing his tongue to the

hind part' of his skull. The courtier improved his status the following year by marrying Lady Anne Percy, the widow of Sir Thomas Hungerford and daughter of the Third Earl of Northumberland. See Gunn, 'Courtiers', p.37.

7   Three Justices of the United States Supreme Court, during a mock trial of Richard III in 1997, ruled in a 3–0 decision that the 'prosecution' had not fulfilled the necessary burden of proof that the princes had been murdered or that Richard III was complicit in their deaths.

8   Tyrell was buried in the Austin Friars' church (see Hampton, pp.9–22). Sir Thomas More, in his *History of Richard III*, claims Tyrell and his accomplice John Dighton (one of those who allegedly smothered the princes) confessed to the murder of the two boys during their interrogation under torture in the Tower, 'but whether the bodies were removed, they could nothing tell' (Marius, p.106). This seems unlikely – why did Henry VII not use this confession as a powerful propaganda weapon against the Yorkists?

9   Thus Suffolk was ritually cursed by the papal Bull and condemned to perpetual hell. The Bull was obtained with the assistance of Adriano Castelli (c.1461–c.1521), Bishop of Hereford (1502–4) and secretary to Alexander VI, who made him a cardinal in May 1503. The papal Bull was later proclaimed in London (Vergil, p.133).

10 Cunningham, *ODNB*, vol. 44, p.698.

11 Joan had married her nephew Ferdinand II of Naples in 1496 when she was eighteen and he twenty-seven. The marriage was short-lived, however; he died on 7 September the same year.

12 A sweet wine from Smyrna (an ancient town in Turkey, now Izmir), flavoured with aromatic spices and then filtered.

13 'Memorials', pp.223–39.

14 She never remarried and died on 27 August 1518.

15 Jointure: an estate settled on a wife to provide income for the period during which she survives her husband.

16 Bentley, p.130.

17 Hall, p.498. Northumberland wore a coat 'of goldsmith's work, garnished with pearl and [precious] stone' and was accompanied by four hundred henchmen. He was esteemed 'both of the Scots and Englishmen, more like a prince than a subject'.

18 The wedding guests sat down to a feast of prodigious proportions, including boar's head, brawn with mustard, charred grouse, baked or stewed capons, roast pork and shoulders of mutton, swan with chowder, roast crane and veal. The 'skynk to potage' sounds less appetising. For the third course, there were jellies, decorated with the royal arms of Scotland and England, and plums, apples and pears with blancmange (Thomas & Thornley, p.324).

19 Ellis, 1st ser., vol. 1, p.41. The marriage was hardly a love match but there are signs of real affection between James and Margaret later on. They had six children, the first being James, Duke of Rothesay, born on 21 February 1507. Of the six, two daughters were stillborn and only one, James, survived infancy. He was later to become James V of Scotland, a few months after his first birthday.

20 *CSP Spain*, vol. 1, pp.329–30.

21 Ehses, pp.xliiiff.

22 Scarisbrick, *Henry VIII*, p.10. The only copy of this letter is contained in a register of briefs in the Vatican archives.

23 Tertian fever may last up to one day and then reappears on the third. The disease is spread by the bite of the female *Anopheles* mosquito, which breeds in stagnant water. This spreads the parasite *Plasmodium falciparum*, which grows in the liver and then enters the bloodstream and invades the red blood cells.

24 Scarisbrick, *Henry VIII*, p.10.

25 Ibid.

26 *CSP Spain*, vol. 1, p.379.

27 Vergil, p.139; 'Greyfriars Chronicle', p.28. The eagle had been renewed in December 1497, being set up 'by a carpenter of London called Godfrey' (Thomas & Thornley, p.286). After being blown off, the weathercock was replaced on its pinnacle 'not without great exertions on account of the vast height'.

28 Vergil, p.135.

29 Hayward, p.91.

30 Hall, p.534.

31 Juana was constantly jealous over her handsome husband's attractiveness to women, indulging in many fiery Spanish tantrums. She cut off the long hair of one of her ladies-in-waiting, whom she suspected of having an affair with Philip, and laid the long tresses on his pillow as a warning to him. She also dismissed all her ladies as being too pretty.

32 *CSP Spain*, Supplement to vols. 1 and 2, pp.132–3.

33 'Greyfriars Chronicle', p.28.

34 *CSP Spain*, vol. 1, p.379, claims that the archduke offered up Suffolk 'unasked'. A century later, Bacon recounts the conversation differently. Henry told Philip: 'Sir, you have been saved upon my coast. I hope you will not suffer me to wreck upon yours.' When the archduke asked for an explanation, the king replied: 'I mean it by that same harebrained wild fellow, my subject, the Earl of Suffolk, who is protected in your country and begins to play the fool when all others are weary of it.' Philip answered: 'I had thought sir your felicity had been above those thoughts, but if it trouble you, I will banish him.' Henry said, 'Those hornets were best in their nests and worst when they did fly abroad' and that his desire was to 'have him delivered'. The archduke then confessed to be 'a little confused' with all these metaphors (Bacon, pp.223–5).

35 Hayward, p.91.

36 *LP Henry VII*, pp.284–5; Starkey, *Henry – Virtuous Prince*, p.217.

37 *CSP Spain*, vol. 4, pt. 1, p.340.

38 Vergil, p.139.

39 BL Add. MS 21,404, f.9. Printed in Byrne, pp.7–8.

40 No copy survives, but years later, Erasmus remembered it began: 'A report has arrived here too sad to be readily believed but so persistent that it cannot appear altogether baseless that Prince Philip has departed this life.' Clearly Erasmus knew of Henry's close relationship with the archduke (Nichols, vol. 1, p.424).

41 Nichols, ibid., pp.424–6 and Byrne, pp.4–5.

42 Lucian (c.AD 125-after AD 180) was the author of the first science fiction story. His *True Story* has the hero transported by a giant waterspout to the surface of the moon.

43 Pollard, *Henry VIII*, p.16.

44 Katherine of Aragon to Ferdinand of Spain, London, 22 April 1506 (BL Egerton MS 616 ff.29v–30).

45 Scarisbrick, *Henry VIII*, p.8.

46 Henry VII to Ferdinand of Spain (*CSP Spain*, vol. 1, pp.406–8).

47 De Puebla to Ferdinand, London, 15 April 1507 (*CSP Spain*, vol. 1, p.409). Juana's maternal grandmother had been declared insane and was locked away in Arévalo. In 1503, after giving birth to her fourth child, Juana ran out of her castle and spent thirty-six hours continually screaming in the open air (see Michael Farquhar, *A Treasury of Royal Scandals*, New York, 2001, p.56). Eventually her son, Charles V of Spain, locked her up in a windowless room in the castle of Torclesillas. She died on 12 April 1555, aged seventy-five, after nearly fifty years of imprisonment.

48 They were married by proxy at Christmas 1508.

49 *CSP Spain*, vol. 1, p.406.

50 Ibid., p.411.

51 Ibid., p.412.

52 Richardson, p.456.

53 Vergil, p.135. Bray was buried in a chantry chapel in the royal mausoleum of St George's Chapel, within Windsor Castle. His image, with a 'sage and grave' countenance, appears amongst three attendants to the king in a stained-glass window in the priory church of Great Malvern, Worcestershire, together with the kneeling figures of Elizabeth of York and Prince Arthur, completed in December 1501 (see Richardson, p.455).

54 Rex, *The Tudors*, p.40.

55 *CSP Spain*, vol. 1, p.206.

56 *CSP Spain*, Supplement to vols. 1 and 2, p.22.

57 Rex, *The Tudors*, p.40. In his will, Henry VII bequeathed the relic to St George's Chapel, Windsor.

58 Now Westminster Abbey.

59 *CCR Henry VII*, pp.138–48.

60 Chrimes, p.305. The hospital stood on the south side of the Strand on a site now occupied by the Savoy Hotel and Savoy Theatre. It was dissolved by Henry VII's grandson Edward VI in 1553, but refounded by his granddaughter Mary I in 1556, with her maids of honour supplying the beds. It was finally closed in the early 1700s (BL Stowe MS 865, f.5r).

61 Anglo, 'Court Festivities', p.20. On 7 December 1507, there is a payment of twenty shillings to 'John Blank, the black trumpeter, for his month's wages of November at eight pence the day'. Anglo points out that a negro musician, probably this politically incorrectly named John Blank, is twice shown amongst the king's trumpets in the *Great Roll of the Tournament* at Westminster in February 1511 (ibid., p.34).

62 TNA LC/2/1/1, ff.73–73v and Starkey, *Henry – Virtuous Prince*, p.173.

63 Guildford (1489–1532) was the son of Sir Richard Guildford, Master of the Ordnance to Henry VII and Comptroller of his household. He was created a banneret for his services fighting the Cornish rebels in 1497 but died in Jerusalem while on pilgrimage.

64 Skelton became Rector of Diss in Norfolk and was probably 'the Duke of York's schoolmaster' who was paid a final forty shillings in April 1502 (Carlson, p.267).

65 Carlson, p.253. For more on Holt, see Orme, pp.283–305.

66 Pollard, *Henry VII*, vol. 3, p.16.

67 Blezzard and Palmer, p.256.

68 Anglo, 'Court Festivities', pp.33, 35 and 36. BL Add MS 31,922 contains sixty-three songs and ballads composed early in the reign of Henry VIII, a third of them attributed to Henry himself. 'Pastime with Good Company' heads the list at f.14r.

69 *LP Henry VIII*, vol. 6, pt. ii, p.2,243.

70 Starkey, *Henry – Virtuous Prince*, p.197.

71 'Casting the bar' involved hurling a heavy iron bar from a standing position, rather like shot-putting in modern athletics field sports.

72 A stout wooden pole, six to eight feet (1.83–2.44 m) in length, frequently iron-tipped at both ends.

73 Hayward, p.91.

74 TNA LC 2/1/1 f.73v.

75 Gunn, 'Courtiers', p.45 and Starkey, *Henry – Virtuous Prince*, p.231.

76 Thomas & Thornley, p.328. The 'master carpenter that framed [the gallery] was punished by imprisonment many days after' (ibid., p.331).

77 Charlton, pp.41–5.

78 *LP Henry VIII*, vol. 13, pt. ii, p.318. He was executed for treason by Henry VIII on 9 December 1539.

79 Ferdinand told him in ?July 1508 that his 'principal objective must always be to endeavour to have the nuptial ceremony between the Prince and Princess of Wales performed as soon as possible'. He should see to this 'with the utmost diligence' (*CSP Spain*, vol. 1, p.458).

80 'Correspondence de Fuensalida', p.449.

81 Peter Foley, 'Retrospective on the Quincentenary of the Death of Henry VII', *Ricardian Bulletin*, December 2009, p.34.

82 Vergil, p.145.

83 Rex, *The Tudors*, p.43.

84 Clifford Brewer, p.110.

85 Bacon, p.229.

86 De Puebla to Ferdinand of Spain, London, 5 October 1507 (*CSP Spain*, vol. 1, p.439).

87 *CSP Venice*, vol. 1, p.330.

88 *CSP Spain*, vol. 1, p.457.

89 'Fisher: Works', vol. 1, pp.271–2.

90 Ibid., p.273.

91 Forty shillings were paid out on 25 March for 'the king's grace for playing money' and on 10 April, two payments totalling the large sum of £53 4s 11d were made to Sir Peter Greves 'for the wages of certain priests singing in diverse places for the king'

(Anglo, 'Court Festivities', p.37).

92 'Fisher: Works', vol. 1, p.274.

93 Badoer faced 'great perils' on his journey: 'his horse fell upon him, subsequently he was well nigh drowned.' Haplessly, he told the Venetian government that 'he would array himself as an ambassador' (*CSP Venice*, vol. 1, p.342).

94 *CSP Venice*, ibid., p.344.

95 TNA E 23/3.

96 Richard Welles was paid 66s 8d on 6 April for writing Henry VII's will (Condon, 'The Last Will of Henry VII ... ', p.105).

97 Condon, ibid., p.112.

98 A marble bust purporting to show Henry VII in the agony of death was in the collection of Horace Walpole at Strawberry Hill. However, the bust, probably Italian and now called 'Shouting Male Head', was carved in the seventeenth century and is unconnected with any royal demise. It is in the collection of the Duke of Northumberland at Syon House and is illustrated in *Horace Walpole's Strawberry Hill*, Michael Snodin (ed.), New Haven and London, 2010, p.129.

99 'Fisher: Works', vol. 1, pp.285–6.

100 Henry to Margaret of Savoy, Westminster, 27 June 1509 (BL Add. MS 21,404, f.10).

101 'Fisher: Works', vol. 1, p.274.

102 BL Add. MS 45,131, f.54; Doran, p.56.

CHAPTER 5: *VIVAT REX*

1 BL Add. MS 21,404, f.10.

2 'Correspondence de Fuensalida', p.513.

3 Gunn, 'The Accession of Henry VIII', p.280. Suffolk and Buckingham had been identified by anonymous 'great personages' in 1504 as possible successors to Henry VII (see *LP Henry VII*, vol. 1, p.233.

4 Sandford, p.472.

5 Later, an efficient clerk cancelled this entry and substituted the word 'nil'. The payment was then listed in Henry VIII's chamber accounts (Gunn, 'The Accession of Henry VIII', p.280).

6 BL Add. MS 45,131, f.52v.

7 Ibid.

8 'Correspondence de Fuensalida', p.516.

9 Ibid., pp.514 and 516.

10 Routh, p.42.

11 Gunn, 'The Accession of Henry VIII', p.282.

12 Thomas & Thornley, p.336.

13 Harris, pp.153–71; Gunn, 'The Accession of Henry VIII', p.284.

14 Holinshed, vol. 3, p.505. This must have been menacing gossip to Henry VIII's ears. The last 'Lord Protector' of the realm had been Richard, Duke of Gloucester, who was appointed to the post on 30 April 1483. On 26 June the following year he became Richard III.

15 Hall, p.512. Henry VIII pardoned him and later created him Earl of Wiltshire.

16 *Report of the Deputy Keeper of Public Records*, vol. 3, London, 1842, appendix 2, p.226.

17 Vergil, p.153.

18 Paul's Cross was a preaching cross on the north side of St Paul's Cathedral. Bishop Thomas Kempe rebuilt it in the late fifteenth century, with a lead-covered roof and a low surrounding wall. There was room inside for three or four persons. The open-air pulpit was destroyed in 1643 by radical Protestants.

19 Hall, pp.503 and 505.

20 Brodie, p.160.

21 Many were put in the pillory, subjected to the jeers of the crowd and pelted with rotten fruit (Vergil, p.153).

22 TNA SP 1/1/3; *LP Henry VIII, vol. 1, 2nd ed., p.7; Hughes & Larkin, nos. 59 and 60, pp.79–83.*

23 Sharpe, p.34. The French printer Pynson (1448–1529) worked in the parish of St Clement Danes, between Westminster and the City of London, but moved inside Temple Bar in 1501, possibly because of riots against foreign traders that year. He became King's Printer in 1506 at a wage of £2 a year, later doubled. He became a naturalised citizen in 1513. See Henry Plomer, 'Two Lawsuits of Richard Pynson', *The Library*, 2nd ser., vol. 10 (1909), pp.115–33 and Pamela Neville, *Richard Pynson, King's Printer: Printing and Propaganda in Early Tudor England*, Diss and London, 1990.

24 'Correspondence de Fuensalida', p.517.

25 TNA C 82/335/6 – Exemptions from the general pardon signed by Henry VIII; Tower of London, 30 April 1509. In an administrative slip, poor Ralph Hackelet of Herefordshire was included in this list of exemptions but the error was quickly spotted the same day and he was included in the general pardon (*LP Henry VIII, vol. 1, p.5). On 30 May, the unfortunately named 'Thomas Thomas' was granted a pardon (LP Henry VIII, vol. 1, 2nd ed., p.33).*

26 *CSP Spain*, vol. 2, pp.7–8. The marriage portion initially was to be paid thus: 65,000 scudos in cash, 15,000 scudos in gold and silver, and 20,000 in jewels and ornaments. A few days later, Ferdinand agreed to pay it all in cash 'in order to show the new king how much more he loved him and how much more he valued his friendship than that of his father'.

27 TNA SP 1/1/18.

28 *CSP Spain*, vol. 2, p.10.

29 Not knowing of his death, Stile had written to Henry VII on 26 April warning that Ferdinand was so enraged by Katherine's harsh treatment that he was considering a declaration of war against England (Ridley, p.40).

30 Four thousand Venetian troops were killed in a defeat inflicted by the French at the Battle of Agnadello, between Milan and Bergamo, on 14 May 1509.

31 *LP Henry VIII*, vol. 1, 1st ed., p.4.

32 The Doge and Senate to Andrea Badoer, Venice, 28 April 1509 (*CSP Venice*, vol. 1, p.345).

33 Doge and Senate to Badoer, Venice, 16 May 1509. *CSP Venice*, ibid., p.346.

34 *CSP Venice*, ibid., p.346.

35 In practice, the English king's writ only ran within a forty-mile (64.37 km) area around Dublin.

36 Starkey, *Henry VIII*, p.13.

37 The population was forbidden to eat butter, cheese and meat during Lent and Advent and on Friday or Saturdays, without obtaining a licence on health grounds.

38 Muller, p.280.

39 'Relation of England', p.21.

40 Ibid., pp.42–3.

41 'Sanuto Diaries', vol. 5, xv, pp.572–5.

42 'The Little Office' or 'Hours of Our Lady' was customarily recited by the pious laity in the pre-Reformation church in England.

43 'Relation of England', pp.22–3.

44 'Wriothesley Chronicle', vol. 1, p.6.

45 'Sanuto Diaries', vol. 5, xvii, p.78.

46 'Relation of England', pp.24–5.

47 *Chronicle of Calais*, p.7.

48 TNA SP 1/1/11.

49 BL Arundel MS 26, f.28; Harley MS 6,079, f.31.

50 Anglo, *Images*, pp.100–1.

51 See C. Galvin and P. Lindley, 'Pietro Torrigiano's Portrait Bust of King Henry VII' in *Gothic to Renaissance: Essays on Sculpture in England*, P. Lindley (ed.), Stamford, 1995, pp.170–87; R. P. Howgrave-Graham, 'Royal Portraits in Effigy: Some New Discoveries in Westminster Abbey', *Journal of the Royal Society of Arts*, vol. 101 (1952–3), pp.465–71; and Frederick Hepburn, 'The 1505 Portrait of Henry VII', *Antiquaries Journal*, vol. 88 (2008), pp.235–6. The effigy remains in the museum of Westminster Abbey.

52 'Fisher: Works', vol. 1, pp.269–70.

53 Anglo, *Images*, pp.101–2.

54 The name is the origin of the vernacular phrase 'in the clink' – meaning being 'in prison'.

55 Leland, vol. 4, p.309.

56 BL Harley MS 6,079, f.31.

57 *LP Henry VIII*, vol. 1, 2nd ed., pp.31–2.

58 Groveley Forest remains the largest area of woodland in South Wiltshire. It is situated on a chalk ridge south of the village of Great Wishford, and lies within the Cranborne Chase and West Wiltshire Downs Area of Outstanding Natural Beauty.

59 *LP Henry VIII*, vol. 1, 2nd ed., p.11. A 'corrody' was provision for maintenance, given regularly by a religious house, rather like an annuity. Both preferments were available because of the death of James Braybroke.

60 *LP Henry VIII*, vol. 1, 2nd ed., p.30.

61 TNA SP 1/1/33. Darcy, the previous Captain of the Guard, acted in that capacity at Henry VII's funeral. He received some compensation by soon after being elected a Knight of the Garter at a meeting of the order's chapter at Greenwich (*LP Henry VIII*, vol. 1, 2nd ed., p.24).

62 Marney (c.1457–1523) had fought at Bosworth and Stoke Field and in the final campaign against Perkin Warbeck in 1497. He was also one of the witnesses to Henry's protestation at the marriage with Katherine of Aragon. Marney was appointed Lord Privy Seal and created Baron Marney shortly before his death.

63 TNA SP 1/1/28.

64 *LP Henry VIII*, vol. 1, 2nd ed., p.24.

65 Ibid., p.11.

66 'Correspondence de Fuensalida', pp.519–20.

67 BL Cotton MS *Vitellius B XII*, f.123v – deposition of Nicholas West, Bishop of Ely, relating to Katherine's marriage with Henry. He recalled a disagreement between Warham and Fox about the legality of the marriage.

68 Lambeth Palace MS CM 51/115. The parchment is sadly torn at its right-hand edge and has thirteen holes.

69 TNA SP 1/1/43 – Ferdinand of Spain to Katherine, Princess of Wales, 18 May 1509.

70 Starkey, *Henry – Virtuous Prince*, p.281. Thomas had previously been in the service of Prince Arthur, also as Groom of the Privy Chamber. He was clearly a new favourite of Henry's; on 17 May he was appointed Keeper of Ockeley Park, Shropshire, and the same day appointed 'troner and pieser' in the port of London. This official oversaw the weighing of produce – rather like a modern-day trading standards inspector (*LP Henry VIII*, vol. 1, 2nd ed., p.29). The following year, he was made Keeper of Netherwood Park, Herefordshire (ibid., p.276).

71 Mattingly, p.97; Antonia Fraser, p.49.

72 TNA SP 1/1/45 – formal words pronounced at wedding of Henry VIII and Katherine of Aragon.

73 *LP Henry VIII*, vol. 6, p.169; *CSP Spain*, Supplement to vols. 1 and 2, p.450.

74 *CSP Spain*, vol. 2, p.20.

75 *LP Henry VIII*, vol. 1, 2nd ed., pp.48–50.

76 BL Cotton MS *Tiberius E VIII*, f.100v.

77 Hayward, p.43.

78 Ibid., p.44.

79 Jones & Underwood, p.236.

80 Thomas & Thornley, pp.339–40.

81 My italics. *LP Henry VIII*, vol. 1, 2nd ed., p.54.

82 Hall, p.508.

83 Ibid.

84 The London chronicler described her crown as a 'circlet of silk, gold and pearl about her head' (Thomas & Thornley, p.340).

85 Hall, p.508.

86 Thomas & Thornley, p.340.

87 Neville Williams, *Henry VIII and his Court*, p.15.

88 *LP Henry VIII*, vol. 1, 2nd ed., p.42.

89 Ibid., p.38.

90 The Coronation Chair was made on the orders of Edward I in 1300–1 to hold the captured Stone of Scone (on which Scottish kings were crowned) beneath its seat.

The Stone was removed to Scotland in 1996. For coronations, the Chair is placed in the sacrarium, facing the abbey's high altar.

91 'Rutland Papers', pp.14–15. This relates to the coronation of Henry VII, but the ritual of that day was closely followed for the crowning of his son, doubtless also in the wording of the oath.

92 BL Harley MS 6,079, f.21v.

93 BL Cotton MS *Tiberius D VIII*, f.89.

94 A vassal owing feudal allegiance and service to their sovereign lord.

95 BL Add. MS 6,113, f.72.

96 Hayward, p.44. During the coronation, she donned two sets of crimson and purple robes.

97 Antonia Fraser, p.50.

98 Miller, p.93.

99 Thomas & Thornley, pp.341–3.

100 Cheyneygates was originally part of the abbot's house of the Benedictine monastery. During Edward IV's reign, his queen Elizabeth Woodville probably lived at Cheyneygates when she sought sanctuary at Westminster. Later in Henry VIII's reign, Sir Thomas More was detained there before his removal to the Tower. The rooms were badly damaged by German bombing in 1941 but have since been rebuilt.

101 BL Add. MS 12,060, f.23v.

102 H. F. Pearce, 'The Death of Lady Margaret' in Rackham, pp.15–20.

103 BL Add. MS 12,060, f.23v and Jones & Underwood, p.237.

104 Pole, vol. 4, pp.94–5. Pole said Henry boasted that 'no other prince had in his kingdom a bishop so endowed with learning and virtue' as John Fisher. The bishop himself said he was more bound to the king than others because Henry was born in his diocese and he had been confessor to his grandmother. Henry VIII still had Fisher beheaded for treason on Tower Hill on 22 June 1535.

105 'Fisher: Works', pp.291, 301.

CHAPTER 6: A GOLDEN WORLD

1 *LP Henry VIII*, vol. 1, 2nd ed., p.27.

2 Addressed to the 'most serene and most mighty, Lord Ferdinand, by the grace of God, King of Aragon, Sicily and Jerusalem, our most beloved Father' (*CSP Spain*, vol. 2, p.20). Henry sent a similar account of the coronation to Cardinal Sixtus della Rovere that July, describing the 'incredible demonstrations of joy and enthusiasm' over the event (*LP Henry VIII*, vol. 1, 2nd ed., p.56).

3 BL Egerton MS 616, f.43. Endorsed: 'pro Johanne Style' – to be delivered by the English ambassador to Ferdinand.

4 *LP Henry VIII*, vol. 1, 2nd ed., p.118.

5 *CSP Spain*, vol. 2, p.20. Henry begged the king to assist in obtaining a legacy left to Mountjoy's wife by Queen Isabella: 'She has sent a power of attorney to some of her relatives.'

6 BL Egerton MS 616, f.45. A jennet is a small Spanish horse, which was ridden by

light cavalrymen. Ferdinand was quick to respond: the English envoy John Stile reported in early September that 'the king your good father has provided a certain goodly horse of this country's jennets that he will send to be presented unto your highness' (BL Cotton MS *Vespasian C l*, f.58v). The jennet and the other horses were sent by land (*LP Henry VIII*, vol. 1, 2nd ed., p.89).

7   *CSP Spain*, vol. 2, pp.21–2.
8   Ferdinand to Katherine, Queen of England; Mansilla, 18 November 1509 (*CSP Spain*, vol. 2, pp.25–6.
9   Henry to Ferdinand; Greenwich Palace, 1 November 1509 (*CSP Spain*, vol. 2, p.23).
10 *LP Henry VIII*, vol. 1, 2nd ed., p.1,473. When Maria married Lord Willoughby, Master of the Royal Hart Hounds, in June 1516, Katherine allowed her to use Greenwich Palace for the ceremony (Neville Williams, *Henry VIII and His Court*, p.32).
11 Vives (1493–1540) wrote a commentary on Augustine's *De Civitate Dei* ('The City of God') published in 1522, dedicated to Henry VIII.
12 *CSP Spain*, vol. 2, p.24.
13 ibid., p.30.
14 Roper, p.11.
15 Allen & Allen, '*Opus Epistolarum*', epistle 215; *LP Henry VIII*, vol. 1, 2nd ed., p.27. Warham gave Erasmus a further £5.
16 Singer, p.79.
17 R. W. Chambers, p.169.
18 BL Cotton MS *Titus D IV* – quarto volume of 138 ff. The poems were published in print in 1518, as an addendum to the Froben edition of More's *Utopia*; f.12v has an illustration with the Tudor rose, Katherine's badge of the pomegranate and the Beaufort portcullis.
19 TNA E 36/228, f.7.
20 *LP Henry VIII*, vol. 1, 1st ed., p.30. It was increased by a further £20 a year from the treasury in July 1515. Luke was one of those gentry who were ordered to create an inventory of the disgraced Empson's possessions in Northamptonshire.
21 *LP Henry VIII*, vol. 1, 2nd ed., p.1,444.
22 A tun of wine held 210 British gallons, or 954·68 litres. Was she a hard drinker or just a generous hostess to her guests?
23 *LP Henry VIII*, vol. 1, 2nd ed., pp.64 and 309.
24 Ibid., p.96.
25 Ibid., p.76.
26 Ibid., p.319.
27 Ibid., p.305.
28 Ibid., p.77; Greenwich, 25 July 1509. The following day Henry gave permission for the executors to found a perpetual chantry for one chaplain within the Collegiate Church of Wimborne, Dorset.
29 TNA SP 1/1/100. These estimates were drawn up during the last two years of Henry VII's reign, but were endorsed by his son in December 1509. They were considerably less than the eventual cost of the work by Torrigiano.

30 Higgins, p.141. See also: R. F. Scott, 'On the Contracts for the Tomb of the Lady Margaret Beaufort . . .', *Archæologia*, vol. 66 (1915), pp.365–76.
31 Darcy (1467–1537) was later executed on 30 June 1537 for his role in the Pilgrimage of Grace rebellion in the North of England, despite a pardon and his plea that he had 'never fainted or feigned' in his service, at home or overseas, to the king or his father in more than fifty years.
32 *LP Henry VIII*, vol. 1, 1st ed., p.29.
33 This is a piece of sixteenth-century black propaganda. Rhys ap Thomas (1448–1525) was a staunch supporter of Henry VII and is traditionally supposed to have killed Richard III at the end of the Battle of Bosworth. After his death, his tomb was moved from the Augustinian priory at Carmarthen at the Dissolution of the Monasteries to St Peter's Church, Carmarthen, where it remains. His grandson, Rhys ap Gruffudd (b.1509), was beheaded by Henry VIII for treason on 4 December 1531.
34 Allen & Allen, *Letters of Richard Fox*, pp.43–4.
35 BL Cotton MS *Vespasian C XIV*, f.106.
36 Sir William Bulmer was rebuked in 1519 for wearing the livery of Edward Stafford, Duke of Buckingham, while he was in the king's service, probably during the king's visit to Buckingham's seat at Penshurst, Kent, in August that year (Thiselton, p.12).
37 BL Cotton MS *Titus A XIII*, f.186. The force was reconstituted by Thomas Cromwell in December 1538 (BL Harley MS 6,807, f.25) under Sir Anthony Browne, later Master of the King's Horse. These 'Gentlemen Pensioners' became the Honourable Corps of Gentlemen-at-Arms on 17 March 1834 and their forty members still accompany the sovereign on state occasions. Their captain is now a political appointment and is normally the government Chief Whip in the House of Lords (see Hutchinson, *Thomas Cromwell*, p.226).
38 *CSP Venice*, vol. 1, p.5; *LP Henry VIII*, vol. 1, 2nd ed., p.75.
39 Neville (1471–1538), brother of George, Third Baron Abergavenny, was a close friend to both Henry and Katherine (Mattingly, p.160) and was an accomplished ballad singer. He occupied many positions at Henry VIII's court – Esquire of the Body, Gentleman of the Privy Chamber, Master of the Hounds and Standard Bearer – but was beheaded for treason on 8 December 1538. Neville's resemblance in looks created the unfounded rumour that he was a bastard son of Henry VII. During a masque at one of his banquets, Wolsey mistook Neville for the king (R. Sylvester, 'Cardinal Wolsey', pp.27–8). Many years later, Elizabeth I met Neville's son Henry during a progress in Berkshire and greeted him jocularly with the words: 'I am glad to see thee, brother Henry' (Scarisbrick, *Henry VIII*, p.18, fn.).
40 Hall, p.513.
41 Kendal was a coarse woollen cloth, normally dyed green.
42 A buckler was a small round shield with a boss on the front and a handle behind.
43 Hall, p.513.
44 BL Add. MS 5,758, f.8; *LP Henry VIII*, vol. 1, 2nd ed., p.156.
45 BL Add. MS 21,481; Stowe MS 146, f.3.
46 1 Henry VIII, cap.7.
47 1 Henry VIII, cap.11.

48 1 Henry VIII, cap.13.

49 1 Henry VIII, cap.14.

50 1 Henry VIII, cap.12. See Elton, 'A Restatement', pp.7–10.

51 Hall, p.513.

52 An alb was an ecclesiastical vestment, a long-sleeved linen tunic worn over a cassock but beneath a chasuble or cope by a priest or bishop.

53 A tippet was a short shoulder cape.

54 Hall, pp.513–14.

55 Among the knights chosen the next day was Sir Henry Marney.

56 Singer, p.79. The grounds of the house – an orchard and twelve separate pleasure gardens – stretched down to the Thames. The site is occupied today by Salisbury Square and Dorset Street.

57 In February, Sir Andrew Windsor, Keeper of the Great Wardrobe, was authorised to deliver 'for the use of our nursery, God willing' crimson cloth of gold to cover the baby's cradle, and to provide 'pillows, sheets, [counter]panes, swaddling bands, including beds for mistress nurse and the two rockers' and hangings for the chamber of the Lady Mistress of the Nursery – probably Elizabeth Denton again, considering her recent preferments (*LP Henry VIII*, vol. 1, 2nd ed., p.178). The following month, payment was made for red say (a fine twill cloth) to cover the steps of a font, and six ells (seven and a half yards or 6.86 m) of linen for 'aprons and napkins for four gentlemen and the sergeant of our vestry, according to the old use and custom' of a christening (*LP Henry VIII*, ibid., p.184).

58 In mid-February, the Venetian ambassador reported Henry's thanks for the Signory's congratulations on the queen's pregnancy (*LP Henry VIII*, ibid., p.167).

59 Also known as St Peter of Verona (1206–52), a thirteenth-century preacher in Lombardy, Italy. He was canonised by Pope Innocent IV 337 days after his martyrdom, the quickest recorded progression to sainthood. Before the new calendar of saints was introduced in the twentieth century, his feast day was 29 April, which may suggest that this was the date that Katherine was in labour.

60 She was listed as a member of Katherine's household in 1500 (see *CSP Spain*, vol. 1, p.246) and wanted to become a nun of the Franciscan Order.

61 The nunnery, founded in 1293, had become impoverished. In 1515, twenty-seven of the nuns died from plague ('Greyfriars Chronicle', p.29), probably leaving only eight alive, and shortly afterwards the nunnery was destroyed by fire. It was rebuilt in the 1520s but dissolved less than twenty years later.

62 Queen Katherine to Ferdinand; Greenwich Palace, 27 May 1510 (*CSP Spain*, vol. 2, p.38; *LP Henry VIII*, vol. 1, 2nd ed., p.285).

63 Caroz to Ferdinand; London, 29 May 1510 (*CSP Spain*, vol. 2, p.44).

64 *CSP Spain*, Supplement to vols. 1 and 2, pp.42–4.

65 Ibid.

66 Loades, p.22.

67 They were married in December 1509. Henry gave an offering of 6s 8d at the wedding. It was Anne's second marriage; she had wed Sir Walter Herbert in March 1503 but he died in September 1507 and there were no children.

68 Emphasis mine. Caroz's words have a flavour almost of the hunting field.

69 His creation as Earl of Wiltshire is described in BL Harley MS 6,074, f.54.

70 Anne and George Hastings clearly kissed and made up: they went on to have eight children.

71 Hart, p.25.

72 *CSP Spain*, Supplement to vols. 1 and 2, pp.42–4. As we have seen, the confessor and Caroz did not get on. In December 1514, the confessor was urging Katherine to 'forget Spain and everything Spanish in order to gain the love of the King of England and of the people', which would not have endeared him to a Spanish ambassador (*CSP Spain*, vol. 2, p.248; Caroz to Friar Juan de Eztuniga, Provincial of Aragon).

73 Signed on 23 March 1510. For its content, see *LP Henry VIII*, vol. 1, 2nd ed., pp.33ff.

74 It was signed on 17 November 1510.

75 Caroz to Ferdinand; London, 29 May 1510 (*CSP Spain*, vol. 2, pp.39–40).

76 Caroz to Ferdinand; London, 29 May 1510 (*CSP Spain*, vol. 2, p.44).

77 Hall, p.515.

78 Ibid., pp.515–16.

79 Brodie, pp.150–1.

80 Harrison, pp.86–92.

81 *Report of the Deputy Keeper of the Public Records*, appendix 2, vol. 3, London, 1852, p.227. His will, which was never proved, is printed in *LP Henry VIII*, vol. 1, 2nd ed., pp.326–7. By his second marriage to Elizabeth – sister and eventually heir of John Grey, Fourth Viscount Lisle – contracted some time in 1501–4, Dudley had three sons. John, the eldest, inherited his maternal grandfather's title in 1542 and rose to become Duke of Northumberland, a power in the government of Henry VIII's son Edward VI, and was executed on Tower Hill on 22 August 1553. John Dudley was the father of the Elizabethan grandees Robert, Earl of Leicester, and Ambrose, Earl of Warwick. See Gunn, 'Edmund Dudley', p.68 and David Loades, *John Dudley, Duke of Northumberland*, London, 1996, p.269.

82 Henry paid £17 16s to hire horses to take Empson to Northampton in October 1509 (*LP Henry VIII*, vol. 1, 2nd ed., p.1,444).

83 From the Old French legal term meaning 'to hear and determine'.

84 Chrimes, pp.315–16.

85 *LP Henry VIII*, vol. 1, 2nd ed., p.106.

86 Ibid., p.133.

87 BL Cotton MS *Galba B III*, f.3.

88 TNA SP 1/3/75.

89 BL Cotton MS *Galba B III*, f.4. Spinelly wanted cash to purchase the sequestered Scottish cannon and Henry VIII promised him £500 to buy them. See Anglo, *Great Tournament Roll*, vol. 1, introduction, p.12, fn.

90 The Gentlemen of the King's Chapel were paid £6 13s 4d for praying 'for the queen's good deliverance'.

91 *LP Henry VIII*, vol. 1, 2nd ed., p.670.

92 BL Add. MS 6,113, f.79v.

93 The Prior of Christchurch, Canterbury, was paid £4 for his servants carrying the

font to and from Richmond.

94 Anglo, *Great Tournament Roll*, vol. 1, introduction, p.51; Ellis, 2nd ser., vol. 1, pp.180–3.

95 TNA E 36/217, f.41.

96 Thomas & Thornley, p.369.

97 Ibid., p.370.

98 Anglo, *Great Tournament Roll*, vol. 1, introduction, pp.54–5; BL Harley Charters 83 H.1; Harley MS 6,079, f.36v.

99 Hall, p.519; TNA E 36/217, f.68; Thomas & Thornley, p.374.

100 Hall, p.520.

101 *LP Henry VIII*, vol. 1, 2nd ed., p.400.

102 Hall, p.519.

CHAPTER 7: THE PURSUIT OF MILITARY GLORY

1 *CSP Spain*, vol. 2, p.165.

2 Patterson, p.15.

3 Vergil, p.161.

4 Henry commissioned a translation of the life of Henry V in 1513 by Titus Livius who urged the king to emulate his predecessor (see *First English Life of King Henry the Fifth* ... , Charles Kingsford (ed.), Oxford, 1911, p.4). In December 1509, the Doge and Senate of Venice, in vainly urging Henry to attack France while her troops were devastating Venetian possessions on the Italian mainland, pointed out that an English invasion would be 'so great an opportunity for the conquest of a crown whose title he bears' and that an expedition against 'his capital and natural enemy, the King of France' would win him 'as much praise and glory as have ever fallen to the lot of any other King of England' (*CSP Venice*, vol. 2, p.24).

5 Vergil, p.161.

6 BL Cotton MS *Titus B I*, f.104v; reprinted in Allen & Allen, *Letters of Richard Fox*, p.54.

7 Allen & Allen, ibid., p.54.

8 Hughes & Larkin, no. 61, pp.83–4. Its preamble referred to the 'peace which, blessed by Jesus, has long continued in this his realm' and acknowledged that Englishmen 'be not so well appointed and provided with horse, harness [armour] and weapons convenient for the war as they have in the time past'.

9 Scarisbrick, *Henry VIII*, p.28.

10 TNA SP 1/2/40v.

11 *LP Henry VIII*, vol. 1, 2nd ed., p.400.

12 TNA SP 1/2/40. Letter from Warham to Darcy, 24 March 1511.

13 Hall, p.522. Ferdinand met some of the cost of the expedition and Henry forgave a loan of £1,000 to Darcy, but he was still financially embarrassed. In January 1514, he complained to Wolsey of his penury, saying that the Spanish expedition and his subsequent military service in France had cost him £4,000 and he was forced to sell his lands and plate 'but only the king [and Wolsey] shall know it'. Loyally, he

volunteered for more military service: 'I was never so meet [ready] for any business and in my life my purse never so weak' (TNA SP 1/7/80).

14 *LP Henry VIII*, vol. 1, 2nd ed., p.449. The papal galleys carrying over this cargo were to collect English tin with which to roof St Peter's in the Vatican.

15 'Sanuto Diaries', vol. 5, xiv, pp.334ff.

16 Scarisbrick, *Henry VIII*, pp.29 and 326.

17 Henry hired German mercenaries to stiffen his forces. In March 1512, one of his Spears, Guyote de Heull, was paid £13 6s 8d for 'retaining Almains [Germans] for the war'; the soldiers were paid four pence a day and their two captains four shillings. Payments of £40,000 were made to John Daunce, treasurer, for 'the wars' in February 1513 and a further £51,000 for the 'victualling and conveying over sea of the army'.

18 From the thirteenth century, the Church taught that those who died without sin – predominantly saints – were believed to enter Heaven immediately after dying. Those who died in mortal sin went straight to Hell. Unbaptised souls were held in Limbo. The souls who still had sins to atone for were held in Purgatory until Judgement Day, unless they worked out their penance in the interim, in which case they too entered Heaven. Indulgences promised a reduced time in Purgatory, normally measured in days and months.

19 'Sanuto Diaries', vol. 5, xiv, p.239.

20 Ibid., p.300.

21 William Knight to Wolsey, King's Almoner; 'from our pavilions beside Reinteria, Ipusqua, 14 June 1512' (*LP Henry VIII*, vol. 1, 2nd ed., p.362).

22 Scarisbrick, *Henry VIII*, p.29. Wolsey reported to Fox in August 1512 that a Spaniard – 'a man full of words' – had 'lately come to the king ... excusing [Ferdinand] his master that his army has not joined with [Henry's] army hitherto, alleging that the danger of Navarre ... [was] the cause of this long delay' (see Allen & Allen, *Letters of Richard Fox*, p.57).

23 *LP Henry VIII*, vol. 1, 2nd ed., pp.571–2.

24 Fuentarrabia, a city and port on the mouth of the River Bidassoa, near the French frontier.

25 Thomas, Lord Howard, to Wolsey; 8 July 1512 (TNA SP 1/2/119).

26 'The flux' was dysentery, which is spread through food contaminated with human faeces and was common in areas of poor sanitation.

27 Hall, p.529.

28 Ibid., pp.530–1.

29 John Stile to Henry VIII; 5 August 1512 (BL *Vespasian C I*, ff.65–77).

30 Dr William Knight to Wolsey; Fuentarrabia, 5 August 1512 (BL *Vespasian C I*, f.79).

31 Dr William Knight to Wolsey; San Sebastian, 4 October 1512 (BL *Vespasian C I*, f.81).

32 J. S. Brewer, vol. 1, p.20.

33 The Guyenne region corresponds to the modern *département* of Gironde.

34 *CSP Spain*, vol. 2, pp.68–9.

35 Poynings to Henry VIII; Brussels, 14 October 1512 (BL *Galba B III*, f.51).

36 Henry VIII to Poynings and other ambassadors, November 1512 (BL *Galba B III*, f.54).

37 Martin de Muxica to Ferdinand of Spain; London, 19 November 1512 (BL Add. MS 32,091, f.92).
38 *LP Henry VIII*, vol. 1, 2nd ed., p.578.
39 Hall, p.525; Hutchinson, *House of Treason*, p.7.
40 *Mary Rose*, 600 tons, and her sister ship *Peter Pomegranate*, 450 tons, were laid down in January 1510 and completed in the summer of the following year. They were the first English warships to be fitted with gun ports (Moorhouse, p.106).
41 St Lawrence was a priest who was martyred by the Roman Emperor Valerian in AD 258, traditionally by being roasted on a gridiron.
42 A carrack was a large merchant ship armed for naval operations.
43 Moorhouse, p.74.
44 Hutchinson, *House of Treason*, p.8.
45 Allen & Allen, *Letters of Richard Fox*, p.58.
46 Ibid.
47 Three days later, Howard's body was recovered from the sea by the French. It was disembowelled, embalmed and buried nearby. His gold whistle also washed up and was found. It was sent to the French queen, Anne of Brittany, in Paris and his armour given to Princess Claude as a war trophy. In his will, Howard had left the whistle to Henry VIII.
48 BL Cotton MS *Caligula D VI*, ff.106–7.
49 Ibid., f.104.
50 BL Cotton MS *Caligula B IV*, f.76 and Doran, p.74.
51 BL Cotton MS *Caligula B IV*, f.83.
52 Scarisbrick, *Henry VIII*, p.33.
53 'Sanuto Diaries', vol. 5, xv, p.305; London, 18 September 1512.
54 A first payment of 35,000 crowns (£8,750) was due to Maximilian within one month of his declaration of war on France and a similar amount fell due once he began hostilities. A further 30,000 crowns were payable after three months of fighting (*LP Henry VIII*, vol. 1, 2nd ed., p.940).
55 *CSP Spain*, vol. 2, pp.79–82. The treaty cementing the attack plans is in BL Cotton MS *Vespasian C VI*, f.375.
56 Allen & Allen, *Letters of Richard Fox*, p.70.
57 *LP Henry VIII*, vol. 1, 2nd ed., p.637.
58 BL Stowe MS 146, f.24.
59 *LP Henry VIII*, vol. 1, 2nd ed., p.919.
60 Hughes & Larkin, nos.65–8, pp.94–101.
61 BL Cotton MS *Vitellius B II*, f.34.
62 'Sanuto Diaries', vol. 5, xviii, p.445.
63 Hughes & Larkin, no.69, p.101. The previous August, Sir Edward Poynings (who had succeeded Henry as Lord Warden of the Cinque Ports) was ordered to muster forces 'when required' to defend against the 'expected invasion of the French' and to erect warning beacons and maintain watches along the Channel shoreline (TNA SP 1/2/146).
64 *CSP Milan*, p.384.

65 There was no trial, although the earl had been attainted in 1504.

66 BL Cotton MS *Faustina E VII*, f.6. Stowe MS 692, f.12 provides the names of the commanders of the three divisions.

67 *CSP Milan*, p.388.

68 Grafton, vol. 2, p.269.

69 Hatfield House MS CP 147/1.

70 BL Cotton MS *Cleopatra B V*, f.64. The gunfire was heard across the Channel in Dover, twenty-two miles (35.41 km) away.

71 Hall, p.539.

72 Carew (1464–1513) was another of Henry VII's loyalists who fought with him at Bosworth (where he was knighted) and drove Perkin Warbeck from Exeter in 1497.

73 BL Cotton MS *Cleopatra B V*, f.64.

74 A contemporary sketch of Calais can be found in BL Cotton MS *Augustus I III*, f.70.

75 Hall, pp.539–40.

76 Cruickshank, p.25.

77 BL Cotton MS *Cleopatra B V*, ff.64–95.

78 Hughes & Larkin, no.73, pp.106–21.

79 Bill men were armed with a variety of long pointed, hooked, spiked and bladed staff or hafted weapons, including partisans, glaives, gisarmes, lugged spears and halberds, some of which were probably developed from agricultural tools. They were particularly useful for infantry in defending against cavalry attacks, but were equally efficacious in hand-to-hand combat on foot.

80 BL Lansdowne MS 818, f.2v. As the troops were falling in, some of the cavalry's horses stampeded and the Captain of the Royal Guard, Sir Henry Marney, had his leg broken when his horse kicked out. Several other gentlemen were hurt.

81 BL Cotton MS *Cleopatra B V*, ff.64–95.

82 Shakespeare, *Henry V*, Act 4, prologue, line 47.

83 BL Cotton MS *Caligula D VI*, f.92.

84 Hall, p.542.

85 Cruickshank, p.37.

86 Hall, p.545.

87 BL Harley MS 2,252, f.41.

88 BL Cotton MS *Cleopatra B V*, ff.64–95.

89 BL Harley MS 787, f.58.

90 Hall, p.549. Specific rules were laid down for the camp before Thérouanne governing the relations between English and German soldiers. The king 'strictly charged and commanded that no Englishman intermeddle or lodge themselves within the ground assigned to the [Germans] for their lodgings or to give them any reproach or unfitting language or words by the which noise or debate might ensue, upon pain of imprisonment' (BL Arundel MS 26, ff.56v–57v).

91 'Sanuto Diaries', vol. 5, xvii, p.76.

92 Ibid., vol. 5, xvii, pp.16–17.

93 BL Cotton MS *Caligula D VI*, f.94.

94   BL Cotton MS *Vitellius B II*, f.51.

95   'Sanuto Diaries', vol. 5, xvii, p.78.

96   Ellis, 3rd ser., vol. 1, p.152. Katherine was about to lead reinforcements north as she wrote this letter. See also: BL Cotton MS *Caligula D VI*, f.93. Her instructions to muster troops in inland shires during her Regency are in Lambeth Palace MS 247, ff.58–60.

97   Cruickshank, p.127.

98   BL Cotton MS *Cleopatra B V*, ff.64–95.

99   *CSP Milan*, p.395.

100 *Chronicle of Calais*, pp.71–4; Gunn, *Charles Brandon*, pp.30–1.

101 *CSP Milan*, p.405.

102 BL Cotton MS *Vespasian F III*, f.15. For a full account of the Battle of Flodden, see Hutchinson, *House of Treason*, pp.15–20. In a letter to Wolsey, Katherine described the battle 'as a great gift that almighty God has sent to the king . . . This matter is so marvellous that it seems to be of God's doing alone' (BL Cotton MS *Caligula B IV*, f.35).

James died excommunicate and Henry sought special permission for him to be buried with royal honours in St Paul's Cathedral, London. This never happened. James IV's body was eventually taken to the Carthusian monastery at Sheen where, wrapped in lead, it lay unburied for many years. The antiquary John Stow reported later in the sixteenth century that after the dissolution of the house in the 1530s, the corpse had been thrown into a lumber room 'amongst the old timber and rubble. Since [such] time, workmen there, for their foolish pleasure, hewed off his head. Lancelot Young [Master Glazier to Elizabeth I] . . . brought [the head] to his house in Wood Street [London] where for a time he kept it for its sweetness. In the end, he caused the sexton [of St Michael's Wood Street] to bury it amongst other bones, taken out of their charnel house' (John Stow, *Survey of London*, 2 vols., Oxford, 1908, vol. 1, p.298).

103 BL Egerton MS 2,014, f.2. Reprinted in part in Byrne, pp.20–1.

104 Hatfield House MS CP 277/1, f.1.

CHAPTER 8: HOME AND ABROAD

1   Greenwich, 3 June 1516 (*CSP Venice*, vol. 2, p.305).

2   It was handed back to France in 1519 but captured by Imperial forces in 1521. For the English occupation of Tournai, see: Mayer, pp.257–77 and Davies, pp.1–26. Charles Brandon, now created Duke of Suffolk, led a 10,000-strong English army in August 1523 to initially capture the French port of Boulogne as a jumping-off point for a major military enterprise planned for the following year. His objectives were changed, however, and the army struck east, coming within fifty miles (80.47 km) of Paris before bad weather bogged down the troops and they retreated to Flanders ('State Papers', vol. 6, pp.221ff. and 233ff.).

3   A total of more than £1 million was paid out by John Heron, Treasurer of Henry's Privy Chamber, between the king's accession and 1518, of which nearly 70 per cent

was spent on preparations for war and hostilities. See TNA E 36/215/257ff. and Scarisbrick, *Henry VIII*, p.54.

4 Scarisbrick, *Henry VIII*, p.39. According to Venetian tittle-tattle, Charles was completely against marrying Mary, saying a little ungallantly that 'he wanted a wife and not a mother' ('Sanuto Diaries', vol. 5, xvii, pp.23–4).

5 *CSP Venice*, vol. 2, p.175.

6 BL Cotton MS *Vitellius B II*, f.56.

7 Henry boasted vainly to the Venetian ambassador in May 1514 that he wanted to go to Jerusalem and 'would take it with 25,000 men' ('Sanuto Diaries', vol. 5, xvii, p.139).

8 *LP Henry VIII*, vol. 1, 2nd ed., p.1,107.

9 The cap of maintenance is also called the 'cap of estate' or 'cap of dignity'.

10 BL Cotton MS *Vitellius B II*, f.69.

11 'Sanuto Diaries', vol. 5, xviii, pp.302–5.

12 *LP Henry VIII*, vol. 1, 2nd ed., p.1,184.

13 Allen & Allen, '*Opus Epistolarum*', vol. 2, epistle 287. His ministers reported in January 1514 that 'the king has been lately visited by a malady named the smallpox but is now recovered and out of danger' (*LP Henry VIII*, vol. 1, 2nd ed., p.1,141). The doctor was probably John Chambre, listed as a member of the Privy Chamber in 1514–5 ('Rutland Papers', p.21).

14 Charles was ill in June 1514 and his doctors claimed the effects of the moon were prolonging his illness (*LP Henry VIII*, vol. 1, 2nd ed., p.1,303. His letter to Princess Mary of 18 December 1513 hardly bursts with affection: he asked a diplomat to inform him of 'the state of your health, which is the best news I can hear' (BL Cotton MS *Galba B XIII*, f.93).

15 'Letters Louis XII', vol. 4, p.335.

16 See L. G. Carr Laughton, 'The Burning of Brighton by the French', *Transactions of the Royal Historical Society*, 3rd ser., vol. 10 (1916), pp.167–73.

17 Surrey reported to the King's Council on 14 June: 'I landed yesterday in Normandy, three miles west of Cherbourg and burned [four] miles west, three miles east and more than [two] inland as far as any house might be seen for great woods, leaving nothing unburnt but abbeys and churches. [We] burned many gentlemen's country houses, well built and stuffed with hangings ... of silk, of which neither they nor our men have little pr[ofit] for all or the more part was burnt.' He had re-embarked without any loss (BL Cotton MS *Caligula D VIII*, f.246).

18 'Sanuto Diaries', vol. 5, xviii, pp.302–5.

19 BL Egerton MS 544, f.158.

20 BL Cotton MS *Caligula D VI*, f.121v.

21 BL Harley MS 3,462, f.142v.

22 BL Add. MS 15,387, f.25.

23 J. S. Brewer, vol. 1, p.10, fn. Elephantiasis grossly enlarged part of the body – usually an arm or leg – due to obstruction of the lymphatic system by filarial worms.

24 *LP Henry VIII*, vol. 1, 2nd ed., p.1,325. Charles of Burgundy, when he heard the news of Mary's jilting, told his councillors: 'Well! Am I to have my wife as you promised me?' They answered him: 'You are young but the King of France is the first king in

Christendom and having no wife, [so] it rests with him to take for his queen any woman he pleases.' Charles then took a young hawk and plucked its feathers and explained: 'Because he is young he is held in small account and because he is young he squeaked not when I plucked him. Thus have you done by me. I am young, you have plucked me at your pleasure and I knew not how to complain. Bear in mind that for the future I shall pluck you' (*CSP Venice*, vol. 2, p.201).

25 BL Harley MS 3,462, f.142.
26 TNA SP 1/5/230, f.266.
27 One of Henry's warships, the 900-ton *Lubeck*, was wrecked on the French coast, and several hundred of the crew drowned.
28 'Rutland Papers', p.25.
29 Knecht, p.80.
30 *LP Henry VIII*, vol. 2, pt. 1, p.74.
31 *CSP Spain*, vol. 2, p.248.
32 'Sanuto Diaries', vol. 5, xix, p.1.
33 BL Cotton MS *Caligula D VI*, f.149.
34 *LP Henry VIII*, vol. 1, 2nd ed., p.1,456 and *CSP Spain*, vol. 2, pp.243–5.
35 Hall, p.572.
36 'Sanuto Diaries', vol. 5, xx, pp.98–9.
37 BL Cotton MS *Caligula D VI*, f.176.
38 *LP Henry VIII*, vol. 2, pt. 1, pp.74–5.
39 BL Cotton MS *Caligula D VI*, f.184.
40 *LP Henry VIII*, vol. 2, pt. 1, p.75.
41 BL Cotton MS *Vespasian F XIII*, f.80.
42 *LP Henry VIII*, vol. 2, pt. 1, p.125.
43 BL Egerton MS 985, f.61v.
44 Scarisbrick, *Henry VIII*, p.76.
45 'Sanuto Diaries', vol. 5, xxix, p.20; Russell, pp.131–2.
46 'Sanuto Diaries', vol. 5, xxix, pp.71–9.
47 Russell, p.176. It was probably intended to be a Welsh dragon.
48 Routh, p.44. See A. J. Geritz, 'The Relationship of Brothers-in-Law Thomas More and John Rastell', *Moreana*, vol. 139–40 (1999), pp.35–48.
49 Routh, ibid. Rastell (*c.*1475–1536) served as coroner in Coventry from 1506 but two years later, possibly because of his Lollard religious beliefs, moved to London where he ran a successful legal practice in addition to printing and publishing mainly law books, although he was the first in England to print musical scores (see A. Hyatt King, 'The Significance of John Rastell in Early Music Printing', *The Library*, 5th ser., vol. 26 (1971), pp.197–214). However, Rastell fell foul of Archbishop Thomas Cranmer in 1535 over his denial of clerical rights to tithes and died in poverty in the Tower of London.
50 Williamson, pp.94ff. and 248ff., and Scarisbrick, *Henry VIII*, p.124.
51 It is generally considered to have been discovered by John Cabot in 1497.
52 Balasses were rubies, coloured faintly red.
53 Granates were yellow-red prismatic garnets.

54 Hatfield House MS CP 245/5, ff.3v–4r.

55 Hatfield House MS CP 245/5, ff.9v–14r. Another copy is in BL Cotton MS *Vitellius C VII*, f.337v.

56 Rut (*fl.* 1512–28) was appointed master of the 800-ton Genoese carrack *Maria de Loreto* in 1512 after it had been seized in Dartmouth, Devon, for service in the French wars.

57 Built in 1524 and named after the wife of Sir Henry Guilford, one-time Master of the Horse and Comptroller of the Royal Household.

58 Andrews, p.55.

59 A league was reckoned to be the distance a man could walk in an hour and is roughly equivalent to three miles (4.8 km).

60 *LP Henry VIII*, vol. 4, p.3,121.

61 Wright, pp.29–40.

62 Hayward, p.6. The average height for men during the Tudor period was around 5 ft 8 in. – although John Fisher, Bishop of Rochester, was the same height as Henry VIII.

63 *LP Henry VIII*, vol. 3, pt. 1, p.142.

64 BL Cotton MS *Caligula D VII*, f.158. Henry had sworn to grow his beard until meeting King Francis of France. His mother, Louise of Savoy, was puzzled by the sudden loss of facial hair and asked the English ambassador, Sir Thomas Boleyn, whether this was a slight to her son. Boleyn hastened to reassure her that Henry's affection for Francis was greater 'than [that for] any king living. She was well appeased and said, "Th[eir] love is not in the beards but in the hearts."'

An illumination in the Chief Justice Rolls in the Court of King's Bench in Trinity Term, 1518, shows Henry as young and clean-shaven, but this may have been a stock image of his father, Henry VII, adapted for the new king (TNA KB 27/1024).

65 Vespers is the evening office or service, beginning in the Latin rite: 'O God, come to my assistance. O Lord, make haste to help me. Glory be to the Father, and to the Son, and to the Holy Spirit. As it was in the beginning is now and ever shall be world without end. Amen.' Compline is the final office of the day.

66 *LP Henry VIII*, vol. 3, pt. 1, p.350.

67 Tennis had its dangers. On 10 July 1525, the city of Valencia gave a banquet to the Marquis of Brandenburg 'after which he played at tennis and caught a fever by overheating himself and died in three days' (BL Cotton MS *Vespasian C III*, f.75).

68 Kybett, p.22. During dancing at a diplomatic reception, eight masked noblemen wore black velvet slippers 'this being done lest the King should be distinguished from the others; as, from the hurt which he lately received on his left foot when playing at tennis, he wears a black velvet slipper' (*LP Henry VIII*, vol. 4, p.clxxv).

69 A payment for 1,000 crowns was made in January 1519 'playing money for the king, Twelfth Eve'.

70 Hall, *Chronicle*, p.520. It is ironic that the Sheriffs of London prohibited the playing of 'tennis, dice and other unlawful games, contrary to the statutes for the maintenance of archery' in a proclamation published in December 1528. A case of one law for the rich and another for the poor? (See BL Harley MS 442, f.97.)

71 *CSP Venice*, vol. 2, pp.557–63.

72 'Dispatches', vol. 1, pp.85ff.

73 Ibid., p.83.

74 J. S. Brewer, vol. 1, p.97.

75 *CSP Venice*, vol. 2, pp.246–7.

76 Ibid., p.325.

77 William Cornish (1465–1523) was the Master of the children of Henry's Chapel Royal. He was also a composer, dramatist and actor, and responsible for the musical and dramatic entertainments at the royal court. See Anglo, *Spectacle*, pp.118–21 and 203–4.

78 *LP Henry VIII*, vol. 2, p.1,246.

79 *CSP Venice*, vol. 2, pp.397–404.

80 *LP Henry VIII*, vol. 4, pp.869–72.

81 Lambeth Palace Library MS 602, p.59.

82 Roper, pp.67ff.

83 Ackroyd, p.226.

84 *LP Henry VIII*, vol. 3, pt. 1, p.468.

85 BL Cotton MS *Vitellius B IV*, f.111.

86 Ayot, p.70, fn.

87 BL Cotton MS *Vitellius B IV*, f.226.

88 Scarisbrick, *Henry VIII*, p.116.

89 35 Henry VIII cap. 3. It was repealed during the reign of Catholic Mary I but restored under Elizabeth (1 Elizabeth cap. 1) and has remained part of the style and title of the English crown ever since.

90 Fuller, book v, p.168.

91 *CSP Venice*, vol. 2, p.560.

92 A felt hat, worn by doctors of divinity in the sixteenth century, the name probably derived from the Latin *pileus*, a conical hat.

93 A red felt cardinal's hat lined with silk, sixteenth century, once owned by Horace Walpole and kept in the Holbein Chamber at Strawberry Hill, was said to have been Wolsey's, having been discovered by Bishop Burnet when he was Clerk of the Closet in the seventeenth century. It is now at Christ Church, University of Oxford.

94 Singer, pp. 96–101 and 104–7.

95 The only English Pope was Adrian IV, or Nicholas Breakspear, who occupied St Peter's throne from 1154 to 1159.

96 Adrian VI was the last non-Italian pope to be elected until John Paul II, 456 years later.

97 See D. S. Chambers, pp.20–30.

98 Guy, p.47.

99 Erasmus to Paulus Bombasius; Basle, 26 July 1518 (Nichols, vol. 3, epistle 805).

100 Roper, p.20.

101 Hall, pp.597–8. See also Walker, pp.1–16.

102 Harris, p.168.

103 His personal accounts for January–April 1521 show income totalling £8,274 for the

four months, or £3·2 million in current spending values (*LP Henry VIII*, vol. 3, pt. 1, pp.500–1). His lands had an annual value of £4,905 15s 5¼d. However, in 1520, he had debts of £10,535 19s (Harris, p.172).

104 In 1500, Buckingham had married Alianore, eldest daughter of Henry Percy, Fourth Earl of Northumberland. Their second son Henry married the daughter of Margaret Pole, Countess of Salisbury, and their eldest daughter Elizabeth wed Thomas Howard, later Earl of Surrey and Third Duke of Norfolk.

105 *CSP Venice*, vol. 2, p.561.

106 Ellis, 3rd ser., vol. 1, pp.214–18.

107 BL Harley MS 283, f.70.

108 Scarisbrick, *Henry VIII*, p.120.

109 BL Add. MS 19,398, f.644.

110 Thornbury Castle is now a hotel.

111 For example, see Vergil, pp.262ff.

112 Tothill Fields were a marshy tract of land between Millbank and Westminster Abbey.

113 Hall, p.622.

114 In 1560, merchant tailor Richard Hall gave £500 for the purchase of the property in Suffolk Lane, off Thames Street, for use as a school. This building was destroyed in the Great Fire of London in 1666 and a new school, housing two hundred boys, was built on the site in brick in 1675.

115 BL Cotton MS *Vitellius B IV*, f.96.

116 The roll and file of the Court of the Lord High Steward is in TNA KB/8/5.

117 The Statute of Treasons of 1352 (25 Edward III cap. 2) included 'compassing or imagining the king's death' as a treasonable offence. See discussion in Tanner, pp.375–81.

118 Under English law, commoners have the right to a trial by a jury of their equals and a statute of 1341 (15 Edward III cap. 1) gave the nobility the right to be tried by their peers. From the Tudor period, the Lord High Steward heard cases when Parliament was not sitting, otherwise trials were conducted in the House of Lords. The last peer to be tried by his peers and executed was Laurence Shirley, Fourth Earl Ferrers, who was hanged for murder in 1760. The last trial in the Lords was of Edward Russell, Twenty-sixth Baron de Clifford, who was acquitted of manslaughter in 1935. The right of the nobility to trial by peers was abolished in 1948.

119 Hall, p.623.

120 *LP Henry VIII*, vol. 3, pt. 1, pp.490–1.

121 Ibid., p.492.

122 BL Harley MS 283, f.70.

123 *LP Henry VIII*, vol. 3, pt. 1, pp.cxxxi–iii.

124 Harris, p.185.

125 Surrey had married Buckingham's daughter Elizabeth early in 1513. It was not a happy marriage. See Hutchinson, *House of Treason*, pp.63–76.

126 BL Cotton MS *Vitellius B IV*, f.84v.

127 BL Stowe MS 163, f.3.

128 Hall, p.624.

129 Ibid.

130 Shorn was rector of North Marston around 1290 and the waters of his holy well were believed to cure cases of malaria and the gout. See Richard Marks, 'A Late Medieval Pilgrimage Cult: Master John Shorn of North Marston and Windsor' in L. Keen and E. Scarff (eds.), *Windsor Medieval Archæology ... British Archæological Association Conference Proceedings*, vol. 25 (2002), pp.192–207.

131 BL Cotton MS *Caligula D VIII*, f.83. The Emperor Maximilian was a little surprised at Buckingham's fate. He told the English envoy Sir Richard Wingfield that 'he knew [Henry's] great virtue and wisdom too well to suppose he would have had the duke executed without great and just cause' (BL Cotton MS *Vitellius B XX*, f.234).

132 14/15 Henry VIII cap. 20.

133 *LP Henry VIII*, vol. 3, pt. 1, p.406.

134 The Battle of Pavia was fought early on the morning of 24 February 1525.

135 Robert Macquereau, *Histoire générale de l'Europe depuis la naissance de Charle-quint jusqu'als cinq juin 1527*, Louvain, 1725, p.231.

CHAPTER 9: THE KING'S 'SCRUPULOUS CONSCIENCE'

1 Hall, p.755.

2 Davies & Edwards, p.895. MacNalty (p.162) gives the sex of the child as male but the date as November 1513.

3 *LP Henry VIII*, vol. 1, 2nd ed., p.1,486. On 4 October 1514, the Wardrobe was ordered to deliver a cradle covered with scarlet 'for the use of a nursery, God willing' (ibid., p.1,403).

4 *CSP Venice*, vol. 2, p.285.

5 BL Harley MS 3,504, f.232.

6 Henry bought New Hall from Thomas Boleyn in 1516 at a cost of £1,000 and spent a further £17,000 on rebuilding it in 1517–21. It is now New Hall School.

7 Illustrated in Thurley, p.102.

8 BL Cotton MS *Vespasian F III*, f.73.

9 *LP Henry VIII*, vol. 2, pt. 2, p.1,328.

10 'Dispatches', vol. 2, p.236.

11 Ibid., p.240.

12 Hutchinson, 'Henry's Reproductive Woes'.

13 See Alan Bideau, Bertrand Desjardins and Hector Pérez Brignoll, *Infant Mortality in Britain: A Survey of Current Knowledge on Historical Trends and Variations in Infant and Child Mortality in the Past*, Oxford, 1997.

14 *CSP Venice*, vol. 2, p.1,287.

15 'Sanuto Diaries', vol. 5, xxvii, p.276.

16 Elizabeth Blount received an annual salary of 100 shillings in 1513.

17 Her copy is BL Egerton MS 1,991.

18 BL Cotton MS *Caligula D VI*, f.149.

19 Philippa Jones, p.79.

20 BL Cotton MS *Vitellius B II*, f.183.

21 *LP Henry VIII*, vol. 6, p.241.

22 See the Revd Alfred Suckling's *Antiquities and Architecture . . . of the County of Essex*, London, 1845, p.27. He adds: 'It is a very remarkable situation to have chosen for the purposes of debauchery as it not only abuts upon the churchyard but is actually within a stone's [throw] of the residence of the monks.'

23 14/15 Henry VIII, cap. 34; Mattingly, p.123. This income was derived from Talboys' father who was declared a lunatic in 1517. Gilbert Talboys was knighted in 1524 and was appointed Sheriff of Lincolnshire the following year. Bessie Blount had two sons and a daughter with Gilbert before his death in 1530. After 1533 she married Edward Clinton and had three daughters by him. She was a lady-in-waiting to Henry's fourth wife Anne of Cleves and died in 1541, probably from tuberculosis.

24 *LP Henry VIII*, vol. 4, p.2,558.

25 BL Add. MS 8,715, f.220v.

26 BL Cotton MS *Caligula B I*, f.232. Margaret told Henry that she knew she would 'never get good from Scotland by fair means and will never willingly stay there with those who do not love her'.

27 Angus wrote to Henry on 19 October 1519, thanking him for sending the friar to Stirling who had 'discharged his mission so well' that Margaret was willing (then) to stay with him (BL Cotton MS *Caligula B I*, f.141). It took seven or eight weeks to convince her (BL Cotton MS *Caligula B II*, f.333).

Henry inherited his father's respect for the Greenwich Friar Observants. He wrote to Pope Leo X declaring his 'deep and devoted affection' for them and finding it impossible to 'adequately describe their zeal, night and day, to win back sinners to God'. Many suffered during the 1530s for refusing the take the Oath of Succession.

28 Byrne, p.68. She married Stewart on 3 March 1528.

29 J. S. Brewer, vol. 2, p.161.

30 Lady Margaret Douglas was the daughter of the king's sister Margaret by her second marriage.

31 Hutchinson, *House of Treason*, pp.77–9.

32 He was entitled to keep four servants and two horses at court ('Rutland Papers', p.101).

33 *LP Henry VIII*, vol. 4, p.991.

34 Warnicke, 'The Rise and Fall of Anne Boleyn', pp.35, 237–8 and A. G. L'Estrange, *Palace and Hospital or Chronicles of Greenwich*, 2 vols., London, 1889, vol. 1, p.192.

35 Flügel, 'On the Character . . .', p.146.

36 Hoskins, pp.347–8.

37 *LP Henry VIII*, vol. 8, p.215.

38 Ibid., p.214.

39 *LP Henry VIII*, vol. 12, pt. 2, pp.332–3; Hutchinson, *Thomas Cromwell*, pp.141–2.

40 *LP Henry VIII*, vol. 4, pp.1,932–3.

41 Henry later ordered Sir Thomas Boleyn to house and maintain Mary – but at least assigned her the annuity of £100 formerly enjoyed by her husband.

42 BL Cotton MS *Vespasian C III*, f.176.

43 After a fire which destroyed large portions of the Palace of Westminster in 1512,

Henry took over Wolsey's building operations at Bridewell and in 1523 completed the brick-built house with two courtyards and a long gallery leading to a water gate on the Thames. See Thurley, pp.40–1.

44 BL Add. MS 6,113, f.61.

45 'State Papers', vol. 1, p.161. Wolsey had two illegitimate children by his mistress Joan Larke: Thomas Winter, born around 1510, and Dorothy, born c.1512.

46 *LP Henry VIII*, vol. 4, p.677.

47 Croke (c.1489–1558) was educated at Eton College and was recruited by John Fisher to teach Greek at Cambridge.

48 BL Cotton MS *Vespasian F III*, f.44.

49 *LP Henry VIII*, vol. 4, pt. 2, p.1,721; Ellis, 3rd ser., vol. 2, p.117.

50 *LP Henry VIII*, vol. 4, pt. 2, p.2,595.

51 'Sanuto Diaries', vol. 5, xxxix, p.167.

52 Plowden, p.54.

53 BL Cotton MS *Vespasian F XIII*, f.140.

54 Paul, p.59. A new translation of *The Education of a Christian Woman*, edited by Charles Fantazzi, was published by the University of Chicago Press in 2000.

55 *CSP Spain*, vol. 3, pt. 1, p.1,018.

56 *LP Henry VIII*, vol. 4, p.1,049.

57 'Sanuto Diaries', vol. 5, xi, p.613.

58 Roper (1496–1578) was the eldest son of John Roper (d.1524), Attorney General to Henry VIII. He was later Clerk of the Pleas to the Court of King's Bench and a Member of Parliament. Roper wrote a biography of his father-in-law Sir Thomas More.

59 More's first wife was Jane Colt. She died in 1511 and within a month he remarried, this time to Alice, the widow of the merchant John Middleton who had died in 1509.

60 Roper, pp.20–1.

61 The ladies kept their bonnets and their headdresses. One had to be repaired at the cost of two shillings.

62 *LP Henry VIII*, vol. 3, p.1,559. The cost of the pageant was £20 16s 4d.

63 Hall, p.631.

64 Sander, p.25.

65 Singer, p.424.

66 Ibid., pp.426–7.

67 It may have been even earlier – in October 1525, as a French envoy, John Brinon, told Louise of Savoy of a conversation with Wolsey, the subject of which 'I cannot write to you, as he made me promise not to mention them' (*LP Henry VIII*, vol. 4, p.769). Whether that subject was the king's marriage must remain a matter of conjecture.

68 Matilda, daughter of Henry I, had at that time been the only female ruler of England – and only for a few months in 1141, before a civil war broke out against her cousin Stephen, a rival claimant to the throne.

69 Hall, p.674 and MacNalty, p.73.

70 Moriarty, p.13 and Hutchinson, *Last Days*, p.127. Vicary was rewarded with a medical

appointment in the royal household at a salary of twenty shillings a year and was promoted to sergeant surgeon in 1536, a post worth £26 13s 4d.

Out of this sore leg was born the widespread belief that the king suffered from syphilis – contracted whilst he was campaigning in France – and that as this venereal disease can damage foetuses, it was a factor in Katherine's poor natal record. However, the thigh is an unusual location for a *gumma* or swelling – a symptom of tertiary syphilis – and these are not normally painful, yet Henry suffered agonies. Moreover, there is no evidence of syphilis amongst his children. Treatment of this disease consisted of six weeks of sweating the patient and the administration of doses of (poisonous) mercury which made gums red and sore and created copious flows of saliva. There are no reports of a prolonged absence of the king from public life or of these symptoms. Therefore Henry having syphilis looks like mere black propaganda.

71 Hall, p.697.
72 MacNalty, p.57. Fear stalked the streets but this outbreak was hardly comparable to the 250,000 who died in Britain during the Spanish Influenza epidemic of March 1918–June 1920.
73 'Love Letters', pp.30–2.
74 Ives, *The Life and Death of Anne Boleyn*, pp.100–1.
75 BL Royal MS 1 E iv.
76 Vergil, p.324; Harpsfield, p.41.
77 *CSP Spain*, vol. 3, pt. 1, p.293.
78 Stow, p.543.
79 Richard Sylvester, 'Cardinal Wolsey', p.179.
80 Harpsfield, p.31.
81 BL Cotton MS *Vitellius B IX*, f.36.
82 *LP Henry VIII*, vol. 4, p.2,588.
83 Mattingly, p.191.
84 J. S. Brewer, vol. 2, pp.187–8 and Scarisbrick, *Henry VIII*, p.155.
85 *LP Henry VIII*, vol. 4, p.1,434.
86 Ibid., vol. 4, p.1,450.
87 *CSP Spain*, vol. 3, pt. 2, p.276.
88 *LP Henry VIII*, vol. 4, pt. 2, p.1,504.
89 'State Papers', vol. 1, p.194.
90 Ibid., pp.230–1.
91 Biblioteca Apostolica Vaticano Vat. Lat. 3731A, f.5.
92 'Love Letters', pp.32–4.
93 Ives, *The Life and Death of Anne Boleyn*, p.85.
94 Ibid., p.91 and TNA SP 1/66/39.
95 *LP Henry VIII*, vol. 4, pt. 2, p.2,003.
96 BL King's MS 9, ff.66v and 231v.
97 Scarisbrick, *Henry VIII*, pp.158–9.
98 'State Papers', vol. 1, pp.278–9.
99 Scarisbrick, *Henry VIII*, p.162.

100 Mattingly, pp.194–5.
101 Gairdner, p.249.
102 Hall, pp.754–5.
103 *LP Henry VIII*, vol. 4, pt. 2, p.2,096.
104 *CSP Spain*, vol. 3, pt. 2, p.877.
105 Ibid., p. 882.
106 *LP Henry VIII*, vol. 4, pt. 2, p.2,210.
107 Ibid., p.2,108.
108 Two volumes of legal opinions on the validity of the marriage by bishops and canon lawyers, drawn up for the legatine trial, are in Lambeth Palace Library, MSS 2341–2. They were probably part of Campeggio's file.
109 BL Cotton MS *Vitellius B XII*, f.208.
110 Starkey, *Six Wives*, pp.237–9.
111 Ibid., p.243.
112 Singer, pp.214–17.
113 Mattingly, p.209.
114 *CSP Spain*, vol. 4, pt. 1, p.352. Anne continued her nagging: 'I see that some fine morning you will succumb to her reasoning and that you will cast me off.'
115 Gairdner, p.250.
116 Ibid., p.248.
117 'Sanuto Diaries', vol. 5, lii, p.176.
118 In a letter to Prior Bernard Salviati, nephew of Clement VII, 5 November 1529, Campeggio writes of the 'various hindrances which met me between London and Dover' (*LP Henry VIII*, vol. 4, p.2,702). Du Bellay, the French ambassador in London, added this postscript to a dispatch of 12 October: 'I have just heard that upon pretence of want of ships they would not let him [Campeggio] pass without consulting about it, for fear he carries off the treasure of the Cardinal of York' (*LP Henry VIII*, vol. 4, p.2,672).
119 *CSP Spain*, vol. 4, pt. i, pp.303–4. This was the second time in ten years that the contents of Campeggio's luggage had been exposed to the rude hoi polloi. In January 1518, when he arrived in London to discuss a crusade against the Turks, the mules carrying his chests bolted in Cheapside and the damaged luggage spilled out his 'broken shoes and roasted flesh, pieces of bread, eggs and much vile baggage, at which sight the boys cried "see my Lord Legate's treasure!" and so the muleteers were ashamed and took up the stuff and passed forth' (see Hall, pp.592–3).
120 Hall, p.759. The commission had been burnt.
121 Campeggio was Bishop of Salisbury.
122 Henry VIII to Campeggio, Windsor, 22 October 1529 (*LP Henry VIII*, vol. 4, p.2,677).
123 Henry was not finished with Campeggio. By Act of Parliament (25 Henry VIII cap. 27) in January 1534, he and another absentee Italian, Geronimo Ghinucci, were deprived, respectively, of their sees of Salisbury and Worcester. Campeggio also lost his cardinal-protectorship of England the same year on Henry's instructions.
124 *CSP Spain*, vol. 4, pt. 1, pp.351–2.

125 'Wriothesley Chronicle', vol. 1, p.16.
126 Biblioteca Apostolica Vaticano ASV A.A. Arm. I-XVIII, 4098A.
127 *CSP Spain*, vol. 4, pt. 2, p.263.
128 For details of the legislation creating the foundation of the break with Rome, see Hutchinson, *Thomas Cromwell*, pp.49–51 and 53–5.
129 Elton, *Policy*, p.278.
130 TNA SP 1/82/151.
131 Ellis, 3rd ser., vol. 2, p.276.
132 *CSP Milan*, p.557.
133 BL Harley MS 283, f.75.

BIBLIOGRAPHY

LIST OF ABBREVIATIONS

ASV	*Archivum Secretum Aposticum Vaticanum*	*Jnl*	*Journal*
BAA	British Archæological Association	*LP*	*Letters and Papers, Foreign & Domestic, Henry VIII, 1509–47*
BL	British Library	MS/MSS	manuscript(s)
Bull.	Bulletin	n.s.	new series
CCR	*Calendar Close Rolls*	*ODNB*	*Oxford Dictionary of National Biography*
CFR	*Calendar of Fine Rolls*		
CP	Cecil Papers, Hatfield House	pt.	part
		PPE	Privy Purse Expenses
CPR	*Calendar of Patent Rolls*	*PROME*	*Parliament Rolls of Medieval England*
CS	Camden Society		
CSP Milan	*Calendar of State Papers, Milan*	RCHM	Royal Commission on Historical Manuscripts
CSP Spain	*Calendar of State Papers, Spain*	r	recto
		rev.	revised
CSP Venice	*Calendar of State Papers, Venice*	RHS	Royal Historical Society
		RP	*Rotuli Parliamentorum*
ed.	edited	TNA	The National Archives
edn.	edition	*Trans.*	*Transactions.*
EETS	Early English Text Society	transl.	translated
EHR	*English Historical Review*	ser.	series
f.	folio	*St. P.*	*State Papers*
fn.	footnote	v	verso
HJ	*Historical Journal*	vol(s).	volume(s)
HR	*Historical Research*		

PRIMARY SOURCES

Manuscript

BIBLIOTHÈQUE DE MÉJANES, AIX-EN-PROVENCE, FRANCE

MS 442 Res MS 20 – Portrait of a boy toddler, inscribed 'le Roy henry d'angleterre'.

BODLEIAN LIBRARY, OXFORD

Selden MS Supra 77 – *De astroruim ui fatali*, a fifty-eight folio book of astrological predictions, by William Parron, dedicated to Henry VII, 1499.

BRITISH LIBRARY

Additional MS

4,822 – Tract in an early sixteenth-century hand of *Coniunccio Arthuri et Veneris*, by Richard Maryng, brother in the house of Bonhommes, Edlington, Wiltshire.

5,758, f.8 – Opening of Henry VIII's first Parliament; Westminster, 21 January 1510.

6,113, f.61 – Ceremony of creating Henry Fitzroy, Duke of Richmond; Bridewell, 18 June 1525.

——f.72 – Names of nobles that did homage at the coronation of Henry VIII.

——f.79v – Account of christening of Prince Henry at Richmond, Sunday 5 January 1511.

7,099, f.129 – Contract for alabaster effigy tomb, to be carved by James Keyley, for Richard III in the church of the Greyfriars, Leicester.

8,715, f.220v – Ridolfo Pio, Bishop of Faenza (Papal Nuncio in France) to Ambrosius de Recalcatis, papal secretary; Da Monte Plaisant, 10 March 1536.

12,060, f.23–23v – Collection of miraculous examples and narratives in support of Transubstantion by Henry Parker, Baron Morley.

15,387, f.25 – Henry VIII to Pope Leo X; Greenwich, 12 May 1514.

19,398, f.644 – Henry VIII to Wolsey; ?late 1520/early 1521.

21,404, f.9 – Prince Henry to Philip I of Castile; Greenwich, 9 April 1506.

——f.10 – Henry VIII to Margaret of Savoy; Westminster, 27 June 1509.

21,481 – King's Book of Household Payments, April 1509–March 1518, signed by Henry VIII on almost every folio.

26,787 – Moral treatise *Speculum Principis* by John Skelton, presented to Henry VIII on his accession.

32,091, f.92 – Modern copy of letter from Martin de Muxica, Spanish ambassador in London, to Ferdinand, describing the interrogation of the English captains by Henry VIII; London, 19 November 1512.

31,922 – Sixty-three songs, ballads and instrumental music composed early in the reign of Henry VIII, roughly a third attributed to the king's composition.

33,772 – Sixty-five folio volume in Latin of the lives of the saints, presented by Giovanni de' Gigli, Bishop of Worcester, to Lady Margaret Beaufort in 1497.

45,131, ff.37–41 – Description of the funeral of Arthur, Prince of Wales.

——ff.41v–47v – Description of the funeral of Elizabeth of York, 1503, with a drawing of the funeral procession at ff.41v–42.

——ff.48v–54 – Funeral of Henry VII, 1509, a description of events after his death, with a drawing of him on his deathbed, f.54.

48,000 (Yelverton MS 1), ff.590–594v – Spanish ratification of the marriage treaty of Prince Henry and Katherine of Aragon, 23 September 1503.

59,899, f.24 – Payment to Robert Vertue for 'platt' [plans] of Greenwich Palace 'devised by the queen', 1502.

Arundel MS

26, f.28 – Description of the removal of Henry VII's corpse at Richmond, May 1509.

——f.56v–57v – Regulations governing the English camp before Thérouanne, August 1513.

Cotton MS

Appendix XXVII, f.145 – Deposition of unidentified witness on marriage of Prince Arthur and Katherine of Aragon.

Augustus I, III, f.70 – Contemporary drawing of the town of Calais from the sea.

Caligula B I, f.141 – Archibald Douglas, Earl of Angus, to Henry VIII; Dalkeith, 19 October 1519.

——f.232 – Queen Margaret to Henry VIII; Edinburgh, April 1519.

Caligula B II, f.333 – Lord Dacre of the North to Wolsey; Harbottle, 22 October 1519.

Caligula B VI, f.35 – Queen Katherine to Thomas Wolsey; Woburn, Bedfordshire, 16 September 1513.

——f.76 – James IV of Scotland to Henry VIII; Edinburgh, 24 May 1513.

——f.83 – Margaret, wife of James IV of Scotland, to Henry VIII; 11 April 1513.

Caligula D VI, f.92 – Katherine of Aragon to Wolsey; Richmond, [2]6 July 1513.

——f.93 – Katherine of Aragon to Wolsey; Richmond, 13 August 1513.

——f.94 – Katherine of Aragon to Wolsey; Richmond, 25 August 1513.

——f.104 – Thomas Lord Howard, Lord High Admiral, to Wolsey, on board *Mary Rose*, Plymouth harbour, May 1513.

——f.106–7 – Thomas Lord Howard, Lord High Admiral, to Henry VIII; on board *Mary Rose*, Plymouth harbour, 7 May 1513.

——f.121v – Henry to Wolsey about his requirements for a French peace treaty – fragmentary, the document damaged by fire; ?June 1514.

——f.149 – Charles Brandon, Duke of Suffolk, to Henry VIII; Beauvais, 25 October 1514.

——f.176 – Charles Brandon, Duke of Suffolk, to Wolsey; Paris, 5 March 1515.

——f.184 – Charles Brandon, Duke of Suffolk, to Henry VIII; Paris, – March 1515.

Caligula D VII, f.158 – Sir Thomas Boleyn to Wolsey; Blois, 16 November 1519.

Caligula D VIII, f.83 – Wolsey to Sir Richard Jerningham, English ambassador to the French court; Westminster, 20 May 1521.

Caligula D VIII, f.246 – Earl of Surrey to King's Council; on board the *Mary Rose*, Portland, 14 June 1514.

Cleopatra B V, ff.64–95 – Diary of John Taylor, king's chaplain and clerk of the Parliament during the invasion of France, 1513.

Cleopatra E III, f.123 – Draft of an oration by an English ambassador to Pope Innocent VIII and the Cardinals, Rome, soon after the marriage of Henry VII to Elizabeth of York, January 1486.

Cleopatra E IV, f.249 – Richard Layton to Thomas Cromwell about 'Our Lady's Girdle' at Bruton Abbey, Somerset, 24 August 1535.

Faustina E VII, f.6 – Order of battle of the king's rearguard for the invasion of France, June 1513.

Galba B III, f.3 – Convenant between Thomas Spinelly, Henry VIII's agent in the Low Countries and the Flemish gunmaker Hans Poppenruyter of Malines to cast forty-eight artillery pieces.

——f.4 – Thomas Spinelly to Henry VIII, 26 January 1510, about artillery manufacture.

——f.51 – Sir Edward Poynings to Henry VIII; Brussels, 14 October 1512.

——f.54 – Henry VIII to Sir Edward Poynings and other ambassadors; November 1512.

Galba B XIII, f.93–Letter from Charles, Prince of Spain to Princess Mary signed 'V're bon Mary, Charles'; Malines, 18 December 1513.

Julius B XII, ff.91–110 – Creation of Henry Duke of York.

Tiberius D VIII, f.89 – Form of coronation oath, 24 June 1509, as amended in his own hand by Henry VIII, probably in the 1530s.

Tiberius E VIII, f.100v – A 'device for the manner and order of the Coronation' of Henry VII 'rightful and undoubted inheritor of the crowns of England and France' by the whole consent of the realm chosen and required to be King and also of the Princess Katherine, daughter of Spain and Aragon, his wife, Queen of England and of France, to be solemnised at Westminster, Sunday 24 June 1509. Interlined later by Henry VIII.

Titus A XIII, f.186 – Ordinances and statutes devised by Henry VIII for a 'retinue of spears'; 20 November 1509.

Titus B I, f.104v – Thomas Wolsey to Bishop Fox; Windsor, 30 September 1511.

Titus D IV, 138 ff. – Quarto volume, the so-called *Coronation Suite* presented to Henry and Katherine, written by Thomas More; 1509.

Vespasian C I, ff.65–77 – Letter in cipher from John Stile, ambassador in Spain to Henry VIII; 5 August 1512.

——f.79 – Dr William Knight to Thomas Wolsey, the king's almoner; Fuentarrabia, 5 August 1512.

——f.81 – Dr William Knight to Wolsey; San Sebastian, Spain, 4 October 1512.

Vespasian C III, f.75 – Report of the death of the Marquis of Brandenburg in Valencia after over-heating himself playing at tennis; 10 July 1525.

——f.176 – Bishop Cuthbert Tunstal, Lord Privy Seal, Sir Richard Wingfield, Richard Sampson, Dean of the Chapel Royal, ambassadors to the Imperial Court, to Henry VIII; Toledo, 8 July 1525.

Vespasian C VI, f.375 – Treaty between Henry VIII and Ferdinand of Spain for the recovery of Aquitaine and the defence of the Pope; February 1513.

Vespasian C XIV, f.106 – Articles and ordinances governing the security of the Tower of London 'that the king's grace has established' signed by the Earl of Surrey and the Bishops of Winchester and Durham; London, 25 July 1509.

Vespasian C L, f.58v – Despatch from the English envoy John Stile to Henry VIII; Valladolid, 9 September 1509.

Vespasian F III, f.15 – Queen Katherine to Henry VIII; Woburn, Bedfordshire, 16 September 1513.

——f.44 – Henry Fitzroy, Duke of Richmond, to Wolsey; Sheriff Hutton, Yorkshire, 4 March ?1526.

——f.73 – Henry VIII to Wolsey; Woodstock, 1 July 1518.

Vespasian F XIII, f.60 – Lady Margaret Beaufort to Henry VII, Collyweston, 14 January ?1501.

——f.80 – Charles Brandon, Duke of Suffolk, to Henry VIII; Montreuil, 22 April 1515.

——f.140 – Katherine of Aragon to Princess Mary; Woburn, October 1525.

Vitellius B II, f.34 – Papal indulgence of Julius II to all who serve in Henry VIII's dominions in the expedition against Louis XII, including those who contribute towards its cost; Rome, December 1512.

——f.51 – Cardinal Bainbridge to Wolsey; Rome, 17 September 1513.

——f.56 – Pope Leo X to Henry VIII; Rome, 17 December 1513.

——f.69 – Pope Leo X to Henry VIII, award of sword and *pileus*; Rome, 1 March 1514.

——f.183 – Silvester de' Gigli, Bishop of Worcester, to Andrea Ammonius, Latin secretary to Henry VIII; Rome, November 1515.

Vitellius B IV, f.84v – Notes by Richard Pace about Buckingham's guilt on the reverse of a letter to him from Rome dated 29 March 1521; May 1521.

——f.111 – The ceremony of publishing Pope Leo X's sentence against Martin Luther, in St Paul's church; 12 May 1521.

——f.96 – Richard Pace to Thomas Wolsey; Greenwich Palace, 16 April 1521.

Vitellius B IX, f.38 – College of Cardinals to Wolsey; Rome, 9 February 1527.

Vitellius B XI, f.207 – Clement VII to Wolsey; Rome, 19 July 1529.

Vitellius B XII, f.85 – Testimony of Sir Anthony Willoughby about Prince Arthur's marriage with Katherine of Aragon.

——f.123v – Deposition of Nicholas West, Bishop of Ely.

——f.208 – Cardinals' rejection of Katherine of Aragon's appeal to Rome and summons to her to appear at the legatine trial.

Vitellius B XX, f.234 – Sir Richard Wingfield, English ambassador at the Imperial court to Wolsey; 'Mayence' (Mainz), 3 June 1521.

Egerton MS

544, f.158 – Ferdinand to Bernard de Mesa, Bishop of Trinopoli; Medina del Campo, 24 July 1514.

616, article 5 – Two letters in Latin from Prince Arthur to Katherine of Aragon, Ludlow Castle, October and November 1499.

——f.29v–30 – Katherine of Aragon to Ferdinand of Spain, London, 22 April 1506.

——f.43 – Henry VIII to Ferdinand of Spain; Greenwich, 26 July 1509.

616, article 5 f.45 – Queen Katherine to Ferdinand of Spain; Greenwich, 29 July 1509.

985, f.61v – Christening of Henry, son of the Duke of Suffolk and Mary his wife; 11 March 1515.

1,651, f.1 – Presentation letter from Erasmus to Henry, Duke of York, 1499.

1,991 – *Confessio amantis*, a poem by John Gower, owned by Elizabeth Blount.

2,014, f.2 – Henry VIII to Maximilian Sforza, Duke of Milan; the English camp before Tournai, 16 September 1513.

2,341 – Instructions for making images in stained glass of Henry VII, Elizabeth of York, their daughter Margaret and of Lady Margaret Beaufort, to be inserted into the windows of the church of the Greyfriars Observant at Greenwich.

2,642, ff.174v – Description of funeral of Arthur, Prince of Wales, 1502.

——f.185v – Description of funeral of Princess Elizabeth, second daughter of Henry VII and Elizabeth of York, 1495.

——ff.189–189v – Description of funeral of Henry VII, 1509.

Harley MS

283, f.70 – Confession of Robert Gilbert, Chancellor to the Duke of Buckingham; May 1521.

——f.75 – Circular letter (addressed to Lord Cobham, Queen Anne's Chamberlain) announcing the birth of a daughter to the queen; Greenwich Palace, 7 September 1533.

442, f.97 – Proclamation by Sheriffs of London banning tennis, dice 'and other unlawful games' contrary to the statutes for the maintenance of archery; London, 4 December 1528.

787, f.58 – Henry VIII to James IV of Scotland; camp before Thérouanne, 12 August 1513.

965, f.41v – Transcript of later inscription on Prince Arthur's tomb in Worcester Cathedral by Capt. Richmond Symonds, a royalist officer, in 1644.

2,252, f.41 – Henry VIII's answer to James IV's ultimatum; camp before Thérouanne, 11 August 1513.

3,462, f.142v – Henry VIII to Pope Leo X, announcing peace treaty with France; Greenwich, 12 August 1514.

——f.142 – Symbolic consummation of the marriage of Princess Mary with Louis XII of France; Greenwich, 13 August 1514.

3,504, f.232 – Christening of Princess Mary at Greenwich; Wednesday 20 February 1515.

——f.264v – 'Manner of bringing Henry VII's corpse from Richmond'.

6,074, f.54 – Description of the creation of Henry Lord Stafford as Earl of Wiltshire; Westminster, 3 February 1510.

6,079, f.21v – Narrative account of the Coronation of Henry VIII, 23 [*sic*] June 1509.

——f.31 – Narrative account of the burial of Henry VII.

——f.36v – Account of celebratory jousts on 12/13 February 1511 and marks obtained by contestants.

7,039, f.34 – Henry VII to his mother, Lady Margaret Beaufort, Greenwich, 17 July ?1507.

Charters 83 H.1 – Record of courses run at the tournament in January 1511 to celebrate the birth of Prince Henry.

King's MS

9, ff.66, 231v – Messages between Henry VIII and Anne Boleyn about their love, written in a *Book of Hour.*

Lansdowne MS

818, f.2v – Order of battle of the king's army on departure from Calais, end of June 1513.

Royal MS

1 E. IV – Thirteenth-century copy of the *Book of Leviticus* from St Augustine's Priory, Canterbury, Kent.

2 A. XVIII – Lady Margaret Beaufort's *Book of Hours.*

12 B. VI – William Parron's *Liber de optimo fato nobilissimi domini Henrici Eboraci ducis ac optimorum parentum.*

14 B. XXXIX – Wardrobe accounts of the royal household, including the costs of escorting Katherine of Aragon from Exeter to London and her wedding with Prince Arthur at St Paul's and eight days of entertainment 'of the Spanish lords at Canon Row'.

Stowe MS

146, f.3 – Exchequer Declarations, year ended Michaelmas (29 September) 24 Henry VII.

——f.24 – Order for 3,000 harnesses for the king's army from Robert Bolt, mercer of London, for delivery at The Tower by 30 April; January 1513.

163, f.3 – Account of the trial of Sir Edward Stafford, third Duke of Buckingham, 13/16 May 1521.

583, ff.27–33v – Description of funeral of Elizabeth of York, 1503, with pen-and-ink drawings of the processions at articles 1, 2 and 4.

692, f.12 – 'The order of the King's army into France' 1513, with names of the commanders of the three divisions.

LAMBETH PALACE LIBRARY

CM 51/115 – Archbishop William Warham's draft licence for the marriage of Henry VIII and Katherine of Aragon in 'any chapel or church', 8 June 1509.

MSS 247, ff.58–60 – Instructions for musters issued inland shires, 6 June–24 October 1513, when Queen Katherine was Regent of England.

MSS 602, p.50 – Richard Pace to Wolsey; Greenwich, 7 April 1521.

MSS 2341–2 – Legal opinions on the validity of Henry VIII's marriage to Katherine of Aragon; probably part of Cardinal Campeggio's file on the case.

MSS OF THE MARQUIS OF SALISBURY

Cecil Papers

CP 147/1 – Henry VIII to William Knight; Dover, 29 June 1513.

CP 227/1 f. 1 – *The Famous Victory of our Invincible King Henry VIII over the French and Scots*, verses by Bernard André, 'Royal Poet'.

CP 245/5 ff.3v–4r – Robert Thorne to Dr Edward Lee, English ambassador to the court of Charles V; Seville, 1527.
——ff. 9v–14r – Robert Thorne's proposal to Henry VIII for a voyage to the North Pole, 1527.

THE NATIONAL ARCHIVES

Court of Chancery records
C 82/335/6 – List of exemptions from the general pardon of 25 April 1509, signed by Henry VIII; Tower of London, 30 April 1509.

Exchequer records
E 23/3 – Last will and testament of King Henry VII; Richmond, 31 March 1509.
E 36/209, f.8v and f.12v – Purchases of clothing for Prince Henry, 6/16 November 1498.
E 26/215/257ff – John Heron, Treasurer of the Chamber's books of payments 1–9 Henry VIII.
E 36/217 f.41 – Revels Account of Richard Gibson for the celebratory joust at Westminster, 12/13 February 1511.
E 36/228 f.7 – *Lawde & Prayse for Our Sovereigne Lord the Kyng*, by John Skelton, 1509.
E 101/403/2, ff.1–4 – Cash delivered on day to John Heron, Treasurer of the Chamber.
E 101/414/6 f.25v – Henry VII's book of payments, by John Heron, Treasurer of the Chamber. Four shillings compensation for a farmyard cock shot by the king's crossbow.
E 101/415/7 no. 15 – Payment for livery for John Williams, footman to Duke of York, 11 October 1511.
——no. 76 – Payment for coat and other clothing to John Goor, 'fool with Duke of York', 26 October 1501.
——no. 83 – Payment for livery to Richard Wiggins, footman to Duke of York, 17 May 1502.
E 404/81/1 – Payment to Anne Oxenbridge as Henry's wet nurse, 31 December 1491.
E 404/81/3 – Payments to the nursery staff for Lord Henry and Princesses Margaret and Elizabeth, 17 September 1493.
E 404/81/4 – Writs for attendance 'upon our dearest second son the Lord Henry to take with and under him the noble order of Knight of the Bath', 2 October 1494.
E 404/82 – Warrant dated 26 October 1495 for funeral expenses of Princess Elizabeth.
E 404/86/1 – Records of Exchequer of Receipt, warrants for issue.
E 404/86/3 – Loan by Henry VII to Sir Roland de Velville, his reputed bastard.

Court of King's Bench records
KB 8/5 – Roll file of the court of the Lord High Steward trying Sir Edward Stafford, third Duke of Buckingham, 13/16 May 1521.
KB 27/1024 – Chief Justice Roll, with illumination showing Henry VIII young and clean shaven; 1518.

Lord Chamberlain's records

LC 2/1/1 ff.4–4v – Allowances for black mourning cloth for Prince Henry's household for the funeral of his brother Edmund.

——f.73–73v – List of members of household of Prince Henry, 1503.

State Papers

SP 1/1/3 – General pardon issued by Henry VIII, 25 April 1509.

SP 1/1/11 – File of warrants for payments by John Heron, Treasurer of the Chamber for black cloth and other expenses for the funeral of Henry VII; Westminster, 11 May 1509.

SP 1/1/18 – King Ferdinand of Spain to Henry VIII; Valladolid, 11 May 1509.

SP 1/1/28 – Appointment of George Talbot, Earl of Shrewsbury, as Chamberlain of the Exchequer, 13 May 1509.

SP 1/1/33 – Appointment of Sir Henry Marney as Captain of Guard and Vice-Chamberlain, 12 May, 1509.

SP 1/1/43 – Ferdinand of Spain to Katherine, Princess of Wales; 18 May 1509.

SP 1/1/45 – Formal words pronounced at wedding of Henry VIII and Katherine of Aragon; Greenwich, 11 June 1509.

SP 1/1/100 – Estimates for the cost of construction of the tomb of Henry VII and Elizabeth of York in Westminster Abbey; endorsed by Henry VIII, December 1509.

SP 1/2/40 – Lord Chancellor Warham to Lord Darcy before his departure to Spain; 24 March 1511.

SP 1/2/40v – Henry VIII's instructions to Lord Darcy before his expedition against the Moors sailed for Spain; March 1511.

SP 1/2/119 – Thomas, Lord Howard, captain of the army, to Wolsey; 8 July 1512.

SP 1/2/146 – Commission of array to Sir Edward Poynings to muster forces against 'the expected invasion of the French'; Otford, Kent, 28 August 1512.

SP 1/3/75 – Account of William Brown of receipts and payments of artillery made at Malines by Hans Poppenruyter, naming the guns, December 1512.

SP 1/5/230, f.266 – Bills witnessing payments by Sir John Daunce for Princess Mary's trousseau; October 1514.

SP 1/7/80 – Thomas Lord Darcy to Wolsey about his military service; Templehurst, 15 January 1514.

SP 1/66/30 – List of jewels delivered to Henry VIII, undated but probably August 1527–May 1528.

SP 1/82/151 – Seditious remarks by the monk John Frances; 22 January 1533.

BIBLIOTECA APOSTOLICA VATICANO

ASV A.A. Arm. I-XVIII, 4098A – Address of the peers of England to Pope Clement VII seeking the annulment of Henry VIII's marriage with Katherine of Aragon.

Vat. Lat. 3731A f.5 – Henry VIII to Anne Boleyn; undated but probably January 1527.

WORCESTERSHIRE RECORD OFFICE

261.4/BA1006/31b/319 – Purchase of bows and arrows by Droitwich, Worcestershire, to arm troops sent when Prince Arthur went into Wales, 1496.

Printed

Allen, P. S., and H. M. (eds.), *Opus Epistolarum des Erasmi Roterdami*, vol. 1, (1484–1514), Oxford, 1906.

——*Letters of Richard Fox 1486–1527*, Oxford, 1929.

Andreas, Bernard, *Historia Regis Henrici Septimi ... necnon alia quædam ad eundem regem spectantia*, ed. James Gairdner, London, 1858.

Antiquarian Repertory, 4 vols., ed. Francis Grose and Thomas Astle, London, 1809.

Bentley, Samuel, *Excerpta Historica, or Illustrations of English History*, London, 1833.

Bull, Richard (ed.), *Manner and Order taken for the Christening of the High and Mighty Prince Arthur*, in *Antiquarian Repertory*, vol. 1 (1807), pp.353–7.

Byrne, Murial St Clare, *Letters of Henry VIII*, London, 1936.

Caius, John, *A Boke or Counseill against the Sweate*, London, 1552.

'Calais Chronicle' – *Chronicle of Calais*, ed. John Gough Nicols, CS, London, 1846.

CCR Henry VIII 1500–09, vol. 2, London, 1963.

CFR Henry VII 1485–1509, London, 1962.

'Correspondence Fuensalida' – *Correspondencia di Gutierre Gomez de Fuensalida*, ed. the duque de Berwick y de Alba, Madrid, 1907.

CPR Henry VII, vol. 1 (1485–94), London, 1914; vol. 2 (1494–1509), London, 1916.

Crowland Chronicle Continuations 1459–86, ed. N. Pronay and J. Cox, London, 1986.

CSP Milan – vol. 1, ed. Allen B. Hinds, London 1912.

CSP Spain – vol. 1 (1485–1509), London, 1862; vol. 2 (1509–25), London, 1866; Supplement to vols. 1 and 2, London, 1868; all ed. by Rawdon Brown. Vol. 3, pt. 1 (1525–26), London 1873; vol. 3, pt. 2 (1527–9) London, 1877; vol. 4, pt. 1 (1529–30), London, 1879; vol. 4, pt. 2 (1531–3), London 1882 and vol. 5, pt. 1 (1534–5), London, 1886, all ed. Pascual de Gayangos. Further Supplement to vols. 1 and 2, ed. by Garrett Mattingly, London, 1947.

CSP Venice – vol. 1 (1202–1509), London, 1864; vol. 2 (1509–19), London, 1867; vol. 3 (1520–6), London, 1869; vol. 4 (1527–33), London 1871, all ed. Rawdon Brown.

'Despatches' – *Four Years at the Court of Henry VIII: A Selection of Despatches written by the Venetian Ambassador Sebastian Giustinian*, 2 vols, London, 1854.

Ellis, Henry, *Original Letters Illustrative of English History*, 1st ser., 3 vols., 2nd edition, London, 1825; 2nd ser. 4 vols., London, 1827.

'Fisher Works' – *English Works of John Fisher*, ed. J. E. B. Mayor, 2 vols., EETS extra ser. 7, London, 1876.

Grafton, Richard, *Chronicle or History of England, 1189–1558*, 2 vols., London, 1808.

'Greyfriars Chronicle' – *Chronicle of the Grey Friars of London*, ed. John Gough Nichols, CS, London, 1852.

Hall, Edward, *Chronicle containing the History of England ... to the end of the Reign of Henry VIII*, London, 1809.

Harpsfield, Nicholas, *Life and Death of Sir Thomas More knight*, ed. E. V. Hitchcock, EETS, London, 1932.

Holinshed, Raphael, *Chronicles of England, Scotland and Ireland*, 6 vols., London, 1809.

Hughes, Paul and Larkin, James, *Tudor Royal Proclamations*, vol. 1, *The Early Tudors, 1485–1553*, New Haven and London, 1964.

Kipling, Gordon (ed.), *The Receyt of the Ladie Kateryne*, EETS, Oxford, 1990.

Leland, John, *De Rebus Britannicis Collectanea*, ed. Thomas Hearne, 6 vols., London, 1774.

'Letters Louis XII' – *Lettres due Roya Louis XIII et du Cardinal Georges d'Amboise, avec plusieurs autres lettres, mémoires et instructions écrities depuis 1504 jusques et compris 1514*, ed. J. Godefroy, 4 vols., Brussels, 1712.

'Love Letters' – *Love Letters of Henry VIII*, ed. Henry Savage, London, 1949.

LP ... Henry VII, ed. James Gairdner (Rolls ser.), London, 1861.

LP Henry VIII, 21 vols. and addenda, ed. J. S. Brewer, R. H. Brodie and James Gairdner, London, 1862–1920.

Madden, F., 'Genealogical and Historical notes in Ancient Calendars', *Collectanea Topographia et Genealogica*, vol. 1 (1834), pp.277–9.

'Materials' – *Materials for a History of the Reign of Henry VII*, ed. W. Campbell, (Rolls ser.), 2 vols., London, 1873 and 1877.

'Memorials' – *Memorials of King Henry the Seventh*, ed. James Gairdner (Rolls ser.), London 1858.

'More Correspondence' – *Correspondence of Sir Thomas More*, ed. E. F. Rogers, Princetown, 1947.

Muller, James, *Letters of Stephen Gardiner*, Cambridge, 1933.

Nichols, Francis (ed.), *The Epistles of Erasmus*, 3 vols., London, 1901.

Paston Letters, ed. James Gairdner, 6 vols., London, 1904.

Pollard, A. F., *The Reign of Henry VII from Contemporary Sources*, 3 vols., London 1913–14.

'Plumpton Correspondence' – *A Series of Letters ... written in the Reigns of Edward IV, Richard III, Henry VII and Henry VIII ... from Sir Edward Plumpton's book of letters*, ed. Thomas Stapleton, CS old. ser, vol. 4, London, 1839.

Pole, Cardinal Reginald, *Epistolarum Reginaldi Poli ... et aliorum ad upsum*, ed. Cardinal Angelo Quirini, Brescia, 5 vols., 1774, reprinted, Farnborough, 1967.

PPE Elizabeth of York, ed. Sir Harry Nicholas, London, 1830.

PPE Henry VIII, November 1529–December 1532, ed. Sir Harris Nicholas, London, 1827.

PROME – ed. C. Given-Wilson et al., 16 vols., Woodbridge, 2005.

'Relation of England' – *A Relation ... of the Island of England about the Year 1500*, transl. Charlotte Sneyd, CS, London, 1847.

Roper, William, *Life of Sir Thomas More*, ed. Elsie Vaughan Hitchcock, EETS, London, 1935.

'Rutland Papers' – *Original Documents illustrative of the Courts and Times of Henry VII and Henry VIII selected from the private archives of ... the Duke of Rutland*, ed. William Jerdan, CS, old s., vol. 21, London, 1842.

'Ryalle Book' *Ceremonies and Services at Court in the time of Henry VII*, in *Antiquarian Repertory*, vol. 1 (1807), pp.296–341.

RP – ed. J. Strachey et al., 6 vols., London, 1767–77.

'Sanuto Diaries' – *Dairii di Marino Sanuto*, ed. Frederigo Stefani, 58 vols., Venice, 1879–1902.

Singer, Samuel, *Life of Cardinal Wolsey*, London, 1827.

St. P. – *State Papers King Henry VIII*, 11 vols., (Record Commission), London, 1830–52.

Stow, John, *Annales of England*, London, 1601.

Sylvester, Richard (ed.), *Life and Death of Cardinal Wolsey by George Cavendish*, EETS, London, 1959.

Tanner, J. R., *Tudor Constitutional Documents 1485–1603*, Cambridge, 1951.

Thomas, A. H. and Thornley, I. D. (eds.), *Great Chronicle of London*, London, 1938.

Vergil, Polydore, *Anglica Historia 1485–1537*, ed. Denys Hay, CS, vol. 74, London, 1950.

Williams, C. H., (ed.), *English Historical Documents 1485–1558*, London, 1967.

Wright, Ian (ed.), *Spanish Documents concerning English Voyages to the Caribbean 1527–68*, Hakluyt Society, 2nd. ser., no. 42, London, 1929.

'Wriothesley Chronicle' – *A Chronicle of England 1485–1559*, ed. William Hamilton, 2 vols., CS, Westminster, 1875–7.

SECONDARY SOURCES

Calculations of modern purchasing power of Tudor spending were derived from Lawrence H. Officer, 'Purchasing Power of British Pounds from 1264 to Present'. URL: http://www.measuringworth.com/ppoweruk/

Ackroyd, Peter, *The Life of Thomas More*, London, 1998.

Andrews, Kenneth, *Trade, Plunder and Settlement*, Cambridge, 1991.

Anglo, Sydney, 'The Court Festivities of Henry VII: A Study Based upon the Account Books of John Heron, Treasurer of the Chamber', *Bull. John Rylands Library*, vol. 43 (1960–1), pp.12–44.

——*The Great Tournament Roll of Westminster*, 2 vols., Oxford, 1968.

——*Spectacle, Pageantry and Early Tudor Policy*, Oxford, 1969.

——*Images of Tudor Kingship*, London, 1992.

Armstrong, C. A. J., 'An Italian Astrologer at the Court of Henry VII', in Ernest Jacob, ed., *Italian Renaissance Studies*, pp.433–55.

Arthurson, Ian, *The Perkin Warbeck Conspiracy 1491–9*, Stroud, 1997.

Ayot, Thomas, 'Transcript of an Original MS containing a Memorandum from George Constantine to Thomas Lord Cromwell', *Archæologia*, vol. 23 (1831), pp.50–78.

Bacon, Francis, *The Historie of the Reigne of King Henry the Seventh*, London, 1629.

Baldwin, R. C. D., 'Robert Thorne', *ODNB*, vol. 54, pp.605–7.

Bezzard, Judith and Palmer, Francis, 'King Henry VIII: Performer, Connoisseur and Composer of Music', *Antiquaries Jnl*, vol. 80 (2000), pp.249–72.

Brewer, Clifford, *The Death of Kings*, London, 2000.

Brewer, J. S., *The Reign of Henry VIII*, ed. James Gairdner, 2 vols., London, 1884.

Brodie, D. M., 'Edmund Dudley, Minister of Henry VII', *Trans. RHS*, 4th ser., vol. 15 (1932), pp.133–61.

Brooks, Richard, *Cassell's Battlefields of Britain and Ireland*, London, 2005.

Burnet, Gilbert, *History of the Reformation of the Church of England*, 2 vols., London, 1841.

Busch, W., *England unter den Tudors: I – König Heinrich VII*, Stuttgart and London, 1899.

Carley, James, *The Books of King Henry VIII and his Wives*, London, 2004.

Carlin, Martha, 'Willian Parron', *ODNB*, vol. 42, pp.861–2.

Carlson, David R., 'Royal Tutors in the Reign of Henry VII', *Sixteenth Century Jnl*, vol. 22 (1991), pp.253–79.

Cavendish, Richard, 'Death of Elizabeth of York', *History Today*, vol. 53 (February 2003), pp.52–3.

Cavill, P. R., *The English Parliaments of Henry VII 1485–1504*, Oxford, 2009.

Charlton, E., 'A Roll of Prayers Belonging to Henry VIII when Prince', *Archæologia Aeliana*, n.s., vol. 2 (1858), pp.41–5.

Chambers, D. S., 'Cardinal Wolsey and the Papal Tiara', *Bulletin of Institute of Historical Research*, vol. 38 (1965), pp.20–30.

Chambers, R. W., *Thomas More*, London, 1935.

Chrimes, S. B., *Henry VII*, London, 1972.

Clough, Cecil, 'John Rastell', *ODNB*, vol. 46, pp.80–2.

Condon, Margaret, 'The Last Will of Henry VII ... ', in Tatton-Brown and Mortimer, *Westminster Abbey: The Lady Chapel of Henry VII*, pp.99–140.

——'God Save the King! Piety, Propaganda and the Perpetual Monument', in Tatton-Brown and Mortimer, *Westminster Abbey: The Lady Chapel of Henry VII*, pp.59–98.

Cooper, Charles, *Memoir of Margaret, Countess of Richmond*, Cambridge, 1874.

Cooper, J. P., 'Henry VII's Last Years Reconsidered', *HJ*, vol. 2 (1959), pp.102–39.

Crawford, A. (ed.), *Letters of the Queens of England, 1100–1547*, Stroud, 1994.

Cruickshank, C. G., *Army Royal: Henry VIII's Invasion of France 1513*, Oxford, 1969.

Cunningham, Sean, 'Edmund de la Pole', *ODNB*, vol. 44, pp.696–8.

Davies, C. S. L., 'Tournai and the English Crown, 1513–19', *HJ*, vol. 41 (1998), pp.1–26.

——and Edwards, John, 'Catherine of Aragon', *ODNB*, vol. 30, pp.892–901.

Doran, Susan (ed.), *Man and Monarch: Henry VIII*, London, 2009.

Elton, G. R., 'Henry VII, Rapacity and Remorse', *HJ*, vol. 1 (1958), pp.21–39.

——'Henry VII: A Restatement', *HJ*, vol. 4 (1961), pp.1–20.

——*The Tudor Revolution in Government*, Cambridge, 1953.

——*Policy and Police*, Cambridge, 1972.

Ehses, Stefan, *Römische Dokumente zur Geschichte der Ehescheidung Heinrichs VIII von England 1527–34*, Paderborn, 1898.

Flügel, J. C., *Men and their Motives: Psycho-analytical studies*, London, 1934.

——'On the Character and Married Life of Henry VIII', in *Psychoanalysis and History*, ed. Bruce Mazlish, rev. ed., New York, 1971.

Fraser, Antonia, *The Wives of Henry VIII*, New York, 1992.

Fraser, Ernest *Italian Renaissance Studies*, London, 1960.

Fuller, Thomas, *Church History of Britain*, London, 1655.

Gairdner, James, 'New Lights on the Divorce of Henry VIII', *EHR*, vol. 11 (1896), pp.230–55; vol. 12 (1897), pp.1–16; 237–53.

Grummett, David, 'Household Politics and Political Morality in the Reign of Henry VII', *HR*, vol. 82 (2009), pp.393–411.

Gunn, Steven, *Charles Brandon, Duke of Suffolk, c.1484–1545*, Oxford, 1988.

——'The Accession of Henry VIII', *HR*, vol. 44 (1991), pp.278–88.

——'The Courtiers of Henry VII', *EHR*, vol. 108 (1993), pp.23–49.

——'Edmund Dudley', *ODNB*, vol. 17, pp.61–9.

——'Perkin Warbeck', *ODNB*, vol. 57, pp.246–8.

——and Monkton, Linda (eds.), *Arthur Tudor, Prince of Wales*, Woodbridge, 2009.

Guy, John, *Thomas More*, London, 2000.

Halsted, Caroline, *Life of Margaret Beaufort, Mother of King Henry VII*, London, 1838.

Hampton, W. E., 'Sir James Tyrell with some notes on the Austin Friars and those buried there', *Ricardian*, vol. 4, (1978) pp.9–22.

Hanham, Alison, 'Edmund de la Pole, defector', *Renaissance Studies*, vol. 2 (2006), pp. 239–50.

Harris, Barbara J., *Edward Stafford, third duke of Buckingham, 1478–1521*, Stamford, 1986.

Harrison, C. J., 'Petition of Edmund Dudley', *EHR*, vol. 87 (1972), pp.82–99.

Hart, Kelly, *The Mistresses of Henry VIII*, Stroud, 2009.

Hayward, Maria, *Dress at the Court of Henry VIII*, Leeds, 2007.

Herbert, Lord Edward of Cherbury, *Life and Reign of King Henry the Eighth*, London, 1672.

Higgins, Alfred, 'On the Work of Florentine Sculptors in England in the early part of the Sixteenth-century with Special Reference to the Tombs of Cardinal Wolsey and King Henry VIII', *Archæological Jnl*, vol. 51 (1894), pp.129–220.

Horowitz, Mark, 'Henry Tudor's Treasure', *HR*, vol. 82 (2009), pp.560–79.

——'Policy and Prosecution in the Reign of Henry VII', *HR*, vol. 82 (2009), pp.412–58.

Hoskins, Anthony, 'Mary Boleyn's Children – Offspring of Henry VIII?', *Genealogists' Magazine*, vol. 25 (1997), pp.345–52.

Hutchinson, Robert, *Last Days of Henry VIII*, London, 2005.

——*Thomas Cromwell*, London, 2007.

——'Henry's Reproductive Woes', *BBC History Magazine*, vol. 9, (October 2008), p.95.

——*House of Treason: The Decline and Fall of a Tudor Dynasty*, London, 2009.

Illingworth, W., 'Draft of an Indenture of Covenant ... for a Monument to Henry VIII and his Queen', *Archæologia*, vol. 16 (1812), pp.80–8.

Ives, Eric, *The Life and Death of Anne Boleyn 'the Most Happy'*, Oxford, 2005.

——'Tudor Dynastic Problems Revisited', *HR*, vol. 81 (2008), pp.255–79.

Jones, Michael and Underwood, Malcolm, *The King's Mother, Lady Margaret Beaufort*, Cambridge, 1992.

Jones, Philippa, *The Other Tudors: Henry VIII's Mistresses and Bastards*, London, 2009.

Kingsford, C. L., 'Historical Notices on Medieval London Houses', *London Topographical Record*, vol. 10 (1916), pp.44–144.

Knecht, R. J., *Rise and Fall of Renaissance France*, London, 1996.

Kybett, Susan, 'Henry VIII, a Malnourished King', *History Today*, vol. 39 (1979), pp.19–22.

Lander, J. R., 'Bonds, Coercion and Fear: Henry VII and the Peerage', *Florelegium Historiale: Essays presented to Wallace K. Ferguson*, Toronto, 1971, pp.328–67.

Loades, David, *The Politics of Marriage: Henry VIII and his Queens*, Stroud, 1994.

Luckett, D. A., 'The Thames Valley Conspiracies Against Henry VII', *HR*, vol. 68 (1995), pp.164–73.

MacNalty, Sir Arthur S., *Henry VIII – a Difficult Patient*, London, 1952.

Marius, Richard, *Thomas More – a Biography*, New York, 1984.

Mattingly, Garrett, *Catherine of Aragon*, London, 1946.

Mayer, T. F., 'Tournai and Tyranny: Imperial Kingship and Critical Humanism', *HJ*, vol. 34 (1991) pp.257–77.

Miller, Helen, *Henry VIII and the English Nobility*, Oxford, 1986.

Moorhouse, Geoffrey, *Great Harry's Navy – How Henry VIII gave England Seapower*, London, 2005.

Moriarty, E. J., 'Henry VIII Medically Speaking', *Historical Bull. Calgary Associate Clinic*, vol. 20 (1955–6).

Nelson, W., *John Skelton Laureate*, New York, 1939.

ODNB, new ed., eds. H. G. G. Matthews and Brian Harrison, 60 vols., Oxford, 2004.

Orme, Nicholas, 'John Holt, Schoolmaster and Grammarian', *The Library*, 6th ser., vol. 18 (1996), pp. 283–305.

Patterson, Angus, *Fashion and Armour in Renaissance Europe*, London, 2009.

Paul, John E., *Catherine of Aragon and her Friends*, London, 1966.

Plenderleith, H. J, 'The Royal Bronze Effigies in Westminster Abbey', *Antiquaries Jnl*, vol. 39 (1959), pp.87–162.

Plowden, Alison, *Tudor Women: Queens and Commoners*, London, 1979.

Pollard, A. F., *Henry VIII*, London and Paris, 1902.

Rackham, Harris (ed.), *Christ's College in Former Days*, Cambridge, 1939.

Rex, Richard, 'The English Campaign against Luther in the 1520s', *Trans. RHS*, 5th ser., vol. 39 (1989), pp.85–106.

——*The Tudors*, Stroud, 2003.

Richardson, W. C., *Tudor Chamber Administration 1485–1507*, Baton Rouge, 1952.

Ridley, Jasper, *Henry VIII*, London, 1984.

Rimer, Graeme, Richardson, Thom and Cooper, J. P. D, (eds.) *Henry VIII: Arms and the Man*, London, 2009.

Robinson, W. R., 'Henry VIII's Household in the 1520s: The Welsh Connection', *HR*, vol. 68 (1995) pp.174–90.

Routh, E. M. G., *Sir Thomas More and his Friends*, London, 1934.

Russell, Joyceline, *The Field of Cloth of Gold: Men and Manners in 1520*, London, 1969.

Salter, F. M., 'Skelton's *Speculum Principis*' *Speculum*, vol. 9, Ann Arbor, Michigan, 1934, pp.25–37.

Sander, Nicolas, *The Rise and Growth of the Anglican Schism*, ed. D. Lewis, London, 1877.

Sandford, Francis, *Genealogical History of the Kings and Queens of England*, 2nd. ed., London, 1707.

Scarisbrick, J. J., *Henry VIII*, new ed., New Haven and London, 1997.

——'The Pardon of the Clergy, 1531', *HJ*, vol. 12 (1956) pp.25ff.

Scattergood, John (ed.), *John Skelton: the Complete English Poems*, New Haven and London, 1983.

Sharpe, Kevin, *Selling the Tudor Monarchy: Authority and Image in Sixteenth-century England*, New Haven and London, 2009.

Southworth, John, *Fools and Jesters at the English Court*, Stroud, 1998.

Stanley, Arthur, *Historical Memorials of Westminster Abbey*, 3rd rev. ed., London, 1869.

Starkey, David, *Six Wives: The Queens of Henry VIII*, London, 2004.

——*Henry – The Virtuous Prince*, London, 2008.

——(ed.), *Henry VIII. A European Court in England*, London, 1991.

Strickland, Agnes, *The Lives of the Queens of England*, 6 vols., London, 1866.

Sylvester, R. S. (ed.), *History of King Richard III and Selections from the English and Latin Poems*, 2 vols., New Haven and London, 1976.

Tatton-Brown, Tim and Mortimer, Richard, *Westminster Abbey, the Lady Chapel of Henry VII*, Woodbridge, 2003.

Taviner, Mark, Thwaites, Guy and Grant, Vanya, 'The English Sweating Sickness 1485–51: A Viral Pulmonary Disease', *Medical History*, vol. 42 (1998), pp.96–8.

Thiselton, T. M., *Regia Insignia, an account of the King's Honorable Band of Gentlemen Pensioners or Gentlemen at Arms*, London, 1819.

Thurley, Simon, *The Royal Palaces of Tudor England*, New Haven and London, 1993.

Walker, Greg, 'Expulsion of the Minions', *HJ*, vol. 32 (1989), pp.1–16.

Wheatley, Henry B., 'Original Plan of Durham House and Gardens, 1628', *London Topographical Record*, vol. 10 (1916), pp.150–61.

Warnicke, Retha, 'Anne Boleyn's Childhood and Adolescence', *HJ*, vol. 28 (1985), pp.939–52.

——*The Rise and Fall of Anne Boleyn: Family Politics at the Court of Henry VIII*, Cambridge, 1989.

——'Anne Boleyn Revisited', *HJ*, vol. 34 (1991), pp.953–4.

Williams, Neville, *Henry VIII and his Court*, London, 1971.

——*The Cardinal and the Secretary*, New York, 1975.

Williamson, J. A., *Voyages of the Cabots and the English Discovery of North America under Henry VII and Henry VIII*, London, 1929.

Wroe, Ann, *Perkin, A Story of Deception*, London, 2003.

INDEX

Bold page numbers indicate entries in the Dramatis Personæ (pages 261–72).
References in end notes are indicated by 'n' (e.g. 314n96).

Arthur Tudor, Prince of Wales—*contd*
marriage to Katherine of Aragon, 33,
51–5, 61–2, 64, 65, 78, 288n2, 289n24,
289n31
titles, 9, 18, 19, 278n35
Arundel, Earl of *see* FitzAlan, Thomas
Ashford, Kent, 15
Aspenden, 280n61
Assertio Septem Sacramentorum ('Defence
of the Seven Sacraments'), 203–4
astrology, 66, 68, 250, 290n48
Audley, Edmund (Bishop of Salisbury and
Chancellor of the Order of
Garter), 70, 291n67
Austin Friars, Church of the, 215, 293n8

Bacon, Francis (Viscount St Albans), 5, 97,
294n34
Badoer, Andrea (Venetian
ambassador), 98–9, 109, 138, 297n93
Bainbridge, Cardinal Christopher
(Archbishop of York and ambassador
in Rome), 159, 160, 171, 180, 189
Baker, Matthew (Esquire of the Body), 100
Barbara (ship), 195
Barlow, Roger (explorer), 196
Barnet, Battle of (1471), 2, 47
Barton, Andrew (Scottish privateer), 167
Bath, Order of the, 11, 19–23, 120, 279n50–51
battles:
Agincourt (1415), 155, 176, 179
Agnadello (1509), 298n30
Barnet (1471), 2, 47
Blackheath (1497), 29–30, 273n5
Bosworth (1485), x, 2–3, 18, 47, 93, 183,
273n9, 275n39, 303n33
Flodden (1513), 182–3, 185–6, 310n102
Mortimer's Cross (1461), 2
Pavia (1525), 216, 316n134
Spurs (1513), 178–80, 183, 185–6
Stoke Field (1487), 7–8, 23, 25, 78, 90,
273n5
Tewkesbury (1471), 2
Bayley, Elizabeth, 92
Baynard's Castle, 45, 244, 285n42
Bayonne, 161
Beaufort, John (First Duke of
Somerset), 273n6, 274n23

Beaufort, Lady Margaret (Countess of
Richmond; mother of Henry
VII), **261–2**
antecedents, 2, 273n6
appearance, 49
Book of Hours, 5, 8, 12, 52, 274n23
at coronation of Henry VIII, 121,
124
death, 126–7, 134
marriages, 47
ordinances for birth and christening of
Henry VIII, 11–12, 13, 276n6
patronage, 49
piety and vow of chastity, 47–8, 49–50,
105
properties, 29, 47–8, 117, 286n58–61
raising of grandchildren, 15, 37, 41, 50,
60, 93
regent for Henry VIII, 103, 104, 105, 114,
115, 117
relationship with Henry VII, 48–9
titles and privileges, 48
tomb, 135
Beaulieu Abbey, Hampshire, 30–31
Beaulieu, Essex, New Hall, 45, 218, 236, 238,
316n6
Beauvais, 191
Becket, St Thomas, 36, 90
Bereworth, Stephen (physician), 274n25
Berryman, William (food taster to Henry
VII), 135
Berwick-upon-Tweed, 27, 81, 136, 171,
280n65
Bewdley, 33, 64
Blackadder, Robert (Archbishop of
Glasgow), 58
Blackfriars, London, 242–3
Blackheath, Battle of (1497), 29–30,
273n5
Blackmore, Essex, St Lawrence Priory, 220,
317n22
Blank, John (trumpeter), 295n61
Blomberg, Barbara (mistress of Charles V,
Holy Roman Emperor), 221
Blount, Elizabeth 'Bessie' (*later* Talboys;
maid of honour to Katherine of
Aragon; mistress of Henry
VIII), 219–20, **266**, 316n16, 317n23

Douglas, Lady Margaret (daughter of
Margaret Tudor), 222, 317n30
Dover, 174, 194, 246, 248, 309n70
Dover Castle, 19
Draughton, Margaret (rocker of the royal
cradle), 13
Droitwich, 278n37
du Bellay, Jean (French ambassador), 241,
245, 320n118
Dublin, 6, 299n35
Christ Church Cathedral, 7
Dudley, Edmund 42–3 (president of Henry
VII's council), 42, 93, 140, **267**
imprisonment and execution, 104–5,
106, 148–50, 305n81
Dudley, John (First Duke of
Northumberland), 305n81
Dunstable, 249–50
Durham, Ushaw College, 94
Durham House, London, 74, 88, 224,
292n78
Dynham, John (First Baron Dynham; Lord
High Treasurer), 24, 28
dysentery, 248, 307n26

Edinburgh, Holyrood House, 81
Edmund Tudor (First Earl of Richmond;
father of Henry VII), 2, 47
Edmund Tudor (Duke of Somerset; brother
of Henry VIII), 33, 39, 41, 66, 282n92,
283n24
Edward the Confessor, St, 123, 124
Edward I, 124
Edward III, 2, 207
Edward IV, 3–4, 6, 16, 261, 274n12, 278n26,
301n100
Edward V, 3–4, 79, 261, 275n37, 293n7–8
Edward VI (*earlier* Prince Edward; son of
Henry VIII), x, 253–4, **263**, 281n72,
289n15
Eleanor of Austria (daughter of Philip,
Archduke of Burgundy), 69, 83,
129–30
Elizabeth I (*earlier* Princess Elizabeth;
daughter of Henry VIII), x, 250, **263**,
273n5
Elizabeth Tudor (sister of Henry VIII), 15,
28, 281n72

Elizabeth of York (mother of Henry VIII)
see York, Elizabeth of
Eltham Palace, 15, 27, 28, 38, 45, 92
Empson, Sir Richard (Chancellor of the
Duchy of Lancaster), 42, 43, 140, 142,
267
imprisonment and execution, 104–5,
106, 116, 148–50, 302n20, 305n82
Erasmus, Desiderius, 69, 87–8, 132, 133, 187,
206, 294n40
meets young Henry, 35, 38–40
Catalogue of Lucubrations, 283n15
Prosopiæ Britanniæ, 39–40, 283n16
Errenteria, 163
Essex, earls of *see* Bourchier, Henry;
Cromwell, Thomas
Étaples, Treaty of (1492), 16–17
Eustace, St, 5, 274n24
'Evil May Day' riots (1517), 112
Exeter, 30
Exeter, Marquis of *see* Courtenay, Henry
Eyton, Shrine of Our Lady of, 210

Falmouth, 84
Farnham Castle, 7, 15
Fécamp, Abbot of (French ambassador),
138
Ferdinand II of Aragon, 50, 80, 97, **270**
betrothal and marriage of Princess
Katherine to Henry VIII, 65, 71, 88–9,
107–8, 118–19, 129–31, 296n79, 298n26
campaign against Moors in North
Africa, 157, 306n13
death, 194
death of Henry VII, 107–8
death of Isabella of Castile, 75
Henry VIII seeks vengeance against,
190–91
marriage of Princess Katherine to Prince
Arthur, 33, 53, 58, 65
marriage to Germaine de Foix, 81
war against French, 164–5, 171, 174, 188
Ferdinand II of Naples, 293n11
Fernández, Friar Diego (confessor to
Katherine of Aragon), 131–2, 142–3,
145, 191, 305n72
Field of Cloth of Gold meeting (1520),
94–5, 209